William Gilmore Simms

Southward Ho!

A Spell of Sunshine

William Gilmore Simms

Southward Ho!
A Spell of Sunshine

ISBN/EAN: 9783743353596

Manufactured in Europe, USA, Canada, Australia, Japa

Cover: Foto ©ninafisch / pixelio.de

Manufactured and distributed by brebook publishing software (www.brebook.com)

William Gilmore Simms

Southward Ho!

SOUTHWARD HO!

A

SPELL OF SUNSHINE

By W. GILMORE SIMMS, Esq.

AUTHOR OF "THE YEMASSEE"—"THE PARTISAN"—"MELLICHAMPE"—
"KATHARINE WALTON"—"THE SCOUT"—"WOODCRAFT," ETC.

"Southward ho!
As the waves bow, as the winds blow.
Spread free the sunny sail, let us go, friends, go."

New York:
A. C. ARMSTRONG & SON,
714 BROADWAY.
1882.

Entered, according to Act of Congress, in the year 1854,
By J. S. REDFIELD,
In the Clerk's Office of the District Court of the United States, in and for the Southern District of New York.

SOUTHWARD HO!

CHAPTER I.

"When the wind is southerly," etc.—HAMLET.

I WAS at New York in the opening of July. My trunks were packed, and I was drawing on my boots, making ready for departure. Everybody was leaving town, flying from the approaching dog-days in the city. I had every reason to depart also. I had certainly no motive to remain. New York was growing inconceivably dull with all her follies. Art wore only its stalest aspects, and lacked all attractions to one who had survived his own verdancy. Why should I linger?

But, in leaving the city, I was about to pursue no ordinary route of travel. While my friends were all flying to the interior, seeking cool and shady glades along the Hudson, deep caves of the Catskills, wild ridges and glens of the Adirondack, or quiet haunts in Berkshire, I had resolved on returning south — going back to Carolina in midsummer. A friend who had heard of my intentions suddenly burst into my chamber with all the fervency of a northeaster.

"What does all this mean?" was his question. "Back to the south? In the name of Capricorn and Cancer, why this most perverse of all determinations? What can you mean by it? Is it suicide you purpose? Is death in the swamps, of malaria, musquito, and *coup de soleil*, preferable to knife or pistol? Can you really prefer black vomit, to an easy and agreeable death from charcoal? Prussic acid will be more easy and more grateful, and you will make a far more agreeable corpse in the eyes of the spectator. Yellow fever spoils the complexion; and the very delay which you make in dying, by such a process—though sufficiently rapid for all mortal purposes—will yet be such a loss of flesh as to lessen your proportions grievously when laid out. Choose some other form of exit. Let it be short, agreeable, and in no ways hurtful to your physique or complexion. Next to the loss of one's friend, is the pain one feels in seeing the ugly changes which a vicious disease, acting through the liver, makes in his personal appearance. Be counselled. If you will die, go with me to the chemist. We will get you something which shall serve your purpose, without producing tedious discomfort and spoiling your visage."

My friend was a genuine Manhattan—a lively rattlepate of good taste and good manners, who had the most unbounded faith in New York; who venerated the ancient Dutch régime of Peter Stuyvesant, hated the Yankees quite as much as the southrons are said to do; but, as usual in Gotham, believed the south to be a realm of swamp only, miasma, malaria, musquito, and other unmentionable annoyances—totally uninhabitable in midsummer—from which all persons commonly fled as from the wrath of Heaven.

"Nay, nay," was my answer. "I am not for suicide. I sha'n't die in Carolina. You forget, I am a native. Our diseases of the south are so many defences. They are of a patriotic influence and character. They never afflict the natives. They only seize upon the spoiler—those greedy birds of passage, who come like wild geese and wild ducks, to feed upon our rice-fields, and carry off our possessions in their crops, when the harvest is ready for the gathering. We are as healthy in Carolina in midsummer, nay much more so, than you are in New York. Charleston, for example, is one of the healthiest seaports in the Union."

"Oh! get out. Tell that to the marines. But, supposing that I allow all that. Supposing you don't die there, or even get your liver out of order—there are the discomforts—the hot, furnace-like atmosphere, the musquitoes—the—the—"

"You multiply our miseries in vain. I grant you the musquitoes, but only along the seaboard. Twenty miles from the coast, I can carry you to the most delicious pineland settlements and climate, where you need to sleep with a blanket, where no epidemic prevails, no sickness in fact, and where a musquito is such a rarity, that people gather to survey him, and wonder in what regions he can harbor; and examine him with a strange curiosity, which they would never exhibit, if he could, then and there, make them sensible of his peculiar powers. When one happens there, driven by stress of weather, he pines away in a settled melancholy, from the sense of solitude, and loses his voice entirely before he dies. He has neither the heart to sing, nor the strength to sting, and finally perishes of a broken heart. His hope of safety, it is said, is only found in his being able to fasten upon a foreigner, when he is reported to fatten up amazingly. The case, I admit, is rather different in Charleston. There he is at home, and rears a numerous family. His name is Legion He is a dragon in little, and a fierce bloodsucker. There he sings, as well as stings, with a perfect excellence of attribute. By the way, I am reminded that I should use the feminine in speaking of the *stinging* musquito. A lady naturalist has somewhere written that it is the male musquito which does the *singing*, while the female alone possesses the stinging faculty. How the discovery was made, she has not told us. But the fact need not be questioned. We know that, among birds, the male is usually the singer. Let it pass. The musquitoes, truly, are the most formidable of all the annoyances of a summer residence in Charleston; but, even there, they are confined mostly to certain precincts. In a fine, elevated, airy dwelling, open to south and west, with double piazzas along the house in these quarters, and with leisure and money in sufficient quantity, I should just as soon, for the comfort of the thing, take up my abode for the summer in the venerable city watered by the Ashley and the Cooper, as in any other region of the world."

"Pooh! pooh! You Charlestonians are such braggers."

"Good! This said by a Manhattan, whose domestic geese are all Cygnets—rare birds, verily!"

"But the horrid heat of Charleston."

"The heat! Why Charleston is a deal cooler than either New York, Philadelphia, or Baltimore, in summer."

"Psha! How you talk."

"I talk truly. I have tried all these cities. The fact is as I tell you; and when you consider all things, you will not venture to doubt. Charleston is directly on the sea. Her doors open at once upon the gulf and the Atlantic. The sea rolls its great billows up to her portals twice in twenty-four hours, and brings with them the pleasantest play of breezes that ever fanned the courts of Neptune, or made music for the shells of Triton. There are no rocky heights on any side to intercept the winds. All is plain sailing to and from the sea. Besides, we build our houses for the summer climate. While you, shuddering always with the dread of ice and winter, wall yourselves in on every hand, scarcely suffering the sun to look into your chambers, and shutting out the very zephyr, we throw our doors wide to the entrance of the winds, and multiply all the physical adjuncts which can give us shade and coolness. A chamber in a large dwelling will have its half dozen windows—these will be surrounded with verandahs—great trees will wave their green umbrellas over these in turn; and, with a shrewd whistle —a magic peculiarly our own—we persuade the breeze to take up its perpetual lodgings in our branches. Remember, I speak for our dwelling-houses—these chiefly which stand in the southern and western portions of the city. In the business parts, where trade economizes space at the expense of health and comfort, we follow your Yankee notions—we jam the houses one against the other in a sort of solid fortress, shutting our faces against the breezes and the light, the only true resources against lassitude, dyspepsia, and a countless host of other disorders."

'I don't believe a word of it."

"Believe as you please, but the case is as I tell you."

"And you persist in going south?"

"I do; but my purpose is only to pass through Charleston, after a brief delay. I am going to spend the summer among our mountains."

"Mountains! Why, what sort of mountains have you in Carolina?"

"Not many, I grant you, but some very noble, very lofty, very picturesque: some, to which your famous Catskill is only a wart of respectable dimensions! Our Table Rock, for example, is a giant who could take his breakfast, with the greatest ease, from your most insolent and conceited summits."

"Why have we never heard of them before?"

"Because you are talking all the while of your own. You hear nothing. Were you to stop your own boasting for a season, and listen to your neighbors, you would scarcely continue to assume, as you do, that the world's oyster, everywhere, was to be opened only by the New York knife. In the matter of mountains, North Carolina, where she borders on South, is in possession of the most noble elevations in the United States proper. Black Mountain is understood to be the loftiest of our summits But there are many that stretch themselves up, in the same region, as if eager for its great distinctions. Here you find a grand sea of mountains; billow upon billow, stretching away into remoter states, on all hands, till the ranging eye loses itself with their blue peaks, among the down-tending slopes of heaven. It is here that I propose to refresh myself this summer. I shall explore its gorges, ascend its heights, join the chase with the mountain hunters, and forget all your city conventionalities, in a free intercourse with a wild and noble nature. Take my counsel and do the same. Go with me. Give up your Newport and Saratoga tendencies, and wend south with me in search of cool breezes and a balmy atmosphere."

"Could I believe you, I should! I am sick of the ancient routes. But I have no faith in your report. You think it patriotism to paint your sepulchres. Their handsome outsides, under your limning, shall not tempt me to approach them, lest they yawn upon me. But, write me as you go. 'Description is your forte.' I shall find your pictures pleasant enough, when not required to believe them truthful. Refresh me with your fictions. Do you really believe you shall see a mountain where you go—anything higher than a hill—anything approaching our Highlands?"

"Go with me. See for yourself."

"Could I persuade myself that I should not be drowned in a morass, eaten up by musq:itoes, have my liver tortured by Yellow Jack, and my skin utterly *cured* for drumheads by your horrid sun—I might be tempted. You would betray me to my fate. I can't trust you."

"Hear me prophesy! Fifteen years will not pass before the mountain ranges of the Carolinas and Georgia will be the fashionable midsummer resort of all people of taste north of the Hudson. They will go thither in search of health, coolness, pure air, and the picturesque."

"You say it very solemnly, yet I should more readily believe in a thousand other revolutions. At all events, if you will go south in July, see that the captain of your steamer takes an iceberg in tow as soon as she gets out to sea. There are several said to be rolling lazily about off Sandy Hook. Write me if you survive; and deal in as much pleasant fiction as you can. I shall look for nothing else. Now that postage is nothing, I am ambitious of a large correspondence."

"You shall hear from me."

"And, by the way, you may do some good in your scribblings, by enlightening others. In truth, your country is very much a *terra incognita*. Let us have a description of manners and customs, scenery and people. A touch of statistics, here and there, will possibly open the way to our capital and enterprise; and, to one so fond of such things as myself, an occasional legend or tradition — the glimpse of an obscure history of the Revolution — or of the time beyond it — will greatly increase the value of your correspondence."

"A good hint! I may inspire that faith in others which you withhold — very unwisely, I must say. Your world does, in truth, need some honest information touching ours, by which to keep it from such sad mistakes as augur much mischief for the future."

"Oh! no politics now, I beg! Leave them to the cats and monkeys — the dogs and demagogues."

"Don't fear! My epistles shall be penned in accordance with my moods and humors — according to passing facts and fancies — and I shall only occasionally take you — *over* the ditch and gutter! This assurance should keep you in good humor."

"Write of what you see, of course."

"And of what I feel."

"And of what you think."

"And of what I hear."

"And of what you know."

"And of what I believe."

"And—"

"What more! One would think these requisitions quite sufficient. I shall try to comply with them—at my leisure."

"Don't forget to give us a story now and then—a legend—fact or fabrication—I don't care which. You may wind up a chapter with a song, and a description with a story."

"You are indulgent! Well, I will do what I can for you. I shall report my daily experiences, and something more. My memory shall have full play, and the events of former progresses shall be made to illustrate the present. I shall exercise perfect freedom in what I write—a liberty I hope always to enjoy—and shall soothe the idle vein, by affording every privilege to Fancy. Without some such privilege, your traveller's narrative is apt to become a very monotonous one; and he who drily reports only what he sees, without enlivening his details by what he feels, or fancies, or remembers, will be very apt, however much he may desire to correspond, to find few friends willing to pay postage on his letters, even at present prices."

"Good! You have the right notion of the thing. Well! You go at three? I shall see you off. *Adios!*"

Sure enough, at the designated hour, my friend waited my arrival on the quarter-deck of the good steamer Marion, Berry master. Our hands grasped.

"I am here," said he.

"I am grateful!"

"Stay! Hear me out! Your words have prevailed. I am anxious to believe your fiction. I am tired of Newport and Saratoga—long for novelty—have insured my life for ten thousand—and now, ho! for the South! I go with you as I am a living man!"

And we sang together the old chant of the Venetian, done into English—

"As the waves flow, as the winds blow,
  Spread free the sunny sail, let us go, brothers, go!
  Southward ic! Southward ho!"

CHAPTER II.

> "Our separation so abides, and flies,
> That thou, residing here, go'st yet with me,
> And I, hence fleeting, here remain with thee."
>
> [*Antony & Cleopatra.*

So sudden had been the determination of my friend to accompany me south, that there was but a single acquaintance to see him off, and he came late, with a quarter-box of cigars under his arm, and a bottle of London-Dock black brandy, rolled up in a blue silk pocket-handkerchief, carried in his hands as gingerly as if a new-born baby. These were to afford the necessary consolations against salt-water. My friend and myself, meanwhile, mounted to the quarter-deck, leaving the gang-way free to the bustling crowds that come and go, like so many striving, crossing, and purposeless billows, on all such occasions. We had not many passengers, at this season of the year, but they had numerous acquaintances to see them off. We watched sundry groups, in which we could detect symptoms of suppressed emotion, not less intelligent and touching because, evidently, kept down with effort.

Even when we know our own restless nature, eager always for change, it is yet wonderful that we should leave home—should tear ourselves away from the living fibres of love which we leave to bleed behind us, and but slowly to close the wounds in our own bosoms.

The strongest heart goes with some reluctance, even when it hurries most. The soul lingers fondly, though the horses grow restiff in the carriage at the door. We look back with longing eyes, while the vessel drops down the stream. If we could endure the shame and self-reproach of manhood, in such a proceeding, we should, half the time, return if we could.

Truly, this parting is a serious business—even where the voyager is, like myself, an old one. To the young beginner it is a great trial of the strength. To tear oneself away from the youthful home — the old familiar faces — the well-remembered haunts and pathways, more precious grown than ever, — when we are about to leave them, perhaps for ever, — is a necessity that compels many a struggle in which the heart is very apt to falter. The very strength of the affections betrays its great deficiency of strength.

The gathered crowd upon the quay — the eagerness, the anxiety, and earnest words and looks of all — the undisguised tears of many — the last broken, tender words of interest — the subdued speech — the sobs which burst from the bosom in the last embrace; — what associations, and pangs, and fears, and losses, do these declare! what misgivings and terrors! True, the harbor smiles in sweetness; the skies look down in beauty; the waves roll along, soft, subdued, with a pleasant murmur; there is not a cloud over the face of heaven — not a voice of threat in the liquid zephyr that stirs the hair upon your forehead: but the prescient soul knows the caprice of wind, and sea, and sky; and the loving heart is always a creature full of tender apprehensions for the thing it loves. Long seasons of delicious intercourse are about to terminate; strong affinities, which can not be broken, are about to be burdened with cruel apprehensions, and doubts which can not be decided till after long delay; and the mutual intercourse, which has become the absolute necessity of the heart, is to be interrupted by a separation which may be final. The deep waters may roll eternal barriers between two closely-linked and bonded lives, and neither shall hear the cry of the other's suffering — neither be permitted to extend the hand of help, or bring to the dying lips the cup of consolation.

Such are the thoughts and fears of those who separate daily. Necessity may excuse the separation; but how is it with those whose chief motive for wandering is pleasure? In diversity of prospect, change of scene, and novel associations, they would escape that *ennui* which, it seems, is apt to make its way even into the abode of love. There is some mystery in this seeming perversity, and, duly examined, it is not without its justification. The discontent which prompts the desire for change in the breast of man, is the fruit, no doubt, of a soul-necessity which is not easy to analyze. We owe to this secret prompter some of the best benefits which the world enjoys; and the temporary sufferings of the affections—the wounds of separation—are not wholly without their compensation, even while the wounds are green.

A similitude has somewhere been traced between the effects of parting and of death. The former has been called a death in miniature. It certainly very often provokes as fond an exhibition of grief and privation. But these declare as much for life as for mortality. There is another side to the picture. The parting of friends is so far grateful, as it gives us the renewed evidences of a warm, outgushing, and acutely-sensitive humanity. We are consoled, through the sorrow, by the love. We see the grief, but it does not give us pain, as we find its origin in the most precious developments of the human nature. We weep, but we feel; and there is hope for the heart so long as it can feel. There are regrets—but O! how sweet are the sympathies which harbor in those regrets! The emotions, the passions,—the more precious interior sentiments,—need occasionally some pressure, some privation, some pang, in order that they may be made to show themselves—in order that we may be assured of our possessions still;—and how warmly do they crowd and gather above us in the moment when we separate from our associates! Into what unexpected activity and utterance do they start and spring, even in the case of those whose ordinary looks are cold, who, like certain herbs of the forest, need to be bruised heavily before they will give out the aromatic sweetness which harbors in their bosoms!

And these are the best proofs of life—not death. Humanity never possesses more keen and precious vitality than while it suffers. It is not, as in the hour of decay and decline—when the blood is chilled by apathy—when the tongue is stilled by palsy—when the exhausted nature gladly foregoes the struggle, and craves escape from the wearying conflict for existence—anxious now for the quiet waters only—imploring peace, and dulled and indifferent in respect to all mortal associations. The thoughts of the mind, the yearnings of the heart, are all of a different nature, at the separation of friends and kindred. They do not part without a hope. The pain of parting is not without a pleasure. There are sweet sorrows, as well as sad, and this is one of that order. There are many fears, it is true; but these speak for life, nay hope, rather than for death. Every impulse, in the hour which separates the voyagers, tells of life—of vague and grateful anticipations—of renovating experiences—of predicted and promised enjoyments, which neutralize the pain of parting, even in the breasts that most warmly love. Those who remain weep, perhaps, more passionately than those who go. Yet how sweet is that silent tear in the solitude—haunted by happy memories—in the little lovely realm of home! The voyager loses these presences and associations of home; but, in place of them, he dreams of discoveries to be made which he shall yet bring home and share with those he leaves. He will gather new associations to add to the delights of home; new aspects; treasures for the eye and mind, which shall make the solitary forget wholly the lonely length of his absence. Nature has benevolently possessed us with promptings, such as these, which disarm remorse and apprehension: else how should enterprise brave the yet pathless waters, or hope retread the wilderness? Where should genius look for the accompanying aid of perseverance? where would ambition seek for encouragement? where would merit find its reward?

It is well to leave our homes for a season. It is wise to go abroad among strangers. The mind and body, alike, become debilitated, and lose their common energies as frequently from the lack of change and new society as from any other cause. Relaxation, in this way, from the toils of one station, serves to enlarge the capacities, to make room for thought, to afford time for the gathering of new materials, and for the exercise of all the faculties of sense and sentiment. As the farther we go in the natural, so in the moral world, a like journey in the same manner yields us a wider horizon. We add to our stock by attrition with strangers. A tacit trade is carried on between us. Our modes of thinking, our thoughts themselves, our manners, habits, aims, and desires—if not exchanged for others—become intermixed with, or modified by them. They gather from us as much, in these concerns, and in this way, as we can possibly derive from them; and thus, by mutual acquaintance with each other, we overcome foolish prejudices, subjugate ancient enmities, make new friends and associations, and all this simply by enlarging the sphere of our observation—by overleaping the boundaries of a narrow education—leaving the ten-mile horizon in which we were born, and to which our errors are peculiar, and opening our eyes upon a true picture of the character of the various man.

Of all tyrants, home ignorance is the worst.

"Home-keeping youth have ever homely wits,"

which subjugate the understanding, enthral the heart, minister to a miserable sectarianism, as well in society as in politics and religion, and which, in the denial to the individual of any just knowledge of his fellows, leaves him in most lamentable ignorance of the proper resources in himself. We should know our neighbor if only in order to know ourselves, and home is never more happily illustrated than when we compare and contrast it with what we see abroad. It is surprising how soon we lose the faculty of reasoning when the province which we survey is contracted to the single spot in which we sleep and eat. We cease to use our eyes when the sphere is thus limited. The disease of moral nearsightedness supervenes, and the mind which, in a larger field of action and survey, might have grasped all humanity within its range, grows, by reason of this one mishap, into the wretched bigot, with a disposition to be as despotic, in degree with the extreme barrenness of his mental condition.

"Ah! clearly," concluded my companion, after we had worked out the meditations together which I have thrown together above as a sort of essay—"clearly, there is no more moral practice in the world than is found in vagabondage; yet if you try to prove its morality, you take from it all its charm. I am for enjoying the vice as such, without arguing for the necessity of evil—which I yet admit.—But, look you, we are to have some lady passengers. That's a graceful creature!"

I soon discovered in the group to which my companion called my attention, some old acquaintances.

"Ay, indeed; and when you have seen her face, and chatted with her, you will account her beautiful as graceful. She is a sweet creature to whom I will introduce you. The family is one of our oldest, highly-esteemed and wealthy. You want a wife—she is the woman for you. Win her, and you are a favorite of the gods. She has already refused a dozen. Ten to one, she is on her way to the very mountain regions to which we go."

"Good!—I shall be glad to know her. Not that I want a wife—though, perhaps, I need one."

The group disappeared in the cabin. Our hour was approaching. The last bell would soon ring—our fellow-passengers—fortunately few in number—some forty only—were all on board. Several of them were known to me, and I promised myself and my companion good-fellowship. Meanwhile, we were taking our last look at the neighborhood. The bay and harbor of New York make a very grateful picture. The amphitheatre is a fine and noble one, but it is a mistake to insist upon the *grandeur* of its scenery. Mr. Cooper, once, in a conversation with me, even denied that it could be called a beautiful one. But he was clearly in error. He had measured its claims by foreign standards, such as the bay of Naples, the adjuncts of which it lacked. But its beauties are nevertheless undeniable. The error of its admirers is in talking vaguely of its sublimity. Grandeur is not the word to apply to any portion of the Hudson. It is a bold and stately stream, ample, noble, rich, but with few of the ingredients of sublimity. It impresses you—is imposing;—your mind is raised in its contemplation, your fancy enlivened with its picturesqueness—but it possesses few or none of the qualities which awe or startle. It has boldness rather than vastness, is commanding rather than striking, and, if impressive, is quite as frequently cold and unattractive. To a Southern eye, accustomed to the dense umbrage, the close coppice, the gigantic forest, the interminable shade, the wilderness of undergrowth, and the various tints and hues of leaf and blossom, which crown our woods with variety and sweetness, the sparseness of northern woods suggests a great deficiency, which the absence of a lateral foliage, where the trees do occur, only increases. Mountain scenery, unless wild and greatly irregular, repels and chills as commonly as it invites and beguiles. There must be a sufficient variety of forest tint and shelter, under a clear blue sky, to satisfy the fancy and the sympathies. That along the Hudson, after the first pleasant transition from the sea, becomes somewhat monotonous as you proceed. For the length of the river, the scenery is probably as agreeable and attractive as any in the country, unless, perhaps, the St. John's, which is quite a wonderful stream—imposing in spite of the absence of all elevations—and I may add, in certain respects, the Tselica, or French-Broad, in North Carolina. The first of these rivers is remarkable for its great openings into noble lakes, and its noble colonnades of trees;—the last for its furious rapids, its precipitous and broken heights, that bear upon their blasted fronts the proofs of the terrible convulsion of storm and fire, that rent their walls apart and gave passage for the swollen torrent. These you may study and pursue, mile after mile, with constant increase of interest. But, along the Hudson, I do not see that the spectator lingers over it with any profound admiration, or expectation, the first hour or two of progress being over. His curiosity seldom lasts beyond West Point. Observe the crowds wayfaring daily in the steamboats, between New York and Albany—as they glide below the Palisade, that excellent wall of *trap*, almost as regularly built, as if by the hand of mortal artificer—as they penetrate the Highlands and dart beneath the frowning masses of Crow Nest, and Anthony's Nose;—watch them as they approch all these points and places —all of them distinguished in song and story, in chronicle and guide-book—and you will perceive but little raised attention— little of that eager enthusiastic forgetfulness of self, which speaks the excited fancy, and the struggling imagination. They will talk to you of beauties, but these do not inflame them; of sublimities, which never inspire awe; and prospects, over which they yawn rather than wonder.

In fact, the exaggerations in regard to this river have done some wrong to its real claims to respect and admiration. The traveller is taught to expect too much. The scenery does not grow upon him. The objects change in their positions, from this hand to that, in height and bulk, but seldom in form, and as infrequently in relation to one another. The groups bear still the same family likenesses. The narrow gorge through which you are passing at one moment, presented you with its twin likeness but a few minutes before; and the great rock which towers, sloping gradually up from the river in which it is moored with steadfast anchorage, is only one of a hundred such, which lack an individual character. The time has not yet arrived when the commanding physical aspects of the scene shall possess an appropriate moral attraction; when the temple shall swell up with its vast range of marble pillars, crowning the eminence with a classic attraction, and addressing equally the taste and patriotism;—when groves and gardens, and palaces, like those of Bagdad, shall appeal to that oriental fancy in the spectator which is clearly the province of our sky and climate.

At present, these are somewhat repelled by the frequent and manifest perversities of taste, as it seeks to minister to pretension, at the expense of fine and imposing situations. The lawn which spreads away upon the shore, terminating at once with a West Indian verandah, a Dutch farmhouse, and probably a Gothic cottage, scarcely persuades you to a second glance; or, if it does, only to prompt you to quarrel with the painful and unfruitful labors of the architect in search of the picturesque. In what is natural, it may be admitted that you find grace and beauty, but somewhat injured by monotony; in what is done by art you are annoyed by newness, and a taste still crude and imperfectly developed.

The bay of New York is much more noble, I am inclined to think, than the Hudson; but the characteristics of the two are not unlike. Depth, fullness, clearness—a *coup d'œil* which satisfies the glance, and a sufficient variety in the groups and objects to persuade the eye to wander—these are the constituents of both; and, in their combination, we find sweetness, grace and nobleness, but nowhere grandeur or sublimity. Green islets rise on either hand, the shore lies prettily in sight, freshened with verdure, and sprinkled by white cottages which you must not examine in detail, lest you suspect that they may be temples in disguise. Here are forts and batteries, which are usually said to frown, but, speaking more to the card, the grin is more frequent than the frown; and here, emerging through the gorge of the Narrows, we gaze on pleasant heights and headlands, which seem the prettiest places in the world for summer dwellings and retreats. No one will deny the beauty of the scene, as it is, or will question its future susceptibilities. Let us adopt the right epithets. In passing out to sea, with the broad level range of the Atlantic before us, glowing purple in the evening sunlight, we find it easy to believe, gazing behind us upon the shore, that, for the charm of a pleasing landscape, a quiet home, a dear retreat for peace and contemplation, no region presents higher attractions than we find along the shores which lead from Sandy Hook to the city of Manhatta, and spread away from that up the valley of the Hudson, till we pass beyond the Catskill ranges.

"You are like all the rest of the outsiders," said my companion, querulously. "It takes a New York eye to see and appreciate the sublimity of the Hudson."

"Precisely. That is just what I say. It is the New York eye only which makes this discovery. But we are off. There goes the gun!—and farewell, for the present, to our goodly Gotham. Ah! there is Hoboken! How changed for the worse, as a picture, from what is was when I first knew it. Twenty years ago, when I first visited New York, Hoboken was as favorite a resort with me, of an afternoon, as it was to thousands of your citizens. Its beautifully sloping lawns were green and shady. Now! oh! the sins of brick and mortar! There, I first knew Bryant and Sands, and wandered with them along the shores, at sunset, or strolled away, up the heights of Weehawken, declaiming the graceful verses of Halleck upon the scene. All is altered now! *Vale!*"

CHAPTER III

"The world's mine oyster,
Which I with sword will open."

Our steamers do not take long in getting out to sea. We have no such tacking and backing, and sidling and idling, as afflicted and embarrassed the movements of the ancient packet-ships, after they had tripped anchors. On the present occasion, our vessel went ahead with a will, and though not the fastest of our steamers, yet with a power of her own, particularly in a heavy sea, and with lively breezes, which enables her, under such circumstances to surge ahead with the bravest. We were soon out of the hook, with our nose set south, a mild setting sun persuading us onward, holding out rosy wreaths and halos in the west, which seemed to promise well for the balmy clime to which our course was bent. The breeze, though fresh, was soft and warm, and the sea as smooth as the blandishments of a popular orator. The scene was sufficiently auspicious to bring all the passengers on deck, where they grouped about together according to their several affinities. I kept my promise to my companion, and introduced him to the interesting lady in dove-colored muslin.

"Miss Burroughs, suffer me to introduce to you my friend, Mr. Edgar Duyckman of New York."

The lady bowed graciously — my friend was superlative in courtesy, and expressed his great delight in making her acquaintance. She smiled, as she replied —

"Mr. Duyckman seems to forget that he enjoyed this pleasure on a previous occasion."

"Indeed! Where, Miss Burroughs?" was the response. Our Edgar was evidently disquieted. The lady smiled again, the smallest possible twinkle of the quiz peeping out from the corner of her eyes.

"Both at Newport and Saratoga. But I can hardly complain that the impression which I made upon his memory was so slight, remembering how many were the eyes, dazzled like his own, by the blaze of Miss Everton's beauty."

Very rich was the suffusion upon Edgar's cheek. He had been one of the heedless beetles, who had his wings singed in that beauty's blaze. Common rumor said that he had been mortified unexpectedly by a rude and single monosyllable, from that young lady, in reply to a very passionate apostrophe. Poor fellow, he was quite cut up—cut down, he phrased it—by the extent of his present companion's knowledge. But she was not the person to press an ungenerous advantage, and the subject was soon made to give way to another which left the galled jade free. He soon recovered his composure, and we got into a pleasant chat mostly about the world in which we found ourselves; suffering a "sea change" in thoughts as well as association. Our fellow-passengers, numbering just enough for good-fellowship and ease, were mostly veteran seafarers, to whom salt water brought no afflictions. We were pleasantly enough occupied for a while, in scanning their visages as they passed, and discussing their appearances, and supposed objects. Of course, a fair proportion of the men were bound south for business purposes. The ladies were but three in number, and, like my young friend and myself, their aim was for the mountain country. As yet, any notion of taking this route in midsummer had not entered into the imagination of summer idlers to conceive. We were, in a measure, the pioneers in a novel progress.

My friend Duyckman, soon becoming interested in the fair Selina Burroughs, began to bring forth all his resources of reading and experience. He had an abundant supply of graceful and grateful resources, and was capable of that pleasant sort of intellectual trifling which is perhaps the most current of all the light coin of society. The moment that he could fairly forget the *malapropos* reference to the beautiful coquette of Newport, he became easy, fluent and interesting, and under his lead the chat became at once lively and interesting, relating particularly to the scenes about, and the prospect before us. These, as I have shown, were sufficiently pleasant and promising. The sun was set, but the shores lay still in sight, a dim edging of coast, a dark stripe of riband along the deep. We were not yet out of our latitude, and the points of shore, as we passed, could still be identified and named. It is easy enough for Americans to pass from the present to antiquity, and, *per saltum*, to make a hurried transition to the future. The orator who does not begin at the flood, or at least with the first voyage of Columbus, scarcely satisfies the popular requisition on this head. Thus, coming out of the mouth of the Hudson, it was matter of course that we should meditate the career of old Hendrick, of that Ilk, the first to penetrate the noble avenue of stream from which we had just emerged. It was no disparagement to the ancient mariner, that my friend dealt with him in a vein not dissimilar to that in which Irving disposed of the great men of the Dutch dynasty, the Van Twillers, the Stuyvesants, and other unpronounceable dignitaries. He passed, by natural transitions, to modern periods.

"Perhaps, the most exciting of recent events is the oyster war between the Gothamites and Jerseyites. The history of this amusing struggle for plunder is one that should be put on record by a becoming muse. It is a fit subject for an epic. I would recommend it to Bayard Taylor, or Dr. Holmes. The first essential is to be found in the opposite characteristics of the rival races. They are sufficiently distinct for contrast — York and Jersey — as much so as Greek and Trojan. A study of details would afford us the Achilles and Hector, the Ulysses, Ajax, and Thersites. Nor should we want for a pious priest or two, since, in modern times, piety is, by a large number, supposed to be only a fit training for habits of peculation."

"It furnishes a frequent mask, at all events."

"Yes, and was not wanting in this contest. The number of persons engaged was sufficient to enlist all varieties of character, and it was a matter of vital interest to one of the parties at least. The smaller republic was largely interested in the subject of debate. The courage and enterprise of the Jerseyans had plucked the rugged oyster from his native abodes, and subjected him to the usual processes of civilization. They had planted him in favorite places, and given due attention to his training. The oyster was grateful, and took his education naturally. He grew and fatted; and the benevolent Jerseyans watched his growth and improvement with daily care, looking fondly forward to the time when he should take his place in the gratified presence of the great and noble of the land. Famously did the oyster grow —thus considerately protected—until he rose conspicuous in every estimation among the gastronomes of Gotham. These looked with equal envy and admiration upon the performances of their neighbors. Little did Jersey suspect the danger that awaited her favorites. But cunning and cupidity, and eager lust, and ravenous appetite, were planning desolation and overthrow to the hopes of these guardians of the innocent. Evil designs were plotted—cruel, treacherous, barbarous, like those which finally routed the poor nuns at midnight from their Charlestown convent. And great was the shock and the horror of Jersey when the assault was finally made under cover of night and darkness."

"Truly, Mr. Duyckman, you make a lively picture of the event. Pray go on: I am interested to know the result. What of the progress of the war? I confess to only a slight knowledge of the affair."

"Without the documents, I can not go into particulars. To collect these would require a life. To depict them properly would demand a Homer. The war between the cranes and frogs would alone furnish a just plan for such a history. I must content myself with a summary. But, were you to have proper portraits of the fierce Sam Jones, the redoubtable Pete Pinnock, Ben the Biter, Barney the Diver, Bill the Raker, Ned the Devourer, and a score or two more, on both sides, who distinguished themselves in the field during this bivalvular campaign, you would feel that there are still provinces for the epic muse, in which she might soar as gloriously as she ever did in the days of Ilium. Jersey rose to the necessities of the occasion. We will say nothing about her *interest* in this event; but her pride was involved in the security of her virgin beds; and when, prompted by cupidity, these were invaded, *vi et armis*, by the grasping Gothamites, who desired to share the spoils which their valor had not been sufficient to achieve, it was not to be wondered at that all Jersey should rise in arms. The public sentiment was unanimous. From Newark to Absecom, but a single cry was heard. From Jersey City to Cape May, the beacons were lighted up. The cry 'To arms!' spread and echoed far and wide, from the heights of Weehawken to the breakers of Barnegat. The feeling of each Jerseyan was that of the North Carolinian from Tar river, on his way to Texas, when he heard of Santa Anna's invasion of the single star republic. They flourished their plover-guns, where the son of the old North State flourished his rifle, preparing, like him, to assert their rights, *in nubibus*. Well might the oyster family become proud of the excitement occasioned by the contemplated invasion of their abodes. The banner of lust and avarice, carried by the Gothamites, was borne forward with sufficient audacity to show the estimated value of the prize."

Here our captain put in with a fragment of one of the ballads made on the occasion :—

"It was Sam Jones, the fisherman, so famed at Sandy Hook,
That, rising proudly in the midst, the oyster-banner took,
And waved it o'er the host, until, convulsed in every joint,
They swore with him a mighty oath to capture Oyster Point:
Such luscious pictures as he drew of treasures hoarded there,
Such prospects of the future stew, the broil and fry to share,
No Greek or Roman, Turk or Goth, with such an eager scent,
By such a fierce marauder led, to raid or slaughter went.
All glory to Sam Jones the Big — a mighty man was he;
And when he next goes forth to fight, may I be there to see."

"Bravo, captain! you are as good as a chronicler. Let us have the rest."

"That is all I recollect of the ballad; but, had I known your wishes in season, we might have got it all out of the pilot. He was in the war, and was one of the wounded — taken with the fine edge of an oyster-shell on the left nostril, where he carries the proof of his valor to this day in a monstrous scar. The only further curious fact I know, in the history, is that the said scar always opens afresh in the 'R' months, — the oyster-season."

The curious fact thus stated led to some discussion of the occult subject of moral and physical affinities, in which we wandered off to the philosophies of Sir Kenelm Digby and Hahnemann. From these we concluded that there is a latent truth in the vulgar proverb which asserts "the hair of the dog to be good 'or the bite" — a proverb which we hold to be the true source of homeopathy. The practical inference from the discussion was that our pilot could do nothing more likely to effect the cure of his abraded nostril, than to subject his nose to an oyster-scraping in all the months which contain the irritating letter. This episode over, our Gothamite continued his narration:—

"The invasion of the oyster-beds of Jersey, thus formidably led by Jones the Big, was at first a surprise. The Jerseyans never dreamed of the malice of their neighbors. But they had been vigilant, and were valiant. The Jersey Blues had enjoyed a very honorable reputation for valor from the Revolutionary period, not exceeded, perhaps scarcely equalled, by any of the neighboring colonies. They had a proper pride in maintaining this reputation. It was at once a question of life and honor, and they rushed fearlessly to the rescue. The slaughter of their innocents had begun, and they were suffered but little time for preparation. Hastily snatching up what weapons and missiles they could lay hands upon, they darted forth by land and sea. For a season, the war consisted of unfruitful skirmishes only, but the two armies at length drew together. The great cities of refuge of the oyster were in sight, the prize of valor. The audacity of the invaders increased with the prospect. Sam Jones led his followers on with a savage desperation peculiarly his own. Very fearful had been Sam's experience. He had slept upon a circle of six feet, on an oyster-bed, with the Atlantic rolling around him. He had enjoyed a hand-to-hand combat with a shark, of sixteen feet, in five-fathom water. He had ceased to know fear, and had learned to snap his fingers at all enemies. No wonder, led by such a hero, that the Gothamites went into the fray with a rush and shout that shook the shores, and made the innocent muscles under water quake to the centre of their terrified beds. They rushed to the attack with a courage which, as the moral historians are apt to say, was worthy of a better cause. The Greeks at Troy, under the conduct of Ajax the Buffalo, never darted under the hills and towers of Ilium with more defiant demeanor."

"I am impatient for the issue," said the lady. "Pray, how did the Jerseyans stand the shock?"

"Most gallantly—as if duly inspired by the innocence which they sought to defend. The Trojans, led by Hector and Troilus, never showed fiercer powers of resistance than did the serried ranks of Jersey under the terrible concussion. Every man became a hero,—every hero a tower of strength—a fortress. Terrible was the encounter. The battle opened with the flight of missiles from the light troops. Shells skated through the air. It was in the play of this light artillery that the nose of Bill Perkins the pilot, suffered its hurts. Another—one of the Joneses. a cousin of Sam—had the bridge of his fairly broken. It has not been held *passable* since. But the sanguinary passions of the two parties were not willing that the fight should long continue at respectful distances. Soon, pike crossed with pike; oyster-rakes grappled with oyster-rakes; forks, that once drove unembarrassed through the luscious sides of fat victims only, now found fierce obstruction, and no fat, from implements of their own structure and dimensions. The conflict was long in suspense, and only determined in the fall of the redoubtable Sam, the monarch of Sandy Hook. He succumbed beneath a blow inflicted by a young turtle, which, caught up in his desperation by Ralph Roger, of Tuckahoe, was whirled about as a stone in a sling, thrice above his head, until it came in contact with that of Jones. Shell against shell. The crack of one of them was heard. For a moment, the question was doubtful which. But, in a jiffy, the gigantic bulk of Jones went over, like a thousand of brick, shaking the clam-beds for sixty miles along the shore. An awful groan went up from the assembled Gothamites. The affair was over. They lost heart in the fall of their hero, and threw down their arms. Jersey conquered in the conflict."

"Oh, I am so rejoiced!" exclaimed Miss Burroughs, her proper sense of justice naturally sympathizing with the threatened innocents, assailed at midnight in their unconscious beds.

"And what punishment was inflicted upon the marauders?"

"A very fearful one. Thirty prisoners were taken; many had fallen in the fight; many more had fled. The missing have never been ascertained to this day."

"Well, but the punishment?"

"This was planned with a painful malice. At first, the vindictive passions of the Jerseyans being uppermost, it was strenuously urged that the captives should be sacrificed as a due warning to evil-doers. It was agreed that nothing short of the

2

most extreme penalties would suffice to prevent the repetition of the offence. The nature of the necessity seemed to justify, with many, the sanguinary decision. The principle urged was, that the punishment was to be graduated rather by the facility of crime than by its turpitude. Thus, horse-stealing is in some regions rated with murder, simply because, from the nature of beast and country, it is supposed that horses may be more easily stolen than men slain. Men are usually assumed to incline to defend their lives; but it would be an extreme case where a horse, once bridled and saddled, would offer any resistance to his own abduction. He would rather facilitate the designs upon his own innocence by the use of his own legs. The oysters, more simple, more confiding than the horse even, are still more at the mercy of the marauder. His crime is, accordingly, in proportion to the weakness, the good faith, the confiding simplicity of the creature, whose midnight slumbers he invades. These arguments were well urged by one of the Jersey oystermen, who had once filled the station of a chancellor of one of the supreme courts in one of the states. A passion for Cognac had lost him his elevation, and, in the caprices of fortune, he had passed from equity to oysters. The transition, now-a-days, is hardly one to surprise or startle. He used his old experience, whenever he could get a chance to practise upon an audience, and made a monstrous long speech upon this occasion; and very touching indeed was the picture which he drew of the tender character, the virgin innocence, the exposed situation, the helplessness of the oyster—its inabilities for self-defence, and the virtues which commended it to all persons of proper sympathies and a genuine humanity—which were of a sort, also, to provoke the horrid appetites of a class of desperates who perpetually roamed about, like the evil beasts described in scripture, seeking only what they might devour. Our ex-chancellor argued that the oyster was to be protected from invasion; that prevention was always better than cure; that the punishment of the criminal was the only proper process of prevention; that law was only valuable for its effects in terrorem; that the rights of eminent domain in Jersey, along the whole oyster region invaded, conferred upon her the right of summary punishment, at her discretion, as the necessary incident of her sovereignty; and he wound up by an eloquent allusion to the oysters as among the benefactors of mankind. They suffered themselves to live and fatten only for our gratification; and the least that could be done would be to put to death all persons who, without legal rights, presumed to penetrate their sleeping-places and tear them from their beds with violence."

"I begin to tremble for the captives," quoth the lady.

"Well you may. The ex-chancellor had gone into the action only after certain free potations, and he was eloquent in the extreme. The situation of the prisoners became a very perilous one. They were permitted to hearken to the keen debate respecting their crimes and probable fate. Roped in boats, or along the shores, they waited in fear and trembling for their doom. Fortunately, the counsels of humanity prevailed. The Jerseyans, satisfied with having asserted their rights, and pleased with victory, were prepared to be magnanimous. They spared the lives of the offenders, but did not suffer them to depart wholly without punishment. It may be said, that, considering the appetites of the Manhattanese, they adopted the severest of all possible punishments. With their captives fast tethered in sight, they prepared to indulge in a feast of oysters in which the Manhattanese were not allowed to share.

"They provided an ample supply, and dressed them in all possible modes by which to taunt the desires of the epicure. The captives inhaled the pleasant fumes of the fried; they beheld the precious liquid which embraced the portly dimensions of the stewed; they inhaled the odors of choice claret as it amalgamated with other select virtues of the stew, and they gloated over the deliciously-brown aspects of a large platter of oyster-fritters. Oysters on all sides, in all shapes, in every style of dressing, rewarded the victors for their toils, while the conquered, permitted to behold, were denied altogether to enjoy. The meat being extracted, the odorous shells were placed before them, and they were bidden to eat. 'You claimed a share in our beds,' was the scornful speech of the conquerors,—'your share is before you. Fall to and welcome.' Violent groans of anguish and mortification burst from the bosoms of the prisoners at this indignity. Sam Jones, with a broken sconce, roared his rage aloud with the breath of a wounded buffalo. But there was no redress—

no remedy. After a twenty-four hours' captivity, the offenders were permitted to go free, with an injunction to 'sin no more' in the way of oysters. It needed no such injunction with many of the party. The terrors which the poor fellows had undergone probably cured them of their tastes, if not their cupidity, and we may fancy them going off, mournfully singing—

> "So we'll go no more an-oystering
> So late into the night."

This, in little, is the history of the war, which, as I have said, deserves to be chronicled for the future in Homeric verse.

Here one of our fellow-passengers put in:—

"The history of the wars between the tribes of Gotham and Jersey, which you have given, has its parallels in other states. I was on a visit to what is called in Virginia, 'The Eastern Shore,' where they give you just such a narrative, and where the oyster-beds are similarly harassed by irresponsible marauding parties, most of whom are Pennsylvanians. The commerce of this region is chiefly in oysters. In all the bays you behold at anchor a suspicious sort of vessel—looking for all the world like the low, long, black-looking craft of the Spanish *flibustier*. From some of the stories told of these vessels, they are really not a whit better than they should be; and their pursuits are held to be almost as illegitimate as those of the ancient buccaneers of Nassau and New Providence. They wage an insatiate war upon one class, the most inoffensive of all the natives of the Eastern Shore. Their most innocent name is 'pungo'—a sort of schooner, hailing mostly from Manhattan and Massachusetts. They prey upon the Virginia oyster banks, ostensibly under the forms of law. By contract, they procure the ordinary 'raccoon oyster'—the meanest of the tribe—an innocent in a perfect state of nature—totally uneducated, at a shilling (York) per bushel. These are carried off in large quantities to the bays and harbors of Pennsylvania, New York, and places farther east, and placed in nurseries, where good heed is taken to their ease, growth, and physical development, until they are fitted to take their places at table, to the satisfaction of appreciative guests. For the better oysters, taken from deep water, and worthy of the immediate attention of the public, the 'pungos' pay three shillings. In the cities farther north they are retailed at this rate by the dozen—that number being a standard allowance, for an able-bodied alderman, of moderate stomach—an Apicius, not an Heliogabalus. This is the only legalized method of robbing the Virginia waters of their natives. By this process the poorer sort of people are employed to gather the oyster, and are thus compensated for their *labor*—nothing being allowed for the value of the 'innocent' victim. As it is thus made a business for a certain portion of the residents, the practice is tolerated, if not encouraged; though it threatens to destroy, in the end, the resources of the region in respect to this commodity. The clam is appropriated in the same manner, to say nothing of large varieties of fish.

"But there are trespassers who pursue another practice; who seize with the strong hand—who make formidable descents, at unreasonable hours and seasons, and rend and carry off immense quantities, without leaving the usual toll. To these forays, the sensibilities and the patriotism of the people are always keenly alive; and fearful issues, tooth and nail, are sometimes the consequence.

"On one occasion, not long ago, the Virginians of that region got an inkling of a formidable invasion by the Pennsylvanians. The 'bale fires' were lighted accordingly;—the horn was blown, and a general gathering took place of all within striking distance. The 'Old Dominion' is not easily roused, being huge of form, indolent, and easily pacified by appeals to her magnitude and greatness. You may take many liberties with her, so long as you do not ruffle her self-esteem—nay, you may absolutely meddle with her pocketbook if you will do the thing adroitly and without disturbing her *siesta;*—but beware how you carry off her oysters without paying the customary' toll. She can't stand that.

"On this occasion, whig and democrat, forgetting old snarls, came forth with a hearty will. They stood shoulder to shoulder, and the same horn summoned equally both parties to the conflict. It was a common cause, and they promptly agreed to go together to the death for their rights in oysters. As in the case of the combatants of Gotham and Jersey, each side had its famous captains—its Ajaxes and Hectors. But the Pennsylvanians suffered from a falling of the heart before they came to blows

Whether it was that their conscientiousness was too active or their courage too dormant, they submitted before they came to blows; and the whole foraging party—'the entire swine'— an entire tribe of that peaceable sachem, Penn—in a body, every mother's son of them—eighty or ninety in number— were driven into an extemporary logpen at the muzzle of the musket. Around this our angry Virginians kept vigilant watch. The Quaker that raised head above the battlements, though but to peep out at the evening sunset, was warned backward with a tap of spear or shilelah. They were held thus trembling for two or three days in durance vile, until they had paid heavy ransom. It required some fifteen hundred dollars, cash, before the foragers were released. This was a famous haul for our guid folk of the Eastern Shore. For some time it had the effect of keeping off trespassers. But when was cupidity ever quieted short of having its throat of greed cut at the carotid? The practice has been resumed, and our Eastern Shore Virginians are again beginning to growl and to show their teeth. When I was there last, they were brushing up their guns, and newly priming. They promise us a new demonstration shortly, both parties, whig and democratic, preparing to unite their forces to prevent their innocent young shellfish from being torn away from their beds at midnight."

"And loving oysters as I do, I am free to say they could not peril their lives in a more noble cause. Stamped paper and tea were nothing to it."

CHAPTER IV.

"With song and story make the long way short."

THE sea never fails to furnish noble studies to those who, by frequent travel, have succeeded in overcoming its annoyances. But the number is few who feel reconciled to calm thought and patient meditation while roaming, at large and lone, on its wilderness of bosom. Those only who have completely undergone that sea change, of which Shakspere tells us in the "Tempest," can yield themselves fairly up to the fancies which it inspires and the subliming thought which it awakens. Unhappily, to the greater number of those the subject has lost all its freshness. When we have so frequently boxed the compass, that we can

"Lay hands upon old ocean's mane,
And play familiar with his hoary locks,"

he forfeits all his mysteries.

It is surprising to note how little there is really visible in the great deeps to those who go down frequently upon the waters. To such eyes they even lose their vastness, their vagueness, the immensity which baffles vision, and fills the mind with its most impressive ideas of eternity. Your "Old Salt" is a notorious skeptic. He wears his forefinger perpetually upon the side of his nose. He is not to be amused with fancies and chimeras. He has outgrown wholly his sense of wonder, and his thought of the sea is somewhat allied with the contemptuous, as was that of the Mississippian for the brown bear whom he had whipped in single combat. As for marvels and mysteries in the creature —beauties of splendor or grandeur—these wholly elude his thoughts and eyes. If he appreciates the sea at all, it is solely because of its sharpening effect upon his appetite!

Most of those wayfarers whom you meet often upon the route belong to this order. You will find them at all times peering into the larder. In their sleep, they dream of it, and you will hear broken speeches from their lips which show their memories still busy with yesterday's feast, or their anticipations preparing for that of the morrow. The steward and cook aboard-ship are the first persons whose acquaintance they make. These they bribe with shillings and civilities. You will scarcely open your eyes in the morning, ere you will see these "hail fellows" with toast and tankard in their clutches; a bowl of coffee and a cracker is the initial appetizer, with possibly a tass of brandy in the purple beverage, as a lacer. Then you see them hanging about the breakfast table, where they take care to plant themselves in the near neighborhood of certain of the choicest dishes. All their little arrangements are made before you get to the table, and there will be a clever accumulation of good things about the plates of these veterans, in the shape of roll and egg, etc., which would seem destined to remind the proprietor, in the language of warning which was spoken daily (though with a far different object) to the monarch of the Medes and Persians—"Remember, thou art mortal."

This is a fact which our veterans of the high seas never forget. They carry within them a sufficient monitor which ever cries, like the daughter of the horse-leech, "Give! Give!" They have no qualms of conscience or of bowels; and it seems to do them rare good to behold the qualms of others. It would seem that they rejoiced in these exhibitions, simply as they are, assured by these, that the larder is destined to no premature invasion on the part of the sufferers.

I have often looked upon this class of travellers—not with envy, Heaven forefend!—though it would have rejoiced me frequently, at sea, to have possessed some of their immunities—that rare insensibility, for example, in the regions of diaphragm and abdomen, which, if unexercised for appetite, might at least suffer other sensibilities to be free for exercise.

But it has provoked my wonder, if not my admiration, that inflexible stolidity of nature, which enables the mere mortal so entirely to obtain the ascendency over the spiritual man. Our gourmand sees no ocean waste around him—follows no tumbling billows with his eye—watches not, with straining eagerness, where the clouds and the waters descend and rise, as it were in an embrace of passion. Sunrise only tells him of his coffee and cracker, noon of lunch, sunset of tea, and the rarely sublimed fires of the moonlight, gleaming from a thousand waves, suggest only a period of repose, in which digestion goes on without any consciousness of that great engine which he has all day been packing with fuel. Tell him of porpoise and shark, and his prayer is that they may be taken. He has no scruples to try a steak from the ribs of the shark, though it may have swallowed his own grandmother. Of the porpoise he has heard as the sea-hog, and the idea of a roast of it, is quite sufficient to justify the painstaking with which he urges upon the foremast man to take his place at the prow, in waiting, with his harpoon. Nay, let a school of dolphins be seen beneath the bows, darting along with graceful and playful sweep, in gold and purple, glancing through the billows, like so many rainbows of the deep, he thinks of them only as a *fry*—an apology for whiting and cavalli, of which he sighs with the tenderest recollections, and for which he is always anxious to find a substitute. I have already observed that we have two or three specimens of this *genus* now on board the Marion.

"I don't know," said our fair companion, "but that steam has robbed the sea very equally of its charms and terrors."

"Ah! we have now no long voyages. Your coastwise travelling seldom takes you from sight of land, and you scarcely step from the pier head in one city, before you begin to look out for the lighthouse of another. Even when crossing the great pond, you move now so rapidly, and in such mighty vessels, that you carry a small city with you—a community adequate to all your social wants—and are thus made comparatively indifferent to your absolute whereabouts."

"Well, there is something pleasant," said one, "to be able to fling yourself into your berth in one city only to awaken in another. I confess that it takes away all motive to thought and survey. Few persons care to look abroad and about in such short periods. There is little to amuse or interest, traversing the ship's decks for a night, in the face of smoke and steam, jostling with strange people wrapped in cloaks, whom you do not care to know, as it is not probable that you are ever to meet again when you part to-morrow. You must be long and lonely on the seas, before the seas will become grateful in your sight and reveal their wonders. Steam has removed this necessity and thus taken away all the wonders of the deep. You now see no mysteries in the surging billows—hear no spiritual voices from the shrouds. The spell has been taken from the waters—the trident is broken in the hands of the great Triton. Steam, a mightier magic, has puffed away, as by a breath, a whole world of unsubstantial, but very beautiful fable. The ocean is now as patient as the wild horse under the lasso—subdued to the will of a rider who was never known to spare whip or spur."

"The worst feature in this improved navigation is its unsocial influence. It deprives you of all motive to break down those idle little barriers of convention which are apt to fetter the very best minds, and cause a forfeiture of some of their sweetest humanities. You seek to know none of the virtues of your companions, and certainly never care to put in exercise your own. One ceases to be amiable in a short voyage. A long one, on the contrary, brings out all that is meritorious as well in yourself as your shipmate. A sense of mutual dependence is vastly promotive of good fellowship.—Then you see something of one another, and hear something of the world. People show what they are, and tell you what they have seen; and intimacies, thus formed, have ripened into friendships, which no after events have been able to rupture. Commend me to the ancient slow-and-easy packet ships that left you time for all these things;—that went between Charleston and New York, and never felt any impatience to get to the end of their journey;—that took every advantage afforded by a calm to nap drowsily on the bosom of the broad element in which they loved to float;—and rocked lazily upon the great billows, as if coquetting with the breezes rather than using them for progress."

"There was leisure then for study and philosophy and poetry; nay, love-making was then an easy and agreeable employment, to such as had the stomach for it. It will not be easy for me to forget my thousand experiences of the tender passion on such voyages—by moonlight and starlight—'with one sweet spirit for my minister,' gazing together on the great mirror-like ocean, or up into the persuasive heavens, till we drank in floods of tenderness, from a myriad of loving eyes."

"Ah!" cried Duyckman archly, "one is reminded of Moore—

> "'Ah! could you heaven but speak as well,
>   As starry eyes can see,
>   Ah! think what tales 'twould have to tell,
>   Of wandering youth like me.'

"By the way, why should we not have some tales of wandering youth to-night—and why not some songs too. Miss Burroughs, it has not escaped my very curious eye that there is a guitar among your luggage. May I hope that you will suffer me to bring it you?"

The lady hesitated. I interposed:—

"Oh! surely; we must not suffer such a night of beauty, such a sea of calm, such a mild delicious evening, to pass unemployed, and in the only appropriate fashion. We are a little world to ourselves—pilgrims to one Canterbury, and we may well borrow a leaf from Boccacio and a lesson from Chaucer. You will sing for us, and we shall strive to requite you, each after his own fashion. Here are several whom I know to be capable of pleasant contribution in the way of song and story, and my friend Duyckman can hardly refuse to follow your example, as he suggests it. In your ear, I may whisper that he is full of romances, and has a whole budget of legends wrought out of Provençal and Troubadour history."

"Fie! Fie! Honor bright."

The lady now gracefully consented.

"The temptation is too great to be resisted. My scruples yield to your persuasions. Will you order the guitar?"

It was brought. We had the music, but not alone. To the great delight of all parties, the fair charmer gave us her lyrics woven in with an historical narrative—a romance in itself, which, in a brief and pleasant introduction, she mentioned that she had gathered herself from the lips of the celebrated General ——— of Venezuela, who was only last year in the country. I must deliver the story, as nearly as possible as it came from the lady's lips, not forgetting to mention that, in the lyrical portions, the guitar contributed the accompaniment, and the effect of the pieces, thus delivered, was singularly dramatic and effective.

Our circle contracted about the fair *raconteur*, silence followed, and fixed attention, and she began.

THE STORY OF THE MAID OF BOGOTA.

CHAPTER I.

Whenever the several nations of the earth which have achieved their deliverance from misrule and tyranny, shall point, as they each may, to the fair women who have taken active part in the cause of liberty, and by their smiles and services have contributed in no measured degree to the great objects of national defence and deliverance, it will be with a becoming and just pride only that the Colombians shall point to their virgin martyr, commonly known among them as La Pola, the Maid of Bogota. With the history of their struggle for freedom her story will always be intimately associated; her tragical fate, due solely to the cause of her country, being linked with all the touching interest of the most romantic adventure. Her spirit seemed to be woven of the finest materials. She was gentle, exquisitively sensitive, and capable of the most true and tender attachments. Her mind was one of rarest endowments, touched to the finest issues of eloquence, and gifted with all the powers of the improvisatrice; while her courage and patriotism seem to have been cast in those heroic moulds of antiquity from which came the Cornelias and Deborahs of famous memory. Well had it been for her country had the glorious model which she bestowed upon her people been held in becoming homage by the race with which her destiny was cast—a race masculine only in exterior, and wanting wholly in that necessary strength of soul which, rising to the due appreciation of the blessings of national freedom, is equally prepared to make, for its attainment, every necessary sacrifice of self. And yet our heroine was but a child in years—a lovely, tender, feeble creature, scarcely fifteen years of age. But the soul grows rapidly to maturity in some countries, and, in the case of women, it is always great in its youth, if greatness is ever destined to be its possession.

Doña Apolinaria Zalabariata—better known by the name of La Pola—was a young girl, the daughter of a good family of Bogota, who was distinguished at an early period, as well for her great gifts of beauty as of intellect. She was but a child when Bolivar first commenced his struggles with the Spanish authorities, with the ostensible object of freeing his country from their oppressive tyrannies. It is not within our province to discuss the merits of his pretensions as a deliverer, or his courage and military skill as a hero. The judgment of the world and of time has fairly set at rest those specious and hypocritical claims, which, for a season, presumed to place him on the pedestal with our Washington. We now know that he was not only a very selfish, but a very ordinary man—not ordinary, perhaps, in the sense of intellect, for that would be impossible in the case of one who was so long able to maintain his eminent position, and to succeed in his capricious progresses, in spite of inferior means, and a singular deficiency of the heroic faculty. But his ambition was the vulgar ambition, and, if possible, something still inferior. It contemplated his personal wants alone; it lacked all the elevation of purpose which is the great essential of patriotism, and was wholly wanting in that magnanimity of soul which delights in the sacrifice of self, whenever such sacrifice promises the safety of the single great purpose which it professes to accomplish.

But we are not now to consider Bolivar, the deliverer, as one whose place in the pantheon has already been determined by the unerring judgment of posterity. We are to behold him only with those eyes in which he was seen by the devoted followers to whom he brought, or appeared to bring, the deliverance for which they yearned. It is with the eyes of the passionate young girl, La Pola, the beautiful and gifted child, whose dream of country perpetually craved the republican condition of ancient Rome, in the days of its simplicity and virtue; it is with her fancy and admiration that we are to crown the *ideal* Bolivar, till we acknowledge him, as he appears to her, the Washington of the Colombians, eager only to emulate the patriotism, and to achieve like successes with his great model of the northern confederacy.

Her feelings and opinions, with regard to the Liberator, were those of her family. Her father was a resident of Bogota, a man of large possessions and considerable intellectual acquirements. He gradually passed from a secret admiration of Bolivar to a warm sympathy with his progress, and an active support—

so far as he dared, living in a city under immediate and despotic Spanish rule — of all his objects. He followed with eager eyes the fortunes of the chief, as they fluctuated between defeat and victory in other provinces, waiting anxiously the moment when the success and policy of the struggle should bring deliverance, in turn, to the gates of Bogota. Without taking up arms himself, he contributed secretly from his own resources to supplying the coffers of Bolivar with treasure, even when his operations were remote — and his daughter was the agent through whose unsuspected ministry the money was conveyed to the several emissaries who were commissioned to receive it. The duty was equally delicate and dangerous, requiring great prudence and circumspection; and the skill, address, and courage, with which the child succeeded in the execution of her trusts, would furnish a frequent lesson for older heads, and the sterner and the bolder sex.

La Pola was but fourteen years old when she obtained her first glimpse of the great man in whose cause she had already been employed, and of whose deeds and distinctions she had heard so much. By the language of the Spanish tyranny which swayed with iron authority over her native city, she heard him denounced and execrated as a rebel and marauder, for whom an ignominious death was already decreed by the despotic viceroy. This language, from such lips, was of itself calculated to raise its object favorably in her enthusiastic sight. By the patriots, whom she had been accustomed to love and venerate, she heard the same name breathed always in whispers of hope and affection, and fondly commended, with tearful blessings, to the watchful care of Heaven.

She was soon to behold with her own eyes this individual thus equally distinguished by hate and homage in her hearing. Bolivar apprized his friends in Bogota that he should visit them in secret. That province, ruled with a fearfully strong hand by Zamano, the viceroy, had not yet ventured to declare itself for the republic. It was necessary to operate with caution; and it was no small peril which Bolivar necessarily incurred, in penetrating to its capital, and laying his snares, and fomenting insurrection, beneath the very hearth-stones of the tyrant. It was to La Pola's hands that the messenger of the Liberator confided the missives that communicated this important intelligence to her father. She little knew the contents of the billet which she carried him in safety, nor did he confide them to the child. He himself did not dream of the precocious extent of that enthusiasm which she felt almost equally for the common cause, and for the person of its great advocate and champion. Her father simply praised her care and diligence, rewarded her with his fondest caresses, and then proceeded with all quiet despatch to make his preparations for the secret reception of the deliverer.

It was at midnight, and while a thunder-storm was raging, that he entered the city, making his way, agreeably to previous arrangement, and under select guidance, into the inner apartments of the house of Zalabariata. A meeting of the conspirators — for such they were — of head men among the patriots of Bogota, had been contemplated for his reception. Several of them were accordingly in attendance when he came. These were persons whose sentiments were well-known to be friendly to the cause of liberty, who had suffered by the hands, or were pursued by the suspicions of Zamano, and who, it was naturally supposed, would be eagerly alive to every opportunity of shaking off the rule of the oppressor.

But patriotism, as a philosophic sentiment, to be indulged after a good dinner, and discussed phlegmatically, if not classically, over sherry and cigars, is a very different sort of thing from patriotism as a principle of action, to be prosecuted as a duty, at every peril, instantly and always, to the death if need be. Our patriots at Bogota were but too frequently of the contemplative, the philosophical order. Patriotism with them was rather a subject for eloquence than use. They could recall those Utopian histories of Greece and Rome which furnish us with ideals rather than facts, and sigh for names like those of Cato, and Brutus, and Aristides. But more than this did not seem to enter their imaginations as at all necessary to assert the character which it pleased them to profess, or maintain the reputation which they had prospectively acquired for the very commendable virtue which constituted their ordinary theme. Bolivar found them cold. Accustomed to overthrow and usurpation, they were now slow to venture property and life upon the predictions and promises of one who, however perfect in their estimation as a patriot, had yet suffered from most capricious fortunes. His past history, indeed, except for its patriotism, offered but very doubtful guarantees in favor of the enterprise to which they were invoked.

Bolivar was artful and ingenious. He had considerable powers of eloquence — was specious and persuasive; had an oily, and bewitching tongue, like Belial; and, if not altogether capable of making the worse appear the better cause, could at least so shape the aspects of evil fortune, that, to the unsuspicious nature, they would seem to be the very results aimed at by the most deliberate arrangement and resolve.

But Bolivar, on this occasion, was something more than ingenious and persuasive; he was warmly earnest, and passionately eloquent. In truth, he was excited much beyond his wont. He was stung to indignation by a sense of disappointment. He had calculated largely on this meeting, and it promised now to be a failure. He had anticipated the eager enthusiasm of a host of brave and noble spirits, ready to fling out the banner of freedom to the winds, and cast the scabbard from the sword for ever. Instead of this, he found but a little knot of cold, irresolute men, thinking only of the perils of life which they should incur, and the forfeiture and loss of property which might accrue from any hazardous experiments.

Bolivar spoke to them in language less artificial and much more impassioned than was his wont. He was a man of impulse rather than of thought or principle, and, once aroused, the intense fire of a southern sun seemed to burn fiercely in all his words and actions.

His speech was heard by other ears than those to which it was addressed. The shrewd mind of La Pola readily conjectured that the meeting at her father's house, at midnight, and under peculiar circumstances, contemplated some extraordinary object. She was aware that a tall, mysterious stranger had passed through the court, under the immediate conduct of her father himself. Her instinct divined in this stranger the person of the deliverer, and her heart would not suffer her to lose the words, or, if possible to obtain it, to forego the sight of the great object of its patriotic worship. Besides, she had a right to know and to see. She was of the party, and had done them service She was yet to do them more.

Concealed in an adjoining apartment—a sort of oratory, connected by a gallery with the chamber in which the conspirators were assembled—she was able to hear the earnest arguments and passionate remonstrances of the Liberator. They confirmed all her previous admiration of his genius and character. She felt with indignation the humiliating position which the men of Bogota held in his eyes. She heard their pleas and scruples, and listened with a bitter scorn to the thousand suggestions of prudence, the thousand calculations of doubt and caution, with which timidity seeks to avoid precipitating a crisis. She could listen and endure no longer. The spirit of the improvvisatrice was upon her. Was it also that of fate and a higher Providence? She seized the guitar, of which she was the perfect mistress, and sung even as her soul counselled and the exigency of the event demanded. Our translation of her lyrical overflow is necessarily a cold and feeble one.

  It was a dream of freedom,
   A mocking dream, though bright,
  That showed the men of Bogota
   All arming for the fight;
  All eager for the hour that wakes
   The thunders of redeeming war,
  And rushing forth, with glittering steel,
   To join the bands of Bolivar.

  My soul, I said, it can not be
   That Bogota shall be denied
  Her Arismendi too—her chief
   To pluck her honor up and pride;
  The wild Llanero boasts his braves
   That, stung with patriot wrath and shame,
  Rushed redly to the realm of graves,
   And rose, through blood and death, to fame.

  How glad mine ear with other sounds,
   Of freemen worthy these that tell!
  Ribas, who felt Caraccas' wounds,
   And for her hope and triumph fell;
  And that young hero, well beloved,
   Giraldat, still a name for song;
   Piar, dying soon,
   For the future living long.

Oh, could we stir with other names,
  The cold, deaf hearts that hear us now,
How would it bring a thousand shames,
  In fire, to each Bogotan's brow!
How clap in pride Grenada's hands,
  How glows Venezuela's heart,
And how, through Cartagena's lands,
  A thousand chiefs and heroes start.

Sodeno, Paez, lo! they rush,
  Each with his wild and Cossack rout
A moment feels the fearful hush,
  A moment hears the fearful shout!
They heed no lack of arts and arms,
  But all their country's perils feel,
And, sworn for freedom, bravely break,
  The glittering legions of Castile.

I see the gallant Roxas clasp
  The towering banner of her sway;
And Monagas, with fearful grasp,
  Plucks down the chief that stops the way;
The reckless Urdaneta rides,
  Where rives the earth the iron hail;
Nor long the Spanish foeman bides,
  The strokes of old Zaraza's flail!

Oh, generous heroes, how ye rise!
  How glow your states with equal fires!
'Tis there Valencia's banner flies,
  And there Cumaria's soul aspires;
There, on each hand, from east to west,
  From Oronook to Panama,
Each province bares its noble breast,
  Each hero—save in Bogota!

At the first sudden gush of the music from within, the father of the damsel started to his feet, and, with confusion in his countenance, was about to leave the apartment. But Bolivar arrested his footsteps, and in a whisper commanded him to be silent and remain. The conspirators, startled if not alarmed, were compelled to listen. Bolivar did so with a pleased attention. He was passionately fond of music, and this was of a sort at once to appeal to his objects and his taste. His eye kindled as the song proceeded. His heart rose with an exulting sentiment. The moment, indeed, embodied one of his greatest triumphs— the tribute of a pure, unsophisticated soul, inspired by Heaven with the happiest and highest endowments, and by earth with the noblest sentiments of pride and country. When the music ceased, Zalabarinta was about to apologize and to explain, but Bolivar again gently and affectionately arrested his utterance.

"Fear nothing," said he. "Indeed, why should you fear? I am in the greater danger here, if there be danger for any; and I would as soon place my life in the keeping of that noble damsel, as in the arms of my mother. Let her remain, my friend; let her hear and see all; and above, do not attempt to apologize for her. She is my ally. Would that she could make these *men* of Bogota feel with herself—feel as she makes even me to feel."

The eloquence of the Liberator received a new impulse from that of the improvisatrice. He renewed his arguments and entreaties in a different spirit. He denounced, in yet bolder language than before, that wretched pusillanimity which, quite as much, he asserted, as the tyranny of the Spaniard, was the curse under which the liberties of the country groaned and suffered.

"And now, I ask," he continued, passionately, "men of Bogota, if ye really purpose to deny yourselves all share in the glory and peril of the effort which is for your own emancipation. Are your brethren of the other provinces to maintain the conflict in your behalf, while, with folded hands, you submit, doing nothing for yourselves? Will you not lift the banner also? Will you not draw sword in your own honor, and the defence of your firesides and families? Talk not to me of secret contributions. It is your manhood, not your money, that is needful for success. And can you withhold yourselves while you profess to hunger after that liberty for which other men are free to peril all—manhood, money, life, hope, everything but honor and the sense of freedom. But why speak of peril in this? Peril is everywhere. It is the inevitable child of life, natural to all conditions—to repose as well as action,—to the obscurity which never goes abroad, as well as to that adventure which for ever seeks the field. You incur no more peril in openly braving your tyrant, all together as one man, than you do thus tamely sitting beneath his footstool, and trembling for ever lest his capricious will may slay as it enslaves. Be you but true to yourselves—openly true—and the danger disappears as the night-mists that speed from before the rising sun. There is little that deserves the name of peril in the issue which lies before us. We are more than a match—united, and filled with the proper spirit—for all the forces that Spain can send against us. It is in our coldness that she warms—in our want of unity that she finds strength. But even were we not superior to her in numbers—even were the chances all wholly and decidedly against us—I still can not see how it is that you hesitate to draw the sword in so sacred a strife—a strife which consecrates the effort, and claims Heaven's sanction for success. Are your souls so subdued by servitude, are you so accustomed to bonds and tortures, that these no longer irk and vex your daily consciousness? Are you so wedded to inaction that you cease to feel? Is it the frequency of the punishment that has made you callous to the ignominy and the pain? Certainly, your viceroy gives you frequent occasion to grow reconciled to any degree of hurt and degradation. Daily you behold, and I hear, of the exactions of this tyrant—of the cruelties and the murders to which he accustoms you in Bogota. Hundreds of your friends and kinsmen, even now, lie rotting in the common prisons, denied equally your sympathies and every show of justice, perishing daily under the most cruel privations. Hundreds have perished by this and other modes of torture, and the gallows and garote seem never to be unoccupied. Was it not the bleaching skeleton of the venerable Hermano, whom I well knew for his wisdom and patriotism, which I beheld, even as I entered, hanging in chains over the gateway of your city? Was he not the victim of his wealth and love of country? Who among you is secure? He dared but to deliver himself as a man—and, as he was suffered to stand alone, he was destroyed. Had you, when he spoke, but prepared yourselves to act, flung out the banner of resistance to the winds, and bared the sword for the last noble struggle, Hermano had not perished, nor were the glorious work only now to be begun. But which of you, involved in the same peril with Hermano, will find the friend, in the moment of his need, to take the first step for his rescue? Each of you, in turn, having wealth to tempt the spoiler, will be sure to need such friendship. It seems you do not look for it among one another—where, then, do you propose to find it? Will you seek for it among the Cartagenians—among the other provinces—to Bolivar *without?* Vain expectation, if you are unwilling to peril anything for yourselves *within!* In a tyranny so suspicious and so reckless as is yours, you must momentarily tremble lest ye suffer at the hands of your despot. True manhood rather prefers any peril which puts an end to this state of anxiety and fear. Thus to tremble with apprehension ever, is ever to be dying. It is a life of death only which ye live—and any death or peril that comes quickly at the summons, is to be preferred before it. If, then, ye have hearts to feel, or hopes to warm ye—a pride to suffer consciousness of shame, or an ambition that longs for better things—affections for which to covet life, or the courage with which to assert and to defend your affections—ye can not, ye will not hesitate to determine, with souls of freemen, upon what is needful to be done. Ye have but one choice as men; and the question which is left for ye to resolve, is that which determines, not your possessions, not even your lives, but simply your rank and stature in the world of humanity and man."

The Liberator paused, not so much through his own or the exhaustion of the subject, as that his hearers should in turn be heard. But, with this latter object, his forbearance was profitless. There were those among them, indeed, who had their answers to his exhortations, but these were not of a character to promise boldly for their patriotism or courage. Their professions, indeed, were ample, but were confined to unmeaning generalities. "Now is the time—now!" was the response of Bolivar to all that was said. But they faltered and hung back at every utterance of his spasmodically-uttered "now! now!" He scanned their faces eagerly, with a hope that gradually yielded to despondency. Their features were blank and inexpressive, as their answers had been meaningless or evasive. Several of them were of that class of quiet citizens, unaccustomed to any enterprises but those of trade, who are always slow to peril wealth by a direct issue with their despotism. They felt the truth of Bolivar's assertions. They knew that their treasures were only so many baits and lures to the cupidity and exactions of the royal emissaries, but they still relied on their habitual caution and docility to keep terms with the tyranny at which they yet trembled. When, in the warmth of his enthusiasm, Bolivar depicted the bloody struggles which must precede their deliverance, they began, indeed, to wonder among themselves how they ever came to fall into that mischievous philosophy of patriotism which had involved them with such a restless rebel as Bolivar! Others of the company were ancient hidalgos, who had been men of spirit in their day, but who had survived the season of enterprise, which is that period only when the heart swells and overflows with full tides of warm and impetuous blood.

"Your error," said he, in a whisper to Señor Don Joachim de Zalabariata, "was in not bringing young men into your counsels."

"We shall have them hereafter," was the reply, also in a whisper.

"We shall see," muttered the Liberator, who continued, though in silence, to scan the assembly with inquisitive eyes, and an excitement of soul, which increased duly with his efforts to subdue it. He had found some allies in the circle — some few generous spirits, who, responding to his desires, were anxious to be up and doing. But it was only too apparent that the main body of the company had been rather disquieted than warmed. In this condition of hopeless and speechless indecision, the emotions of the Liberator became scarcely controllable. His whole frame trembled with the anxiety and indignation of his spirit. He paced the room hurriedly, passing from group to group, appealing to individuals now, where hitherto he had spoken collectively, and suggesting detailed arguments in behalf of hopes and objects, which it does not need that we should incorporate with our narrative. But when he found how feeble was the influence which he exercised, and how cold was the echo to his appeal, he became impatient, and no longer strove to modify the expression of that scorn and indignation which he had for some time felt. The explosion followed in no measured language.

"Men of Bogota, you are not worthy to be free. Your chains are merited. You deserve your insecurities, and may embrace, even as ye please, the fates which lie before you. Acquiesce in the tyranny which offends no longer, but be sure that acquiescence never yet has disarmed the despot when his rapacity needs a victim. Your lives and possessions—which ye dare not peril in the cause of freedom—lie equally at his mercy. He will not pause, as you do, to use them at his pleasure. To save them from him there is but one way—to employ them against him. There is no security against power but in power; and to check the insolence of foreign strength you must oppose to it your own. This ye have not soul to do, and I leave you to the destiny you have chosen. This day, this night, it was yours to resolve. I have perilled all to move you to the proper resolution. You have denied me, and I leave you. To-morrow—unless indeed I am betrayed to-night"—looking with a sarcastic smile around him as he spoke—"I shall unfurl the banner of the republic even within your own province, in behalf of Bogota, and seek, even against your own desires, to bestow upon you those blessings of liberty which ye have not the soul to conquer for yourselves."

CHAPTER II.

Hardly had these words been spoken, when the guitar again sounded from within. Every ear was instantly hushed as the strain ascended—a strain, more ambitious than the preceding, of melancholy and indignant apostrophe. The improvvisatrice was no longer able to control the passionate inspiration which took its tone from the stern eloquence of the Liberator. She caught from him the burning sentiment of scorn which it was no longer his policy to repress, and gave it additional effect in the polished sarcasm of her song. Our translation will poorly suffice to convey a proper notion of the strain.

Then be it so, if serviles ye will be,
　　When manhood's soul had broken every chain,
'Twere scarce a blessing now to make ye free,
　　For such condition tutored long in vain:
Yet may we weep the fortunes of our land,
　　Though woman's tears were never known to take
One link away from that oppressive band
　　Ye have not soul, not soul enough to break!

Oh! there were hearts of might in other days,
　　Brave chiefs, whose memory still is dear to fame;
Alas for ours!—the gallant deeds we praise
　　But show more deeply red our cheeks of shame:

As from the midnight gloom the weary eye,
  With sense that can not the bright dawn forget,
Looks sadly hopeless, from the vacant sky,
  To that where late the glorious day-star set!

Yet all's not midnight dark if, in your land,
  There be some gallant hearts to brave the strife;
One single generous blow from Freedom's hand
  May speak again our sunniest hopes to life;
If but one blessed drop in living veins
  Be worthy those who teach us from the dead,
Vengeance and weapons both are in your chains,
  Hurled fearlessly upon your despot's head!

Yet, if no memory of the living past
  Can wake ye now to brave the indignant strife,
'Twere nothing wise, at least, that we should last
  When death itself might wear a look of life!
Ay, when the oppressive arm is lifted high,
  And scourge and torture still conduct to graves,
To strike, though hopeless still — to strike and die!
  They live not, worthy freedom, who are slaves!

As the song proceeded, Bolivar stood forward as one rapt in ecstacy. The exultation brightened in his eye, and his manner was that of a soul in the realization of its highest triumph. Not so the Bogotans by whom he was surrounded. They felt the terrible sarcasm which the damsel's song conveyed — a sarcasm immortalized to all the future, in the undying depths of a song to be remembered. They felt the humiliation of such a record, and hung their heads in shame. At the close of the ballad, Bolivar exclaimed to Joachim de Zalabarietta, the father: —

"Bring the child before us. She is worthy to be a prime minister. A prime minister? No! the hero of the forlorn hope! a spirit to raise a fallen standard from the dust, and to tear down and trample that of the enemy. Bring her forth, Joachim. Had your *men* of Bogota but a tithe of a heart so precious! Nay, could her heart be divided among them — it might serve a thousand — there were no viceroy of Spain within your city now!"

And when the father brought her forth from the little cabinet, that girl, flashing with inspiration — pale and red by turns — slightly made, but graceful — very lovely to look upon — wrapped in loose white garments, with her long hair, dark and flowing unconfined, and so long that it was easy for her to walk upon it*—the admiration of the Liberator was insuppressible.

"Bless you for ever," he cried, "my fair Princess of Freedom! You, at least, have a free soul, and one that is certainly inspired by the great divinity of earth. You shall be mine ally, though I find none other in all Bogota sufficiently courageous. In you, my child, in you and yours, there is still a redeeming spirit which shall save your city utterly from shame!"

While he spoke, the emotions of the maiden were of a sort readily to show how easily she should be quickened with the inspiration of lyric song. The color came and went upon her soft white cheeks. The tears rose, big and bright, upon her eyelashes—heavy drops, incapable of suppression, that swelled one after the other, trembled and fell, while the light blazed, even more brightly from the showers in the dark and dilating orbs which harbored such capacious fountains. She had no words at first, but, trembling like a leaf, sunk upon a cushion at the feet of her father, as Bolivar, with a kiss upon her forehead, released her from his clasp. Her courage came back to her a moment after. She was a thing of impulse, whose movements were as prompt and unexpected as the inspiration by which she sung. Bolivar had scarcely turned from her, as if to relieve her tremor, when she recovered all her strength and courage. Suddenly rising from the cushion, she seized the hand of her father, and with an action equally passionate and dignified, she led him to the Liberator, to whom, speaking for the first time in that presence, she thus addressed herself:—

"*He* is yours—he has always been ready with his life and money. Believe me, for I know it. Nay more! doubt not that there are hundreds in Bogota—though they be not here—who, like him, will be ready whenever they hear the summons of your trumpet. Nor will the women of Bogota be wanting. There will be many of them who will take the weapons of those who use them not, and do as brave deeds for their country as did the dames of Magdalena when they slew four hundred Spaniards."†

---

* A frequent case among the maids of South America.

† This terrible slaughter took place on the night of the 16th of June, 1816, under the advice and with the participation of the women of Mompox, a bea

"Ah! I remember! A most glorious achievement, and worthy to be written in letters of gold. It was at Mompox, where they rose upon the garrison of Morillo. Girl, you are worthy to have been the chief of those women of Magdalena. You will be chief yet of the women of Bogota. I take your assurance with regard to them; but, for the men, it were better that thou peril nothing even in thy speech."

The last sarcasm of the Liberator might have been spared That which his eloquence had failed to effect was suddenly accomplished by this child of beauty. Her inspiration and presence were electrical. The old forgot their caution and their years The young, who needed but a leader, had suddenly found a genius. There was now no lack of the necessary enthusiasm. There were no more scruples. Hesitation yielded to resolve. The required pledges were given—given more abundantly than required; and, raising the slight form of the damsel to his own height, Bolivar again pressed his lips upon her forehead, gazing at her with a respectful delight, while he bestowed upon her the name of the Guardian Angel of Bogota. With a heart bounding and beating with the most enthusiastic emotions—too full for further utterance—La Pola disappeared from that imposing presence which her coming had filled with a new life and impulse

CHAPTER III.

It was nearly dawn when the Liberator left the city. That night the bleaching skeleton of the venerable patriot Hermano was taken down from the gibbet where it had hung so long, by hands that left the revolutionary banner waving proudly in its place. This was an event to startle the viceroy. It was followed by other events. In a few days more, and the sounds of

tiful city on an island in the river Magdalena. The event has enlisted the muse of many a native patriot and poet, who grew wild when they recalle l th e courage of

> "Those dames of Magdalena,
> Who, in one fearful night,
> Slew full four hundred tyrants,
> Nor shrunk from blood in fright."

Such women deserve the apostrophe of Macbeth to his wife:—

> "Bring forth men children only."

insurrection were heard throughout the province — the city still moving secretly — sending forth supplies and intelligence by stealth, but unable to raise the standard of rebellion, while Zamano, the viceroy, doubtful of its loyalty, remained in possession of its strong places with an overawing force. Bolivar himself, under these circumstances, was unwilling that the patriots should throw aside the mask. Throughout the province, however, the rising was general. They responded eagerly to the call of the Liberator, and it was easy to foresee that their cause must ultimately prevail. The people in conflict proved themselves equal to their rulers. The Spaniards had been neither moderate when strong, nor were they prudent now when the conflict found them weak. Still, the successes were various. The Spaniards had a foothold from which it was not easy to expel them, and were in possession of resources, in arms and material, derived from the mother-country, with which the republicans found it no easy matter to contend. But they did contend, and this, with the right upon their side, was the great guarantee for success. What the Colombians wanted in the materials of warfare, was more than supplied by their energy and patriotism; and, however slow in attaining their desired object, it was yet evident to all, except their enemies, that the issue was certainly in their own hands.

For two years that the war had been carried on, the casual observer could, perhaps, see but little change in the respective relations of the combatants. The Spaniards still continued to maintain their foothold wherever the risings of the patriots had been premature or partial. But the resources of the former were hourly undergoing diminution, and the great lessening of the productions of the country, incident to its insurrectionary condition, had subtracted largely from the temptations to the further prosecution of the war. The hopes of the patriots naturally rose with the depression of their enemies, and their increasing numbers, and improving skill in the use of their weapons, not a little contributed to their endurance and activity. But for this history we must look to other volumes. The question for us is confined to an individual. How, in all this time, had La Pola redeemed her pledge to the Liberator — how had she whom he had described as the "guardian genius of Bogota."

adhered to the enthusiastic faith which she had voluntarily pledged to him in behalf of herself and people?

Now, it may be supposed that a woman's promise, to participate in the business of an insurrection, is not the thing upon which much stress is to be laid. We are apt to assume for the sex a too humble capacity for high performances, and a too small sympathy with the interests and affairs of public life. In both respects we are mistaken. A proper education for the sex would result in showing their ability to share with man in all his toils, and to sympathize with him in all the legitimate concerns of manhood. But what, demands the caviller, can be expected of a child of fifteen? and should her promises be held against her for rigid fulfilment and performance? It might be enough to answer that we are writing a sober history. There is the record. The fact is as we give it. But a girl of fifteen, in the warm latitude of South America, is quite as mature as the northern maiden of twenty-five; with an ardor in her nature that seems to wing the operations of the mind, making that intuitive with her, which, in the person of a colder climate, is the result only of long calculation and deliberate thought. She is sometimes a mother at twelve, and, as in the case of La Pola, a heroine at fifteen. We freely admit that Bolivar, though greatly interested in the improvvisatrice, was chiefly grateful to her for the timely rebuke which she administered, through her peculiar faculty of lyric song, to the unpatriotic inactivity of her countrymen. As a matter of course, he might still expect that the same muse would take fire under similar provocation hereafter. But he certainly never calculated on other and more decided services at her hands. He misunderstood the being whom he had somewhat contributed to inspire. He did not appreciate her ambition, or comprehend her resources. From the moment of his meeting with her she became a woman. She was already a politician as she was a poet. Intrigue is natural to the genius of the sex, and the faculty is enlivened by the possession of a warm imagination. La Pola put all her faculties in requisition. Her soul was now addressed to the achievement of some plan of co-operation with the republican chief, and she succeeded, where wiser persons must have failed, in compassing the desirable facilities.

Living in Bogota—the stronghold of the enemy—she exercised a policy and address which disarmed suspicion. Her father and his family were to be saved and shielded, while they remained under the power of the viceroy, Zamano—a military despot who had already acquired a reputation for cruelty scarcely inferior to that of the worst of the Roman emperors in the latter days of the empire. The wealth of her father, partly known, made him a desirable victim. Her beauty, her spirit, the charm of her song and conversation, were exercised, as well to secure favor for him, as to procure the needed intelligence and assistance for the Liberator. She managed the twofold object with admirable success—disarming suspicion, and, under cover of the confidence which she inspired, succeeding in effecting constant communication with the patriots, by which she put into their possession all the plans of the Spaniards. Her rare talents and beauty were the chief sources of her success. She subdued her passionate and intense nature—her wild impulse and eager heart—employing them only to impart to her fancy a more impressive and spiritual existence. She clothed her genius in the brightest and gayest colors, sporting above the precipice of feeling, and making of it a background and a relief to heighten the charm of her seemingly wilful fancy. Song came at her summons, and disarmed the serious questioner. In the eyes of her country's enemies she was only the improvvisatrice—a rarely gifted creature, living in the clouds, and totally regardless of the things of earth. She could thus beguile from the young officers of the Spanish army, without provoking the slightest apprehension of any sinister object, the secret plan and purpose—the new supply—the contemplated enterprise—in short, a thousand things which, as an inspired idiot, might be yielded to her with indifference, which, in the case of one solicitous to know, would be guarded with the most jealous vigilance. She was the princess of the tertulia—that mode of evening entertainment so common, yet so precious, among the Spaniards. At these parties she ministered with a grace and influence which made the house of her father a place of general resort. The Spanish gallants thronged about her person, watchful of her every motion, and yielding always to the exquisite compass, and delightful spirituality of her song. At worst, they suspected her of no greater offence than of being totally heartless, with all her charms, and of aiming at no treachery more dangerous than that of making conquests, simply to deride them. It was the popular qualification of all her beauties and accomplishments that she was a coquette, at once so cold, and so insatiate. Perhaps, the woman politician never so thoroughly conceals her game as when she masks it with the art which men are most apt to describe as the prevailing passion of the sex.

By these arts, La Pola fulfilled most amply her pledges to the liberator. She was, indeed, his most admirable ally in Bogota. She soon became thoroughly conversant with all the facts in the condition of the Spanish army—the strength of the several armaments, their disposition and destination—the operations in prospect, and the opinions and merits of the officers—all of whom she knew, and from whom she obtained no small knowledge of the worth and value of their absent comrades. These particulars, all regularly transmitted to Bolivar, were quite as much the secret of his success, as his own genius and the valor of his troops. The constant disappointment and defeat of the royalist arms, in the operations which were conducted in the province of Bogota, attested the closeness and correctness of her knowledge, and its vast importance to the cause of the patriots.

CHAPTER IV.

Unfortunately, however, one of her communications was intercepted, and the cowardly bearer, intimidated by the terrors of impending death, was persuaded to betray his employer. He revealed all that he knew of her practices, and one of his statements, namely, that she usually drew from her shoe the paper which she gave him, served to fix conclusively upon her the proofs of her offence. She was arrested in the midst of an admiring throng, presiding with her usual grace at the tertulia, to which her wit and music furnished the eminent attractions. Forced to submit, her shoes were taken from her feet in the presence of the crowd, and in one of them, between the sole and the lining, was a memorandum designed for Bolivar, containing the details, in anticipation, of one of the intended movements of the viceroy. She was not confounded, nor did she sink beneath this discovery. Her soul seemed to rise rather into an unusual degree of serenity and strength. She encouraged her friends with smiles and the sweetest seeming indifference, though she well knew that her doom was certainly at hand. She had her consolations even under this conviction. Her father was in safety in the camp of Bolivar. With her counsel and assistance he would save much of his property from the wreck of confiscation. The plot had ripened in her hands almost to maturity, and, before very long, Bogota itself would speak for liberty in a formidable *pronunciamento*. And this was mostly her work! What more was done, by her agency and influence, may be readily conjectured from what has been already written. Enough, that she herself felt that in leaving life she left it when there was little more left for her to do.

La Pola was hurried from the tertulia before a military court—martial law then prevailing in the capital—with a rapidity corresponding with the supposed enormity of her offences. It was her chief pang that she was not hurried there alone. We have not hitherto mentioned that she had a lover, one Juan de Sylva Gomero, to whom she was affianced—a worthy and noble youth, who entertained for her the most passionate attachment. It is a somewhat curious fact that she kept him wholly from any knowledge of her political alliances; and never was man more indignant than he when she was arrested, or more confounded when the proofs of her guilt were drawn from her person. His offence consisted in his resistance to the authorities who seized her. There was not the slightest reason to suppose that he knew or participated at all in her intimacy with the patriots and Bolivar. He was tried along with her, and both condemned—for at this time condemnation and trial were words of synonymous import—to be shot. A respite of twelve hours from execution was granted them for the purposes of confession. Zamano, the viceroy, anxious for other victims, spared no means to procure a full revelation of all the secrets of our heroine. The priest who waited upon her was the one who attended on the viceroy himself. He held out lures of pardon for both, here and hereafter, upon the one condition only of a full declaration of her secrets and accomplices. Well might the leading people of Bogota tremble all the while. But she was firm in her refusal. Neither promises of present mercy, nor threats of the future, could extort from her a single fact in relation to her proceedings. Her lover, naturally desirous of life, particularly in the possession of so much to make it precious, joined in the entreaties of the priest; but she answered him with a mournful severity that smote him like a sharp weapon—

"Gomero! did I love you for this? Beware, lest I hate you ere I die! Is life so dear to you that you would dishonor both of us to live? Is there no consolation in the thought that we shall die together?"

"But we shall be spared—we shall be saved," was the reply of the lover.

"Believe it not—it is false! Zamano spares none. Our lives are forfeit, and all that we could say would be unavailing to avert your fate or mine. Let us not lessen the value of this sacrifice on the altars of our country, by any unworthy fears. If you have ever loved me, be firm. I am a woman, but I am strong. Be not less ready for the death-shot than is she whom you have chosen for your wife."

Other arts were employed by the despot for the attainment of his desires. Some of the native citizens of Bogota, who had been content to become the creatures of the viceroy, were employed to work upon her fears and affections, by alarming her with regard to persons of the city whom she greatly esteemed and valued, and whom Zamano suspected. But their endeavors were met wholly with scorn. When they entreated her, among other things, "to give peace to her country," the phrase seemed to awaken all her indignation.

"Peace! peace to our country!" she exclaimed. "What peace! the peace of death, and shame, and the grave, for ever!" And her soul again found relief only in its wild lyrical overflow.

> What peace for our country, when ye've made her a grave,
> A den for the tyrant, a cell for the slave;
> A pestilent plague-spot, accursing and curst,
> As vile as the vilest, and worse than the worst!
>
> The chain may be broken, the tyranny o'er,
> But the sweet charms that blessed her ye may not restore;
> Not your blood, though poured forth from life's ruddiest vein
> Shall free her from sorrow, or cleanse her from stain!

'Tis the grief that ye may not remove the disgrace,
That brands with the blackness of hell all your race;
'Tis the sorrow that nothing may cleanse ye of shame,
That has wrought us to madness, and filled us with flame.

Years may pass, but the memory deep in our souls,
Shall make the tale darker as Time onward rolls;
And the future that grows from our ruin shall know
Its own, and its country's, and liberty's foe.

And still, in the prayer at its altars shall rise,
Appeal for the vengeance of earth and of skies;
Men shall pray that the curse of all time may pursue
And plead for the curse of eternity too!

Nor wantonly vengeful in spirit their prayer,
Since the weal of the whole world forbids them to spare
What hope would there be for mankind if our race,
Through the rule of the brutal, is robbed by the base?

What hope for the future, what hope for the free,
And where would the promise of liberty be,
If Time had no terror, no doom for the slave,
Who would stab his own mother, and shout o'er her grave!

Such a response as this effectually silenced all those cunning agents of the viceroy who urged their arguments in behalf of their country. Nothing, it was seen, could be done with a spirit so inflexible; and in his fury Zamano ordered the couple forth to instant execution. Bogota was in mourning. Its people covered their heads, a few only excepted, and refused to be seen or comforted. The priests who attended the victims received no satisfaction as concerned the secrets of the patriots; and they retired in chagrin, and without granting absolution to either victim. The firing party made ready. Then it was, for the first time, that the spirit of this noble maiden seemed to shrink from the approach of death.

"Butcher!" she exclaimed to the viceroy, who stood in his balcony, overlooking the scene of execution. "Butcher! you have then the heart to kill a woman!"

These were the only words of weakness. She recovered herself instantly, and, preparing for her fate, without looking for any effect from her words, she proceeded to cover her face with the *saya*, or veil, which she wore. Drawing it aside for the purpose, the words "*Vive la Patria!*" embroidered in letters of gold, were discovered on the *basquina*. As the signal for execution was given, a distant hum, as of the clamors of an approaching army, was heard fitfully to rise upon the air.

"It is he! He comes! It is Bolivar! It is the Liberator!" was her cry, in a tone of hope and triumph, which found its echo in the bosom of hundreds who dared not give their hearts a voice. It was, indeed, the Liberator. Bolivar was at hand, pressing onward with all speed to the work of deliverance; but he came too late for the rescue of the beautiful and gifted damsel to whom he owed so much. The fatal bullets of the executioners penetrated her heart ere the cry of her exultation had subsided from the ear. Thus perished a woman worthy to be remembered with the purest and proudest who have done honor to nature and the sex; one who, with all the feelings and sensibilities of the woman, possessed all the pride and patriotism, the courage, the sagacity and the daring of the man.

CHAPTER V.

"We did keep time, sir, in our catches."
[*Twelfth Night.*

As a matter of course, the contribution of our fair companion was received with warmest thanks and congratulations. She had delivered herself of the pleasant labor, as if there had been a pleasure in the service—unaffectedly, with equal ease, modesty and spirit. Her narrative was graceful, while her lyrical efforts were marked by an enthusiasm which was regulated, in turn, by the nicest delicacy and good taste. My Gothamite friend was all in raptures, and I fancied that his praises were by no means of ungracious sound in the ears of Miss Burroughs. Selina, by the way--the name which my long intimacy with her permitted me to use familiarly—was young enough for sentiment—was, as I believed, quite free of any attachments; and, though too quiet to figure conspicuously in a fashionable jam, was here just in the situation which could most effectually exhibit her more charming qualities. My friend Duyckman was evidently touched. There was a probability, indeed—so I fancied—that each of them, before long, would be inclined to say, in the language of Nicholas Bottom, "I shall desire you of more acquaintance, good master Pease Blossom." I could look on such a growth of liking between the parties with great complaisancy. To one who is no longer in the field, the sweetest picture in the world is in the gradual approach of two young fond hearts to one another—they themselves, perhaps, quite unconscious of the tendency, yet as docile as the ductile needle to the directing finger of the pole.

For awhile the conversation became general among the group. The night was passing insensibly. It was so calm, soft, seductive, that sleep was forgotten. The cares of trade, the tasks of toil, the intensity of study, affected none of us.

Each, with a fresh sense of freedom, was free also from all sense of physical exhaustion. Why sleep? There were listeners, and each unlocked his stores. The oyster war was re-called, and other anecdotes given. As we swept along by the shores of New Jersey, which we could no longer see, her people, character, and history, furnished our topics. It was admitted that the Jerseyans were a sterling sort of people. They had shown good pluck in the Revolution, and their country had furnished the battle-fields of some of our most glorious actions —Monmouth, Princeton, Trenton. These recalled Washington, and Lee, and Lafayette, and many others. It was admitted that—

"The Jerseyan, when a gentleman, was of the best models; and even when not exactly a gentleman, was still to be recognised as a good fellow. Without being the swashing, conceited Gothamite, he was yet very far from resembling the prim, demure broad-brims of the Quaker city. In other words, he was gay and gallant, without rudeness or foppery; and firm and thoughtful, without being strait-laced and puritanical. In brief, he had a character of his own, and was not made up of the odds and ends of all sorts of people."

Our son of Gotham did not exactly relish the comparison thus made by one of the group, and replied in a rather stale sarcasm:—

"The less said by way of comparison between Jersey, as between New York and Philadelphia, the better. As old Franklin phrased it—she is the barrel on tap at both ends."

The retort followed from the former speaker.

"These two cities are the sewers of Jersey. She uses them for common purposes—employing them where needful for her common uses, without being responsible for their morals, or troubled with their nuisances. She is fortunate in escaping the evils of great cities, which she can nevertheless use at pleasure."

This was a new view of the case which had never occurred to our Gothamite, and required reflection. He had no immediate answer. The other speaker continued, and made his contributions to our entertainment by a statement of certain facts which might be wrought into story.

"Jersey," he said, "even along the shores, and, in recent periods, is not without its picturesque and romantic. It is not long, since that the coast which we are passing was distinguished infamously by a class of cruel outlaws, who were not the less murderous because they performed their crimes under the cover of night and tempest. Here, in situations favorable to their accursed trade, dwelt a race of land pirates, such as roved the wastes of the Mississippi—such as not many years ago occupied the Keys of Florida—such as still mislead and prey upon the innocent and unsuspecting, on the dreary land routes to Oregon and California. These were wreckers, who lived upon waifs cast up by the sea, and who hung out false lights, when the nights were dark and stormy, to beguile the unwary and exhausted mariner. Everybody is aware of the sort of life which they pursued, for many years, during a period still fresh within the memories of men; though no one can conjecture the extent to which they carried their nefarious traffic. I heard a story, not long ago, told by a sea-captain along this route, which he assured me he had from the very best authority."

We were all agog to hear, and our Jerseyan thus proceeded:—

"It appears that some twenty years ago there suddenly appeared a stranger in the country along shore—in a lonely and sequestered spot—of whom nobody knew anything. Briefly, no one was particularly curious to inquire. He was moody, reserved, somewhat sullen, and a person whose aspect gave warning of irritable passions, while his physique was one of great muscular activity and power. He described himself as an Englishman, and went by the name of Dalton. As far as the people could gather from himself and others, he was understood to have been a sailor, and a deserter from the royal navy. This was, to a small degree, a source of sympathy for him— particularly as he had been cruelly treated in the service. Some accounts spoke of him as one who, in sudden fray, had used a marlin-spike with a little too heavy a hand upon an insolent and brutal lieutenant. In leaving the service, however, in disgust, and at short notice, he yet took up another trade which still kept him in daily commerce with the ocean. The sight of this field was, perhaps, more natural to his eyes than any other. He made his way along shore to a portion of the coast where the restraints of society and law were fewest. Here he naturally became a wrecker, and gathered his spoils along the sea side, after a fashion but too common with his neighbors. Every storm brought him tribute, and his accumulations began to be considerable. Wrecks increased fearfully after his appearance in the neighborhood; and, for the goods thus brought to these wild outlaws, by a wretched fortune, they had but one duty to perform—to bury out of sight the human sufferers who were quite as frequently the victims of their cruel snares as of the treacherous shores and tempests.

"Dalton prospered in the horrid trade; and the rude cabin in which he dwelt alone, and which was visited but rarely, began to improve in its furniture. Bedsteads and beds, beyond what he himself could use or seemed to need, were accumulated in his solitary chamber. Chairs and tables and mirrors followed. Supplies of crockery, and other things, implying the presence of woman, were gradually brought from the cities; and conjecture exaggerated the value of his stores and treasures. At length, the mystery of these proceedings was explained. Dalton was now heard to speak of mother, wife, and sister—all of whom he expected from England—to whom he had written, and sent the necessary money for emigration. He spoke of these relations with a show of feeling which occasionally softened, and even sweetened, his savage aspect and utterance; and seemed to entertain for them severally a degree of affection, which could hardly have been expected from his nature. He was a coarse, uneducated man, and the villanous scrawl which declared his wishes to his kindred, was revised by one of his neighbors, better read than himself, from whom, it seems, these particulars were afterward obtained. His letter was despatched, and he spoke frequently of the family which he expected, and for which he had prepared his dwelling, filling it with comforts, to which, in all probability, they had never before been accustomed.

"But months elapsed, bringing him no answer to his entreaties. Meanwhile, he still continued his fearful and criminal employments. Still he prospered in all merely pecuniary respects. He became the envy of those who regarded his accumulations as the proper and permanent objects of desire. But the wages of sin and death are delusions also;—mockeries, which mortify the very meanest hearts, even when they are most sought, and most in possession.

"One dark and threatening evening in September, the wind blowing a gale which increased in fury as the night came on, a sail was dimly descried in the distance. In the growing darkness she disappeared. But, through the night, at intervals, the boomings of a cannon might be heard. These appeals of terror soon ceased; swallowed up in the united roar of sea and storm and thunder. The billows, in mountain rollers, came in upon the sandy shore. But the tempest did not affright our wreckers. They welcomed the increasing violence of the storm. They were abroad and busy — one of them at least.

"Dalton had marked the vessel, dimly seen at sunset, for his prey. The course of the wind, the season, the violence of the gale, the proximity of the fated craft to the leeshore, all contributed to fill him with the horrid hope of plunder at the expense of life and humanity. He stole out from his hovel, under cover of the darkness, heedless of the driving fury of the wind, to an elevated hammock of sand, where he fired a beacon of tar-barrels. What mocking hopes did this blaze awaken in the bosoms of the hapless creatures in that barque? He thought nothing of them. Possibly, other lights were kindled, like those of Dalton, and with like charitable purposes. The diabolical purpose was aptly answered by the watchful Fates!

"That night, while Dalton crouched in his cabin, he fancied that he heard human voices appealing to him, above all the voices of the storm. It was not the lingering human feeling within his heart, which made him listen and tremble with strange and stifling sensations. But, he fancied that he was called by name. He fancied that the voices were familiar, and it seemed to him that, in his very ears were syllabled in shrieks, the several words —'brother,' 'husband,' 'son.' He was paralyzed. A cold sweat covered his frame. He could not stir. He could not speak. He sat beside his chimney in a strange stupor, which forbade that he should either sleep or go forth!

"But habitual guilt is a thing of rare powers of hardihood and endurance. Cupidity came to his relief. He meditated the great gains of his trade. The prey was in the toils, beyond possibility of escape, and before the dawn its struggles would have ceased. The morning came. With the first gray streak of light he was forth and upon the sands. The storm had subsided, the sun had opened his eyes, all brightness, upon the beautiful world. But the seas were still tumultuous, and Dalton could see that a large fragment of the stranded ship, was still tossing in their wild embraces in a little cove which the waves had eaten into the sands. Everywhere before him were the proofs of wreck and ruin. Here a mast and spar, there a bit of deck and bulwark; there rolled a barrel in upon the reef, and there floated away a naked raft and hammock.

"As he wandered, seeking and picking up his spoils, he happened suddenly upon other trophies of the storm. On the very edge of the sea, where it blended with the shore in comparative calm, lay two human bodies locked closely in a last embrace. Both were females. Their heads rested upon the sands. Their garments, and the arms of one, were lifted to and fro by the billows. Did they live? He approached them with feelings, strange to him, of equal awe and curiosity. He had a fearful presentiment of the truth. He drew them from the waters. He unclasped them from that strong embrace which they had taken in death. He beheld their faces.

"'Mother! Sister!'

"He knew them at a glance!

"And it was his hand that had fired the beacon which had conducted both to death.

"'My wife! my wife! I have drowned my wife!'

"Where was she! He looked for *her* in vain. The remorseless sea gave up no other of its victims. But he found a box in which were his own letters. They told her fate.

"His horror and remorse, too lately awakened, suffered him to keep no secrets. His first outcry revealed the whole terrible history. He had avenged humanity upon himself. Even among the wild creatures with whom he herded, the terrible judgment upon his own miserable soul, inflicted by his own deed, was too awful to seem to need other penalties. He was suffered to go free. He remained only long enough in the neighborhood to see the poor corses deposited in earth, and then fled, leaving all behind him,—fled into the interior, and, it was said, nine years afterward, that he was then to be found, somewhere in Ohio, a sad, gray-headed man, a devout Christian, reconciled to the Church, and waiting humbly for that change, which, it was *his* hope—and should be ours,—might witness the purification of his stains through the saving grace of his Redeemer."

Our Jerseyan, having finished his voluntary yarn, was voted the thanks of the company; and it was then unanimously agreed that our Gothamite should take up the reel, and see what he could do, at warp and woof, in the business of invention.

"We were promised a story of the troubadours, I think, sir," said Miss Burroughs.

We all concurred in the subject thus indicated, and, after certain modest preliminaries, Duyckman gave us a curious picture of the fantastical sentiment—serious enough in its way—of which we may find so many remarkable examples in the history of chivalry and the crusades. It may not be amiss to apprise the reader that he will find an actual biography in what follows.

THE PILGRIM OF LOVE.

> ————"Sails, oars, that might not save,
> The death he sought, to Geoffrey Rudel gave."
> PETRARCH.

The history of the Provençal troubadours is full of grateful and instructive material—curious as history, instructive as developing a highly-artificial state of society, and full of interest as literary biography. To the young poet, the study is one which will teach many useful lessons of his art. To the passionate dreamer of romance, it will yield delicious provocations to revery, in which all his ideals will be satisfied. These biographies should be written out by poets; not in verse, for that might suggest doubts of their veracity, but in a prose at once sparkling and sentimental; uniting the oriental fancy of Curtis, with the sighing pathos of a Norton or a Landon. We commend the idea to study and examination; and will content ourselves, in the meantime, with a brief sketch of one of the most remarkable troubadours of his age and order.

Geoffrey Rudel was a prince of Blaye, as well as a troubadour. In those days, nobility was not inconsistent with letters.

Our poet was one of those who could wield the sword as well as the lyre. He was a knight of high reputation, and a gentleman; and, as such, wore the honors of chivalry with all the grace of one "to the manner born." But, with all these possessions, there was one deficiency, which was considered fatal to the perfection of his character. His grace and courtesy were acknowledged in court and chamber. He could make his enemy tremble in the field. As a poet he had fire and sentiment, and was peculiarly sensible to the glories of the visible world. He was the favorite of princes, and was ranked among the friends of no less a personage than Richard Cœur de Lion. But he had never once been troubled with the tender passion. He had never been beguiled to love by beauty. He acknowledged the charms of woman, but he remained unenslaved. He could sing of the attractions which he did not feel. He had his muse, perhaps his ideal perfection, and to her he sung. He portrayed her charms, but he neither found nor seemed to seek them. Tradition vaguely hints at efforts which he made, to discern a likeness in the living world to the exquisite creation embodied in his mind. But he seemed to search for her in vain. His wanderings, seeking for this perfect creature, were wholly without profit. It does not seem that he exulted in his insensibility. An object of universal admiration himself, he himself constantly strove to admire. He did admire, but he did not love. The object of pursuit eluded his grasp. In those days, it was deemed no impropriety, on the part of the fairer sex, to seek openly the conquest of the brave knight and the noble poet. Beauty sought Geoffrey Rudel in his solitude. She brought him rarest tribute. She spoke to him in songs, sweet as his own, and with oriental flowers more precious than any which his care had cultured. She did not conceal the passion which his accomplishments had inspired; but she declared her secret in vain. His heart seemed invulnerable to every shaft. His soul remained inaccessible to all the sweet solicitings of love.

It must not be thought that he found pride in this insensibility. He felt it as a misfortune. For the troubadour not to love, was to deprive his verses of that very charm which alone could secure them immortality. For the knight to be untouched by the charms of woman, was to wither the greenest chaplet which valor had ever fixed upon his brow. He declared his griefs at the insusceptibility of his heart. His prayer embodied a petition that he might be made to love. But he prayed for heavenly succor, and he looked for earthly loveliness, in vain. His mind was greatly saddened by his condition. His isolation impaired his energies. He ceased to sing, to seek the tourney and the court, and delivered himself up to a musing and meditative life, which was only not utter vacancy. At a season of general bustle among the nations, he sank into apathy. He had served in arms with Richard, but the entreaties of that impetuous and powerful monarch no longer succeeded in beguiling him from his solitude. The world was again arrayed in armor — the whole wide world of Christendom — moving under the impulses of religious fanaticism, at the wild instance of St. Bernard. Preparations were in progress for the second crusade, but the stir of the multitude aroused no answering chord in his affections. He put on no armor; his shield hung upon his walls; his spear rusted beneath it, and no trumpet was sounded at his gates. Like one overcome with sloth, Geoffrey Rudel lay couched within the quiet retreats of his castle near Bourdeaux, and gave no heed to the cries and clamors of the world without. But his soul had not lapsed away in luxuries. He was immersed in no pleasures more exciting than those of song. His soul was full of sadness rather than delight. His lyre sent forth the tenderest pleading, and the most touching lamentation. His heart was filled with sorrow, as he entreated vainly that it should be filled with love. Very sweet were his ballads; plaintive always, and teeming with fancies, which faintly sought to ally themselves to affections. With a soul given up to contemplations, which, if not loving, were not warlike, he gave no heed to the movements, or even the reproaches of his brethren — knights and troubadours. The preaching of St. Bernard touched not him. We do not know that he ever listened once to that great apostle of the crusades; nor, indeed, can we pretend to assert that his conversion ever formed a special object with the preacher. But the entreaties of others were urged upon him, and without success. He answered them with a melancholy denial, which declared his regrets more than his indifference. Some of his ditties, written at this period, have been preserved to us. They are remarkable for their delicacy, their plaintiveness of tone, the nice taste by which his spirit was informed, and the grief of those yearnings, the denial of which was the true cause of his lethargy. The muse to which he now yielded himself was that of a latent affection. The wild spirit of warfare had no voice for his soul. He sung—but why not suffer him to speak for himself, those tender sensibilities which he has put into verse, not wholly unworthy of his renown? Our rude English version may show the character of his sentiment, if not the peculiar art and the ingenuity of his strain. He speaks in this sonnet of his despondency, and of that ideal which he despairs to find in life.

> " From nature comes the lesson of true love—
>   She teaches me, through flowers and fruits, to grace
> My form in gay apparel, and to prove
>   For how much heart my own can furnish place.
> The nightingale his tender mate caresses,
>   Caressed in turn by mutual look and strain;
> Ah! happy birds, whom genial love thus blesses,
>   Ye teach me what to seek, yet teach in vain.
> I languish still in silence—your delight—
>   The shepherd with his pipe—the eager child,
>   That makes his labor speak in pleasures wild—
> All that I hear, and all that lives in sight—
>   Still mock me with denial. In my woes
> The whole world triumphs. Still the image glows,
> More and more brightly on my yearning eye—
>   A thousand passionate hopes deny repose,
> And warm me still with promises that fly!
>   Oh! my soul's image, when shall these be o'er,
>   When shall I see thee near, and seek thee never more."

This is a sweet murmur, not overstrained, and happily expressed. It should have silenced the reproaches which were at length showered upon his head. It shows him to have possessed a soul at once tender and passionate, if not susceptible; and such now was the usual burden of his song. But it failed to convince his neighbors. Beauty, disappointed in all her endeavors, proclaimed him an insensible. We little know, at this day, how keen and terrible was such a reproach, at a period when love was the very soul of chivalry. Knighthood regarded him as a recreant to its order, which insisted upon a mistress as the first and most powerful incentive to valor. He was called by many cruel epithets—cold, selfish, ungentle; barren of heart, capricious and peevish; loving himself only, like another Narcissus, when a whole world, worthy of a better heart, crowded around him soliciting his love; and this, too, at the very moment when he was repining with the tenderest yearnings, for some one object, precious over all, upon whom to expend the whole wealth of his affections. But he was not long to yearn thus hopelessly. The fates were about to give an answer to the cruel reproaches under which he had suffered. They were about to show that his passion was intense in proportion to the infrequency of its exercise. His destiny was quite as curious as it is touching: we say this by way of warning. The reader must know that we are writing sober history. We are not now practising with artful romances upon his fancy. The chronicles are before us as we write. We are fettered by the ancient record, in complexion of the most sombre black-letter.

It was while Geoffrey Rudel thus lay, sad and sighing, at his castle of Blaye, near Bordeaux, that news came from the Holy Land, which set Christendom once more in commotion. The Crusaders had gone forward in iron legions. They had been successful in every battle, and their triumphs were upon every tongue. Jerusalem, the Holy City, had fallen before their arms, after prodigies of valor had been shown in its defence. But the deeds of knighthood, and the bloody triumphs of the battle-field, were not alone the theme of the troubadour and the traveller. The story which, above all, had served to enliven the imagination, and charm the lyre of Europe, was that of a certain countess of Tripoli—a lady, whose bravery, under circumstances of particular difficulty and peril, was deemed the subject of greatest wonder and delight. Her beauty had been already sung. It was now ennobled in Provençal minstrelsy, by instances of courage, magnanimity, and greatness of soul, such as had seldom been shown by her sex before. Her elastic spirit, the firmness of her soul, the grace of her carriage, the loveliness of her face and person, were duly recorded in a thousand ditties. The pilgrims from the Holy Land could speak of nothing else. The troubadour caught up the grateful history, and found new inspiration in the recital. Faint echoes of the story reached our disconsolate poet, and fell with a renovating influence upon his spirit. He heard, and hearkened with a greedy interest. The recital touched the dormant chords of his nature. He grew excited as he listened, suddenly flung off his lethargy, and soon his lyre began to emulate and excel all others, in rehearsing the charms of her person and the beauties of her soul. He all at once realized his ideal. The countess of Tripoli was the creature of all his imaginings. The image in his soul had found a living likeness. It had long been the image in his dreams—it was now the object of his waking passion. It filled the measure of his hopes; it heightened the glory of his dreams. He loved— he was no longer without a soul.

II.

THE imagination of our troubadour thus powerfully excited, it was not surprising that he should enjoy a glorious vision of the lady of his thoughts. He lay sleeping, during a slumberous summer evening, in a favorite bower of his garden: his lute, resting beside him, was silent also; but he still clasped between his fingers the illuminated missal, in which the wandering monk, scarcely less infatuated than himself, had sought to enshrine the beauties of the Lady of Tripoli in the character of the Blessed Virgin. In the deep draughts of delirious passion which the picture had helped to enliven, the troubadour might well lapse away from delicious fancies into as delicious dreams. The warm sun of his region helped the influence. The birds of Provence ministered also—singing overhead those sweet *capriccios*, half play, half sentiment, which seem to have furnished the model for many of the best specimens of Provençal poetry. The flowers gave forth a soft, persuasive fragrance. The leaves floated to and fro upon the slenderest green vines, under the balmy influence of the southern breeze, ever and anon stooping to his floating hair, and trembling over his somewhat pallid cheek. A favorite greyhound slept at his feet, his long brown nose resting upon the gayly-wrought slippers which enclosed them. Warm fancies, working with the season and the scene, proved to our poet as deliciously narcotizing as those fabled breezes that sweep with delirium the poppy gardens of Yemen. The protracted denial of his previous life was all compensated in the intoxicating fancy of the hour. The creature of his imperfect waking desires, grew to a perfect being in his dreams. He was transported to Paradise, a region which, at that moment, he could find at Tripoli only. And she came forth, the first, to bid him welcome. His reception was not only one of blessing but of ceremonial. The lady of his love was environed by state; but this did not lessen the benignity of her favor. Princes were grouped around her—the severe and stately forms of the Knights of the Temple—the humbler, but not less imposing Brothers of the Hospital—and many others, knights and nobles, with their banners and their shields. And he himself—he, Geoffrey Rudel, prince of Blaye—was in the midst of the splendid circle—the person to whom all eyes were drawn—upon whom her eye was specially fastened—she, the nearest to his heart and person, the lovely countess of Tripoli. But a moment was the glorious vision vouchsafed him; but, even as it began to fade away—growing momentarily more and more dim, without growing less beautiful—he caught the whispered words of her parting salutation—"Hither to me, Rudel—hither to me—and the love that thou seekest, and the peace—shall they not both be thine?"

III.

This was a bliss too great for slumber. It was a bliss too precious to lose at waking. Rudel necessarily awakened with the excess of rapture. He started to his feet with a new impulse. The birds sang, but vainly, from his trees. The flowers in vain stretched forth to his hand. He heeded not the endearments of his greyhound, who started up at the same moment with his master, and whined, and lifted his paws to receive the accustomed caresses. He saw these things no longer. The old temptations and pleasures were discarded or forgotten. A new soul seemed to inform his spirit. A new hope was embodied in his heart. He had received in that dream an inspiration. What was tenderness simply in his heart before, was now passion. His dream was reality. He no longer sighed—he felt. He lived

at last; for, until one loves, he can not be said to live. The
life of humanity is love. The new passion prompted new energies. Geoffrey Rudel was still at Blaye, but he might soon be
at Tripoli. He made his preparations for Tripoli accordingly.
Once more his good steed was put in exercise. His shield was
taken from the wall. His lance was cleansed of its rust, and
glittered gayly in the sunbeams, as if rejoicing in its resumed
employments. The proud spirit of knighthood was once more
rekindled in the bosom of our hero. He was again a living man,
with all the tenderness which inspires bravery to seek adventure. It was easy now to feel all the enthusiasm at which it
was his wont to smile; and he could now look with regret and
mortification at those days of apathy which kept him in repose
when St. Bernard went through the land, preaching his mission
of power. He could now understand the virtue of leaving home
and family, friends and fortune, to fight for the Holy Sepulchre.
The spirit of the crusade suddenly impregnated his soul. Solemnly he took up the cross—literally, in the figure upon his
garments—and made his preparations for embarking for the
East. Never had a change so sudden been wrought in human
bosom. Nor did he conceal the true occasion of the miracle.
When did troubadour ever withhold the secret of his passion?
It was his pride to reveal. Geoffrey Rudel loved at last. He,
too, could be made to yield to the spells of beauty. His lyre
was not silent. He unfolded himself in the most exquisite improvvisations, which we should but coldly render in our harsh
language of the North. He who had been all apathy before,
was now all excitement. His limbs trembled with the wild fever
in his veins. A deep spot of red grew suddenly apparent on
his faded cheek. A tone of nervous impatience now distinguished the utterance which had hitherto been gentle and for-
bearing always. His muse spoke more frequently, and with
a spasmodic energy, which had not been her usual characteris-
tic. We preserve another of his sonnets, feebly rendered into
our dialect, which he penned just before leaving Provence for
the East:—

"She I adore, whom, save in nightly dreams,
These eyes have ne'er beheld, yet am I sure
She is no other than the thing she seems—
A thing for love and worship evermore

Oh! not your dark-eyed beauties of the East,
   Jewish or Saracen — nor yet the fair,
Your bright-cheeked maids of Christendom, the best
   For saintly virtues and endowments rare —
May rank with her whom yet I do not see,
   To whom I may not speak — who does not know
My homage, yet who nightly comes to me,
   And bids my hopes revive, my passion glow.
With day she disappears, and then alone,
   I know that she is distant: — I will fly;
Pierce the deep space between that foreign sky,
And bare to her the heart so much her own.
   The seas will not betray me, when they know
Love is my guide and bids me death defy."

His preparations were not long delayed. His soul was too eager in its new passion to permit of any unnecessary waste of time. His flame had become a frenzy — the leading idea of his mind, which reason had ceased to resist, and which friends no longer ventured to combat. His preparations completed, and the bark ready, his pen records one of the usual vows of knight-errantry. In the following sonnet, he professes that humility which was commonly set forth quite too ostentatiously to be sincere always; but which, in his case, the sequel of our story will show to have been deeply seated in his soul. We shall not find it necessary to call the attention particularly to the delicacy of the sentiments contained in these selections — a delicacy, we may add, which speaks more certainly for the particular instance before us, than it ordinarily did, at that period, for the general character of chivalry: —

" 'Tis sworn that I depart — and clad in wool
   With pilgrim staff before her eyes I go —
   Glad, if with pity for my love and wo,
She suffers me within her palace rule.
   But this were too much joy. Enough to be
Near the blest city which she keeps, though there,
   The triumph of the Saracen I see,
And fall a captive to his bow and spear.
   Heaven grant me the sweet blessing in the prayer! —
Transport me thither — let me, in her sight,
   The rapture, born of her sweet presence, share,
And live so long within her happy light,
   The love that fills my soul, to pour into her ear."

The sentiment that touched the soul of Geoffrey Rudel, was certainly no common one. It may have been a fanaticism, but it was such a fanaticism as could only happen to a poet. In inferior degree, however, the frenzy was not an unusual one. It belonged to the age and to his profession, if the performances of the troubadour, at any time, could properly deserve this title! Common to his order, it was heightened as well as refined by the peculiar temper of his individual mind, and by that contemplative, inner or spiritual life which he had lived so long. Though spoken aloud, and fondly and frequently reiterated, it was no momentary ebullition. The passion had fastened upon his mind and his affections equally, and was fixed there by the grateful image that informed his dreams. These, repeated nightly, according to the tradition, gave him no time to cool. Their visitation was periodical. Their exhortation was pressing. They preyed upon his strength, and his physical powers declined in due degree with the wondrous increase of his mental energies. He set sail for Palestine with all the fervor of his enthusiasm upon him, as warm and urgent as when it had seized upon him first. The voyage was protracted, and the disease of our pilgrim underwent increase from its annoyances. But, if his frame suffered, the energies of his soul were unimpaired. His muse was never in better wing or vigor. Still he sung, and with all the new-born exultation of a lover. The one hope of his heart, the one dream of his fancy, gave vitality to every utterance. The image of the beautiful and noble Countess of Tripoli was reflected from, and through, all his sonnets, as through a mirror of magic. Of their usual burden, a single specimen will suffice:—

"When my foot presses on those sacred shores—
 To me thrice sacred, as they bear the sign,
That, lifted high, all Christendom adores—
 And the proud beauty I have loved as mine—
My song shall speak my passion—she shall hear
 How much I love—how powerful is the sway,
 Her charms maintain o'er heart so far away,
That, until now, no other chains could wear.
Ah, sure, she will not let me sing in vain—
 Such deep devotion, such abiding trust,
 Love, so wholly born of her own beauty, must
Touch her sweet spirit with a pleasing pain!

> Shoul*l* she prove ruthless—no, it can not be
> My god-sire gave such evil fate to me."

The last allusion in this poem may not be so readily understood in our times. It is still a subject of some discussion. It is thought by some to have reference to the old tradition of gifts bestowed by fairies upon persons in their infancy. Our own notion is, that it is taken from one of the institutions of chivalry. A knight was said to be *born* only when he had received the honors of knighthood. At this ceremony he had a god-father or sponsor. This person was usually chosen by the novice in consideration of his high renown, his bravery and good fortune. A certain portion of these good qualities were naturally supposed capable of transmission. The sponsor answered for the good qualities of the youthful squire, and bestowed on him his blessing with his counsel. The allusion in the verses quoted is not obscure, if we remember the relationship between the parties.

IV.

But we must not linger. The excitement of our troubadour increased with the voyage. It was hardly restrainable within the bounds of sanity as the ship approached her port of destination. Rudel was beloved by all on board. His grace, talent, gallantry, and enthusiasm, had touched all hearts. The curious history of his passion had lifted him in their admiration and wonder. They saw, with many misgivings, that it was growing momently at the peril of his life and reason. But it was vain to expostulate with one so completely lifted by his fervor beyond the reach of ordinary argument. He ate but little and had no appetite. His ailments, derived wholly from the strange flame by which he was possessed, were yet stimulating influences which gave him strength in the absence of mortal nutriment. Very thin, indeed, were the cheeks which yet brightened with the liveliest intelligence. The skin of his face had become so delicately white and transparent, that the blue veins stood out prominent upon his forehead, and you might trace everywhere the progress of the fiery blood through his face and hands. His eye wore a wild, unnatural intensity that seemed to dart through the beholder. And yet it was apparent, even then, that the glance which seemed to penetrate your soul, was full of intelligence to which you were not a party. The soul of that glance was elsewhere, far in advance of the slowly-sailing ship, in search of the mistress of his desires.

Fearful was the fever that preyed upon his enfeebled frame. Yet, while momently sinking in the sight of all, his heart was full of hope and courage. There was a cheering and surprising elasticity in his tones — an exulting consciousness of assured success in voice and aspect — which made him superior to all human anxieties. While no one even supposed he could over reach the shore alive, he himself had no doubts that he would certainly do so. His confidence in this destiny raised strange supernatural convictions in his brother knights, the companions of his voyage. Their interest in his fate increased as they beheld and listened. He spoke to them freely, and poured forth, at frequent moments, the sentiments which were inspired by his passion. The exquisite sonnets which were thus delivered, seemed to them the utterance of a being already released from human bonds; they were so tender, so hopeful, and withal so pure. The extravagance of his flame was forgotten in its purity. The wildness of his delirium was sweet, because of its grace and delicacy. They spread their fruits before him, and poured forth their beakers of Greek wine, to persuade him to partake of more nourishing food than any which his passion could provide; and he smiled as he tasted of their fruits, and lifting the goblet to his lips, he chanted: —

> "Ay, bring me wine of Cyprus,
> The sweetest of the grove,
> And we will drink, while passing.
> A brimful draught of love,—
> The laughing wine of Cyprus,
> A brimful draught for me;
> And I will yield while passing
> The goblet to the sea!
> Yes! Bring me wine of Cyprus!

And, without quaffing, he flung the beaker into the deep. He needed not the stimulus of wine. As he had no longer a relish for earthly nourishment, so it had no power upon his blood or spirit.

They were cheered at length with the sight of the shores of Palestine,—the Promised Land, indeed, to him. But such an enthusiasm as that which had possessed his soul could not have been entertained by any mortal, except at vital hazard. His joy became convulsion. Lifted from the vessel and placed with his feet upon the earth, he sank down in a swoon, to all appearance dead. But the faith which he had in the promise of his dream, was sufficient to reanimate his strength. Borne on a litter to the nearest dwelling, the wonderful story of his passion, and of his voyage in pursuit of its object, was soon borne through Tripoli. It reached, among others, the ears of the noble lady who had been so innocently the cause of his misfortunes. Then it was that he realized the vision that blessed him while he slept at Blaye. The princess of Tripoli was sensible to all his sorrows. She was touched by the devotion of the troubadour, and, even as he lay in a state of swoon that looked the image of death itself, his ears caught once more the endearing summons, and the accents of that melodious voice, which had aroused him from his despondency and dreams. Once more it whispered to his exulting soul the happy invitation: "Hither to me, Rudel, hither to me; and the love that thou seekest—and the peace—shall they not both be thine?"

V.

THESE dear words aroused him from his swoon. He opened his eyes upon the light, but it was only to close them for ever. But they had gained all that was precious in that one opening The single glance around him, by the dying troubadour, showed him all that he had sought. Her holy and sweet face was the first that he beheld. Her eyes smiled encouragement and love. It was her precious embrace that succored his sinking frame. These tender offices, let it not be forgotten, were not, in those days, inconsistent with the purest virtue. The young maiden was frequently nurse and physician to the stranger knight. She brought him nourishment and medicine, dressed his wounds, and scrupled at no act, however delicate, which was supposed necessary to his recovery. Our countess had been taught to perform these offices, not merely as acts of duty, but as acts of devotion.

It is probable that a deeper interest in the sufferer before her gave a warmer solicitude to her ministrations. She had heard the whole story of our troubadour, and of the influence which she had possessed in rousing him from his apathy into life, even though that awakening had been, finally, fatal to life itself. Of his graces and virtues she knew before, and many were the admirers who had already taught her how sweet and passionate, and how purely due to herself, were the songs and sonnets of Rudel. It was even whispered that their offices were by no means necessary to her knowledge. There were those who insisted that there had been some strange spiritual commerce between the parties, though so many leagues asunder. The story ran that Geoffrey Rudel had been as much the object of her dreaming fancies as she had been of his. They said that while he beheld her in the inspiring vision of the noonday, in his garden at Blaye, she herself, in a state of prolonged trance at Tripoli, was conscious of his presence, and of her own interest in his fate, elsewhere. It is certain that she betrayed no surprise when she heard his story from mortal lips. She betrayed no surprise at his coming, and she was among the first to attend the bedside of the dying man. He felt her presence, as one, even in sleep, feels the sudden sunshine. He breathed freely at her approach, as if the flitting soul were entreated back for a moment, by her charms, to its prison-house of mortality. She embraced him as he lapsed away, while her eyes, dropping the biggest tears, were lifted up to heaven in resignation, but with grief. He, in that mysterious moment, gazed only upon her. His fading glance was filled with exultation. His hope was realized. He expired, thrice happy, since he expired in her arms. The prophetic vision had deceived him in no single particular. She was one of the first to receive and welcome him. His reception had been one of state and sympathizing ceremonial. He beheld, even as he died, the very groups which his dream had shown him. There were the severe and stately aspects of the Knights of the Temple—there again were the humbler Brothers of the Hospital. Princes and barons drew nigh in armor and resting upon their shields, as at a solemn service; and he was in the midst, the figure to whom all eyes were addressed, and she, the nearest to his heart, was also the nearest to his person. The love and the peace which she had promised him completed the full consciousness of his exulting spirit.

All these things had really come to pass. But the stately ceremonial, which his flattering fancies had persuaded him was his bridal, was in truth his funeral. Dying, thus surrounded, he felt that it was a bridal also. In the brief communion which his eyes enjoyed with those of her he loved, he felt that their souls were united. She said to him, as plainly as eyes could speak — "The love and the peace thou seekest, shall they not be thine?" and in this happy faith he yielded up his spirit on her bosom. He was magnificently buried among the Knights Templars at Tripoli. Scarcely had this last ceremonial taken place, when the woman he had so worshipped made a sign, which seemed to confirm the previous rumors of their strange spiritual sympathies. Her heart was certainly more deeply interested in his fate than might well have been the case, had their mutual souls not communed before. The very day of his death, she who had lived a princess, in the very eye of pleased and wondering nations, suddenly retired from the world. She buried her head, if not her secret, beneath the hood of the cloister. "They were placed to sleep apart," says the ancient chronicle, "but, by the Virgin's grace, they wake together!"

An old Provençal author, whose name is unknown, writes: "The Viscount Geoffrey Rudel, in passing the seas to visit his lady, voluntarily died for her sake." His passion has been deemed worthy of the recording muse of Petrarch, who says: "By the aid of sails and oars, Geoffroi Rudel obtained the boon of death which he desired." We have furnished the ample history of this event. In one of the ancient metaphysical discussions so common in the Courts of Love, during the prevalence of chivalry, one of the questions proposed for discussion was as follows:—

"Which contributes most powerfully to inspire love — sentiment or sight? — the heart or the eyes?"

The case was at once decided in favor of sentiment when the story of our troubadour was told. Once more, this narrative is no fiction, though of the purest school of fiction. Its facts are all to be found in the sober records of a period, when, however, society was not quite sober.

CHAPTER VI.

> " O, the sacrifice,
> How ceremonious, solemn, and unearthly,
> It was i' the offering."— *Winter's Tale.*

THE ladies had retired, but midnight still found a sufficiently large group gathered together on the upper deck. By this time others of the party had added themselves to the circle of *raconteurs*, and from one of these we obtained another curious history from the pages of chivalric times, and the troubadours of Provence. The narrator assured us that it was a veritable biography.

LOVE'S LAST SUPPER;

A TRUE STORY OF THE TROUBADOURS.

CHAPTER .

IN the first conception of the institution of chivalry it was doubtless a device of great purity, and contemplated none but highly proper and becoming purposes. Those very features which, in our more sophisticated era, seem to have been the most absurd, or at least fantastic, were, perhaps among its best securities. The sentiment of love, apart from its passion, is what a very earnest people, in a very selfish period, can not so well understand; but it was this very separation of interests, which we now hold to be inseparable, that constituted the peculiarity of chivalry — the fanciful in its characteristics rendering sentiment independent of passion, and refining the crude desire by the exercise and influence of tastes, which do not usually accompany it. Among the Provençal knights and troubadours, in the palmy days of their progress, love was really the most innocent and the most elevated of sentiments. It seems to have been nursed without guile, and was professed, even when seemingly in conflict with the rights of others, without the slightest notion of wrong-doing or offence. It did not vex the temper, or impair the marital securities of the husband, that the beauties of his dame were sung with enthusiasm by the youthful poet; on the contrary, he who gloried in the possession of a jewel, was scarcely satisfied with fortune unless she brought to a just knowledge of its splendors, the bard who alone could convey to the worl' a similar sense of the value of his treasure. The narrative which we have gathered from the ancient chronicles of Provence, and which we take occasion to say is drawn from the most veracious sources of history, will illustrate the correctness of these particulars.

One of the most remarkable instances of the sentiment of love, warmed into passion, yet without evil in its objects, is to be found in the true and touching history of Guillaume de Cabestaign, a noble youth of Roussillon. Though noble of birth, Guillaume was without fortune, and it was not thought improper or humiliating in those days that he should serve, as a page, the knight whose ancestors were known to his own as associates. It was in this capacity that he became the retainer of Raymond, lord of Roussillon. Raymond, though a haughty baron, was one who possessed certain generous tastes and sentiments, and who showed himself capable of appreciating the talents and great merits of Guillaume de Cabestaign. His endowments, indeed, were of a character to find ready favor with all parties. The youth was not only graceful of carriage, and particularly handsome of face and person, but he possessed graces of mind and manner which especially commended him to knightly sympathy and admiration. He belonged to that class of *improvvisatori* to whom the people of Provence gave the name of troubadour, and was quite as ready to sing the praises of his mistress, as he was to mount horse, and charge with sword and lance in her defence and honor. His muse, taking her moral aspect from his own, was pure and modest in her behavior—indulging in no song or sentiment which would not fall becomingly on the most virgin ear. His verses were distinguished equally by their delicacy and fancy, and united to a spirit of the most generous and exulting life a taste of the utmost simplicity and purity. Not less gentle than buoyant, he was at once timid in approach, and joy-giving in society; and while he compelled the respect of men by his frank and fearless manhood, he won the hearts of the other sex by those gentle graces which, always prompt and ready, are never obtrusive, and which leave us only to the just appreciation of their value, when they are withdrawn from our knowledge and enjoyment.

It happened, unfortunately for our troubadour, that he won too many hearts. Raised by the lord of Roussillon to the rank of gentleman-usher to the Lady Marguerite, his young and beautiful wife, the graces and accomplishments of Guillaume de Cabestaign, soon became quite as apparent and agreeable to her as to the meanest of the damsels in her train. She was never so well satisfied as in his society; and her young and ardent soul, repelled rather than solicited by the stern nature of Raymond, her lord, was better prepared and pleased to sympathize with the more beguiling and accessible spirit of the page. The tenderest impressions of love, without her own knowledge, soon seized upon her heart; and she had learned to sigh as she gazed upon the person that she favored, long before she entertained the slightest consciousness that he was at all precious to her eyes. He himself, dutiful as devoted, for a long season beheld none of these proofs of favor on the part of his noble mistress. She called him her servant, it is true, and he, as such, sung daily in her praises the equal language of the lover and the knight. These were words, however, of a vague conventional meaning, to which her husband listened with indifferent ear. In those days every noble lady entertained a lover, who was called her servant. It was a prerogative of nobility that such should be the case. It spoke for the courtliness and aristocracy of the party; and to be without a lover, though in the possession of a husband, was to be an object of scornful sympathy in the eyes of the sex. Fashion, in other words, had taken the name of chivalry; and it was one of her regulations that the noble lady should possess a lover, who should of necessity be other than her lord. In this capacity, Raymond of Roussillon, found nothing of which to complain in the devotion of Guillaume de Cabestaign to Marguerite, his wife. But the courtiers who gathered in her train were not so indulgent, or were of keener sight. They soon felt the preference which she gave, over all others, to our troubadour. They felt, and they resented it the more readily, as they were not insensible to his personal superiority. Guillaume himself, was exceeding slow in arriving at a similar consciousness. Touched with a fonder sentiment for his mistress than was compatible with his security, his modesty had never suffered him to suppose that he had been so fortunate as to inspire her with a feeling such as he now knew within himself. It was at a moment when he least looked for it, that he made the perilous discovery. It was in the course of a discussion upon the various signs of love—such a discussion as occupied the idle hours, and the wandering fancies of chivalry—that she said to him, somewhat abruptly—

"Surely thou, Guillaume, thou, who canst sing of love so tenderly, and with so much sweetness, thou, of all persons, should be the one to distinguish between a feigned passion and a real one. Methinks the eye of him who loves truly, could most certainly discover, from the eye of the beloved one, whether the real flame were yet burning in her heart."

And even as she spoke, the glance of her dark and lustrous eye settled upon his own with such a dewy and quivering fire, that his soul at once became enlightened with her secret. The troubadour was necessarily an *improvrisatore*. Guillaume de Cabestaign was admitted to be one of the most spontaneous in his utterance, of all his order. His lyre took for him the voice which he could not well have used at that overpowering moment. He sung wildly and triumphantly, inspired by his new and rapturous consciousness, even while her eyes were yet fixed upon him, full still of the involuntary declaration which made the inspiration of his song. These verses, which embodied the first impulsive sentiment which he had ever dared to breathe from his heart of the passion which had long been lurking within it, have been preserved for us by the damsels of Provence. We translate them, necessarily to the great detriment of their melody, from the sweet South, where they had birth, to our harsher Runic region. The song of Guillaume was an apostrophe.

   Touch the weeping string!
    Thou whose beauty fires me;
   Oh! how vainly would I sing
    The passion that inspires me.

> This, dear heart, believe,
>   Were the love I've given,
> Half as warm for Heaven as thee,
>   I were worthy heaven!
>
> Ah! should I lament,
>   That, in evil hour,
> Too much loving to repent
>   I confess thy power.
> Too much blessed to fly,
>   Yet, with shame confessing,
> That I dread to meet the eye,
>   Where my heart finds blessing.

Such a poem is beyond analysis. It was simply a gush of enthusiasm — the lyrical overflow of sentiment and passion, such as a song should be always. The reader will easily understand that the delicacy of the sentiment, the epigrammatic intenseness of the expression, is totally lost in the difficulty of subjugating our more stubborn language to the uses of the poet. A faint and inferior idea of what was sung at this moment of wild and almost spasmodical utterance, is all that we design to convey.

The spot in which this scene took place was amid the depth of umbrageous trees, in the beautiful garden of Chateau Roussillon. A soft and persuasive silence hung suspended in the atmosphere. Not a leaf stirred, not a bird chirrupped in the foliage; and, however passionate was the sentiment expressed by the troubadour, it scarcely rose beyond a whisper — harmonizing in the subdued utterance, and the sweet delicacy of its sentiment with the exquisite repose and languor of the scene. Carried beyond herself by the emotions of the moment, the feeling of Marguerite became so far irresistible that she stooped ere the song of the troubadour had subsided from the ear, and pressed her lips upon the forehead of her kneeling lover. He seized her hand at this moment and carried it to his own lips, in an equally involuntary impulse. This act awakened the noble lady to a just consciousness of her weakness. She at once recoiled from his grasp.

"Alas!" she exclaimed, with clasped hands, "what have I done?"

"Ah, lady!" was the answer of the troubadour, "it is thy goodness which has at length discovered how my heart is devoted to thee. It is thy truth, and thy nobleness, dear lady, which I love and worship."

"By these shalt thou know me ever, Guillaume of Cabestaign," was the response; "and yet I warn thee," she continued, "I warn and I entreat thee, dear servant, that thou approach me not so near again. Thou hast shown to me, and surprised from me, a most precious but an unhappy secret. Thou hast too deeply found thy way into my heart. Alas! wherefore! wherefore!" and the eyes of the amiable and virtuous woman were suffused with tears, as her innocent soul trembled under the reproaches of her jealous conscience. She continued—

"I can not help but love thee, Guillaume of Cabestaign, but it shall never be said that the love of the Lady Marguerite of Roussillon was other than became the wife of her lord. Thou, too, shalt know me, by love only, Guillaume; but it shall be such a love as shall work neither of us trespass. Yet do not thou cease to love me as before, for, of a truth, dear servant, the affections of thy heart are needful to the life of mine."

The voice of the troubadour was only in his lyre. At all events, his reply has been only preserved to us in song. It was in the fullness of his joy that he again poured forth his melody:—

> Where spreads the pleasant garden,
>   Where blow the precious flowers,
> My happy lot hath found me
>   The bud of all the bowers.
> Heaven framed it with a likeness,
>   Its very self in sweetness,
> Where virtue crowns the beauty,
>   And love bestows completeness.
> Still humble in possessions,
>   That humble all that prove her,
> I joy in the affections,
>   That suffer me to love her;
> And in my joy I sorrow,
>   And in my tears I sing her,
> The love that others hide away,
>   She suffers me to bring her.
> This right is due my homage,
>   For while they speak her beauty,
> 'Tis I alone that feel it well,
>   And love with perfect duty.

CHAPTER II.

It does not appear that love trespassed in this instance beyond the sweet but narrow boundaries of sentiment. The lovers met daily, as usual, secretly as well as publicly, and their professions of attachment were frankly made in the hearing of the world; but the vows thus spoken were not articulated any longer in that formal, conventional phraseology and manner, which, in fact, only mocked the passion which it affectedly professed. It was soon discovered that the songs of Guillaume de Cabestaign were no longer the frigid effusions of mere gallantry, the common stilt style of artifice and commonplace. There was life, and blood, and a rare enthusiasm in his lyrics. His song was no longer a thing of air, floating, as it had done, on the winglets of a simple fancy, but a living and a burning soul, borne upward and forward, by the gales of an intense and earnest passion. It was seen that when the poet and his noble mistress spoke together, the tones of their voices mutually trembled as if with a strange and eager sympathy. When they met, it was noted that their eyes seemed to dart at once into each other, with the intensity of two wedded fires, which high walls would vainly separate, and which, however sundered, show clearly that they will overleap their bounds, and unite themselves in one at last. Theirs was evidently no simulated passion. It was too certainly real, as well in other eyes as their own. The world, though ignorant of the mutual purity of their hearts, was yet quick enough to discern what were their real sentiments. Men saw the affections of which they soon learned, naturally enough, to conjecture the worst only. The rage of rivals, the jealousy of inferiors, the spite of the envious, the malice of the wantonly scandalous, readily found cause of evil where in reality offence was none. To conceive the crime, was to convey the cruel suspicion, as a certainty, to the mind of him whom the supposed offence most affected. Busy tongues soon assailed the ears of the lord of Roussillon, in relation to his wife. They whispered him to watch the lovers — to remark the eager intimacy of their eyes — the tremulous sweetness of their voices, and their subdued tones whenever they met — the frequency of their meetings — the reluctance with which they separated; and they dwelt with emphasis upon the pointed and passionate declarations, the intensity and ardor of the sentiments which now filled the songs of the troubadour—so very different from what they had ever been before. In truth, the new passion of Guillaume had wrought wondrously in favor of his music. He who had been only a clever and dextrous imitator of the artificial strains of other poets, had broken down all the fetters of convention, and now poured forth the most natural and original poetry of his own, greatly to the increase of his reputation as a troubadour.

Raymond de Roussillon hearkened to these suggestions in silence, and with a gloomy heart. He loved his wife truly, as far as it was possible for him to love. He was a stern, harsh man, fond of the chase, of the toils of chivalry rather than its sports; was cold in his own emotions, and with an intense self-esteem that grew impatient under every sort of rivalry. It was not difficult to impress him with evil thoughts, even where he had bestowed his confidence; and to kindle his mind with the most terrible suspicions of the unconsciously offending parties. Once aroused, the dark, stern man, resolved to avenge his supposed wrong; and hearing one day that Guillaume had gone out hawking, and alone, he hastily put on his armor, concealing it under his courtly and silken vestments, took his weapon, and rode forth in the direction which the troubadour had taken. He overtook the latter after a while, upon the edge of a little river that wound slowly through a wood. Guillaume de Cabestaign approached his lord without any misgiving; but as he drew near, a certain indefinable something in the face of Raymond, inspired a feeling of anxiety in his mind, and, possibly, the secret consciousness in his own bosom added to his uneasiness. He remembered that it was not often that great lords thus wandered forth unattended; and the path which Raymond pursued was one that Guillaume had taken because of its obscurity, and with the desire to find a solitude in which he might brood securely over his own secret fancies and affections. His doubts, thus awakened, our troubadour prepared to guard his speech. He boldly approached his superior, however, and was the first to break silence.

"You here, my lord, and alone! How does this chance!"

"Nay, Guillaume," answered the other, mildly; "I heard that you were here, and hawking, and resolved to share your amusement. What has been your sport?"

"Nothing, my lord. I have scarcely seen a single bird, and you remember the proverb—'Who finds nothing, takes not much.'"

The artlessness and simplicity of the troubadour's speech and manner, for the first time, inspired some doubts in the mind of Raymond, whether he could be so guilty as his enemies had reported him. His purpose, when he came forth that morning, had been to ride the supposed offender down, wherever he encountered him, and to thrust his boar-spear through his body. Such was the summary justice of the feudal baron. Milder thoughts had suddenly possessed him. If Raymond of Roussillon was a stern man, jealous of his honor, and prompt in his resentment, he at least desired to be a just man; and a lurking doubt of the motives of those by whom the troubadour had been slandered, now determined him to proceed more deliberately in the work of justice. He remembered the former confidence which he had felt in the fidelity of the page, and he was not insensible to the charm of his society. Every sentence which had been spoken since their meeting had tended to make him hesitate before he hurried to judgment in a matter where it was scarcely possible to repair the wrong which a rash and hasty vengeance might commit. By this time, they had entered the wood together, and were now concealed from all human eyes. The Lord of Roussillon alighted from his horse, and motioned his companion to seat himself beside him in the shade. When both were seated, and after a brief pause, Raymond addressed the troubadour in the following language:—

"Guillaume de Cabestaign," said he, "be sure I came not hither this day to talk to you of birds and hawking, but of something more serious. Now, look upon me, and, as a true and loyal servant, see that thou answer honestly to all that I shall ask of thee."

The troubadour was naturally impressed by the stern simplicity and solemnity of this exordium. He was not unaware that, as the knight had alighted from his steed, he had done so heavily, and under the impediment of concealed armor. His doubts and anxieties were necessarily increased by this discovery, but so also was his firmness. He felt that much depended upon his coolness and address, and he steeled himself, with all his soul, to the trial which was before him. The recollection of Marguerite, and of her fate and reputation depending upon his own, was the source of no small portion of his present resolution. His reflections were instantaneous; there was no unreasonable delay in his answer, which was at once manly and circumspect.

"I know not what you aim at or intend, my lord, but—by Heaven!—I swear to you that, if it be proper for me to answer you in that you seek, I will keep nothing from your knowledge that you desire to know!"

"Nay, Guillaume," replied the knight, "I will have no conditions. You shall reply honestly, and without reserve, to all the questions I shall put to you."

"Let me hear them, my lord—command me, as you have the right," was the reply of the troubadour, "and I will answer you, with my conscience, as far as I can."

"I would then know from you," responded Raymond, very solemnly, "on your faith and by your God, whether the verses that you make are inspired by a real passion?"

A warm flush passed over the cheeks of the troubadour; the pride of the artist was offended by the inquiry. That it should be questioned whether he really felt what he so passionately declared, was a disparaging judgment upon the merits of his song.

"Ah! my lord," was the reply, expressed with some degree of mortification, "how could I sing as I do, unless I really felt all the passion which I declare. In good sooth, then, I tell you, love has the entire possession of my soul."

"And verily I believe thee, Guillaume," was the subdued answer of the baron; "I believe thee, my friend, for, unless a real passion was at his heart, no troubadour could ever sing as thou. But, something more of thee, Guillaume de Cabestaign. Prithee, now, declare to me the name of the lady whom thy verses celebrate."

Then it was that the cheek of our troubadour grew pale, and his heart sunk within him; but the piercing eye of the baron was upon him. He had no moment for hesitation. To falter now, he was well assured, was to forfeit love, life, and everything that was proud and precious in his sight. In the moment of exigency the troubadour found his answer. It was evasive, but adroitly conceived and expressed.

"Nay, my lord, will it please you to consider? I appeal to your own heart and honor—can any one, without perfidy, declare such a secret?—reveal a thing that involves the rights and the reputation of another, and that other a lady of good fame and quality? Well must you remember what is said on this subject by the very master of our art—no less a person than the excellent Bernard de Ventadour. He should know— what says he?"

The baron remained silent, while Guillaume repeated the following verses of the popular troubadour, whose authority he appealed to:—

> "The spy your secret still would claim,
> And asks to know your lady's name;
> But tell it not for very shame!

> "The loyal lover sees the snare,
> And neither to the waves nor air
> Betrays the secret of his fair.

> "The duty that to love we owe,
> Is, while to her we all may show,
> On others nothing to bestow."

Though seemingly well adapted to his object, the quotation of our troubadour was unfortunate. There were yet other verses to this instructive ditty, and the Baron of Roussillon, who had listened very patiently as his companion recited the preceding, soon proved himself to have a memory for good songs, though he never pretended to make them himself. When Guillaume had fairly finished, he took up the strain after a brief introduction.

"That is all very right and very proper, Guillaume, and I gainsay not a syllable that Master Bernard hath written; nay, methinks my proper answer to thee lieth in another of his verses, which thou shouldst not have forgotten while reminding me of its companions. I shall refresh thy memory with the next that follows." And without waiting for any answer, the baron proceeded to repeat another stanza of the old poem, in very creditable style and manner for an amateur. This remark Guillaume de Cabestaign could not forbear making to himself, though he was conscious at the same time that the utterance of the baron was in singularly slow and subdued accents—accents that scarcely rose above a whisper, and which were timed as if every syllable were weighed and spelled, ere it was confided to expression. The verse was as follows:—

> "We yield her name to those alone,
> Who, when the sacred truth is shown,
> May help to make the maid our own."

"Now, methinks," continued the baron, "here lieth the wisdom of my quest. Who better than myself can help to secure thee thy desires, to promote thy passion, and gain for thee the favor of the fair? Tell me, then, I command thee, Guillaume, and I promise to help thee with my best efforts and advice."

Here was a dilemma. The troubadour was foiled with his own weapons. The quotation from his own authority was conclusive against him. The argument of Raymond was irresistible. Of his ability to serve the young lover there could be no question; and as little could the latter doubt the readiness of that friendship — assuming his pursuit to be a proper one — to which he had been so long indebted for favor and protection. He could excuse himself by no further evasion; and, having admitted that he really and deeply loved, and that his verses declared a real and living passion, it became absolutely necessary that our troubadour, unless he would confirm the evident suspicions of his lord, should promptly find for her a name. He did so. The emergency seemed to justify a falsehood; and, with firm accents, Guillaume did not scruple to declare himself devoted, heart and soul, to the beautiful Lady Agnes de Tarrascon, the sister of Marguerite, his real mistress. At the pressing solicitation of Raymond, and in order to render applicable to this case certain of his verses, he admitted himself to have received from this lady certain favoring smiles, upon which his hopes of future happiness were founded. Our troubadour was persuaded to select the name of this lady, over all others, for two reasons. He believed that she suspected, or somewhat knew of, the mutual flame which existed between himself and her sister; and he had long been conscious of that benevolence of temper which the former possessed, and which he fondly thought would prompt her in some degree to sympathize with him in his necessity, and lend herself somewhat to his own and the extrication of Marguerite. After making his confession, he concluded by imploring Raymond to approach his object cautiously, and by no means to peril his fortunes in the esteem of the lady he professed to love.

CHAPTER III.

BUT the difficulties of Guillaume de Cabestaign were only begun. It was not the policy of Raymond to be satisfied with his simple asseverations. The suspicions which had been awakened in his mind by the malignant suggestions of his courtiers, were too deeply and skilfully infixed there, to suffer him to be soothed by the mere statement of the supposed offender. He required something of a confirmatory character from the lips of Lady Agnes herself. Pleased, nevertheless, at what he had heard, and at the readiness and seeming frankness with which the troubadour had finally yielded his secret to his keeping, he eagerly assured the latter of his assistance in the prosecution of his quest; and he, who a moment before had coolly contemplated a deliberate murder to revenge a supposed wrong to his own honor, did not now scruple to profess his willingness to aid his companion in compassing the dishonor of another. It did not matter much to our sullen baron that the victim was the sister of his own wife. The human nature of Lord Raymond, of Roussillon, his own dignity uninjured, had but little sympathy with his neighbor's rights and sensibilities. He promptly proposed, at that very moment, to proceed on his charitable mission. The castle of Tarrascon was in sight; and, pointing to its turrets that rose loftily above the distant hills, the imperious finger of Raymond gave the direction to our troubadour, which he shuddered to pursue, but did not dare to decline. He now began to feel all the dangers and embarrassments which he was about to encounter, and to tremble at the disgrace and ruin which seemed to rise, threatening and dead before him. Never was woman more virtuous than the lady Agnes. Gentle and beautiful, like her sister Marguerite, her reputation had been more fortunate in escaping wholly the assaults of the malignant. She had always shown an affectionate indulgence for our troubadour, and a delighted interest in his various accomplishments; and he now remembered all her goodness and kindness only to curse himself, in his heart, for the treachery of which he had just been guilty. His remorse at what he had said to Raymond was not the less deep and distressing, from the conviction that he felt that there had been no other way left him of escape from his dilemma.

We are bound to believe that the eagerness which Raymond, of Roussillon, now exhibited was not so much because of a desire to bring about the dishonor of another, as to be perfectly satisfied that he himself was free from injury. At the castle of Tarrascon, the Lady Agnes was found alone. She gave the kindest reception to her guests; and, anxious to behold things through the medium of his wishes rather than his doubts and fears, Raymond fancied that there was a peculiar sort of tenderness in the tone and spirit of the compliments which she addressed to the dejected troubadour. That he was disquieted and dejected, she was soon able to discover. His uneasiness made itself apparent before they had been long together; and the keen intelligence of the feminine mind was accordingly very soon prepared to comprehend the occasion of his disquiet, when, drawn aside by Raymond at the earliest opportunity, she found herself cross-examined by the impatient baron on the nature and object of her own affections. A glance of the eye at Guillaume de Cabestaign, as she listened to the inquiries of the suspicious Raymond, revealed to the quick-witted woman the extent of his apprehensions, and possibly the danger of her sister. Her ready instinct, and equally prompt benevolence of heart, at once decided all the answers of the lady.

"Why question me of lovers?" she replied to Raymond, with a pretty querulousness of tone and manner; "certainly I have lovers enow — as many as I choose to have. Would you that I should live unlike other women of birth and quality, without my servant to sing my praises, and declare his readiness to die in my behalf?"

"Ay, ay, my lady," answered the knight, "lovers I well

know you possess; for of these I trow that no lady of rank and beauty, such as yours, can or possibly should be without;—but is there not one lover, over all, whom you not only esteem for his grace and service, but for whom you feel the tenderest interest—to whom, in fact, you prefer the full surrender of your whole heart, and, were this possible or proper, of your whole person?"

For a moment the gentle lady hesitated in her answer. The question was one of a kind to startle a delicate and faithful spirit. But, as her eyes wandered off to the place where the troubadour stood trembling—as she detected the pleading terror that was apparent in his face—her benevolence got the better of her scruples, and she frankly admitted that there really was one person in the world for whom her sentiments were even thus lively, and her sympathies thus warm and active.

"And now, I beseech you, Lady Agnes," urged the anxious baron, "that you deal with me like a brother who will joy to serve you, and declare to me the name of the person whom you so much favor."

"Now, out upon it, my lord of Roussillon," was the quick and somewhat indignant reply of the lady, "that you should presume thus greatly upon the kindred that lies between us. Women are not to be constrained to make such confession as this. It is their prerogative to be silent when the safety of their affections may suffer from their speech. To urge them to confess, in such cases, is only to compel them to speak unnecessary falsehoods. And know I not you husbands all? you have but a feeling in common; and if I reveal myself to you, it were as well that I should go at once and make full confession to my own lord."

"Nay, dearest Lady Agnes, have no such doubt of my loyalty. I will assure thee that what you tell me never finds it way to the ear of your lord. I pray thee do not fear to make this confession to me; nay, but thou must, Agnes," exclaimed the rude baron, his voice rising more earnestly, and his manner becoming passionate and stern while he grasped her wrist firmly in his convulsive fingers, and, drawing her toward him, added, in the subdued but intense tones of half-suppressed passion, "I tell thee, lady, it behooves me much to know this secret."

The lady did not immediately yield, though the manner of Raymond, from this moment, determined her that she would do so. She now conjectured all the circumstances of the case, and felt the necessity of saving the troubadour for the sake of her sister. But she played with the excited baron awhile longer, and, when his passion grew so impatient as to be almost beyond his control, she admitted, as a most precious secret, confided to his keeping only that he might serve her in its gratification, that she had a burning passion for Guillaume de Cabestaign, of which he himself was probably not conscious.

The invention of the lady was as prompt and accurate as if the troubadour had whispered at her elbow. Raymond was now satisfied. He was relieved of his suspicions, turned away from the Lady of Tarrascon, to embrace her supposed lover, and readily accepted an invitation from the former, for himself and companion, to remain that night to supper. At that moment the great gate of the castle was thrown open, and the Lord of Tarrascon made his appearance. He confirmed the invitation extended by his wife; and, as usual, gave a most cordial reception to his guests. As soon as an opportunity offered, and before the hour of supper arrived, the Lady Agnes contrived to withdraw her lord to her own apartments, and there frankly revealed to him all that had taken place. He cordially gave his sanction to all that she had done. Guillaume de Cabestaign was much more of a favorite than his jealous master; and the sympathies of the noble and the virtuous, in those days, were always accorded to those who professed a love so innocent as — it was justly believed by this noble couple — was that of the Lady Marguerite and the troubadour. The harsh suspicions of Raymond were supposed to characterize only a coarse and brutal nature, which, in the assertion of its unquestionable rights, would abridge all those freedoms which courtliness and chivalry had established for the pleasurable intercourse of other parties.

A perfect understanding thus established between the wife and husband, in behalf of the troubadour, and in misleading the baron, these several persons sat down to supper in the rarest good humor and harmony. Guillaume de Cabestaign recovered all his confidence, and with it his inspiration. He made several improvvisations during the evening, which delighted the company—all in favor of the Lady Agnes, and glimpsing faintly at his attachment for her. These, unhappily, have not been preserved to us. They are said to have been so made as to correspond to the exigency of his recent situation; the excellent Baron Raymond all the while supposing that he alone possessed the key to their meaning. The Lady Agnes, meanwhile, under the approving eye of her husband, was at special pains to show such an interest in the troubadour, and such a preference for his comfort, over that of all persons present, as contributed to confirm all the assurances she had given to her brother-in-law in regard to her affections. The latter saw this with perfect satisfaction; and leaving Guillaume to pass the night where he was so happily entertained, he hurried home to Roussillon, eager to reveal to his own wife, the intrigue between her lover and her sister It is quite possible that, if his suspicions of the troubadour were quieted, he still entertained some with regard to Marguerite. It is not improbable that a conviction that he was giving pain at every syllable he uttered entered into his calculations, and prompted what he said. He might be persuaded of the innocence of the parties, yet doubtful of their affections; and though assured now that he was mistaken in respect to the tendency of those of Guillaume, his suspicions were still lively in regard to those of his wife. His present revelations might be intended to probe her to the quick, and to gather from her emotions, at his recital, in how much she was interested in the sympathies of the troubadour.

How far he succeeded in diving into her secret, has not been confided to the chronicler. It is very certain, however, that he succeeded in making Marguerite very unhappy. She now entertained no doubt, after her husband's recital, of the treachery of her sister, and the infidelity of her lover; and though she herself had permitted him no privilege, inconsistent with the claims of her lord, she was yet indignant that he should have proved unfaithful to a heart which he so well knew to be thoroughly his own. The pure soul itself, entirely devoted to the beloved object, thus always revolts at the consciousness of its fall from its purity and its pledges; and though itself denied—doomed only to a secret worship, to which no altar may be raised, and to which there is no offering but the sacrifice of constant privation — yet it greatly prefers to entertain this sacred sense of isolation, to any enjoyment of mere mortal happiness. To feel that our affections are thus isolated in vain — that we have yielded them to one who is indifferent to the trust, and lives still for his earthly passions — is to suffer from a more than mortal deprivation. Marguerite of Roussillon passed the night in extreme agony of mind, the misery of which was greatly aggravated by the necessity, in her husband's presence, of suppressing every feeling of uneasiness. But her feelings could not always be suppressed; and when, the next day, on the return of the troubadour from Tarrascon, she encountered him in those garden walks which had been made sacred to their passion by its first mutual revelation, the pang grew to utterance, which her sense of dignity and propriety in vain endeavored to subdue. Her eyes brightened indignantly through her tears; and she whose virtue had withheld every gift of passion from the being whom she yet professed to love, at once, but still most tenderly, reproached him with his infidelity.

"Alas! Guillaume," she continued, after telling him all that she had heard, "alas! that my soul should have so singled thine out from all the rest, because of its purity, and should find thee thus, like all the rest, incapable of a sweet and holy love such as thou didst promise. I had rather died, Guillaume, a thousand deaths, than that thou shouldst have fallen from thy faith to me."

"But I have not fallen — I have not faltered in my faith, Marguerite! I am still true to thee — to thee only, though I sigh for thee vainly, and know that thou livest only for another. Hear me, Marguerite, while I tell thee what has truly happened. Thou hast heard something truly, but not all the truth."

And he proceeded with the narrative to which we have already listened. He had only to show her what had passed between her lord and himself, to show how great had been his emergency. The subsequent events at Tarrascon, only convinced her of the quick intelligence, and sweet benevolence of purpose by which her sister had been governed. Her charitable sympathies had seen and favored the artifice in which lay the safety equally of her lover and herself. The revulsion of her feelings from grief to exultation, spoke in a gush of tears, which relieved the distresses of her soul. The single kiss upon his forehead, with which she rewarded the devotion of the troubadour, inspired his fancy. He made the event the subject of the sonnet, which has fortunately been preserved to us;—

MARGUERITE.

"That there should be a question whom I love,
  As if the world had more than one so fair?
  Would'st know her name, behold the letters rare,
  God-written, on the wing of every dove!
Ask if a blindness darkens my fond eyes,
  That I should doubt me whither I should turn;
Ask if my soul, in cold abeyance lies,
  That I should fail at sight of her to burn.
That I should wander to another's away,
  Would speak a blindness worse than that of sight,
  Since here, though nothing I may ask of right,
Blessings most precious woo my heart to stay.
  High my ambition, since at heaven it aims,
  Yet humble, *since a daisy's all it claims.*"

The lines first italicised embody the name of the lady, by a periphrasis known to the Provençal dialect, and the name of the daisy, as used in the closing line, is Marguerite. The poem is an unequivocal declaration of attachment, obviously meant to do away with all adverse declarations. To those acquainted with the previous history, it unfolds another history quite as significant; and to those who knew nothing of the purity of the parties, one who made no allowance for the exaggerated manner in which a troubadour would be apt to declare the privileges he had enjoyed, it would convey the idea of a triumph inconsistent with the innocence of the lovers, and destructive of the rights of the injured husband.

Thus, full of meaning, it is difficult to conceive by what imprudence of the parties, this fatal sonnet found its way to the hands of Raymond of Roussillon. It is charged by the biographers, in the absence of other proofs, that the vanity of Marguerite, in her moments of exultation — greater than her passion — proud of the homage which she inspired, and confident in the innocence which the world had too slanderously already begun to question — could not forbear the temptation of showing so beautiful a testimony of the power of her charms. But the suggestion lacks in plausibility. It is more easy to conceive that the fond heart of the woman would not suffer her to destroy so exquisite a tribute, and that the jealousy of her lord, provoked by the arts of envious rivals, conducted him to the place of safe-keeping where her treasure was concealed. At all events, it fell into his hands, and revived all his suspicions. In fact, it gave the lie to the artful story by which he had been lulled into confidence, and was thus, in a manner, conclusive of the utter guilt of the lovers. His pride was outraged as well as his honor. He had been gulled by all upon whom he had relied — his wife, his page, and his sister. He no longer doubted Marguerite's infidelity and his own disgrace; and, breathing nothing but vengeance, he yet succeeded in concealing from all persons the conviction which he felt, of the guilt which dishonored him, and the terrible vengeance which he meditated for its punishment. He was a cold and savage man, who could suppress, in most cases, the pangs which he felt, and could deliberately restrain the passions which yet occupied triumphant place in his heart and purpose.

It was not long before he found the occasion which he desired. The movements of the troubadour were closely watched, and one day, when he had wandered forth from the castle seeking solitude, as was his frequent habit, Raymond contrived to steal away from observation, and to follow him out into the forest. He was successful in his quest. He found Guillaume resting at the foot of a shady tree, in a secluded glen, with his tablets before him. The outlines of a tender ballad, tender but spiritual, as was the character of all his melodies, were already inscribed upon the paper. The poet was meditating, as usual, the charms of that dangerous mistress, whose beauty was destined to become his bane. Raymond threw himself upon the ground beside him.

"Ah! well," said he, as he joined the troubadour, "this love of the Lady Agnes is still a distressing matter in thy thoughts."

"In truth, my lord, I think of her with the greatest love and tenderness," was the reply of Guillaume.

"Verily, thou dost well," returned the baron; "she deserves requital at thy hands. Thou owest her good service. And yet, for one who so greatly affecteth a lady, and who hath found so much favor in her sight, methinks thou seek'st her but seldom. Why is this, Sir Troubadour?"

Without waiting for the answer, Raymond added, "But let me see what thou hast just written in her praise. It is by his verses that we understand the devotion of the troubadour."

Leaning over the poet as he spoke, as if his purpose had been to possess himself of his tablets, he suddenly threw the whole weight of his person upon him, and, in the very same moment, by a quick movement of the hand, he drove the *couteau de chasse*, with which he was armed, and which he had hitherto concealed behind him, with a swift, unerring stroke deep down into the bosom of the victim. Never was blow better aimed, or with more energy delivered. The moment of danger was that of death. The unfortunate troubadour was conscious of the weapon only when he felt the steel. It was with a playful smile that Raymond struck, and so innocent was the expression of his face, even while his arm was extended and the weight of his body was pressing upon Guillaume, that the only solicitude of the latter had been to conceal his tablets. One convulsive cry, one hideous contortion, and Guillaume de Cabestaign was no more. The name of Marguerite was the only word which escaped in his dying shriek. The murderer placed his hand upon the heart of the victim. It had already ceased to beat.

CHAPTER IV.

"Thou wilt mock me no more!" he muttered fiercely, as he half rose from the body now stiffening fast. But his fierce vengeance was by no means completed. As if a new suggestion had seized upon his mind, while his hand rested upon the heart of the troubadour, he suddenly started and tore away the garments from the unconscious bosom. Once more he struck it deeply with the keen and heavy blade. In a few moments he had laid it open. Then he plunged his naked hand into the gaping wound, and tore out the still quivering heart. This he wrapped up with care and concealed in his garments. With another stroke he smote the head from the body, and this he also concealed, in fragments of dress torn from the person of his victim. With these proofs of his terrible revenge, he made his way, under cover of the dusk, in secret to the castle. What remains to be told is still more dreadful—beyond belief, indeed, were it not that the sources of our history are wholly above discredit or denial. The cruel baron, ordering his cook into his presence, then gave the heart of the troubadour into his keeping, with instructions to dress it richly, and after a manner of dressing certain favorite portions of venison, of which Marguerite was known to be particularly fond. The dish was a subject of special solicitude with her husband. He himself superintended the preparation, and furnished the spices. That night, he being her only companion at the feast, it was served up to his wife, at the usual time of supper. He had assiduously subdued every vestige of anger, unkindness, or suspicion, from his countenance. Marguerite was suffered to hear and see nothing which might provoke her apprehensions or arrest her appetite. She was more than usually serene and cheerful, as, that day and evening, her lord was more than commonly indulgent. He, too, could play a part when it suited him to do so; and, like most men of stern will and great experience, could adapt his moods and manners to that livelier cast, and more pliant temper, which better persuade the feminine heart into confidence and pleasure. He smiled upon her now with the most benevolent sweetness; but while he earnestly encouraged her to partake of the favorite repast which she so much preferred, he himself might be seen to eat of any other dish. The wretched woman, totally unsuspicious of guile or evil, undreaming of disaster, and really conscious of but little self-reproach, ate freely of the precious meat which had been placed before her. The eyes of Raymond greedily followed every morsel which she carried to her lips. She evidently enjoyed the food which had been spiced for her benefit, and as she continued to draw upon it, he could no longer forbear to unfold the exultation which he felt at the entire satisfaction of his vengeance.

"You seem very much to like your meats to-night, Marguerite. Do you find them good?"

"Verily," she answered, "this venison is really delicious."

"Eat then," he continued, "I have had it dressed purposely for you. You ought to like it. It is a dish of which you have always shown yourself very fond."

"Nay, my lord, but you surely err. I can not think that I have ever eaten before of anything so very delicious as this."

"Nay, nay, Marguerite, it is you that err. I *know* that the meat of which you now partake, is one which you have always found the sweetest."

There was something now in the voice of the speaker that made Marguerite look up. Her eyes immediately met his own and the wolfish exultation which they betrayed confounded and made her shudder. She felt at once terrified with a nameless fear. There was a sudden sickness and sinking of her heart She felt that there was a terrible meaning, a dreadful mystery in his looks and words, the solution of which she shrunk from with a vague but absorbing terror. She was too well acquainted with the sinister expression of that glance. She rallied herself to speak.

"What is it that you mean, my lord? Something dreadful! What have you done? This food—"

"Ay, this food! I can very well understand that you should find it delicious. It is such as you have always loved a little too much. It is but natural that you should relish, now that it is dead, that which you so passionately enjoyed while living. Marguerite, the meat of that dish which you have eaten was once the heart of Guillaume de Cabestaign!"

The lips of the wretched woman parted spasmodically. Her jaws seemed to stretch asunder. Her eyes dilated in a horror akin to madness. Her arms were stretched out and forward. She half rose from the table, which she at length seized upon for her support.

"No!" she exclaimed, hoarsely, at length. "No! no! It is not true. It is not possible. I will not—I dare not believe it."

"You shall have a witness, Marguerite! You shall hear it from one whom, heretofore, you have believed always, and who will find it impossible now to lie. Behold! This is the head of him whose heart you have eaten!"

With these dreadful words, the cruel baron raised the ghastly head of the troubadour, which he had hitherto concealed beneath the table, and which he now placed upon it. At this horrible spectacle the wretched woman sunk down in a swoon, from which, however, she awakened but too quickly. The wan and bloody aspect of her lover, the eyes glazed in death but full still of the tenderest expression, met her gaze as it opened upon the light. The savage lord who had achieved the horrid butchery stood erect, and pointing at the spectacle of terror. His scornful and demoniac glance—the horrid cruelty of which he continued to boast—her conscious innocence and that of her lover—her complete and deep despair—all conspired to arm her soul with courage which she had never felt till now. In the ruin of her heart she had grown reckless of her life. Her eye confronted the murderer.

"Be it so!" she exclaimed. "As I have eaten of meat so precious, it fits not that inferior food should ever again pass these lips! This is the last supper which I shall taste on earth!"

"What! dare you thus shamelessly avow to me your passion?"

"Ay! as God who beholds us knows, never did woman more passionately and truly love mortal man, than did Marguerite of Roussillon the pure and noble Guillaume de Cabestaign. It is true? I fear not to say it now! Now, indeed, I am his only, and for ever!"

Transported with fury at what he heard, Raymond drew his dagger, and rushed to where she stood. But she did not await his weapon. Anticipating his wrath, she darted headlong through a door which opened upon a balcony, over the balustrade of which, with a second effort, she flung herself into the court below. All this was the work of but one impulse and of a single instant. Raymond reached the balcony as the delicate frame of the beautiful woman was crushed upon the flag-stones of the court. Life had utterly departed when they raised her from the ground!

This terrible catastrophe struck society everywhere with consternation. At a season, when not only chivalry, but the church, gave its most absolute sanction to the existence and encouragement of that strange conventional love which we have sought to describe, the crime of Raymond provoked a universal horror. Love, artificial and sentimental rather than passionate, was the soul equally of military achievement and of aristocratic society. It was then of vast importance, as an element of power, in the use of religious enthusiasm. The shock given to those who cherished this sentiment, by this dreadful history, was felt to all the extremities of the social circle. The friends and kindred of these lovers—the princes and princesses of the land—noble lords, knights and ladies, all combined, as by a common impulse, to denounce and to destroy the bloody-minded criminal. Alphonso, king of Arragon, devoted himself to the work of justice. Raymond was seized and cast into a dungeon. His castle was razed to the ground, under a public decree, which scarcely anticipated the eager rage of hundreds who rushed to the work of demolition. The criminal himself was suffered to live; but he lived, either in prison or in exile, with loss of caste and society and amidst universal detestation!

Very different was the fate of the lovers whom man could no more harm or separate. They were honored, under the sanction of Alphonso, with a gorgeous funeral procession. They were laid together, in the same tomb, before the church of Perpignan, and their names and cruel history were duly engraven upon the stone raised to their memory. According to the Provençal historians, it was afterward a custom with the knights of Roussillon, of Cerdagne, and of Narbonnois, every year to join with the noble dames and ladies of the same places, in a solemn service, in memory of Marguerite of Roussillon, and William of Cabestaign. At the same time came lovers of both sexes, on a pilgrimage to their tomb, where they prayed for the repose of their souls. The anniversary of this service was instituted by Alphonso. We may add that romance has more than once seized upon this tragic history, out of which to weave her fictions. Boccacio has found in it the material for one of the stories of the Decameron, in which, however, while perverting history, he has done but little to merit the gratulation of Art. He has failed equally to do justice to himself, and to his melancholy subject.

CHAPTER VII.

"Ole Baginny nebber tire."
Æthiopic Muse.

We are now off the capes of Virginia, and you begin to smell the juleps. When the winds are fair, they impregnate the atmosphere — gratefully I must confess — full forty miles at sea, even as the Mississippi gives its color to the Gulf, the same distance from the Balize. Should your vessel be becalmed along the coast, as mine has been frequently, you will be compensated by the grateful odor, morning and evening, as from gardens where mint and tobacco grow together in most intimate communion.

The Virginian has always been a good liver. He unites the contradictory qualities which distinguished the English squire when he drew sword for the Stuarts. He has been freed from the brutal excesses which debased the character of his ancestor as described by Macaulay; but he has lost none of the generous virtues, which, in the same pages, did honor to the same character. He has all the loyalty and faith of the past — he still believes in the antique charms of his home and parish. He is brave and hardy, though indolent, and has a martial swagger peculiarly his own, which gives an easy grace to his courage while taking nothing from what is wholesome in his social demeanor.

The Virginian is a lounger. He will sleep for days and weeks, but only to start into the most energetic and performing life. See him as he drowses at ease in the shade of his piazza, his legs over the balustrade; observe him as he dawdles at the tavern, in a like attitude, with a sympathetic crowd of idlers around him. There he sits, as you perceive, in a ricketty chair, of domestic fashion, the seat of which is untanned bull's hide — his head thrown back, his heels in the air over an empty barrel, a huge plantation cigar protruded from his left cheek, and a pint goblet of julep, foaming amid green leaves and ice, beside him. There he will sit, and swear famously, and discuss politics by the hour, and talk of his famous horses, orators, and warriors—for he is a good local chronicler always, and has a wonderful memory of all that has happened in the "Old Dominion." You will, if you know nothing of him, fancy him a mere braggart and a sluggard. But wait. Only sound the trumpet—give the alarm—and he is on his feet. If a sluggard, he is like the Black Sluggard in Ivanhoe. He only waits the proper provocation. Like the war-horse, the blast of the trumpet puts his whole frame in motion. He kicks the chair from under him. He rolls the barrel away with a single lurch. The cigar is flung from his jaw; and, emptying his julep, he is prepared for action—ready to harangue the multitude, or square off against any assailant.

His fault in war is want of caution. He never provides against an enemy because he never fears one. He is frequently caught napping, but he makes up for it, in the end, by extra exertions. There is a dash of Raleigh and John Smith both in his character, as when the "Old Dominion," when it had not a gunboat or a piece of ordnance, defied Cromwell, and declared at all hazard for the Stuarts. His loyalty is as indisputable as his courage—provided you let him show it as he pleases. He is as self-willed as Prince Rupert, who, in most respects, was no bad representative of the Virginian;—bold, headlong, dashing, full of courage and effrontery, fond of a *rouse*, and mixing fun, fight and devotion, together, in a rare combination, which does not always offend, however it may sometimes startle. A proud fellow, who loves no master, and who only serves because it is his humor to do so.

He is profligate beyond his means. His hospitality, which was once his virtue, is, like that of some of his neighbors further south, becoming a weakness and a vice. He will not, however, *repudiate*, though his gorge rises at the thought of bankruptcy. He is too much of an *individual* for that—has too much pride *as a Virginian*. But, I fear that his profligacy of life has tainted the purity of his politics. I could wish that Virginians were less solicitous of the flesh-pots of the national government.

The mention of Virginia recalls one of the most interesting of our state histories. It is the pride of Virginia to have been one of the maternal states of this country. She shares this distinction with Massachusetts and the Carolinas. I do not mean to say, simply, that her sons have contributed to form the population of other states. It is in the formation of their *character* that she has been conspicuous. She has given tone and opinion to the new communities that have arisen along her frontier. She has equally influenced their social habits and courage. It would be a pleasant study, for the social philosopher, to inquire into the degree in which she has done this. It is enough that I suggest the inquiry."

"What a misfortune to Virginia that she is so near to the District of Columbia."

"And that she has given five presidents to the confederacy."

"Yes! this effect is to make office a natural craving; while, it is thought that every male-child born since the days of Monroe, is born with a sort of natural instinct for, and a right to the presidency."

"Yet, how curious now-a-days are the *materiel* for a president!"

"Curious, indeed! yet this would be no great evil—this change in the sort of clay supposed essential for the manufacture—if states preserved their integrity, their principles and pride, with their passion. But we grow flexible in moral in proportion to our appetites, and one who is constantly hungering will never scruple at any sort of food. The eagle descends to the garbage of the kite, and the race who once wrought their gods out of marble, soon content themselves with very rude imitations in putty."

"They need not be imitations either. We have reached that condition when it is no longer held essential, the counsel of Hamlet to his mother, 'assume a virtue if you have it not.' It is not only no longer held essential to keep up the appearances of truth and patriotism, but one is apt to be laughed at for his pains. Even to seem patriotic at Washington is held to be a gratuitous greenness."

"Let us not speak of it. How much more grateful is it to look back to the rough, wild, half savage, but brave and honest past. What a pity it is that our people do not read their own old chronicles. It is now scarcely possible to pick up any of the old histories of the states, which a sincere people, with any veneration left, would be careful to keep in every household."

"What an equal pity it is that these chronicles have been so feebly exemplified by the local historians. These have usually shown themselves to be mere compilers. They were, in fact, a very dull order of men among us. They were wholly deficient in imagination and art; and quite incapable of developing gracefully, or even of exhibiting fairly, the contents of the chronicle. They merely accumulated or condensed the records; they never *displayed* them. This is the great secret by which histories are preserved to the future and kept popular through time. Art is just as necessary in truth as in fiction — a fact of which critics even do not always appear conscious. See now the wonderful success and attraction of Mr. Prescott's labors. His secret consists chiefly in the exercise of the appropriate degree of art. His materials, in the main, are to be found in a thousand old volumes, available to other writers; but it was in his art that the lumbersome records became imbued with life. His narratives of the conquest of Peru and Mexico are so many exquisite pictures — action, scene, portrait, all harmoniously blended in beautiful and symmetrical connection. His details, which, in common hands, were usually sadly jumbled, constitute a series of noble dramas — all wrought out in eloquent action. His events are all arranged with the happiest order. His *dramatis personæ* play their parts according to the equal necessities of the history and of their individual character. The parts harmonize, the persons work together, and the necessary links preserved between them, the action is unbroken to the close. All irrelevant matter, calculated to impair this interest, is carefully discarded; all subordinate matter is dismissed with a proper brevity, or compressed in the form of notes, at the bottom of his page. Nothing is dwelt upon at length, but that which justifies delineation, either from the intrinsic value of the material, or from its susceptibilities for art. Suppose the historian were to employ such a rule in the development of such chronicles as those of Virginia? What a beautiful volume might be made of it! How full of admirable lessons, of lovely sketches, of fine contrasts, and spirit-stirring actions. The early voyagers, down to the time of Smith, would form the subject of a most delightful chapter; and then we open upon the career of Smith himself—that remarkable man, excellent politician, and truly noble gentleman and soldier. He seems to have been the last representative of an age which had passed from sight before he entered upon the stage. He was the embodiment of the best characteristics of chivalry. How manly his career—with what a noble self-esteem did he prepare for the most trying issues—how generous his courage—how disinterested his virtues—how devoted to the sex—a *preux chevalier*, not unworthy to have supped with Bayard after the battle of Marignano. Neither England nor America has ever done justice to the genius or the performances of this man, and I fear that his name was somewhat in the way of his distinctions. It is difficult to believe in the heroism of a man named Smith. Men do not doubt that he will fight, but mere fighting is not heroism. Heroism is the model virtue; and we are slow to ally it with the name of Smith—indeed, with any name of a single syllable. There are really few or no flaws in the character of the founder of Virginia."

"I am not sure of that! What do you say to his treatment of the beautiful daughter of Powhatan? His coldness—"

"You have simply stumbled in the track of a popular error. It is a vulgar notion that he encouraged and slighted the affections of Pocahontas. All this is a mistake. He neither beguiled her with false shows of love, nor was indifferent to her beauties or her virtues. Pocahontas was a mere child to Smith, but twelve years old when he first knew her, and he about forty."

"But his neglect of her when she went to England"

"He did not neglect her."

"She reproached him for it."

"Yes; the poor savage in her unsophisticated child-heart, knew nothing of that convention which, in Europe, lay as burdensomely upon Smith as upon herself. Even then, however, he treated her as tenderly as if she were his own child, with this difference, that he was required to approach her as a princess. His reserves were dictated by a prudent caution which did not venture to outrage the pedantic prejudices of the Scottish Solomon, then upon the throne, who, if you remember, was very slow to forgive Rolfe, one of his subjects, for the audacity which led him to marry the princess of Virginia."

"By the way, you have yourself made Smith an object of the love of Pocahontas."

"It was the sin of my youth; and was the natural use to be made of the subject when treating it in verse."

"Come—as one of your contributions to our evening, give us your legend. Miss Burroughs will no doubt be pleased to hear it, and your verse may very well serve as a relief to our prose."

"What do you say, Selina?"

"Oh! by all means—the legend."

"To hear is to obey."

The circle closed about me, and, with many natural misgivings, and a hesitation which is my peculiar infirmity, I delivered myself as well as I could of the fabrication which follows:—

POCAHONTAS; A LEGEND OF VIRGINIA.

I.

Light was her heart and sweet her smile,
   The dusky maid of forest-bower,
Ere yet the stranger's step of guile
   Bore one soft beauty from the flower;
The wild girl of an Indian vale,
   A child, with all of woman's seeming,
And if her cheek be less than pale,
   'Twas with the life-blood through it streaming.
Soft was the light that fill'd her eye,
   And grace was in her every motion,
Her voice was touching, like the sigh,
   When passion first becomes devotion;—
And worship still was hers—her sire
   Beloved and fear'd, a prince of power,
Whose simplest word or glance of ire
   Still made a thousand warriors cower.
Not such her sway,—yet not the less,
   Because it better pleased to bless,
And won its rule by gentleness;
   Among a savage people, still
She kept from savage moods apart,
   And thought of crime, and dream of ill
    Had never sway'd her maiden heart.

A milder tutor had been there,
  And, midst wild scenes and wilder men,
Her spirit, like her form, was fair,
  And gracious was its guidance then.
Her sire, that fierce old forest king
  Himself had ruled that she should be
A meek, and ever gentle thing,
  To clip his neck, to clasp his knee;
To bring his cup when, from the chase,
  He came o'erwearied with its toils;
To cheer him by her girlish grace,
  To sooth him by her sunniest smiles:—
They rear'd her thus a thing apart
  From deeds that make the savage mirth,
And haply had she kept her heart
  As fresh and gentle as at birth;
A Christian heart, though by its creed
  Untaught, yet, in her native wild,
Free from all evil thought or deed,
  A sweet, and fond, and tearful child;
Scarce woman yet, but haply nigh
  The unconscious changes of the hour
When youth is and, unknowing why,—
  The bud dilating to the flower,
And sighing with the expanding birth
  Of passionate hopes, that, born to bless,
May yet, superior still to earth,
  Make happy with their pure impress.
Such, in her childhood, ere the blight
  Of failing fortunes touch'd her race,
Was Pocahontas still,—a bright
  And blessing form of youth and grace;—
Beloved of all, her father's pride,
  His passion, from the rest apart,
A love for which he would have died,
  The very life-blood of his heart.

II.

The king would seek the chase to-day,
And mighty is the wild array
That gathers nigh in savage play,—
  A nation yields its ear;
A bison herd — so goes the tale —
Is trampling down the cultured vale,
And none who love the land may fail
  To gather when they hear.

He goes—the father from his child,
To seek the monster of the wild,
But, in his fond embraces caught,
Ere yet he goes, he hears her thought—
Her wish—the spotted fawn—the prize,
The pet most dear to girlhood's eyes,
Long promised, which the chase denies.
Stern is the sudden look he darts
  Among the assembled crowd, as now
His footstep from the threshold parts,
  And dark the cloud about his brow.

"We hunt no timid deer to-day,
And arm for slaughter, not for play—
Another season for such prey,
  My child, and other prey for thee:
A captive from the herd we seek,
Would bring but sorrow to thy cheek,
Make thee forget what peace is here,
  Of bird, and bloom, and shady tree,
And teach thine eyes the unknown tear.—
No more!"
            He puts her from his grasp,
Undoes, with gentle hand, the clasp
She takes about his neck, and then,
  Even as he sees her silent grief,
He turns, that stern old warrior-chief,
And takes her to his arms again.
"It shall be as thou wilt—the fawn,
Ere from the hills the light is gone,
  Shall crouch beneath thy hands."
How sweetly then she smiled—his eye
Once more perused her tenderly,
Then, with a smile, he put her by,
  And shouted to his bands.

III.

They came!—a word, a look, is all—
  The thicket hides their wild array;
A thousand warriors, plumed and tall,
  Well arm'd and painted for the fray.
The maiden watch'd their march,—a doubt
  Rose in her heart, which, as they went,
Her tongue had half-way spoken out,
  Suspicious of their fell intent.
'A bison herd—yet why the frown
  Upon my father's brow, and why

THE WAR PARTY.

The war-tuft on each warrior's crown,
 The war-whoop as they gather'd nigh?
They tell of stranger braves,—a race,
With thunder clad, and pale of face,
And lightnings in their grasp—who dart
 The bolt unseen with deadliest aim—
 A sudden shock, a rush of flame—
Still fatal, to the foeman's heart.
Ah! much I fear, with these to fight,
 Our warriors seek the woods to-day;
And they will back return by night
 With horrid tokens of the fray;—
With captives doom'd in robes of fire
 To sooth the spirits of those who fell,
And glut the red and raging ire
 Of those who but avenge too well!
Ah! father, could my prayer avail,
 Such should not be their sport and pride;
It were, methinks, a lovelier tale,
 Of peace along our river's side;
And groves of plenty, fill'd with song
Of birds that crowd, a happy throng
 To hail the happier throngs below;
That tend the maize-fields and pursue
The chase, or urge the birch canoe,
 And seek no prey and have no foe!
Ah! not for me—if there should come
A chief to bear me to his home—
Let him not hope, with bloody spear,
 To win me to his heart and will—
Nor boast, in hope to please mine ear,
 Of victims he has joy'd to kill.
No! let me be a maiden still;
I care not if they mock, and say
 The child of Powhatan sits lone,
And lingers by the public way
 With none to hearken to her moan—
She'll sit, nor sigh, till one appears
Who finds no joy in human tears."

IV.

Now sinks the day-star, and the eve
With dun and purple seems to grieve;
Sudden the dark ascends, the night
Speeds on with rapid rush and flight;
The maiden leaves her forest bowers,
Where late she wove her idle flowers,

Chill'd by the gloom, but chill'd the more
  As from the distant wood she hears
A shriek of death, that, heard before,
  Hath grown familiar to her ears;
And fills her soul with secret dread
  Of many a grief the young heart knows,
In loneliness, by fancy fed,
  That ever broods o'er nameless woes,
And grieves the more at that relief
Which finds another name for grief.
Too certain now her cause of fear,
  That shout of death awakes again;
The cry which stuns her woman ear,
  Is that of vengeance for the slain.
Too well she knows the sound that speaks
  For terrors of the mortal strife;
The bitter yell, whose promise reeks
  With vengeance on the captive life.

" No bison hunt," she cried, " but fight,
Their cruel joy, their sad delight;
They come with bloody hands to bring
Some captive to the fatal ring;
There's vengeance to be done to-day
For warrior slaughter'd in the fray;
Yet who their foe, unless it be
The race that comes beyond the sea,
The pale, but powerful chiefs who bear
  The lightnings in their grasp, and fling
Their sudden thunder through the air,
  With bolts that fly on secret wing?
The Massawomek now no more
Brings down his warriors to the shore;
  And 'twas but late the Monacan,
O'ercome in frequent fight, gave o'er,
  And bow'd the knee to Powhatan.
Scarce is gone three moons ago
Since they laid the hatchet low,
Smoked the calumet, that grew
  To a sign for every eye,
And by this the warriors knew
That the Spirit from above,
As the light smoke floated high.
Bless'd it with the breath of love.
'Tis the pale-face, then, and he,—
Wild in wrath, and dread to see,—
Terrible in fight,— ah ! me !—

If against my father's heart
He hath sped his thunder-dart.

V.

Now gather the warriors of Powhatan nigh,
    A rock is his throne,
    His footstool a stone;
Dark the cloud on his brow, keen the fire in his eye;
To a ridge on his forehead swells the vein;—
    His hand grasps the hatchet, which swings to and fro
As if ready to sink in the brain,
    But seeking in vain for the foe!
Thus the king on the circle looks round,
With a speech that hath never a sound;
His eye hath a thirst which imparts
    What the lip might but feebly essay,
And it speaks like an arrow to their hearts,
    As if bidding them bound on the prey.
The brow of each chief is in air,
    With a loftiness born of his own;
And the king, like the lion from his lair,
    Looks proud on the props of his throne.
His eagle and his tiger are there,
    His vulture, his cougar, his fox,—
    And, cold on the edge of his rocks,
The war-rattle rings his alarum and cries,
    "I strike, and my enemy dies!"

Lifts the soul of the monarch to hear,
    Lifts the soul of the monarch to see,
And, quick at his summons, the chieftains draw near,
    And, shouting they sink on the knee,—
    Then rise and await his decree.

VI.

The king in conscious majesty
Roll'd around his fiery eye,
As some meteor, hung on high,
Tells of fearful things to be,
    In the record roll of fate,
    Which the victim may not flee—
It may be to one alone,
    Of the thousand forms that wait,
At the footstool of the throne!
Parts his lips for speech, but ere
    Word can speak to human sense,
Lo! the circle opens—there—

One descends, a form of light,
As if borne with downward flight,
  You may hardly gather whence;
Slight the form, and with a grace
Caught from heaven its native place;
Bright of eye, and with a cheek,
In its glowing ever meek,
With a maiden modesty,
That puts Love, a subject, by;—
And such soft and streaming tresses,
That the gazer stops and blesses,
Having sudden dreams that spell
  Reason on her throne, and make
All the subject thoughts rebel,
  For the simple fancy's sake!

Such the vision now! The ring
Yields,—and lo! before the king,
Down she sinks beneath the throne
Where he sits in strength alone,—
She upon a lowly stone!
And her tresses settle down
Loosely on her shoulders brown
Heedless she, the while, of aught
But the terror in her thought.
Eager in her fears, her hand
  Rests upon his knee — her eye —
Gazing on the fierce command
  Throned in his with majesty —
She alone at that dark hour,
Dare approach the man of power.

VII.

Dread the pause that followed then
In those ranks of savage men;
Fain would Powhatan declare
  What is working in his soul;
But the eye that meets him there,
As the maiden upward looks,
  Spells him with a sweet control:
Never long his spirit brooks
  Such control — his angry eye —
Seeks her with reproving fire,
  And her lips, with fond reply,
Part to calm the rising ire;
Soft the accents, yet the sound
Strangely breaks the silence round.

VIII.

"Is't thus thou keep'st thy word with me?
  I see not here the spotted fawn,
Which thou didst promise me should be,
  Ere daylight from the hills was gone,
A captive all unharmèd caught.
For this, to wreathe its neck, I sought
  The purple flower that crowns the wood,—
And gather'd from the sandy shore
The singing shell with crimson core,
  As it were dropp'd with innocent blood.
To thee I know the task were light
  To rouse the silver-foot and take,
Even in its weeping mother's sight,
  The bleating captive from the brake.
Yet, here, no captive waits for me;
  No trophy of thy skill and toil;
Not even the bison-head I see,
  The youthful hunter's proper spoil.
But, in its stead—ah! wherefore now,—
  My father! do not check thy child!
Why is the dark spot on thy brow,
  And why thy aspect stern and wild?
What may this mean? no bison chase,
  Nor failing sport, not often vain,
Hath fix'd that sign upon your face,
  Of passionate hate and mortal pain!
Ah! no! methinks the fearful mood
Hath found its birth in hostile blood—
The war-whoop, shouted as ye went,
This told me of your fell intent;
The death-whoop, chanted as ye came,
Declared, as well, defeat and shame!"

IX.

"Ay!" cried the monarch, "well ye speak·
I feel the words upon my cheek,
In burning characters that cry
For vengeance on mine enemy.
'Tis true as thou hast said, my child,
We met our foemen in the wild,
And from the conflict bear away
But death and shame to prove the fray.
Vainly our warriors fought,—our sires,
  Withhold their blessings on our arms;

SOUTHWARD HO!

The pale-face with his thunder-fires,
  His lightning-shafts, and wizard charms
Hath baffled strength and courage.—We
    May fold our arms—the glorious race,
      That from the day-god took their birth
    Must to the stranger yield the place,
Uproot the great ancestral tree,
    And fling their mantles down on earth.
Yet shall there be no vengeance? Cries,
From earth demand the sacrifice;
Souls of the slaughter'd warriors stand,
And wave us with each bloody hand;
Call for the ghost of him who slew—
In bloody rites, a warrior true,—
  And shall they call in vain?
To smooth the path of shadows, Heaven
A victim to the doom hath given,
Whose heart, with stroke asunder riven,
  Shall recompense the slain!"

X.

While fury took the place of grief,
Impatient then the monarch chief,
A stalwart savage summon'd nigh;—
  "The pale-faced warrior bring—the brave
  Shriek o'er the valley for their slave,—
I hear them in the eagle's cry,
The wolf's sharp clamors—he must die!
No coward he to shrink from death,
But, shouting in his latest breath,
  Its pangs he will defy.—
  It joys my soul at such a fate,
Which, though the agony be great,
  Can still exulting sing,—
Of braves, the victims to his brand,
Whose crowding ghosts about him stand,
To bear him to the spirit-land
  On swift and subject wing!"

XI.

The block is prepared,
  The weapon is bared,
And the warriors are nigh with their tomahawks rear'd;
  The prisoner they bring
  In the midst of the ring,
And the king bids the circle around him be clear'd.

THE VICTIM AT THE STAKE.

The wrath on his brow at the sight
  Of the prisoner they bring to his doom,
Now kindles his eye with a lordly delight,
  As the lightning-flash kindles the gloom.
He rises, he sways, with a breath,
And hush'd grows the clamor of death;
Falls the weapon that groan'd with the thirst
  To drink from the fountain accurst;
Stills the murmur that spoke for the hate
That chafed but to wait upon fate.

XII.

How trembled then the maid, as rose
  That captive warrior calm and stern,
Thus girded by the wolfish foes
  His fearless spirit still would spurn;
  How bright his glance, how fair his face,
  And with what proud and liberal grace
His footsteps free advance, as still
  He follows firm the bloody mace
  That guided to the gloomy place
Where stood the savage set to kill!
How fills her soul with dread dismay,
  Beholding in his form and air
How noble is the unwonted prey
  Thus yielded to the deathsman there!
Still fearless, though in foreign land,
No weapon in his fettered hand,
Girt by a dark and hostile band
  That never knew to spare!
His limbs, but not his spirit bound,
How looks the god-like stranger round!
As heedless of the doom, as when,
In sight of thirty thousand men,
He stood by Regall's walls, and slew
The bravest of her chiefs that came
  His best in beauty's sight to do,
And seeking honor, finding shame!
As little moved by fate and fear,
  As when, in fair Charatza's smile
Exulting, he was doom'd to bear
  The Tartar's blows and bondage vile;—
  And slew him in his resolute mood,
  Though Terror's worst beside him stood,
And all her sleuthhounds follow'd fast,
  Death, hunger, hate, a venomous brood,

Where'er his flying footsteps past."*
Not now to shrink, though, in his eyes,
  Their eager hands, at last, elate,
Have track'd him where the bloodstone lies,
  And mock him with the shaft of fate!
With courage full as great as theirs,
He keeps a soul that laughs at fears;
Too proud for grief, too brave for tears,
Their tortures still he mocks, and boasts
His own great deeds, the crowding hosts,
That witness'd, and the shrieking ghosts
  His violent arm set free;
And, while his heart dilates in thought
Of glorious deeds in lands remote,
  The pride of Europe's chivalry,
It seem'd to those who gazed, that still
The passion of triumph seem'd to fill,
While nerving with a deathless will,
  The exulting champion's heart!
Half trembled then the savage foe,
Lest sudden, from the unseen bow,
He still might send the fatal blow,
  He still might wing the dart.
But soon—as o'er the captive's soul,
Some tender memories seem'd to roll,
Like billowy clouds that charged with streams,
Soon hide in saddest gloom the gleams
Of the imperial sun, and hush,
In grief, the day's dilating flush
Of glory and pride,—the triumph fell—
The soul obey'd the sudden spell!—
A dream of love that, kindled far,
In youth, beneath the eastern star,
Is passing from his hope, to be
The last best light of memory.
Soft grew the fire within his eyes,
One tear the warrior's strength defies,—
His soul a moment falters—then,
  As if the pliancy were shame,
  Dishonoring all his ancient fame,
He stood!—the master-man of men!

XIII.

That moment's sign of weakness broke
  The spell that still'd the crowd! The chief,

---

* See the Life of Captain John Smith, the founder of Virginia; his wondrous adventures among the Turks, &c.

AT THE STAKE

With mockery in his accent spoke —
  For still the savage mocks at grief —
"No more! why should th' impatient death
Forbear, till with the woman's breath,
Her trembling fear, her yearning sigh
  For life but vainly kept with shame,
  He wrongs his own and people's name! —
I would not have the warrior die,
Nor to the last, with battle cry,
  Exulting, shout his fame!
Spare him the crime of tears that flow,
A sign of suffering none should know
But him who flings aside the bow,
  And shrinks the brand to bear,
Let not our sons the weakness see,
Lest from the foe in shame they flee,
And by their souls no longer free,
  Grow captive to their fear:
For him! — I pity while I scorn
The tribe in which the wretch was born;
  And, as I gaze around,
I glad me that mine aged eye
Sees none of all who gather nigh,
Who dreads to hear the war-whoop's sound,
  Not one who fears to die!"

XIV.

They cast the prisoner to the ground,
With gyves from neighboring vines they bound.
His brow upon the ancient rock
They laid with wild and bitter mock,
That joy'd to mark the deep despair
  That moment in the prisoner's eye,
As sudden, swung aloft in air,
  He sees the bloody mace on high!
But not for him to plead in fear —
No sign of pity comes to cheer,
And, with one short unwhisper'd prayer,
  He yields him up to die.
Keen are the eyes that watch the blow,
Impatient till the blood shall flow,
A thousand hearts that gloating glow,
  In eager silence hush'd:
The arm that wields the mace is bending,
The instrument of death descending, —
A moment, and the mortal sinks.

A moment, and the spirit soars,
The earth his parting life-blood drinks,
  The spirit flies to foreign shores:
A moment!—and the maiden rush'd
From the low stone where still affrighted,
  Scarce dreaming what she sees is true—
With vision dim, with thoughts benighted,
  She sate as doom'd for slaughter too;—
And stay'd the stroke in its descent,
While on her childish knee she bent,
Flings one arm o'er the captive's brow,
  Above his forehead lifts her own,
Then turns—with eye grown tearless now,
  But full of speech—as eye alone
Can speak to eye and heart in prayer—
  For mercy to her father's throne!
Ah! can she hope for mercy there?

XV.

And what of him that savage sire?
  Oh! surely, not in vain she turns
To where his glance of mortal ire,
  In lurid light of anger burns.
A moment leaps he to his feet,
  When first her sudden form is seen,
Across the circle darting fleet,
  The captive from the stroke to screen.
Above his head, with furious whirl,
  The hatchet gleams in act to fly;—
But, as he sees the kneeling girl,
  The pleading glances of her eye.—
The angel spirit of mercy waves
  The evil spirit of wrath away,
And all accords, ere yet she craves
  Of that her eye alone can pray.
Strange is the weakness born of love,
  That melts the iron of his soul,
And lifts him momently above
  His passions and their dark control;
And he who pity ne'er had shown
  To captive of his bow and spear,
By one strong sudden sense has grown
  To feel that pity may be dear
As vengeance to the heart,—when still
  Love keeps one lurking-place, and grows,
Thus prompted by a woman's will,
  Triumphant o'er a thousand foes.

LOVE'S TRIUMPH.

'Twas as if sudden, touch'd by Heaven,
The seal that kept the rock was riven;
As if the waters slumbering deep,
　　Even from the very birth of light,
Smote by its smile, had learn'd to leap,
　　Rejoicing to their Maker's sight.

How could that stern old king deny
The angel pleading in her eye?—
How mock the sweet imploring grace,
That breathed in beauty from her face,
And to her kneeling action gave
　　A power to soothe, and still subdue,
Until, though humble as the slave.
　　To more than queenly sway she grew?

Oh! brief the doubt,—O! short the strife!
She wins the captive's forfeit life.
She breaks his bands—she bids him go,
Her idol, but her country's foe;
And dreams not, in that parting hour,
　　The gyves that from his limbs she tears,
Are light in weight, and frail in power,
　　To those that round her heart she wears.

CHAPTER VIII.

Nest egg of the Old Dominion.

WITH joined hands, Smith and Pocahontas conduct you naturally to Jamestown, that abandoned nest of the Sire of Eagles. James river is one of the classic regions of the country. We should all of us, once in a life, at least, make it the object of a pilgrimage! It is full of associations, to say nothing of it as a fine spacious stream, which, when a better spirit and knowledge of farming shall prevail and a denser population shall inhabit its borders, will become a channel of great wealth, and present a throng of quiet beauties to the eye wherever its currents wander.

"But the imputation of a sickly climate rests upon James river."

"This is due wholly to the sparseness of the settlements, the lack of drainage, the want of proper openings in the woods for the progress of the winds, and to the presence of a cumbrous and always rotting undergrowth. Population will cure all this. It is doing it already. The farming settlements are improving, and the health of the river is said to be improving along with them. You will have pointed out to you, along the route, a number of well-cultivated plantations, some containing four or five thousand acres, which are represented as being among the best managed and most profitable in the state. With the substitution of farming for staple culture, this progress would be rapid."

"But the genius of the Southron, particularly the Virginian, has always inclined more to extensive than to careful cultivation. His aims were always magnificent. He must have large estates. He can not bear to be crowded. Like his cattle, he must get all the range he can; and, in the extent of his territory, he neglects its improvement. Indeed, his force — that is, his labor — was never equal to his estates. The New York farmers have been farming upon his waste domains. Their policy differs from his in one essential particular. They concentrate the energies which he diffuses. They require but small territory, and they make the most of it. Lands which, in the hands of the Virginian, were no longer profitable for tobacco, the New-Yorkers have limed for wheat; and what he sold at a dollar per acre, in many instances will now command seventy-five dollars. The character of the Southron is bold and adventurous. This leads him to prefer the wandering to the stationary life. He needs excitement, and prefers the varieties and the vicissitudes of the forest, to the tame drudgery of the farmstead. His mission is that of a pioneer. The same farmer who now makes his old fields flourish in grain, thirty bushels to the acre, would never have set foot in the country, until the brave Virginian had cleared it of its savage inhabitants, the wild beast, and the red man."

"James river conducts you to Jamestown. Jamestown and St. Augustine are among the oldest landmarks of civilization in Anglo-Norman America. You approach both, if properly minded, with becoming veneration. The site of Jamestown is an island, connected by a bridge with the main. The spot is rather a pleasing than an imposing one. It was chosen evidently with regard to two objects, security from invasion by the sea, and yet an easy communication with it when desirable. Here, squat and hidden like a sea-fowl about to lay her eggs, the colony escaped the vigilant eyes and ferocious pursuit of the hungry Spaniard."

"What a commentary upon the instability of national power is the fact, that, at this day, this power has no longer the capacity to harm. In the time of Elizabeth, the Spaniard was the world's great Tiger Shark. Now, he is little better than a skipjack in the maw of that Behemoth of the nations, whose seagrowth he certainly did something to retard. In the time of Roundhead authority, the Dutch were a sort of corpulent swordfish of the sea; now you may better liken them to the great lazy turtle, fat and feeble, whom more adroit adventurers turn upon their backs to be gathered up at leisure. Both of these nations may find their revenges, and recover position in other days, when the powers by which they were overcome shall fall into their errors, and contrive, through sheer blindness, their own emasculation."

"Did you ever read 'Purchas, his Pilgrims?' He has a description of Jamestown in 1610, written by William Strachey. If you are curious to see it, I have it in my berth, and marked the passage only this morning."

Some curiosity being expressed, the book was brought, and the extract read. It may possibly interest others, in this connection, to see where the first tree was hewn in the New World by the hands of the Anglo-Norman.

"A low levell of ground about halfe an acre, or (so much as *Queene Dido* might buy of King *Hyarbas*, which she compassed about with the thongs cut out of one bull's, and therein built her castle of Byrsa) on the North side of the river is cast almost into the forme of a triangle, and so pallazadoed. The South side next the river (howbeit extended in a line, or curtaine six score foote more in lengthe, than the other two by reason of the advantages of the ground doth so require), contains one hundred and forty yards: the West and East side a hundred only. At every angle or corner, where the lines meet, a bulwarke or watchtower is raised, and in each bulwarke a piece of ordnance or two well mounted. To every side, a proportionate distance from the pallisado, is a settled streete of houses, that runs along, so as each line of the angle hath his streete. In the midst is a market place, a storehouse and a *corps du garde*, as likewise a pretty chappelle, though (at this time when we came in) as ruined and unfrequented: but the Lord, Governor and Captaine Generall, hath given order for the repairing of it, and at this instant many hands are about it. It is in lengthe three-score foote, in breadth twenty-four, and shall have a chancell in it of cedar, and a communion table of the blacke walnut—and all the pews of cedar, with fair broad windows, to shut and open, as the weather shall occasion: a pulpit of the same wood, with a font hewn hollow like a canoa; with two bells at the West end. It is so cast as it be very light within, and the Lord Governor and Captaine Generall doth cause it to be passing sweete and trimmed up with divers flowers;—with a sexton belonging to it."

"So much for the Church—the first English Church, be it remembered, ever raised in America. This should render the description an interesting one. And now something for the uses to which it was put. We see that Strachey found it in a ruinous condition. This was in 1610. You are not to suppose that the ruin of the church arose from the neglect of the worshippers. It was rather the result of the more pressing misfortunes of the colonists. Smith was superseded by Lord Delaware in 1609, who brought with him a host of profligate adventurers, some of whom Smith had sent out of the colony, tied neck and heels, as criminals. It was an evil augury to him and to the colony that they were brought back. They brought with them faction, confusion, and misery. Insurrection followed—the Indians revolted and commenced the work of indiscriminate massacre, and the church and religion necessarily suffered all the disasters which had befallen society. But, with the restoration of the church under Delaware, let us see what followed. Our Puritans make a great outcry about their devotions. They are perpetually raising their rams' horns, perhaps quite as much in the hope of bringing down the walls of their neighbors, as with the passion of religion. Our Virginia colonists boast very little of what they did in the way of devotion. Let us hear Strachey still further on this subject:—

"'Every Sunday we have sermons twice a day, and every Thursday a sermon—having two preachers which take their wekely turnes—and every morning at the ringing of a bell, about ten of the clocke, each man addresseth himself to prayers, and so, at four of the clocke before supper.'

"Verily, but few of the 'guid folk' of Virginia or New England are so frequent now-a-days at their religious exercises! The authorities of Virginia set the example:—

"'Every Sunday, when the Lord Governor and Captain Generall goeth to church, he is accompanied with all the Counsaillors, Captains, other officers, and all the gentlemen, and with a guard of Halberdiers, in his lordship's livery, faire red cloaks, to the number of fifty, both on each side and behind him: and being in the church, his lordship hath his seate in the *Quier* in a green velvet chair, with a cloath, with a velvet cushion spread on a table before him on which he kneeleth, and on each side sit the Counsell, Captains, and officers, each in their place; and when he returneth home again, he is waited on to his house in the same manner.'

"Something stately, these devotions, but they were those of

the times, and of—the politician. Religion has a twofold aspect, and concerns society as well as the individual, though not in the same degree. And this, would you believe it, was just ten years before the Puritans landed at Plymouth. Our Virginians were clearly not wholly regardless of those serious performances which their more youthful neighbors, farther East, claim pretty much to have monopolized. But to return. It may interest many readers to see what Strachey further says of the ancient city of Jamestown.

"'The houses first raised were all burnt, by a casualty of fire, the beginning of the second year of their siat [settlement] and in the second voyage of Captain Newport; which have been better rebuilted, though as yet in no great uniformity, either for the fashion or the beauty of the streete. A delicate wrought fine kind of mat the *Indians* make, with which (as they can be trucked for, or *snatched up**) our people so dress their chambers and inward rooms, which make their homes so much the more handsome. The houses have large and wide country chimnies in the which is to be supposed (in such plenty of wood) what fires are maintained; and they have found the way to cover their houses, now (as the *Indians*), with barkes of trees, as durable and good proofs against stormes and winter weather as the best tyle, defending likewise the piercing sunbeams of summer and keeping the inner lodgings coole enough which before would be in sultry weather like stoves, whilst they were, as at first, pargetted and plaistered with bitumen or tough clay; and thus armed for the injury of changing times, and seasons of the the year, we hold ourselves well apaid, though wanting array

---

* This *snatching* up bothered us in the case of a people so devout in their attendance upon church, but, turning to the Journal of the Plymouth Pilgrims (Cheever's) we found at their very first entrance upon Indian land a similar case of snatching up, which proves the practice to have been no ways improper, even if not exactly religious. At page 34, we read, that our beloved Pilgrims found where the "naked salvages" had put away a basket of corne, four or five bushels. "We were in suspense what to do with it," says our simple chronicler, but the long and short of the suspense and consultation resulted in their taking off the commodity—in other words, "snatching up," which they did, with the avowed determination if they ever met with the owner to satisfy him for his grain. Our Virginians, I fancy, did their snatching precisely on the same terms.

hangings, tapestry, and guilded Venetian cordovan, or more spruce household garniture, and wanton city ornaments, remembering the old Epigraph —

> "'We dwelt not here to build us Barnes
> And Halls for pleasure and good cheer,
> But Halls we build for us and ours
> To dwell in them while we live here.'

"The Puritans could not have expressed themselves more devoutly. Here are texts to stimulate into eloquence a thousand annual self-applausive orators, for a thousand years to come. That this was the prevailing spirit of those who gave tone to the colony, and not the sentiments of a single individual, hear further of the manner in which that most excellent ruler, the Lord Delaware, first made his approaches to the colony. This, be it remembered, was in 1610, ten years before the Plymouth pilgrims brought religion to the benighted West :—

"'Upon his lordship's landing, at the south gate of the Pallesado (which looks into the river) our governor caused his company to stand in order and make a guard. It pleased him that I (William Strachey) should bear his colours for that time;— His lordship landing, fell upon his knees, and before us all made a long and silent prayer to himself, and after marching up into the town: when at the gate, I bowed with the colours and let them fall at his Lordship's feet, who passed into the chapelle, where he heard a sermon by Master Bucke, our Governor's preacher,' &c.

"To pray to himself, perhaps, was not altogether in the spirit of that very intense religion which some portions of our country so love to eulogize; but methinks it was not bad for our Virginia Governor, whom their better neighbours were wont to suppose never prayed at all. But they worked, too, as well as prayed, these rollicking Virginians: and their works survive them. The conversion of Pocahontas — the possession of that bright creature of a wild humanity — has been long since envied to Virginia by all the other colonies. Take the account of her conversion from a letter of Sir Thomas Dale :—

"'Powhatan's daughter I caused to be carefully instructed in the Christian religion, who after she had made some good progresse therein, renounced publickly her Country's Idolatry openly confessed her Christian Faith, was, as she desired, baptized, and is since married to an English Gentleman of good understanding — as by his letter unto me, containing the reasons of his marriage unto her, you may perceive. Another knot to bind the knot the stronger. Her father and friends gave approbation of it, and her uncle gave her to him in the Church: she lives civilly and lovingly with him, and I trust will increase in goodnesse as the knowledge of God increaseth in her. She will goe into England with mee, and were it but the gaining of this one such, I will think my time, toile, and present stay, well spent'

"Enough of our old chronicler for a single sitting. I trust the taste will lead to further readings: too little is really known of our early histories. We gather the leading facts, perhaps, from the miserable abridgments that flood the country, and too frequently pervert the truth; but, at best, the tone, the spirit of the history is sadly lacking. We want books which shall not only see the doings of our fathers, but trace and appreciate their sympathies and feelings also. But the bell rings for supper, and the captain signalizes us with an especial leer and wave of the hand. With you in a moment, Señor, as soon as I have laid old Purchas on his pillow."

CHAPTER IX.

"To serve bravely is to come halting off you know."
King Henry IV

"One lingers thoughtfully among the ruins of Jamestown. It is, of course, the mere *site* which will now interest you in its contemplation. There is little or nothing to be seen. It is the association only, the *genius loci*, that offers provocation to the contemplative spirit. You behold nothing but an empty and long-abandoned nest; but it is the nest of one of those maternal birds whose prolific nature has filled the nations. The ruins which remain of Jamestown consist only of a single tower of the old church. In the dense coppice near it, you see the ancient piles which cover the early dead of the settlement. The tower is a somewhat picturesque object by itself, though it depends for its charm chiefly on its historical associations. It is enough of the ruin for the romantic, and, seen by moonlight, the arches and the "rents of ruin," through which ivy and lichen, shrub and creeper, make their appearance, are objects which fancy will find precious to those even who never turn the pages of our musty chronicles, and hear nothing of the mournful whispers of the past. What stores of tradition, wild song and wilder story, are yet to be turned up with the soil of this neighborhood, or laid bare in the search among the ruins of this ancient tower. Could it only speak, what a fascinating history would it reveal. What glorious traditions ought to invest the locality. What memories are awakened by its simple mention. What pictures does it not paint to the fancy and the thought!"

"Talking of traditions of the 'Old Dominion,' I am reminded of one which was told me many years ago by a fellow traveller, as we pursued our way up James river. He insisted that there were good authorities for the story which I had rashly imputed to his own invention. He was one of those persons who never scruple at a manufacture of their own, when the thing wanted is not exactly ready to their hands, and I dare not answer for the chronicle."

"Let us have it by all means."

The ladies seconded the entreaty, and our fellow-voyager began.

"You are aware," said he, "that in the early settlement of Virginia, as perhaps in the case of all colonists in a new country, there is always at first a lamentable dearth of women. The pioneers were greatly at a loss what to do for wives and housekeepers. Nothing could be more distressing."

"As Campbell sings it, of a more select region—

"'The world was sad, the garden was a wild,
And man the hermit sighed—till woman smiled.'"

"Precisely! Our Virginians felt particularly lonesome along the wildernesses of James river, as is the case even now with our Californians along the Sacramento and other golden waters."

"Nay, they are much more charitable now. The gold regions are not so barren of beauty as you think. This may be owing to the greater safety of the enterprise. In 1600 a young woman incurred some peril of losing a scalp while seeking a swain in the territories of that fierce Don of Potomacke, Powhatan."

"'The danger certainly was of a sort to demand consideration. It was one which the old girls might be permitted to meditate almost as cautiously as the young ones. At all events, our 'guid folk' in the Old Dominion felt the need of a supply, the demand being no less earnest than pressing. They commissioned their friends and agents in England to supply their wants with all despatch, making the required qualifications as moderate and few as possible, the better to insure the probability of being provided. The proprietaries, after a solemn counsel together, arrived at the conclusion that the requisition was by no means an unreasonable one; a conclusion to which they arrived more readily from the great interest which their own wives respectively took in the discussion. Efforts were accordingly made for meeting the wishes of the colonists. Advertisements, which, it is said, are still to be found in the news organs of the day—were put forth in London and elsewhere, announcing the nature of the demand and soliciting the supply. Much, of course, was said in favor of the beauty and resources of the country in which they were expected to seek a home. Much also was urged in behalf of the individual settlers, whose demands were most urgent. 'They were of good health and body, very able and diligent, men of moral and muscle, very capable of maintaining church and state, and contributing in a thousand ways to the growth and good of both.' Certain of them were especially described with names given, not omitting sundry cogent particulars in respect to their moneyed means, employments, and general worldly condition. In brief, able-bodied, well-limbed and well-visaged young women, were assured of finding themselves well matched and honorably housed within the sylvan paradise of Powhatan, as soon as they should arrive. The advertisements prudently forbore to insist upon any special certificates — so necessary when housemaids are to be chosen — of character and manners. A small bounty, indeed, was offered with outfit and free passage.

"The appeal to the gentle hearts and Christian charities of the sex, was not made in vain. A goodly number soon offered themselves for the adventure, most of whom were supposed likely to meet the wishes of the hungry colonists. The standards were not overly high — the commissioners, appreciating the self-sacrificing spirit which governed the damsel — were not disposed to be exacting. There were some of the damsels of much and decided growth — some were distinguished more by size than sweetness: others again might — though they modestly forebore to do so — this is the one failing of the sex — boast of their ripe antiquity; none of them were remarkable for their beauty, but as all parties agreed to evade this topic — for reasons no doubt good enough in those days — we will not make it a subject of discussion in ours. There was one only, among two score, about whom the commissioners came to a dead pause — an absolute halt — and finally to a grave renewal of their deliberations.

"The party thus in danger of rejection, was comely enough to the eye, according to the standards adopted in the general recognition of applicants. She was fair enough, and strong enough, and there could be no doubt that she was quite old enough, but there was not quite enough of her.

"She was minus a leg!

"Was this a disqualification or not? That was the difficult question. When first presenting herself, it was observed that she had advanced a foot. The foot was a good one — a foot of size and character, and the leg which accompanied it, and of which more was exhibited than was absolutely necessary to the examination, was admitted to be an unobjectionable leg. But somehow, one of the commissioners begged leave to see the other. This literally occasioned a halt. In place of the required member, she thrust forward a stick of English oak, which might have served to splice the bowsprit of a Baltimore clipper.

"There was a sensation — a decided sensation. The commissioners were taken all aback. They hemmed and hawed. A consideration of the peculiar case was necessary.

"'My good woman,' quoth one of the commissioners, who served as spokesman. 'You have but one leg.'

"'You see, your honor. But it's sure I shall be less apt to run away from the guid man.'

"'True; but whether that consideration will be sufficient to reconcile him to the deficiency.'

"'Why not?' answered the fair suitor, 'seeing that I am a woman for all that.'

"'But you are not a perfect woman.'

"'Will your honor be so good as to mention if you ever did meet with a perfect woman?'

"This was a poser. The commissioners were men of experience. They had seen something of the world. They were all women's men. The woman was too much for them. They went again into consultation. The question was a serious one. Could a woman be a *complete* woman — a perfect one was not now the question — who had but a single leg? The subject of discussion was reduced to this: what are the requisites of a wife in Virginia? The result was, that they resolved to let the woman go, and take her chance. They could not resist a will so determined. They were naturally dubious whether any of the sturdy adventurers in the realm of Powhatan would be altogether willing to splice with a lame damsel not particularly charming, or attractive in any respect: but women for such an expedition were not in excess. The demand from James river for wives was exceedingly urgent; the woman's frankness pleased the commissioners, and her confidence of success finally encouraged them with a similar hope on her behalf. They gave her the necessary funds and certificate, partially persuaded that—

> "'There swims no goose, however grey in state,
> Who can not find some gander for her mate.'
>
> And the cripple went on her way swimmingly."

"And the event?"

"Justified the faith of the legless damsel in the bounty of Providence. Very great was the rejoicing in James river, when the stout vessel wearing English colors was seen pressing up the stream. They knew what they had to expect, and each was eager for his prize. The stout yeomanry of Jamestown turned out *en masse*, each in his best costume and behavior; and as each had yet to make his choice, and as a wife is always, more or less, the subject of some choice, each was anxious to get on board the ship in advance of his comrades. Never was there such a scramble. Wives rose in demand and value; and but little time was consumed in seeing the parties paired, and, two by two, returning from the vessel to the shore. How proudly they departed—our brave adventurers, each with his pretty commodity tucked under his arm! The supply fell short of the demand. There were several who retired with sad hearts, and lonely as they came. All were snatched up except our lame girl; but she was not the person to despair. She put on her sweetest smiles, as the unsupplied seekers circled about her. They had no objection to her face. Her smiles were sufficiently attractive; but that leg of English oak, which she in vain strove to pucker up under her petticoats. The truth had leaked out; and it was no go. Though grievously in want of the furniture so necessary to a warm household, it was rather too much to require our well-shaped and dashing Virginians to couple with a damsel of but one leg; and after circling her with wobegone visages, half-doubting what to do, they at length disappeared, one by one, resolved to await a new ship, and a bride of adequate members. The prospect for our lame duck became rather unpromising; but Fortune, amid all her blindnesses and caprices, is usually governed by a certain sense of propriety and fitness. It so happened that there was a cobbler in the colony, whose trade had been chosen with reference to the painful fact that he had no leg at all. He, poor fellow, needing a wife as much as any of the rest, had but little hope of having his wants supplied by the present consignment. It was doubtful whether he could have ventured to hope under any circumstances — still more absurd to hope when the supply was small, the seekers many, and all in the market before himself. And when he saw those returning who had failed to secure companions, he naturally gave up all notion, if he had ever dared to entertain any, of gratifying his domestic ambition. But as these disappointed adventurers crossed him on their return, and saw the wistful eyes which he cast upon the vessel, they bade him derisively go and seek his fortune.

"'Now's your chance, old fellow!' He soon gathered the intelligence, and at first his soul revolted at the idea of coupling with a lame woman.

"'A woman,' said he to himself, 'gains enough when she gets a husband. She ought to be finished at the least. Nothing should be wanting.'

"But a moment's reflection made him more indulgent. He seized his crutches and made toward the vessel. Then he bethought himself again and made toward his cabin. But the tempter prevailed, and he hobbled slowly forward. With help he was at length brought into the vessel and the presence of the waiting spinster.

"She had been long enough on the anxious benches. They had been a sort of torture to her patience as well as her hope.

"'Why,' said he — as if only now apprized of her deficiency — you've got but one leg.'

"'And you've got none,' she answered pertly.

"This threw him into a cold sweat. He now feared that he should lose his prize. 'What of that?' said he — 'better a lame donkey than no horse. Is it a match? I'm for you.'

"It was now her time to demur. She walked all round him, he wheeling about the while with the utmost possible effort, to show how agile he could be, legless or not. The man was good-looking enough, *minus* his pins; and after a painful pause — to one of the parties at least — she gave him her hand.

"The cobbler's rapture was complete. A chair was slung down the ship's side. Scarcely had this been done wher one of the former seekers reappeared. He was now willing to take the lame damsel; but our cobbler suffered no time for deliberation. He did not dare exercise any foolish generosity in leaving it to her to choose between the two.

"His choler was roused. It was *his* betrothed to whom the wooer came, and, with a tremendous flourish of one of his crutches, our cripple made at the intruder. This demonstration was sufficient. He was allowed to retain his prize. The candidate hurried off, cooling his thirst with whatever philosophy he could muster. When the bridal took place, many were the jests at the expense of our cripple couple. Even the priest who united them was not unwilling to share in the humor of the scene, making puns upon the occasion, such as have been cheapened somewhat by a too frequent circulation.

"'I know not, good people,' he said, 'whether you can properly contract marriage, seeing that you both lack sufficient understanding.'

"'No man should marry with a woman,' said one of the spectators, 'who teaches the utter uselessness of his own vocation.'

"'And why they should be married under a Christian dispensation, I can not see,' was the comment of a third, 'seeing that neither of them are prepared to give proper heed to their *soles*.'

"'It will be a marriage to bind,' said a fourth, 'seeing that neither can well run away from the other.'

"'She won't trouble him long,' said he who had come a moment too late,—'she has already one foot in the grave.'

"The crutch of the cripple was again uplifted.

"'Parson,' said he, 'make us fast, please, as soon as possible. I reckon, if there's but one leg between us, there's no law agin our children having a full complement.'

"Whereat the betrothed blushed prettily, and the ceremony proceeded."

Our companion's narrative might be all true, for what we know. Its elements were all probable enough. But the story rather whet than pacified the appetite; other legends were called for, and the following legend of Venice, founded also on history, succeeded to that of the Virginian.

THE BRIDE OF FATE.

CHAPTER I.

It was a glad day in Venice. The eve of the Feast of the Purification had arrived, and all those maidens of the Republic, whose names had been written in the "Book of Gold," were assembled with their parents, their friends and lovers—a beautiful and joyous crowd—repairing, in the gondolas provided by the Republic, to the church of San Pietro di Castella, at Olivolo, which was the residence of the patriarch. This place was on the extreme verge of the city, a beautiful and isolated spot, its precincts almost without inhabitants, a ghostly and small priesthood excepted, whose grave habits and taciturn seclusion seemed to lend an additional aspect of solitude to the neighborhood. It was, indeed, a solitary and sad-seeming region, which to the thoughtless and unmeditative, might be absolutely gloomy. But it was not the less lovely as a place suited equally for the picturesque and the thoughtful; and, just now, it was very far from gloomy or solitary. The event which was in hand was decreed to enliven it in especial degree, and in its consequences, to impress its characteristics on the memory for long generations after. It was the day of St. Mary's Eve—a day set aside from immemorial time for a great and peculiar festival. All, accordingly, was life and joy in the sea republic. The marriages of a goodly company of the high-born, the young and the beautiful, were to be celebrated on this occasion, and in public, according to the custom. Headed by the doge himself, Pietro Candiano, the city sent forth its thousands. The ornamented gondolas plied busily from an early hour in the morning, from the city to Olivolo; and there, amidst music and merry gratulations of friends and kindred, the lovers disembarked. They were all clad in their richest array. Silks, which caught their colors from the rainbow, and jewels that had inherited, even in their caverns, their beauties from the sun and stars, met the eye in all directions. Wealth had put on all its riches, and beauty, always modest, was not satisfied with her intrinsic loveliness. All that could delight the eye, in personal decorations and nuptial ornaments, was displayed to the eager gaze of curiosity, and, for a moment, the treasures of the city were transplanted to the solitude and waste.

But gorgeous and grand as was the spectacle, and joyous as was the crowd, there were some at the festival, some young, throbbing hearts, who, though deeply interested in its proceedings, felt anything but gladness. While most of the betrothed thrilled only with rapturous anticipations that might have been counted in the strong pulsations that made the bosom heave rapidly beneath the close pressure of the virgin zone, there were yet others, who felt only that sad sinking of the heart which declares nothing but its hopelessness and desolation. There were victims to be sacrificed as well as virgins to be made happy, and girdled in by thousands of the brave and goodly—by golden images and flaunting banners, and speaking symbols—by music and by smiles—there were more hearts than one that longed to escape from all, to fly away to some far solitude, where the voices of such a joy as was now present could vex the defrauded soul no more. As the fair procession moved onward and up through the gorgeous avenues of the cathedral to the altar-place, where stood the venerable patriarch in waiting for their coming, in order to begin the solemn but grateful rites, you might have marked, in the crowding groups, the face of one meek damsel, which declared a heart very far removed from hope or joyful expectation. Is that tearful eye—is that pallid cheek—that lip, now so tremulously convulsed—are these proper to one going to a bridal, and that her own? Where is her anticipated joy? It is not in that despairing vacancy of face—not in that feeble, faltering, almost fainting footstep—not, certainly, in anything that we behold about the maiden, unless we seek it in the rich and flaming jewels with which she is decorated and almost laden down; and these no more declare for her emotions than the roses which encircle the neck of the white lamb, as it is led to the altar and the priest. The fate of the two is not unlike, and so also is their character. Francesca Ziani is decreed for a sacrifice. She was one of those sweet and winning, but feeble spirits, which know how to submit only. She has no powers of resistance. She knows that she is a victim; she feels that her heart has been wronged even to the death, by the duty to which it is now commanded; she feels that it is thus made the cruel but unwilling instrument for doing a mortal wrong to the heart of another; but she lacks the courage to refuse, to resist, to die rather than submit. Her nature only teaches her submission; and this is the language of the wo-begone, despairing glance, but one which she bestows, in passing up the aisle, upon one who stands beside a column, close to her progress, in whose countenance she perceives a fearful struggle, marking equally his indignation and his grief.

Giovanni Gradenigo was one of the noblest cavaliers of Venice—but nobleness, as we know, is not always, perhaps not often, the credential in behalf of him who seeks a maiden from her parents. He certainly was not the choice of Francesca's sire. The poor girl was doomed to the embraces of one Ulric Barberigo, a man totally destitute of all nobility, that alone excepted which belonged to wealth. This shone in the eyes of Francesca's parents, but failed utterly to attract her own. She saw, through the heart's simple, unsophisticated medium, the person of Giovanni Gradenigo only. Her sighs were given to him, her loathings to the other. Though meek and finally submissive, she did not yield without a remonstrance, without mingled tears and entreaties, which were found unavailing. The ally of a young damsel is naturally her mother, and when she fails her, her best human hope is lost. Alas! for the poor Francesca! It was her mother's weakness, blinded by the wealth of Ulric Barberigo, that rendered the father's will so stubborn. It was the erring mother that wilfully beheld her daughter led to the sacrifice, giving no heed to the heart which was breaking, even beneath its heavy weight of jewels. How completely that mournful and desponding, that entreating and appealing glance to her indignant lover, told her wretched history. There he stood, stern as well as sad, leaning, as if for support, upon the arm of his kinsman, Nicolo Malapieri. Hopeless, helpless, and in utter despair, he thus lingered, as if under a strange and fearful fascination, watching the progress of the proceedings which were striking fatally, with every movement, upon the sources of his own hope and happiness. His resolution rose with his desperation, and he suddenly shook himself free from his friend.

"I will not bear this, Nicolo," he exclaimed, "I must not suffer it without another effort, though it be the last."

"What would you do, Giovanni," demanded his kinsman, grasping him by the wrist as he spoke, and arresting his movement.

"Shall I see her thus sacrificed—delivered to misery and the grave! Never! they shall not so lord it over true affections to their loss and mine. Francesca was mine—is mine—even now, in the very sight of Heaven. How often hath she vowed it! Her glance avows it now. My lips shall as boldly declare it again; and as Heaven has heard our vows, the church shall hear them. The patriarch shall hear. Hearts must not be wronged—Heaven must not thus be defrauded. That selfish, vain woman, her mother—that mercenary monster, miscalled her father—have no better rights than mine—none half so good. They shall hear me. Stand by me, Nicolo, while I speak!"

This was the language of a passion, which, however true, was equally unmeasured and imprudent. The friend of the unhappy lover would have held him back.

"It is all in vain, Giovanni! Think! my friend, you can do nothing now. It is too late; nor is there any power to prevent this consummation. Their names have been long since written in the 'Book of Gold,' and the doge himself may not alter the destiny!"

"The Book of Gold!" exclaimed the other. "Ay, the 'Bride of Gold!' but we shall see!" And he again started forward. His kinsman clung to him.

"Better that we leave this place, Giovanni. It was wrong that you should come. Let us go. You will only commit some folly to remain."

"Ay! it is folly to be wronged, and to submit to it, I know! folly to have felt and still to feel! folly, surely, to discover, and to live after the discovery, that the very crown that made life precious is lost to you for ever! What matter if I should commit this folly! Well, indeed, if they who laugh at the fool, taste none of the wrath that they provoke."

"This is sheer madness, Giovanni."

"Release me, Nicolo."

The kinsman urged in vain. The dialogue, which was carried on in under tones, now enforced by animated action, began to attract attention. The procession was moving forward. The deep anthem began to swell, and Giovanni, wrought to the highest pitch of frenzy by the progress of events, and by the opposition of Nicolo, now broke away from all restraint, and hurried through the crowd. The circle, dense and deep, had already gathered closely about the altar-place, to behold the ceremony. The desperate youth made his way through it. The crowd gave way at his approach, and under the decisive pressure of his person. They knew his mournful history—for when does the history of love's denial and defeat fail to find its way to the world's curious hearing? Giovanni was beloved in Venice. Such a history as his and Francesca's was sure to beget sympathy, particularly with all those who could find no rich lovers for themselves or daughters, such as Ulric Barberigo. The fate of the youthful lovers drew all eyes upon the two. A tearful interest in the event began to pervade the assembly, and Giovanni really found no such difficulty as would have attended the efforts of any other person to approach the sacred centre of the bridal circle. He made his way directly for the spot where Francesca stood. She felt his approach and presence by the most natural instincts, though without ever daring to lift her eye to his person. A more deadly paleness than ever came over her, and as she heard the first sounds of his voice, she faltered and grasped a column for support. The patriarch, startled by the sounds of confusion, rose from the sacred cushions; and spread his hands over the assembly for silence; but as yet he failed to conceive the occasion for commotion. Meanwhile, the parents and relatives of Francesca had gathered around her person, as if to guard her from an enemy. Ulric Barberigo, the millionaire, put on the aspect of a man whose word was law on 'change. He, too, had his retainers, all looking daggers, at the intruder. Fortunately for Giovanni, they were permitted to wear none at these peaceful ceremonials. Their looks of wrath did not discourage the approach of our lover. He did not seem, indeed, to see them, but gently putting them by, he drew near to the scarcely conscious maiden. He lifted the almost lifeless hand from her side, and pressing it within both his own, a proceeding which her mother vainly endeavored to prevent, he addressed the maiden with all that impressiveness of tone which declares a stifled but still present and passionate emotion in the heart. His words were of a touching sorrow.

"And is it thus, my Francesca, that I must look upon thee for the last time? Henceforth, are we to be dead to one another? Is it thus that I am to hear that, forgetful of thy virgin vows to Gradenigo, thou art here calling Heaven to witness that thou givest thyself and affections to another?"

"Not willingly, O! not willingly, Giovanni, as I live! I have not forgotten—alas! I can not forget—that I have once vowed myself to thee. But I pray thee to forget, Giovanni. Forget me and forgive—forgive!"

Oh! how mournfully was this response delivered. There was a dead silence throughout the assembly; a silence which imposed a similar restraint even upon the parents of the maiden, who had shown a desire to arrest the speaker. They had appealed to the patriarch; but the venerable man was wise enough to perceive that this was the last open expression of a passion which must have its utterance in some form, and if not this, must result in greater mischief. His decision tacitly sanctioned the interview as we have witnessed it. It was with increased faltering, which to the bystanders seemed almost fainting, that the unhappy Francesca thus responded to her lover. Her words were little more than whispers, and his tones, though deep, were very low and subdued, as if spoken while the teeth were shut. There was that in the scene which brought forward the crowd in breathless anxiety to hear, and the proud heart of the damsel's mother revolted at an exhibition in which her position was by no means a grateful one. She would have wrested, even by violence, the hand of her daughter from the grasp of Giovanni; but he retained it firmly, the maiden herself being scarcely conscious that he did so. His eye was sternly fixed upon the mother, as he drew Francesca toward himself. His words followed his looks:—

"Have you not enough triumphed, lady, in thus bringing about your cruel purpose, to the sacrifice of two hearts—your child's no less than mine? Mine was nothing to you—but hers! what had she done that you should trample upon hers? This hast thou done! Thou hast triumphed! What wouldst thou more? Must she be denied the mournful privilege of saying her last parting with him to whom she vowed herself, ere she vows herself to another! For shame, lady; this is a twofold and needless tyranny!"

As he spoke, the more gentle and sympathizing spirits around looked upon the stern mother with faces of the keenest rebuke and indignation. Giovanni once more addressed himself to the maiden.

"And if you do not love this man, my Francesca, why is it that you so weakly yield to his solicitings? Why submit to this sacrifice at any instance? Have they strength to subdue thee?—has he the art to ensnare thee?—canst thou not declare thy affections with a will? What magic is it that they employ which is thus superior to that of love?—and what is thy right—if heedless of the affections of *thy* heart—to demand the sacrifice of *mine*? Thou hadst it in thy keeping, Francesca, as I fondly fancied I had thine!"

"Thou hadst—thou hadst!—"

"Francesca, my child!" was the expostulating exclamation of the mother; but it failed, except for a single instant, to arrest the passionate answer of the maiden.

"Hear me, and pity, Giovanni, if you may not forgive! Blame me for my infirmity—for the wretched weakness which has brought me to this defeat of thy heart—this desolation of mine—but do not doubt that I have loved thee—that I shall ever—"

"Stay!" commanded the imperious father.

"What is it thou wouldst say, Francesca? Beware!" was the stern language of the mother.

The poor girl shrunk back in trembling. The brief impulse of courage which the address of her lover, and the evident sympathy of the crowd, had imparted, was gone as suddenly as it came. She had no more strength for the struggle; and as she sunk back nerveless, and closed her eyes as if fainting under the terrible glance of both her parents, Giovanni dropped her hand from his grasp. It now lay lifeless at her side, and she was sustained from falling by some of her sympathizing companions The eyes of the youth were bent upon her with a last look.

"It is all over, then," he exclaimed. "Thy hope, unhappy maiden, like mine, must perish because of thy weakness. Yet there will be bitter memories for this," he exclaimed—and his eye now sought the mother—"bitter, bitter memories! Francesca, farewell! Be happy if thou canst!"

She rushed toward him as he moved away, recovering all her strength for this one effort. A single and broken sentence—"Forgive me, O forgive!"—escaped her lips, as she sunk senseless upon the floor. He would have raised her, but they did not suffer him.

"Is this not enough, Giovanni?" said his friend, reproachfully. "Seest thou not that thy presence but distracts her?"

"Thou art right, Nicolo; let us go. I am myself choking—undo me this collar!—There! Let us depart."

The organ rolled its anthem—a thousand voices joined in the hymn to the Virgin, and as the sweet but painful sounds rushed to the senses of the youth, he darted through the crowd, closely followed by his friend. The music seemed to pursue him with mockery. He rushed headlong from the temple, as if seeking escape from some suffocating atmosphere in the pure breezes of heaven, and hurried forward with confused and purposeless footsteps. The moment of his disappearance was marked by the partial recovery of Francesca. She unclosed her eyes, raised her head, and looked wildly around her. Her lips once more murmured his name.

"Giovanni!"

"He is gone," was the sympathizing answer from more than one lip in the assembly; and once more she relapsed into unconsciousness.

CHAPTER II.

Giovanni Gradenigo was scarcely more conscious than the maiden whom he left. He needed all the guidance of his friend.

"Whither?" asked Nicolo Malapiero.

"What matter! where thou wilt!" was the reply.

"For the city, then;" and his friend conducted him to a gondola which was appointed to await them. In the profoundest silence they glided toward the city. The gondola stopped before the dwelling of Nicolo, and he, taking the arm of the sullen and absent Giovanni within his own, ascended the marble steps, and was about to enter, when a shrill voice challenged their attention by naming Giovanni.

"How now, signor," said the stranger. "Is it thou? Wherefore hast thou left Olivolo? Why didst thou not wait the bridal?"

The speaker was a strange, dark-looking woman, in coarse woollen garments. She hobbled as she walked, assisted by a heavy staff, and seemed to suffer equally from lameness and from age. Her thin depressed lips, that ever sunk as she spoke into the cavity of her mouth, which, in the process of time, had been denuded of nearly all its teeth; her yellow wrinkled visage, and thin gray hairs, that escaped from the close black cap which covered her head, declared the presence of very great age. But her eye shone still with something even more lively and oppressive than a youthful fire. It had a sort of spiritual intensity. Nothing, indeed, could have been more brilliant, or, seemingly, more unnatural. But hers was a nature of which we may not judge by common laws. She was no common woman, and her whole life was characterized by mystery. She was known in Venice as the "Spanish Gipsy;" was supposed to be secretly a Jewess, and had only escaped from being punished as a sorceress by her profound and most exemplary public devotions. But she was known, nevertheless, as an enchantress, a magician, a prophetess; and her palmistry, her magic, her symbols, signs and talismans, were all held in great repute by the superstitious and the youthful of the ocean city. Giovanni Gradenigo himself, obeying the popular custom, had consulted her; and now, as he heard her voice, he raised his eyes, and started forward with the impulse of one who suddenly darts from under the griding knife of the assassin. Before Nicolo could interfere, he had leaped down the steps, and darted to the quay from which the old woman was about to step into a gondola. She awaited his coming with a smile of peculiar meaning, as she repeated her inquiry:—

"Why are not you at Olivolo?"

He answered the question by another, grasping her wrist violently as he spoke.

"Did you not promise that she should wed with me—that she should be mine—mine only?"

"Well," she answered calmly, without struggling or seeking to extricate her arm from the strong hold which he had upon it.

"Well! and even now the rites are in progress which bind her to Ulric Barberigo!"

"She will never wed Ulric Barberigo," was the quiet answer. "Why left you Olivolo?" she continued.

"Could I remain and look upon these hated nuptials?—could I be patient and see her driven like a sheep to the sacrifice? I fled from the spectacle, as if the knife of the butcher were already in my own heart."

"You were wrong; but the fates have spoken, and their decrees are unchangeable. I tell you I have seen your bridal with Francesca Ziani. No Ulric weds that maiden. She is reserved for you alone. You alone will interchange with her the final vows before the man of God. But hasten, that this may find early consummation. I have seen other things! Hasten—but hasten not alone, nor without your armor! A sudden and terrible danger hangs over San Pietro di Castella, and all within its walks. Gather your friends, gather your retainers. Put on the weapons of war and fly thither with all your speed. I see a terrible vision, even now, of blood and struggle! I behold terrors that frighten even me! Your friend is a man of arms. Let your war-galleys be put forth, and bid them steer for the Lagune of Caorlo. There will you win Francesca, and thenceforth shall you wear her—you only—so long as it may be allowed you to wear any human joy!"

Her voice, look, manner, sudden energy, and the wild fire of her eyes, awakened Giovanni to his fullest consciousness. His friend drew nigh—they would have conferred together, but the woman interrupted them.

"You would deliberate," said she, "but you have no time! What is to be done must be done quickly. It seems wild to you, and strange, and idle, what I tell you, but it is nevertheless true; and if you heed me not now bitter will be your repentance hereafter. You, Giovanni, will depart at least. Heed not your friend—he is too cold to be successful. He will always be safe, and do well, but he will do nothing further. Away! if you can but gather a dozen friends and man a single galley, you will be in season. But the time is short. I hear a fearful cry—the cry of women—and the feeble shriek of Francesca Ziani is among the voices of those who wail with a new terror! I see their struggling forms, and floating garments, and dishevelled hair! Fly, young men, lest the names of those whom Venice has written in her Book of Gold shall henceforth be written in a Book of Blood."

The reputation of the sybil was too great in Venice to allow her wild predictions to be laughed at. Besides, our young Venetians—Nicolo no less than Giovanni—in spite of what the woman had spoken touching his lack of enthusiasm—were both aroused and eagerly excited by her speech. Her person dilated as she spoke; her voice seemed to come up from a fearful depth, and went thrillingly deep into the souls of the hearers. They were carried from their feet by her predictions. They prepared to obey her counsels. Soon had they gathered their friends together, enough to man three of the fastest galleys of the city. Their prows were turned at once toward the Lagune of Caorlo, whither the woman had directed them. She, meanwhile, had disappeared, but the course of her gondola lay for Olivolo.

CHAPTER III.

It will be necessary that we should go back in our narrative but a single week before the occurrence of these events. Let us penetrate the dim and lonesome abode on the confines of the "Jewish Quarter," but not within it, where the "Spanish Gipsy" delivered her predictions. It is midnight, and still she sits over her incantations. There are vessels of uncouth shape and unknown character before her. Huge braziers lie convenient, on one of which, amid a few coals, a feeble flame may be seen to struggle. The atmosphere is impregnated with a strong but not ungrateful perfume, and through its vapors objects appear with some indistinctness. A circular plate of brass or copper—it could not well be any more precious metal—rests beneath the eye and finger of the woman. It is covered with strange and mystic characters, which she seems busily to explore, as if they had a real significance to her mind. She evidently united the highest departments of her art with its humblest offices; and possessed those nobler aspirations of the soul, which, during the middle ages, elevated in considerable degree the professors of necromancy. But our purpose is not now to determine her pretensions. We have but to exhibit and to ascertain a small specimen of her skill in the vulgar business of fortune-telling—an art which will continue to be received among men, to a greater or less extent, so long as they shall possess a hope which they can not gratify, and feel a superstition which they can not explain. Our gipsy expects a visitor. She hears his footstep. The door opens at her bidding, and a stranger makes his appearance. He is a tall and well-made man, of stern and gloomy countenance, which is half concealed beneath the raised foldings of his cloak. His beard, of enormous length, is seen to stream down upon his breast; but his cheek is youthful, and his eye is eagerly and anxiously bright. But for a certain repelling something in his glance, he might be considered a very handsome man—perhaps by many persons he was thought so. He advanced with an air of dignity and power. His deportment and manner—and, when he spoke, his voice—all seemed to denote a person accustomed to command. The woman did not look up as he approached: on the contrary, she seemed more intent than ever in the examination of the strange characters before her. But a curious spectator might have seen that a corner of her eye, bright with an intelligence that looked more like cunning than wisdom, was suffered to take in all of the face and person of the visiter that his muffling costume permitted to be seen.

"Mother," said the stranger, "I am here."

"You say not who you are," answered the woman.

"Nor shall say," was the abrupt reply of the stranger. "That, you said, was unnecessary to your art—to the solution of the questions that I asked you."

"Surely," was the answer. "My art, that promises to tell thee of the future, would be a sorry fraud could it not declare the present—could it not say who thou art, as well as what thou seekest."

"Ha! and thou knowest!" exclaimed the other, his hand suddenly feeling within the folds of his cloak as he spoke, as if for a weapon, while his eye glared quickly around the apartment, as if seeking for a secret enemy.

"Nay, fear nothing," said the woman, calmly. "I care not to know who thou art. It is not an object of my quest, otherwise it would not long remain a secret to me."

"It is well! mine is a name that must not be spoken among the homes of Venice. It would make thee thyself to quail couldst thou hear it spoken."

"Perhaps! but mine is not the heart to quail at many things, unless it be the absolute wrath of Heaven. What the violence or the hate of man could do to this feeble frame, short of death, it has already suffered. Thou knowest but little of human cruelty, young man, though thy own deeds be cruel."

"How knowest thou that my deeds are cruel?" was the quick and passionate demand, while the form of the stranger suddenly and threateningly advanced. The woman was unmoved.

"Saidst thou not that there was a name that might not be spoken in the homes of Venice? Why should thy very name make the hearts of Venice to quail unless for thy deeds of cruelty and crime? But I see further. I see it in thine eyes that thou art cruel. I hear it in thy voice that thou art criminal. I know, even now, that thy soul is bent on deeds of violence and blood; and the very quest that brings thee to me now is less the quest of love than of that wild and selfish passion which so frequently puts on its habit."

"Ha! speak to me of that! This damsel, Francesca Ziani! 'Tis of her that I would have thee speak. Thou saidst that she should be mine; yet lo! her name is written in the 'Book of Gold,' and she is allotted to this man of wealth, this Ulric Barberigo."

"She will never be the wife of Ulric Barberigo."

"Thou saidst she should be mine."

"Nay, I said not that."

"Ha!—but thou liest!"

"No! Anger me not, young man! I am slower, much slower to anger than thyself—slower than most of those who still chafe within this mortal covering—yet am I mortal like thyself, and not wholly free from such foolish passions as vex mortality. Chafe me, and I will repulse thee with scorn. Annoy me, and I close upon thee the book of fate, leaving thee to the blind paths which thy passions have ever moved thee to take."

The stranger muttered something apologetically.

"Make me no excuses. I only ask thee to forbear and submit. I said not that Francesca Ziani should be *thine!* I said only that I beheld her in thy arms."

"And what more do I ask!" was the exulting speech of the stranger, his voice rising into a sort of outburst, which fully declared the ruffian, and the cruel passions by which he was governed.

"If that contents thee, well!" said the woman, coldly, her eye perusing with a seeming calmness the brazen plate upon which the strange characters were inscribed.

"That, then, thou promisest still?" demanded the stranger.

"Thou shalt see for thyself," was the reply. Thus speaking the woman slowly arose and brought forth a small chafing-dish, also of brass or copper, not much larger than a common plate. This she placed over the brazier, the flame of which she quickened by a few smart puffs from a little bellows which lay beside her. As the flame kindled, and the sharp, red jets rose like tongues on either side of the plate, she poured into it something like a gill of a thick, tenacious liquid, that looked like, and might have been, honey. Above this she brooded for a while with her eyes immediately over the vessel; and the keen ear of the stranger, quickened by excited curiosity, could detect the muttering of her lips; though the foreign syllables which she employed were entirely beyond his comprehension. Suddenly, a thick vapor went up from the dish. She withdrew it from the brazier and laid it before her on the table. A few moments sufficed to clear the surface of the vessel, the vapor arising and hanging languidly above her head.

"Look now for thyself and see!" was her command to the visiter; she herself not deigning a glance upon the vessel, seeming thus to be quite sure of what it would present, or quite indifferent to the result. The stranger needed no second summons. He bent instantly over the vessel, and started back with undisguised delight.

"It is she!" he exclaimed. "She droops! whose arm is it that supports her — upon whose breast is it that she lies — who bears her away in triumph?"

"Is it not thyself?" asked the woman, coldly.

"By Hercules, it is! She is mine! She is in my arms!

She is on my bosom! I have her in my galley! She speeds with me to my home! I see it all, even as thou hast promised me!"

"I promise thee nothing. I but show thee only what is written."

"And when and how shall this be effected?"

"How, I know not," answered the woman; "this is withheld from me. Fate shows what her work is, only as it appears when done, but not the manner of the doing."

"But when will this be?" was the question.

"It must be ere she marries with Ulric Barberigo, for him she will never marry."

"And it is appointed that he weds with her on the day of St. Mary's Eve. That is but a week hence, and the ceremony takes place—"

"At Olivolo."

"Ha! at Olivolo!" and a bright gleam of intelligence passed over the features of the stranger, from which his cloak had by this time entirely fallen. The woman beheld the look, and a slight smile, that seemed to denote scorn rather than any other emotion, played for a moment over her shrivelled and sunken lips.

"Mother," said the stranger, "must all these matters be left to fate?"

"That is as thou wilt."

"But the eye of a young woman may be won—her heart may be touched—so that it shall be easy for fate to accomplish her designs. I am young; am indifferently well-fashioned in person, and have but little reason to be ashamed of the face which God has given me. Beside, I have much skill in music, and can sing to the guitar as fairly as most of the young men of Venice. What if I were to find my way to the damsel—what if I play and sing beneath her father's palace? I have disguises, and am wont to practice in various garments: I can—"

The woman interrupted him.

"Thou mayst do as thou wilt. It is doubtless as indifferent to the fates, what thou doest, as it will be to me. Thou hast seen what I have shown—I can no more. I am not permitted to counsel thee. I am but a voice; thou hast all that I can give thee."

The stranger lingered still, but the woman ceased to speak, and betrayed by her manner that she desired his departure. Thus seeing, he took a purse from his bosom and laid it before her. She did not seem to notice the action, nor did she again look up until he was gone. With the sound of his retreating footsteps, she put aside the brazen volume of strange characters which seemed her favorite study, and her lips slowly parted in soliloquy:—

"Ay! thou exultest, fierce ruffian that thou art, in the assurance that Fate yields herself to thy will! Thou shalt, indeed, have the maiden in thy arms, but it shall profit thee nothing; and that single triumph shall exact from thee the last penalties which are sure to follow on the footsteps of a trade like thine. Thou thinkest that I know thee not, as if thy shallow masking could baffle eyes and art like mine; but I had not shown thee thus much, were I not in possession of yet further knowledge — did I not see that this lure was essential to embolden thee to thy own final overthrow. Alas, that in serving the cause of innocence, in saving the innocent from harm, we can not make it safe in happiness. Poor Francesca! beloved of three, yet blest with neither. Thou shalt be wedded, yet be no bride; shall gain all that thy fond young heart craveth, yet gain nothing — be spared the embraces of him thou loathest, yet rest in his arms whom thou hast most need to fear; and shalt be denied, even when most assured, the only embrace which might bring thee blessing! Happy at least that thy sorrows shall not last thee long — their very keenness and intensity being thy security from the misery which holds through years like mine."

Let us leave the woman of mystery — let us once more change the scene. Now pass we to the pirate's domain at Istria, a region over which, at the period of our narrative, the control of Venice was feeble, exceedingly capricious, and subject to frequent vicissitudes. At this particular time, the place was maintained by the fiercest band of pirates that ever swept the Mediterranean with their bloody prows.

CHAPTER IV.

It was midnight when the galley of the chief glided into the harbor of Istria. The challenge of the sentinel was answered from the vessel, and she took her place beside the shore, where two other galleys were at anchor. Suddenly her sails descended with a rattle; a voice hailed throughout the ship, was answered from stem to stern, and a deep silence followed. The fierce chief of the pirates, Pietro Barbaro—the fiercest, strongest, wisest, yet youngest, of seven brothers, all devoted to the same fearful employment—strode in silence to his cabin. Here, throwing himself upon a couch, he prepared rather to rest his limbs than to sleep. He had thoughts to keep him wakeful. Wild hopes, and tenderer joys than his usual occupations offered, were gleaming before his fancy. The light burned dimly in his floating chamber, but the shapes of his imagination rose up before his mind's eye not the less vividly because of the obscurity in which he lay. Thus musing over expectations of most agreeable and exciting aspect, he finally lapsed away in sleep.

He was suddenly aroused from slumber by a rude hand that lay heavily on his shoulder.

"Who is it?" he asked of the intruder.

"Gamba," was the answer.

"Thou, brother?"

"Ay," continued the intruder, "and here are all of us."

"Indeed! and wherefore come you? I would sleep—I am weary. I must have rest."

"Thou hast too much rest, Pietro," said another of the brothers. "It is that of which we complain—that of which we would speak to thee now."

"Ha! this is new language, brethren! Answer me—perhaps I am not well awake—am I your captain, or not?"

"Thou art—the fact seems to be forgotten by no one but thyself. Though the youngest of our mother's children, we made thee our leader."

"For what did ye this, my brothers, unless that I might command ye?"

"For this, in truth, and this only, did we confer upon thee

this authority. Thou hadst shown thyself worthy to command—"

"Well!"

"Thy skill—thy courage—thy fortitude—"

"In brief, ye thought me best fitted to command ye?"

"Yes."

"Then I command ye hence! Leave me, and let me rest!"

"Nay, brother, but this can not be," was the reply of another of the intruders. "We must speak with thee while the night serves us, lest thou hear worse things with the morrow. Thou art, indeed, our captain; chosen because of thy qualities of service, to conduct and counsel us; but we chose thee not that thou shouldst sleep! Thou wert chosen that our enterprises might be active and might lead to frequent profit."

"Has it not been so?" demanded the chief.

"For a season it was so, and there was no complaint of thee."

"Who now complains?"

"Thy people—all!"

"And can ye not answer them?"

"No! for we ourselves need an answer! We, too, complain."

"Of what complain ye?"

"That our enterprises profit us nothing."

"Do ye not go forth in the galleys? Lead ye not, each of you, an armed galley? Why is it that your enterprises profit ye nothing?"

"Because of the lack of our captain."

"And ye can do nothing without me; and because ye are incapable, I must have no leisure for myself!"

"Nay, something more than this, Pietro. Our enterprises avail us nothing, since you command that we no longer trouble the argosies of Venice. Venice has become thy favorite. Thou shieldest her only, when it is her merchants only who should give us spoil. This, brother, is thy true offence. For this we complain of thee; for this thy people complain of thee. They are impoverished by thy new-born love for Venice, and they are angry with thee. Brother, their purpose is to depose thee."

"Ha! and ye—'

"We are men as well as brethren. We cherish no such attachment for Venice as that which seems to fill thy bosom. When the question shall be taken in regard to thy office, our voices shall be against thee, unless—"

There was a pause. It was broken by the chief.

"Well, speak out. What are your conditions?"

"Unless thou shalt consent to lead us on a great enterprise against the Venetians. Hearken to us, Brother Pietro. Thou knowest of the annual festival at Olivolo, when the marriage takes place of all those maidens whose families are favorites of the Signiory, and whose names are written in the 'Book of Gold' of the Republic."

The eyes of the pirate chief involuntarily closed at the suggestion, but his head nodded affirmatively. The speaker continued.

"It is now but a week when this festival takes place. On this occasion assemble the great, the noble, and the wealthy of the sea city. Thither they bring all that is gorgeous in their apparel, all that is precious among their ornaments and decorations. Nobility and wealth here strive together which shall most gloriously display itself. Here, too, is the beauty of the city — the virgins of Venice — the very choice among her flocks Could there be prize more fortunate? Could there be prize more easy of attainment? The church of San Pietro di Castella permits no armed men within its holy sanctuaries. There are no apprehensions of peril; the people who gather to the rites are wholly weaponless. They can offer no defence against our assault; nor can this be foreseen. What place more lonely than Olivolo? Thither shall we repair the day before the festival, and shelter ourselves from scrutiny. At the moment when the crowd is greatest, we will dart upon our prey. We lack women; we desire wealth. Shall we fail in either, when we have in remembrance the bold deeds of our ancient fathers, when they looked with yearning on the fresh beauties of the Sabine virgins? These Venetian beauties are our Sabines. Thou, too — if the bruit of thy followers doth thee no injustice — thou, too, hast been overcome by one of these. She will doubtless be present at this festival. Make her thine, and fear not that each of thy brethren will do justice to his tastes and thine own. Here, now, thou hast all. Either thou agreest to that which thy people demand, or the power departs from thy keeping. Fabio becomes our leader!"

There was a pause. At length the pirate-chief addressed his brethren.

"Ye have spoken, ye threaten, too! This power of which ye speak, is precious in your eyes. I value it not a zecchino; and wert thou to depose me to-morrow, I should be the master of ye in another month, did it please me to command a people so capricious. But think not, though I speak to ye in this fashion, that I deny your demand. I but speak thus to show ye that I fear ye not. I will do as ye desire; but did not your own wishes square evenly with mine own, I should bide the issue of this struggle, though it were with knife to knife."

"It matters not how thou feelest, or what moveth thee, Pietro, so that thou dost as we demand. Thou wilt lead us to this spoil?"

"I will."

"It is enough. It will prove to thy people that they are still the masters of the Lagune—that they are not sold to Venice."

"Leave me now."

The brethren took their departure. When they had gone, the chief spoke in brief soliloquy, thus:—

"Verily, there is the hand of fate in this. Methinks I see the history once more, even as I beheld it in the magic liquor of the Spanish Gipsy. Why thought I not of this before, dreaming vainly like an idiot boy, as much in love with his music as himself, who hopes by the tinkle of his guitar to win his beauty from the palace of her noble sire, to the obscure retreats of his gondola! These brethren shall not vex me. They are but the creatures of my fate!"

CHAPTER V.

LET us now return to Olivolo, to the altar-place of the church of San Pietro di Castella, and resume the progress of that strangely-mingled ceremonial—mixed sunshine and sadness—which was broken by the passionate conduct of Giovanni Gradenigo. We left the poor, crushed Francesca, in a state of un consciousness, in the arms of her sympathizing kindred. For a brief space the impression was a painful one upon the hearts of the vast assembly; but as the deep organ rolled its ascending anthems, the emotion subsided. The people had assembled for pleasure and an agreeable spectacle; and though sympathizing, for a moment, with the pathetic fortunes of the sundered lovers, quite as earnestly as it is possible for mere lookers-on to do, they were not to be disappointed in the objects for which they came. The various shows of the assemblage—the dresses, the jewels, the dignitaries, and the beauties—were quite enough to divert the feelings of a populace, at all times notorious for its levities. from a scene which, however impressive at first, was becoming a little tedious. Sympathies are very good and proper things; but the world seldom suffers them to occupy too much of its time. Our Venetians did not pretend to be any more humane than the rest of the great family; and the moment that Francesca had fainted, and Giovanni had disappeared, the multitude began to express their impatience of any further delay by all the means in their possession. There was no longer a motive to resist their desires, and simply reserving the fate of the poor Francesca to the last, or until she should sufficiently recover to be fully conscious of the sacrifice which she was about to make, the ceremonies were begun. There was a political part to be played by the doge, in which the people took particular interest; and to behold which, indeed, was the strongest reason of their impatience. The government of Venice, as was remarked by quaint and witty James Howell, was a compound thing, mixed of all kinds of governments, and might be said to be composed of "a *grain* of monarchy, a *dose* of democracy, and a *dram*, if not an *ounce* of optimacy." It was in regard to this *dose* of democracy that the government annually assigned marriage portions to twelve young maidens, selected from the great body of the people, of those not sufficiently opulent to secure husbands, or find the adequate means for marriage, without this help. To bestow these maidens upon their lovers, and with them the portions allotted by the state, constituted the first, and in the eyes of the masses, the most agreeable part of the spectacle. The doge, on this occasion, who was the thrice-renowned Pietro Candiano. "did his spiriting gently," and in a highly edifying manner

The bishop bestowed his blessings, and confirmed by the religious, the civil rites, which allied the chosen couples. To these succeeded the *voluntary* parties, if we may thus presume upon a distinction between the two classes, which we are yet not sure that we have a right to make. The high-born and the wealthy, couple after couple, now approached the altar, to receive the final benediction which committed them to hopes of happiness which it is not in the power of any priesthood to compel. No doubt there was a great deal of hope among the parties, and we have certainly no reason to suppose that happiness did not follow in every instance.

But there is poor Francesca Ziani. It is now her turn. Her cruel parents remain unsubdued and unsoftened by her deep and touching sorrows. She is made to rise, to totter forward to the altar, scarcely conscious of anything, except, perhaps, that the worthless, but wealthy, Ulric Barberigo is at her side. Once more the mournful spectacle restores to the spectators all their better feelings. They perceive, they feel the cruelty of that sacrifice to which her kindred are insensible. In vain do they murmur "shame!" In vain does she turn her vacant, wild, but still expressive eyes, expressive because of their very soulless vacancy, to that stern, ambitious mother, whose bosom no longer responds to her child with the true maternal feeling. Hopeless of help from that quarter, she lifts her eyes to heaven, and, no longer listening to the words of the holy man, she surrenders herself only to despair.

Is it Heaven that hearkens to her prayer? Is it the benevolent office of an angel that bursts the doors of the church at the very moment when she is called upon to yield that response which dooms her to misery for ever? To her ears, the thunders which now shake the church were the fruits of Heaven's benignant interposition. The shrieks of women on every hand—the oaths and shouts of fierce and insolent authority—the clamors of men—the struggles and cries of those who seek safety in flight, or entreat for mercy—suggest no other idea to the wretched Francesca, than that she is saved from the embraces of Ulric Barberigo. She is only conscious that, heedless of her, and of the entreaties of her mother, he is the first to endeavor selfishly to save himself by flight. But her escape from Barberigo is only the prelude to other embraces. She knows not, unhappy child, that she is an object of desire to another, until she finds herself lifted in the grasp of Pietro Barbaro, the terrible chief of the Istriote pirates. He and his brothers have kept their pledges to one another, and they have been successful in their prey. Their fierce followers have subdued to submission the struggles of a weaponless multitude, who, with horror and consternation, behold the loveliest of their virgins, the just wedded among them, borne away upon the shoulders of the pirates to their warlike galleys. Those who resist them perish. Resistance was hopeless. The fainting and shrieking women, like the Sabine damsels, are hurried from the sight of their kinsmen and their lovers, and the Istriote galleys are about to depart with their precious freight. Pietro Barbaro, the chief, stands with one foot upon his vessel's side and the other on the shore. Still insensible, the lovely Francesca lies upon his breast. At this moment the skirt of his cloak is plucked by a bold hand. He turns to meet the glance of the Spanish Gipsy. The old woman leered on him with eyes that seemed to mock his triumph, even while she appealed to it.

"Is it not even as I told thee—as I showed thee?" was her demand.

"It is!" exclaimed the pirate-chief, as he flung her a purse of gold. "Thou art a true prophetess. Fate has done her work!"

He was gone; his galley was already on the deep, and he himself might now be seen kneeling upon the deck of the vessel, bending over his precious conquest, and striving to bring back the life into her cheeks.

"Ay, indeed!" muttered the Spanish Gipsy, "thou hast had her in thy arms, but think not, reckless robber that thou art, that fate has *done* its work. The work is but *begun*. Fate has kept its word to thee; it is thy weak sense that fancied she had nothing more to say or do!"

Even as she spoke these words, the galleys of Giovanni Gradenigo were standing for the Lagune of Caorlo. He had succeeded in collecting a gallant band of cavaliers who tacitly yielded him the command. The excitement of action had served, in some measure, to relieve the distress under which he suffered. He was no longer the lover, but the man; nor the man merely, but the leader of men. Giovanni was endowed for this by nature. His valor was known. It had been tried upon the Turk. Now that he was persuaded by the Spanish Gipsy, whom all believed and feared, that a nameless and terrible danger overhung his beloved, which was to be met and baffled only by the course he was pursuing, his whole person seemed to be informed by a new spirit. The youth, his companions, wondered to behold the change. There was no longer a dreaminess and doubt about his words and movements, but all was prompt, energetic, and directly to the purpose. Giovanni was now the confident and strong man. Enough for him that there *was* danger. Of this he no longer entertained a fear. Whether the danger that was supposed to threaten Francesca was still suggestive of a hope — as the prediction of the Spanish Gipsy might well warrant — may very well be questioned. It was in the very desperation of his hope, that his energies became at once equally well-ordered and intense. He prompted to their utmost the energies of others. He impelled all his agencies to their best exertions. Oar and sail were busy without intermission, and soon the efforts of the pursuers were rewarded. A gondola, bearing a single man, drifted along their path. He was a fugitive from Olivolo, who gave them the first definite idea of the foray of the pirates. His tidings, rendered imperfect by his terrors, were still enough to goad the pursuers to new exertions. Fortune favored the pursuit. In their haste the pirate galleys had become entangled in the lagune. The keen eye of Giovanni was the first to discover them. First one bark, and then another, hove in sight, and soon the whole piratical fleet were made out, as they urged their embarrassed progress through the intricacies of the shallow waters.

"Courage, bold hearts!" cried Giovanni to his people; "they are ours! We shall soon be upon them. They can not now escape us!"

The eye of the youthful leader brightened with the expectation of the struggle. His exulting, eager voice declared the strength and confidence of his soul, and cheered the souls of all around him. The sturdy oarsmen "gave way" with renewed efforts. The knights prepared their weapons for the conflict.

Giovanni *signalled* the other galleys by which his own was followed.

"I am for the red flag of Pietro Barbaro himself. I know his banner. Let your galleys grapple with the rest. Cross their path—prevent their flight, and bear down upon the strongest. Do your parts, and fear not but we shall do ours."

With these brief instructions, our captain led the way with the Venetian galleys. The conflict was at hand. It came. They drew nigh and hailed the enemy. The parley was a brief one. The pirates could hope no mercy, and they asked none. But few words, accordingly, were exchanged between the parties, and these were not words of peace.

"Yield thee to the mercy of St. Mark!" was the stern summons of Giovanni, to the pirate-chief.

"St. Mark's mercy has too many teeth!" was the scornful reply of the pirate. "The worthy saint must strike well before Barbaro of Istria sues to him for mercy."

With the answer the galleys grappled. The Venetians leaped on board of the pirates, with a fury that was little short of madness. Their wrath was terrible. Under the guidance of the fierce Giovanni, they smote with an unforgiving vengeance. It was in vain that the Istriotes fought as they had been long accustomed. It needed something more than customary valor to meet the fury of their assailants. All of them perished. Mercy now was neither asked nor given. Nor, as it seemed, did the pirates care to live, when they beheld the fall of their fearful leader. He had crossed weapons with Giovanni Gradenigo, in whom he found his fate. Twice, thrice, the sword of the latter drove through the breast of the pirate. Little did his conqueror conjecture the import of the few words which the dying chief gasped forth at his feet, his glazed eyes striving to pierce the deck, as if seeking some one within.

"I have, indeed, had thee in my arms, but—"

There was no more—death finished the sentence! The victory was complete, but Giovanni was wounded. Pietro Barbaro was a fearful enemy. He was conquered, it is true, but he had made his mark upon his conqueror. He had bitten deep before he fell.

The victors returned with their spoil. They brought back the captured brides in triumph. That same evening preparations were made to conclude the bridal ceremonies which the morning had seen so fearfully arrested. With a single exception, the original distribution of the "brides" was persevered in. That exception, as we may well suppose, was Francesca Ziani. It was no longer possible for her unnatural parents to withstand the popular sentiment. The doge himself, Pietro Candiano, was particularly active in persuading the reluctant mother to submit to what was so evidently the will of destiny. But for the discreditable baseness and cowardice of Ulric Barberigo, it is probable she never would have yielded. But his imbecility and unmanly terror in the moment of danger, had been too conspicuous. Even his enormous wealth could not save him from the shame that followed; and, however unwillingly, the parents of Francesca consented that she should become the bride of Giovanni, as the only proper reward for the gallantry which had saved her, and so many more, from shame.

But where was Giovanni? His friends have been despatched for him; why comes he not? The maid, now happy beyond her hope, awaits him at the altar. And still he comes not. Let us go back to the scene of action in the moment of his victory over the pirate-chief. Barbaro lies before him in the agonies of death. His sword it is which has sent the much-dreaded outlaw to his last account. But he himself is wounded — wounded severely but not mortally, by the man whom he has slain. At this moment he received a blow from the axe of one of the brothers of Barbaro. He had strength left barely to behold and to shout his victory, when he sank fainting upon the deck of the pirate vessel. His further care devolved upon his friend, Nicolo, who had followed his footsteps closely through all the paths of danger. In a state of stupor he lies upon the couch of Nicolo, when the aged prophetess, the "Spanish Gipsy," appeared beside his bed.

"He is called," she said. "The doge demands his presence. They will bestow upon him his bride, Francesca Ziani. You must bear him thither."

The surgeon shook his head.

"It may arouse him," said Nicolo. "We can bear him thither on a litter, so that he shall feel no pain."

"It were something to wake him from this apathy," mused the surgeon. "Be it as thou wilt."

Thus, grievously wounded, was the noble Giovanni borne into the midst of the assembly, for each member of which he had suffered and done so much. The soft music which played around, awakened him. His eyes unclosed to discover the lovely Francesca, tearful, but hopeful, bending fondly over him. She declared herself his. The voice of the doge confirmed the assurance; and the eyes of the dying man brightened into the life of a new and delightful consciousness. Eagerly he spoke; his voice was but a whisper.

"Make it so, I pray thee, that I may live!"

The priest drew nigh with the sacred unction. The marriage service was performed, and the hands of the two were clasped in one.

"Said I not?" demanded an aged woman, who approached the moment after the ceremonial, and whose face was beheld by none but him whom she addressed. "She is thine!"

The youth smiled, but made no answer. His hand drew that of Francesca closer. She stooped to his kiss, and whispered him, but he heard her not. With the consciousness of the sweet treasure that he had won after such sad denial, the sense grew conscious no longer—the lips of the youth were sealed for ever. The young Giovanni, the bravest of the Venetian youth, lay lifeless in the embrace of the scarcely more living Francesca. It was a sad day, after all, in Venice, since its triumph was followed by so great a loss; but the damsels of the ocean city still declare that the lovers were much more blest in this fortune, than had they survived for the embrace of others less beloved.

"Have I not read something like this story in a touching and romantic episode given in the 'Italy' of Rogers?" asked Salkm Burroughs.

"Yes! Rogers got it from the history. It is one of those incidents which enrich and enliven for romance the early progress of most states and nations that ever arrived at character and civilization. Of course, like the famous legends of infant Rome, it undergoes the artist touch of successive historians all of whom, in early periods, exercised in some degree the privileges of the artist, if not the romancer."

"The event occurs in the first periods of Venetian story, somewhere about A. D. 932, the reigning doge being Candiano the Second. It is good material for the dramatist. I should commend it to Mr. Boker, as the subject of an operatic melodrama. In the hands of our young friend Marvel, it could be wrought into a very pretty and delicate and dreamy work of sentimental fiction."

CHAPTER X.

A LONG. and to us a comparatively interesting, conversation followed,—Virginia, her resources, characteristics, scenery, and general moral, affording the principal subject. In this conversation, which occasionally ran into politics—in which some of the party showed their teeth very decidedly—the whole of our group was brought out, the ladies excepted. They had retired for the night. Most of us had rambled in Virginia at different periods; and it was in the delivery of recollections and impressions that we passed naturally into discussion. I propose to give *bits* only of this conversation, leaving out the bites—confining my report to the innocuous portions of the dialogue, and omitting certain sharp passages which occasionally followed the thoughtless or the wanton shaft. One of our "Down-East" brethren threw down the ball of provocation, dealing in a wholesale, if not wholesome, diatribe against all Southern agriculture. As his opinions are those of a somewhat numerous class, and as they are working no little mischief at the present day, it may be as well to record, with tolerable fullness, the portion of the dialogue which ensued upon their utterance.

"You pass through Virginia," said he, "as through a desert. The towns are few, and these all look old and wretched. The houses need paint, and are frequently in dilapidation. The culture is coarse and clumsy, the implements rude, and the people seem entirely ignorant of all improvements. They plough plant, and reap, precisely as their fathers did a hundred years ago, and without doing any justice to their lands. The lands have never been properly worked, and manures are but little known, and less esteemed. In favorite regions, along watercourses easily accessible, the plantations have been abandoned as entirely exhausted—sold for a song, at an average, perhaps, of a dollar an acre. The same lands, in the hands of New York farmers, have been bought up, improved, made valuable for wheat-crops, and raised to a value ranging from fifteen to seventy-five dollars per acre. Thirty bushels of wheat have been raised to the acre, on tracts which have been thrown out as barren. A like history belongs to North and South Carolina, where similar ignorance of farming, and of agricultural implements, similar coarseness and clumsiness in the cultivation of the soil, have led to similar results—the disparaged value of the lands, their abandonment, and the neglect and dilapidation of towns and houses."

"You simply know nothing about the matter," said one of the party sharply in reply—" or rather, you know just enough of the truth to involve yourself in a monstrous error. I too have travelled in the regions of which you speak, and can venture to say something on the subject, which has its bright as well as gloomy aspects. It is not all gloomy, though it is seldom that the hurrying traveller sees or suspects any other. That you see few or no towns, and that these look desolate, are the natural effects of the life of a people purely agricultural. The southern people do not live in towns if they can avoid them. The culture and command of extensive tracts of land and forest give them a distaste to city life, where they feel restrained by a sense of confinement, and by manners of artificial character—a rigid conventionalism imposing fetters upon that ease and freedom of bearing which belongs to the forest population. Besides, public opinion in the South is unfriendly to the growth of large cities, which many of their leading minds hold to be always of the most mischievous moral tendency—as, indeed, the *North* begins also to discover. Mr. Jefferson pronounced them the *sinks* and sewers of the commonwealth, to be tolerated only as among the dirty national necessities; and the *instincts* of the great body of the agricultural population have led them rightly in the same direction. They have learned to doubt the wholesomeness of the atmosphere of city life. Regarding towns as the mere agencies of the producer, they do not desire to see them absorbing a larger population than is necessary to the actual business which they have to perform.

"You, at the North, on the contrary, look to your flourishing towns, your fine houses, great masses of brick and stone, with thousands jostling in the thoroughfares, as proofs of prosperity and civilization; though, of these thousands, thousands live by beggary, by theft, chicanery, and the constantly active exercise of a thousand evil arts—the inevitable consequence of necessities which could not arise to the community were the unnecessary members driven to an honest, healthy, industrious occupation in neglected fields of agriculture. You judge mostly by externals, which rarely show the truth—the people in cities being chiefly learned in the art of concealing their true condition, and making the best *show* to their neighbors; while the Southern agriculturists know nothing of this art, exhibit themselves precisely as they are; use no white paint to cover old boards—no stucco to make common brick look like stone; and satisfied with the real comforts of their condition, never busy themselves in the endeavor to impose upon their neighbors with the splendors of a season which would only lead to bankruptcy.

"The dilapidated Virginia farmhouse, for example, will receive more guests, at the family table, in one month, than the marble palace in Broadway or Fifth Avenue will entertain in one year. There will be always plenty and a generous welcome, though the service be of delph and not of silver.

"That we have not towns and villages is the inevitable result of staple cultivation. *Every plantation is a village*, and where it is a large one, it will be found provided with all the essential elements of progress and performance, precisely as they are to be found in a village. Here, for example, is always a blacksmith and a carpenter, possibly a wheelwright, and frequently a shoemaker; while, in place of a hotel, for the reception of the stranger, is the mansion-house of the planter—wanting in paint, I grant—of ancient fashion, uncouth architecture—the floors, perhaps, not carpeted, and the furniture of that dark, massive mahogany which the city of New York would revolt at, but which carries to my mind an idea of the dignity of an ancient race, and that reverence for the antique which is, perhaps, too much wanting in every part of our country, except the *old states of the South*.

"This ancient mansion will be found usually with its doors thrown wide—in sign of welcome. Lest you should doubt, as you approach it, you behold the planter himself descending the old brick steps to welcome you. You will be confounded to see that his costume is neither fine nor fashionable—that he wears a great broad-brimmed white hat, exceedingly ample, which may have been manufactured for his grandfather. His coat may be of white flannel, and out at the elbows; and his pantaloons will be of domestic manufacture, homespun or nankin cotton. If you are wise enough to look below the externals, you will see, perhaps, that he has learned to despise them—at all events, you will perceive that he has sacrificed for these none of the essentials of the host, the gentleman, or the patriot. His hospitality is unimpaired by his antiquity—nay, it forms a part of it—and in the retention of the one, he has retained the other as a matter of necessity. As a gentleman, he is frank and easy of manner, unaffected in his bearing, and always solicitous of your comfort and satisfaction. He does not suffer you to perceive that he would have been better pleased that you should have admired his fine house, and passed on without tasking its hospitality. These are characteristics which must be taken as an offset to those respects which you select for censure. These, I have said, are the natural consequence of staple culture. It is the farming culture which exhibits and requires much nicety of detail. In the hands of the planter of a staple, lands are held in bodies too large to be handled minutely. It is the small plat only which you can put in bandbox condition. Lands in staple countries are of less value than labor—in farming countries, of greater value than labor. In proportion as the population becomes dense, they rise in value. But few southern planters desire a dense population. One secret of their hospitality is the extensiveness of their ranges. A wealthy planter, having from fifty to five hundred slaves, will have from a hundred to a thousand head of cattle. He kills so many beeves per annum, from four to forty, according to his *force*. That he can order a *mutton* to be slaughtered, even though but a single guest claims his hospitality, is due to his extensive tracts of field and forest. He seldom sends any of his sheep, cattle, corn, or other provisions to market. These are all retained for the wants of the homestead.

" It will not do for you, recognising the peculiar characteristics of his mode of life—their elegances, comforts, and bounties—to cavil at deficiencies, which could only be remedied by his abandonment of habits which are grateful to the virtues, and which maintain in him the essentials of all high character—dignity and reverence."

"But there must be an end to all this hospitality. The southern planter is not prosperous. His fields are failing him—his staples are no longer valuable."

"Sufficient for the day is the evil thereof. Give us time. Let time answer your prophecy; for it is prediction—not argument, not fact—which you assert. There is no need that his hospitality should be at an end. It only needs that it should be more discriminating, and that the southern planter should steadily close his door against those who come to eat his bread only to denounce the manner in which it is made, and to sleep securely beneath his roof only to leave curses rather than prayers behind them. He must only be sure that his guest, when a stranger, is a gentleman and an honest man; and he will probably, with this modification of his hospitality, never be wanting in the necessary means for satisfying it.

"But, touching his prosperity, I hold it to be the greatest mistake in the world—examining things by just and intrinsic laws—to suppose that he is not prosperous. The southern planter does not derive from his labors so large a *money* income as he formerly did, when the culture of his great staple was comparatively in few hands. It is something different, certainly, to receive twenty cents instead of one hundred for long cottons, and six cents instead of thirty for short. But, in fact, the difference does not substantially affect his prosperity, *if he be not already in debt.* In the period of high prices for his staples, he could readily abandon farming culture to his less prosperous neighbors, leaving it to other states to supply his grain, his forage, his vegetables, his cattle, mules, and horses, for which he could well afford to pay from the excess of his income. But with his resources reduced, his policy necessarily changes, and is changing hourly, in recognition of new laws and new necessities. This change effected, his property will continue as before, though actually no great amount of money passes through his hands. His fields, that *were* failing him when he addressed them wholly to the culture of a single staple, are recovering, now that he alternates his crops, and economizes, prepares, and employs his manure. He ceases to buy grain and provisions. He raises his own hogs and cattle, and his ploughs are driven by mules and horses foaled in his own pastures. He discovers that he is not worse off now, in raising the commodities themselves, for the purchase of which he simply raised the cash before; and he further discovers that, under the present system, he learns to economize land and labor, to improve the quality of the land, and the excellence of the labor; land rises in value with the introduction of thorough tillage; and a cleanlier, more compact method of culture, increases the health of the climate as well as the prosperity of the planters. With thorough tillage he can feed his stock, and thus lessen the extent of his ranges; and this results in a gradually-increasing denseness of the settlements, which are all that is necessary to rendering the state as prosperous as the individual has been."

"What do you mean by this distinction?"

"It is one that politicians do not often make, and it constitutes the grand feature in which the southern states are deficient to a northern eye. It occasions some of the difficulties in your modes of reasoning. The wealth of the state must depend mostly upon its numbers. The wealth of the individual will depend chiefly upon himself. The people of a state may be all in the enjoyment of comfort and affluence, yet the state may be poor. This is the case with all the southern states, the government of which has a sparsely-settled population on which to act. Where the population is thinly planted, the roads will be inferior, the public works infrequent and of mean appearance, and the cities (which depend wholly upon a contiguous back country for support) will stagnate in visible decline, wanting enterprise and energy. The roads, the public buildings, and the cities, by which the stranger judges of the prosperity of a people, will all depend upon the population of a state. If this be large — if the soil is well covered — the powers of taxation are necessarily enlarged, without, perhaps, growing burdensome to any; but the means of life will be correspondingly diminished in the hands of the greater number. Want and poverty will trouble thousands; a few will grow rich at the expense of the rest; with the greater number, the struggle will be incessant from morning to night, to supply the most limited wants of a painful existence.

But in the southern states, where the public works are few, the public buildings humble, and the cities of difficult growth or of stagnating condition, the great body of the people—nay, all the people, bond and free—live in the enjoyment of plenty always, and, in most cases, of a wondrous degree of comfort.

"To illustrate this more completely by parallels: Great Britain and France are, of course, immeasurably superior, not only to the southern states of the Union, but to *all* the states, North and South, in the wonders of art, the great thoroughfares, the noble buildings, and the gigantic cities. These are erroneously assumed to be the proofs of prosperity in a nation, when it is somewhat doubtful if they can be even regarded as just proofs of its civilization. But, in Great Britain and France, millions rise every morning, in doubt where they shall procure the daily bread which shall satisfy the hunger of nature through the next twelve hours. No such apprehension ever troubles the citizen of the rural districts of the South. Rich and poor, black and white, bond and free, are all superior to this torturing anxiety; and the beggar, who in the great cities of Europe and America is as frequent as their posts, is scarcely ever to be seen, even, in a southern city—and then he is chiefly from a northern city, whence he flies to a region, of the hospitality of which (in spite of its failing fortunes) some vague rumors have reached his ears. He flies from the proud and prosperous cities of the North, seeking his bread at the hands of a people whom you profess to despise for their decline."

"With these convictions, why do you repine and complain?"

"I do neither. To do either is unmanly. That the southern people do complain, more than is proper and needful, is surely a something to be regretted; since he who pauses to complain will probably never overtake his flying prosperity. But, that there should be gloom and despondency is but natural with a people who, without positively suffering in fortune or comfort, are yet compelled, by large transitions of fortune, to contrast their present with their past. It is not that we are ruined now, but that we remember how fortunate we were before. If we compare ourselves with other people, and not with ourselves, we shall probably congratulate ourselves rather than complain."

"With your views, you are then satisfied that your people

should continue rural occupations exclusively, to the rejection of manufactures.'

"By no means I am anxious, on the contrary, that our people should embark in every department of art and trade for which they themselves or our climate may be fitted, if only that we may be perfectly independent of our northern brethren. We have abundance of water-power, all over the South; we have the operatives on the spot; and we raise all the raw materials necessary for manufactures. Our water-power never congeals with frost; our operatives never work short, or strike for increased wages, for we always keep them well fed and well clothed; we pension their aged; we protect and provide for their young; and, instead of being sickly at the toils we impose— puny and perishing—they are always fat and frolicsome, and always on the increase; and cotton is every day passing into more general use, as clothing for the poorer races of mankind. But, in the introduction of manufactures, I do not propose that we should neglect or abandon any of our staples: I propose that we should only employ our surplus population and lands for the purpose. There are large tracts of territory, for example, in the Carolinas, which answer for neither cotton, tobacco, nor the smaller grains. In these very regions, there is water-power in abundance; and where this is not the case, there is fuel in inexhaustible abundance, for the use of steam-power. I propose to increase the wealth of the state by the application of these regions to their proper use."

"But if your whole country should become manufacturing, why not? The profits of manufactures are vastly greater than those of the cotton culture. I have seen some statistics of South Carolina, where it is estimated that seven hundred operatives will realize as large a result, in working up the cotton, as a whole district of twenty-five thousand people in making the raw material. They will work up seven thousand bales, triplicating its value, while the twenty-five thousand average but a single bale to each inhabitant."

"This is the sort of statistics which delude the world. It is perhaps true that a district of South Carolina having twenty-five thousand people will send but twenty-five thousand bags of cotton to market. It is also true, perhaps, that eight hundred operatives in a manufactory will, by their labor, increase threefold the value of eight thousand bales, making a total of marketvalues equal to the twenty-five thousand bales. But when the operatives have done this, they have done nothing more than feed and clothe themselves, while, in fact, the cotton-planter has sent nothing but his *surplus* crop into the market. He has lived and fed well, with all his operatives besides. Of the twenty-five thousand persons in agriculture, twelve thousand enjoy luxuries, as well as comforts, which are not common to the cities. They have more leisure; they enjoy more society; most of them ride on horseback, and the greater number of families keep carriage or buggy. Nothing is said of the variety of food which they command, or may command—the delights of their own homes, in their own grounds, their own gardens and firesides; and the ease, the independence and elasticity, which belong to him who lives in the air and sunshine; in exercises which are grateful; and retires from his toils at an early hour, to the enjoyments of his homestead and his sleep. But talking of sleep reminds me of supper. Captain, if my nose does not greatly err, we are in the latitude of the old North State. I have been smelling tar and turpentine for the last half hour."

CHAPTER XI.

Our discussion had taken an essayical form, and was fast losing its interest. Continued desultorily, it became descriptive.

"I was travelling through North Carolina last season," said one of the South-Carolinians present, "and was assailed upon the route by a hale and rather pursy old farmer, with a long and curious examination on the subject of South Carolina politics. It was the time of the threatened secession movement.

"'Well,' said he, 'what are you people gwine to do in South Car'lina! Air you in airnest *now* ?'—'I think so !'—'And what will you do—cut loose ?'—'It is not improbable.'—'But you're not all for it.'—'No! by no means. It is yet to be decided whether there's a majority for separate state secession; there is very little doubt that a vast majority favors the formation of a Southern Confederacy.'—'And do you reckon that the Federal Government will let you go off quietly.'—'It is so thought by certain among us.'—'But you ?'—'I think otherwise. I think they can hardly suffer us to do so. It would be fatal to their revenue system.'—'Well, and if they try to put you down—what are you gwine to do ?'—'I suppose we shall have to carry the attack into the enemy's country, and put them down in turn.'—'That's right, and I'm one of them that stand ready to take a hand whenever you want help. I aint of the way of thinking of Mr. Dockery (it may be Dickery —Dickery, Dickery, Dock—something of the sort it is), who says he's for j'ining the Federal government agin you, and voting men and money to put you down. I reckon there's very few in the Old State to agree with him. He's a native from your country, too, I'm a-thinking. We are a rether slow people in North Carolina, but I reckon we're sure and sound, and true grit, and true South. We don't think you're right, in what you're a-doing, owing to the fact that South Carolina's always a leetle too fast, and mighty apt to go off at a half cock ; but ef she's too quick, we believe it's a quickness pretty much on the right side. I'm a-thinking there's no chance for us in the eend, unless we cut loose from the whole Yankee consarn. Old Isaac Coppidge, one of my neighbors, he said more than twenty years ago, when you was for Nullifying—that you would do right to break up the Union, you South-Carolinians—that the Union was jest a sort of Union between a mighty fat frog and a hungry blacksnake—that the fat frog was the South, and the hungry snake the North. And, says he, it's because the frog is so big and so fat, that the snake kaint swallow him all at once. But the snake's got fast hold, and the frog's a-gitting weaker every day—and every day a little more of him goes down; when the day comes that the frog gives up and lies quiet, the snake'll finish him. That was what old Ike Coppidge used to say, and jest what he says now. As I said, my friend, we don't altogether like your doings, but there's a many among us, who didn't like 'em in the Nullification times. But we see that the thing's getting worse, the frog's gitting lower and lower in the snake's swallow, and we've hafe a notion that you're pretty nigh to be right efter all. We'd like you to wait a bit on us; but ef you don't, we'll have a turn at the pump-handle, whenever there's a fire in your house. There's mighty few that think with Squire Dickery (or Dockery), and we'll git right side up before we're swallowed. I kin tell you that Clingman will distance his man by three thousand votes, or I'm a sinner in mighty great danger.'"

The anecdote brought out one of our passengers from North Carolina, who had not before spoken. He showed himself equally jealous of Virginia on one hand, and South Carolina on the other. The Virginian dashed in; and in a little while the conversation became general. But we soon subsided again into description,

"Harper's Ferry disappointed me," said one of the party. In fact, the traveller wonders at that extravagance of admiration, which, in the case of Mr. Jefferson and others, dilated in terms of such wonder and admiration, upon the sublimity and grandeur of a scene, which in no place rises above the picturesque. It is impossible for anybody to identify any spot in this neighborhood with the scene described by the sage of Monticello. But Jefferson, though a very great man, in certain respects, was, also, no little of a humbug. His superlatives were apt to be bestowed, even where his imagination was unexcited. It is barely possible that he himself felt the wonders which he described as visible in this region; but to most other persons his description appears to be the superb of hyperbole. The scene is undoubtedly a fine one—pleasing and picturesque. The junction, of two broad rivers, at the feet of double mountain ranges, can not be otherwise. Beauty is here, and dignity, and the eye lingers with gratification upon the sweet pictures which are made of the scene, at the rising and the setting of the sun. Standing upon a jagged peak below the junction, and suffering the eye to sweep over the two broad gorges within its range— green slopes gradually ascending from, or abrupt rocks sullenly hanging above, the shallow waters glittering in the sunlight, you will naturally choose a hundred different spots upon which you would fancy the appearance of a Gothic or Grecian cottage. But no ideas of majesty, grandeur, force, power or sublimity, lift you into the regions of enthusiasm. The rivers are shallow and forceless. There are no impetuous rages, no fierce, impulsive gushings, no fearful strifes with crag, and boulder—no storms, no torrents, no agonies of conflict between rock and river. The waters are not only placid, but quiet even to tameness. They seem to have made their way through the rocks insidiously; with the gliding sinuosity of the snake, rather than the wild flight of the eagle, or the mighty rush of the tiger. They have sapped the mountain citadels, not stormed them; and never could have possessed the volume to have done otherwise. The description of Mr. Jefferson would better suit the French Broad in North Carolina, to which the scene at Harper's Ferry can not for a moment compare, whether as regards beauty, majesty, or sublimity. In contrast, the streams are absolutely sluggish. They neither rive, nor rend, nor rage, nor roar among the rocks. They have no wild rapids, no foaming wrath, no headlong plunges, no boiling abysses, and to him who goes thither, with his mind full of Mr. Jefferson's description, there is nothing in reserve but disappointment.

"But what of the Shenandoah Valley as a whole?"

"The valley of the Shenandoah might realize to the youthful romancer his most perfect idea of Arcadia. Reposing cosily in the bosom of protecting mountains, she unfolds to the embrace of the sun the most prolific beauties. Her charms are of a sort to inspire the most perfect idylls, and to mature the mind for contemplation, and to enliven the affections for enjoyment. A dream of peace, sheltered by the wings of security, seems to hallow her loveliness in the sight of blue mountains, and the smiling heavens. On every hand spread out favorite places for retreat and pleasure, the most grateful of all, in which life suffers no provocations inconsistent with mental revery, and where the daily necessities harmonize pleasantly with the most nutritious fancies. Here the farmer may become the poet; here solitude may yield proper occasion for thought: and thought, enlivened by the picturesque, may rise to a constant enjoyment of imagination. There is no scene so uniform as to induce monotony or weariness. Green fields terminate in gentle heights, heights are rendered musical with companionable voices, by the perpetual murmur of rills and waterfalls. The eye that rests upon the rock is charmed away by the *sunny shadows* that chase each other, in perpetual sport, over valleys and sloping lawns; and the heart feels that here, if it be not the case, it should be, that the spirit of man may be as divine as the region in which he finds his abode. That the heart is not here sufficiently subdued to appreciate justly its possessions of nature—that the tastes have not here sufficiently refined, in accordance with the sweetness, simplicity, beauty and sincerity of the place—is only due to the freshness of the scene and the newness of society. In proportion as the sense awakens to what it enjoys—as the means of life increase, and as prosperity leads to leisure, will be the improvement, mentally and spiritually, of a region, which only needs to be justly known, in all its charms and treasures. Time will bring about the necessary improvement. As it is, the scene is one where the heart, already matured, and the tastes already cultivated, may find a thousand abodes, in which life may pass away as a long and grateful sunny day, lapsing sweetly into sleep at last, in a couch hung with purple, and under a sky of blue, draped with the loveliest hues and colors of a peaceful sunset."

Somehow, we got back to the "Eastern Shore," which we had already left behind us, both in ship and story. One of the party was an advocate for modest scenery, that which required you to seek its beauties in the shade, and never sought to compel your admiration by its own obtrusiveness. He had found pictures for the eye where few persons seek them. Thus:— The argument depending upon moral, really, and not physical aspects:—

"In approaching the 'Eastern Shore' of Virginia," said he, "passing from 'Old Point' across the bay, you find yourself gliding toward such scenes of repose, delicacy, and quiet beauty, as always commend themselves to eyes which are studious of detail. To value the beautiful, apart from the sublime, requires the nicely discriminating eye. Here, you pass, in rapid succession, from headland to harbor.—Gentle promontories shoot forth to welcome you, crowded with foliage, and affording protection to sweet waters, and the most pleasant recesses for timid nymphs. You almost look to see the naiads darting through the rippling waters, in fond pursuit, with shouts and laughter. The ocean arrested by the headlands, which have been mostly upheaved from its own sandy hollows, subsides here into so many lakelets, whose little billows just suffice to break pleasantly the monotony of their glassy surface. These bays are scooped out from the shore, scooped into it, rather, in the half-moon form, leaving to each a sandy margin, and a hard beach, upon which you see the gentleman's yacht, or the fisherman's boat drawn up, while the children of both are rollicking together, rolling out among the rollers of the deep. Peace and sweetness and love, seem to be the guardian genii of these secluded places; repose and contemplation are natural occupations; one feels that the passions here do not exercise themselves madly and suicidally—that they are economized and employed only under the guidance of the affections—and that it is possible still to realize in fact the fictions of the Golden Age."

"You should be a poet."

"One can hardly escape such fancies, beholding such a scene."

"And the solitude of the region, though along the Atlantic shore, and contiguous to great marts of civilization, is quite as profound as among the gorges of our own Apalachian mountains."

"Yes, indeed; and the proof may be found in the character and manners of the people of the 'Eastern Shore.' These have scarcely undergone any vital change in the last hundred years. They will tell you that here you find the best specimens of the old Virginian: one of the 'Lions' of the 'Eastern shore' by the way, is an ancient vault, to which I was conducted with considerable interest. It lies upon an ancient farmstead, looking out upon the 'bay,' and occupies the centre of an old field, of which, sheltered by some old trees, it is the only prominent object. It belonged to a member of the Custis family, a branch of the same stock with which Washington intermarried. Its curious feature is to be found in its inscription. The vault, which is now in a state of dilapidation, is of white marble, made in London and curiously carved. Old Custis, the incumbent, was a queer old codger, and rather hard upon the fair sex, if we may judge by his epitaph, which runs literally as follows:—

"Under this marble tomb lies the body of the
Hon. JOHN CUSTIS, Esq.,
of the City of Williamsburg and Parish of Burton; formerly of Hungar's Parish, on the Eastern shore of Virginia, and County of Northampton: aged 71 years, *and yet lived but seven years, which was the space of time he kept* A BACHELOR'S HOME at Arlington, on the Eastern shore of Virginia.

This inscription, we are told by another, on the opposite side, "was put on the tomb by his own positive orders." The *gist* of it, as the ladies will painfully perceive, consists in the line we have italicised; the force of which will be better felt and understood from the additional fact, which does not appear, that this bachelor, who *lived* only in his bachelor condition, *was actually married three times.* His experience, if we are to believe his epitaph, was greatly adverse to the idea of any happiness in the marriage state; yet how strange that he should have ventured thrice upon it! The natural conclusion is that the Hon. John Custis was a singularly just and conscientious man, who, unwilling to do the sex any wrong by a premature judgment, gave them a full and fair trial, at the expense of his own happiness, and pronounced judgment only after repeated experiments. Tradition has preserved some anecdotes of the sort of experience which he enjoyed in the marriage state, one of which I will relate. It appears that he was driving in his ancient coach toward

Cape Charles, with one of his wives—and, to do him justice, we must assure the reader that, unlike our modern Brighamites, he had but one at a time. A matrimonial discussion ensued between the pair, which warmed as they proceeded. The lord grew angry, the lady vociferous.

"It was the diamond," said one—and "I insist," quoth the other, "that it was the club."

"You will drive me mad!" cried John Custis.

"I should call that admirable driving?" retorted the wife.

"By ——!" he exclaimed, "if you say another word I will drive down into the sea!" They were even then upon the beach!

"Another word!" screamed the lady. "Drive where you please," she added—"into the sea—I can go as deep as you dare go any day!"

He became furious, took her at her word, and drove the horses and chariot into the ocean. They began to swim. He held in, looked into her face, and she—laughed in his.

"Why do you stop?" she demanded, exultingly—not a whit alarmed.

"You are a devil!" he exclaimed flinging the horses about, and making for the shore with all expedition.

"Pooh! pooh!" laughed his tormentor. "Learn from this that there is no place where you dare to go, where I dare not accompany you."

"Even to h—!" he groaned.

"The only exception," she answered with a chuckle—"there my dear, I leave you." She had conquered. He never drove in at Cape Charles again, but groaned with the recollection of the seven years bachelor-life at Arlington.

When this little narration had ended, an intelligent German of the party, from whose grave features and silent tongue we had expected nothing, now pleasantly surprised us by volunteering a legend of his own country—a domestic legend of dark and gloomy character. We expressed our gratification at the offer, drew our chairs into the circle, lighted fresh cigars, and listened to the following tale, which, as if parodying the title of a previous story, he called—

THE BRIDE OF HATE: OR, THE PASSAGE OF A NIGHT.

> "Thou and I long since are twain;
> Nor think me so unwary or accursed,
> To bring my feet again into the snare
> Where once I have been caught; I know thy trains,
> Though dearly to my cost; thy gins and toils;
> Thy fair enchanted cup, and warbling charms,
> No more on me have power; their force is nulled;
> So much of adder's wisdom I have learned,
> To fence my ear against thy sorceries."—*Samson Agonistes.*

I.

At length I was permitted to behold my benefactress. The messenger who brought my quarterly remittance was the bearer of a letter, the first which had ever been addressed by her to myself, in which this grateful permission was accorded. I read and reread it a thousand times. My first emotions were those of pleasure—a pleasure enhanced by the hope of satisfying a curiosity, which, awakened in my earliest boyhood, had never yet been gratified. Why had I been so kindly treated, so well provided for, so affectionately considered, in all the changes of my brief existence, my sickness and my health, by a lady of such high condition? Why, again, should she, whose care and consideration had been so unvarying and decided, have shown so little desire to behold the object of her bounty? Years had elapsed since I had become her charge;—years, to me, of continued satisfaction—if one small matter be excepted. There was one alloy to my enjoyments, which, in its most rapturous moments, my boyhood did not cease to feel. It was the mystery which overhung my origin. Who am I? was the question, not so natural to the boy, yet natural enough to the sensitive and thoughtful. I was both sensitive and thoughtful; and my boyish associates, contrived on this very subject, to keep me so. Their inquiries disordered me; their surprise at my ignorance alarmed me; their occasional doubts gave me pain, and the suspicions of their minds readily passed into my own. 'Who am I?' was the perpetual inquiry which my mind was making of itself. I could address it nowhere else. My tutor, with whom I also lodged, declared his ignorance; and I believed him. He was too good a man, too kind, and himself betrayed too great an interest in the question, not to have spoken sincerely. He saw my disquiet, and endeavored to allay it; and the endeavor added to the burden, since it sufficiently declared his equal inability and desire. His anxiety, though unequal to, was not unlike, my own. I know not if his conjectures led him to like conclusions with myself. I only know that mine were sufficiently painful to extort my tears and tremors.

Vainly, at each quarterly return of the agent of the baroness, did I endeavor, by question and insinuation, to gather from him some clue to the facts of which I sought to be possessed. He had been the person who brought me to the school — who made the contract for my education and support with my tutor — and who alone, through each successive period of my life afterward, had been the medium for conveying the benefactions of my friend. To whom, then, could I so naturally apply? whence could I hope to obtain better information? Besides, he always treated me with marked affection. I can remember, when a mere child, how frequently he took me upon his knee, how kindly he caressed me, what affectionate words he poured into my ear; the gentleness of his tones, the tenderness of his regards! Nor, as I advanced in years, did his attentions alter, though they assumed different aspects. He was more reserved, though not less considerate. If he no longer brought me toys, he brought me books; if he no longer took me on his knee, he lingered with me long, and seemed to regret the hour that commanded his departure. There was something too — so I fancied — in what he said, did, and looked, that betrayed the fondness of one who had known me with a tender interest from the beginning. His arms, perhaps, had dandled me in infancy; he had been my follower, my attendant. But why linger on conjectures such as these? My speculations ran wild, as I thought over the circumstances of my condition, and painfully resolved, hour after hour, the secret of my birth.

From Bruno, however, I could obtain nothing. When questioned, he affected a stolid simplicity which, even to my boyish understanding, seemed wholly inconsistent with his. I knew that he was no fool — still less was I willing to consider him a churl. My conclusion was natural. He knew something

He could tell me much. Could he not tell me all, and where could be the motive for concealment? The answer to this question inevitably overwhelmed me for a time, until the elasticity of the youthful heart could disencumber itself from the desponding tendency of a premature activity of thought. The only motive of concealment must be guilt. I was the child of sin— I was the foredoomed of suffering. My present anxieties gave a gravity and intensity of expression to my features which did not become one so youthful. I felt this: I felt the seeming unnaturalness of my looks and carriage; but how could I relieve myself? I felt the pain of thought—thought unsatisfied—and could already imagine how natural was the doom which visited the sins of the father to the third and fourth generation.

When I failed to extort from the cunning of Bruno the secret which I was persuaded he yet possessed, I turned naturally to the letter of my benefactress. I read and reread it, each time with the hope of making some discoveries—of finding some slight clue to the truth—which might relieve my anxiety. An ambiguous sentence, the latent signification of a passage (and how many of these did my desire enable me to discover in a billet of twenty lines?) awakened my hopes and caused my heart to bound with double pulsation. But when I had gone through it again and again, until my head ached, and my senses seemed to swim, I was compelled to acknowledge to myself that there was nothing in the epistle that I had not readily comprehended at the first. It simply expressed the writer's gratification at the improvement and good conduct of the youth whom she had thought proper to educate and provide for, until manhood should bring around the period of independence; and expressed—though without emphasis (and how earnestly did I look for this quality in every word, syllable and point!)—a very natural desire to remark, with her own eyes, the personal deportment and carriage of her protégé—subjects which she seemed to regard as equally important with my intellectual improvement, and of which neither my letters nor my exercises— which were duly transmitted to her by my tutor—could give her much, if any, satisfaction. Failing to find any occult signification in the language, I next addressed my scrutiny to the style and manner of the letter—the handwriting, the air, the round ings equally of letters and periods. How soon, where the hopes and anxieties are awakened, will the boy learn to think, examine, and become analytical! To trace the mind of the writer in his penmanship is a frequent employment with the idly curious; but a deep interest led me to the same exercise. The style of the composition was clear and strong, but it struck me as quite too cold for the benevolent tenor which the note conveyed. Why should one speak the language of reserve whose deeds are the very perfection of generosity? Why should the tones be frigid where the sentiments are as soft as summer and sweet as its own bird-music? There was, to my mind, some singular contradiction in this. I could very well understand how one, doing, or about to do, a benevolent or generous action, should speak of it as slightly and indifferently as possible — nay, should avoid to speak of it at all, if to avoid it be within the nature of the occasion; — but this did not apply to the character of the epistle I examined. The writer spoke freely of her friendly purposes; but her language to the recipient was cold and freezing. If she had said nothing of what she had done and still meditated, and had spoken to me in more elaborate tones, I should have been better satisfied. But there was not an unnecessary word in the whole epistle — not one which I could fancy put in at the moment when the current of feeling, being at its height, forbade the reserve of prudence, or the cautious considerateness of deliberate and calculating purposes. There was evidently considerable pains taken — so my youthful judgment inferred — in the reserved language and manner of this letter; and why should my benefactress, moved only in what she had done by a high but ordinary sentiment of charity, strive to express herself in such language to a boy? This question led me into newer intricacies, from which, I need scarcely add, I did not readily extricate myself. The penmanship of the writer did not call for a less earnest examination than the language which she employed. It was evidently feminine in its character, but how masculine in its tone. The utter absence of ornament was a deficiency, which struck me as forming a surprising feature in the handwriting of a lady. She used capitals constantly in beginning words as well as sentences; but these capitals exhibited the cold Gothic aspects of the Roman, rather than the lively ornamented outlines of the Italian letters. The T of her signature, for example, was a simple perpendicular stroke carried much below the line, with a thick heavy cap upon it, having a dip at each end almost as great as that of an umbrella. The letters were remarkably clear, but how irregular! They seemed to have been written under a determination to write, even against desire and will—dashed spasmodically down upon the paper not coherent, and leaving wide gaps between the several words, into which an ingenious hand might readily have introduced other words, such, as I fondly conjectured, might have given to the composition that friendly warmth and interest in my fate, which it seemed to me it needed more than anything besides. My grand conclusion, on finishing my study, was this, that the writer had taken some pains to write indifferently; that the studied coldness of the letter was meant to conceal a very active warmth and feeling in the writer; and (though I may not be able to define the sources of this conjecture so well as the rest) that this feeling, whatever might be its character, was not such as could compel the admiration or secure the sympathy of mine. This conclusion may seem strange enough, when it is recollected that the baroness was my benefactress, who had always carefully anticipated my wishes; provided for my wants; afforded me the best education which the condition of the palatinate afforded; and, in all respects, had done, through charity, those kindly deeds which could not have been exacted by justice. The next moment I reproached myself for ingratitude—I prayed for better thoughts and more becoming feelings—but my prayer was not vouchsafed me. The conclusion which I have already declared had taken a rooted possession of my mind, and I commenced my journey to the castle of T—— with a mixed feeling of equal awe, anxiety, and expectation.

II.

I now remarked some alteration in the looks and bearing of my companion, Bruno, which also surprised me and awakened my curiosity. Hitherto, he had always seemed a person of little pretension, having few objects, and those of an humble class; a mere yeoman; a good retainer, in which capacity he served at T—— castle; modest in his deportment, without arrogance of any kind; and, in all respects, a very worthy personage. I I do not mean to say that he now assumed the appearance of one who had become less so; but he certainly was no longer the quiet, subdued and somewhat melancholy man whom I had heretofore been wont to find him. A certain boyish lightness of manner and gayety of speech distinguished him as we rode together;—and, though these qualities might not be altogether inconsistent with what is becoming in a man of forty, yet were they, at the same time, very far from corresponding with the usual characteristics which he had borne in our previous intimacy. Until now I should have called him a dull person, possessed of good, benevolent feelings; rather grave and sombre in his discourse; and, altogether, having no qualities to recommend him to a higher destination than that which he filled in the castle of the baroness. Now, he suddenly became the man of spirit; his words were mirthful, his voice musical, his opinions playful and even witty; and, not unfrequently, he would burst into little catches of song, that sounded unpleasantly in my ears, since I could neither conjure up cause of merriment in my own mind, nor conjecture the sources for so much of it in his. Nor did this conduct seem the result of simple natural feelings—the play of health in an exercise which was agreeable, or of sensations which lie beneath the surface only, and obedient to the summons of any cheerful wayfarer, who, having no cares, is susceptible of the most ordinary pleasures. There was an air of positive exultation in his looks, a triumphant consciousness in his manner, which he vainly strove to hide, and in the business of which I quickly inferred, from his frequent smile and searching gaze upon me, I myself had no little interest. When I commented upon his gayety and spirit, he would suddenly control himself, relapse, as it were by an effort, into his ancient gravity, and possibly mutter a few clumsy words of denial. But his struggle to contain himself did not long continue, and before we reached the end of our journey, he had fully surrendered himself to the joyous mood which possessed him on our setting out.

Having no knowledge of Castle T——, I endeavored by a series of direct questions to obtain from him as much information as possible in respect to it and the lady thereof. He seemed to be surprised at the avowal of my ignorance on the subject of the castle, and surprised me even more by expressing his wonder at the fact; concluding by assuring me that I was born in it—at least he had been told so. His mention of my place of birth necessarily provoked an eager renewal of my old inquiries, but to these I obtained no satisfactory answers. Enough, however, was shown me by what he said, and still more by what he looked, that he knew much more than he was willing, or permitted, to reveal. His reserve increased the mystery; for if any of my acquaintance had ever convinced me of their unequivocal regard, it was my old friend Bruno. That he should know, yet withhold, the secret, the desire for which was making my cheek paler every day, and filling my heart with the gloom that seldom afflicts the young, argued, to my understanding, a painful history, which, perhaps, when heard, I should wish for ever buried in oblivion. When I inquired after my benefactress, as I had frequently done before, his brow became clouded, and it was only at such moments that he seemed to part easily with that gayety of manner which had striven to cheer our tedious journey. Stern glances shot from beneath his bushy gray eyebrows, and his lips became compressed, as closely as if some resolute purpose of hostility was gathering in his mind.

"It seems to me, Bruno, that you love me no longer. You will not answer my questions—questions which seriously affect my happiness—and yet it is clear to me that you can do so. Why is this? Why should there be any mystery in the case of one so poor, so humble, such a dependant as myself?"

"Love you, Herman! Do I not love you!" he exclaimed; and I could see a big tear gathering within his eye, as he replied in reproachful accents—"Ah, my son, you know not how much I love you; you know not now—perhaps you will shortly know—and when you do, you will see that what I have withheld from you was wisely withheld. There is a season given for truth, Herman, and if Bruno forbears the truth in your ears, it is only that he may wait for a season."

"But why should you not tell me of the baroness? I should like to form some idea of, and to love her, before I see her."

"Then you do *not* love her?" he demanded with some quick

ness; and I could perceive a smile gleam out upon his countenance, in which I fancied there was even an expression of bitter satisfaction. His question confused me—it conveyed a reproach which he certainly never intended. Could it be possible that I did not love my benefactress—one to whom I owed so much—to whom, indeed, I owed everything? I blushed, hesitated, stammered, and, before I could reply, he again spoke, and anticipated the feeble excuse which I was preparing.

"But how should you love her?" he exclaimed, in tones rather of soliloquy than conversation. "How, indeed! It would have been wonderful, indeed, if you did."

Here he arrested himself in the manner of one who thinks he has said too much. The true feeling with which he spoke I gathered rather from the tone of his utterance than from what he said. The words, however, might have been made to apply much more innocently than the emphasis permitted me to apply them.

"How! what mean you, Bruno?" I demanded, with an astonishment which was sufficiently obvious. He endeavored to evade the effects of his error with the adroitness of a politician.

"How could you be expected to love a person whom you had never seen—whom you do not know—of whom, indeed, you know nothing?"

"Except by her bounties, Bruno."

"True, these demand gratitude, but seldom awaken love, unless by other associations. Mere charity, gifts and favors, have but little value unless the donor smiles while he is giving—speaks kind words, and looks affection and regard. The baroness has erred, if your affection was an object in her sight, in not personally bestowing her bounty and showing, to your own eyes, the concern which she felt in your success, and the benevolence she intended. Without these, her bounty could scarce secure your love; and the feeling which dictates it might have no such motive for its exercise—might be dictated by pride, vanity, the ostentation of a virtue; or, indeed, might be the consequence of a simple sense of duty."

"Duty! How should it be the duty of the baroness to provide for my support and education?"

"Nay, I say not that such is the case. I simply suggest one

of the causes of that favor which men are very apt, when they name, to confound with benevolence."

"But why should you speak as if it were doubtful that the baroness really desires to secure my affection? Do you know, Bruno, that she does not?"

"He or she who aspires to secure the affection of another will scarcely succeed by the mere act of giving in charity. The gift must be accompanied by other acts, other expressions, which shall exhibit the attachment which the giver desires to awaken. It must be shown that there is a pleasure felt in the benevolence, that the heart which bestows enjoys a kindred satisfaction with that which receives. As for any knowledge on the subject of the feelings of the baroness, I pretend none. I but state a general truth when I say, that, if her object had been to make you love her, she should have carried her gifts in person, shown herself frequently to you, counselled you from her own lips, exhorted your industry and diligence, prompted your ambition, cheered your labors, and encouraged all your honorable desires."

"Ah, if she *had* done this, Bruno?"

"Doubtless, you would then have loved her, and then she would have been—"

He paused abruptly; the same stern expression of countenance denoted the suppression of a sentiment, such as more than once before, during our dialogue, had seemed to fill his mind with bitterness. I eagerly demanded of him the conclusion of the sentence, and, with a smile which was half a sneer, he replied:—

"Then she would have been—secure of your love."

I smiled also, and, perhaps, a like sarcastic sneer passed over my own lips, as he came to this lame and impotent conclusion.

"Bruno, you deceive me, and possibly wrong my benefactress. You know more than you will tell me. There is some strange mystery in this business—"

"Which I believe, Herman, but—"

"Which you know, Bruno."

"Perhaps so; but let me ask you, Herman, my dear Herman, do you believe me to be your friend?"

"I do."

'That I have ever shown you kindness, watched over you,

counselled you, guided you, protected you, done all, in short, that a father could have done for the son he most loved?"

"Truly, good Bruno, I believe, I think, I know, that you have been all this to me. You have supplied those performances, which, if your thinking be right, the benevolence of the baroness imprudently omitted."

"Enough, Herman. Believe then a little more. Believe that he who has been friendly and faithful hitherto, without hesitation, without exception, without going back, and without sign of reluctance, will still be true, faithful, and affectionate. There is something that I might say, but not wisely, not beneficially for you, and therefore I forbear to say it. But the time will come, I think it will come very soon, and all my knowledge shall then be yours. Meanwhile, be patient and learn the first best lesson of youth—learn to wait! By learning to wait, you learn to endure, and in learning to endure, you learn one of the principal arts of conquest. I speak to you the lesson of experience, of my own experience. Never did a young man pass through a more trying term of endurance than myself. I have suppressed my nature, stifled the passions of my heart, kept down those struggles of my soul which, as they would have vainly striven for any release, were premature; and, after twenty years of bondage I am at length free. Your visit to the castle of T——, is the epoch of my emancipation."

III.

Having thus spoken, Bruno became suddenly silent, and no effort that I could make could induce him to resume the conversation. Yet, how had this conversation excited me!—what strange commotion did it occasion among the thoughts and fancies of my mind. Where had he obtained the power to speak with so much authority, words so full of animation, thoughts so far beyond his seeming condition? His words seemed to lift and expand himself. His eye glittered with the fire of an eagle's as he spoke, his lip quivered with equal pride and enthusiasm, and his form, it seemed to rise and tower aloft in all the majesty of a tried and familiar superiority. The mystery which enwrapped my own fate, seemed of a sudden to envelop this man also. He had dropped words which indicated an alliance of our destinies, and what could he mean, when, at the close of this speech, he said, that my visit to the castle of T—— was the epoch of his emancipation. The words rang in my ears with the imposing solemnity of an oracle; but, though I felt, in vain did I strive to find something in them beyond their solitary import. They increased the solemnity and anxiety of those feelings which oppressed me on my nearer approach to the gloomy towers of T—— castle. As we came in sight of them I could perceive that the countenance of my companion assumed an expression of anxiety also. A dark cloud, slowly gathering, hung about his brows, and at length spread over and seemed to settle permanently upon his face. He now seldom spoke, and only in answer to my inquiries and in monosyllables. Something of this, in the case of each of us, may have been derived from the sombre and gloomy tone of everything in the immediate neighborhood of this castle. The country was sterile in the last degree. We had travelled the whole day and had scarcely encountered a human being. But few cottages skirted the cheerless and little-trodden pathway over which we came, and a general stuntedness of vegetation and an equally general poverty of resource in all respects, fully accounted to us for, and justified the absence of, inhabitants. Bruno, however, informed me that the country on the other side of the lake on which the castle stood, and from which it derived its resources, was as fertile and populous as this was the reverse. A succession of little hills, rugged and precipitous, which were strewed thickly over our pathway, added to the difficulties of our approach, and the cheerlessness of the prospect. The castle was gray with years —one portion of it entirely dismantled and deserted—the residue in merely habitable condition—the whole presenting such a pile as would be esteemed a ruin among a people of romantic temperament, but carefully avoided by the superstitious as better calculated for the wanderings of discontented ghosts, than as a dwelling for the living. The wall which was meant to protect it from invasion on the side we came, was in a worse state of dilapidation than even the deserted portions of the castle, and we entered the enclosure through a fissure, and over the overthrown masses of lime and stone by which it had been originally filled. There were too many of these openings to render formal ports or gateways necessary. Within the enclosure I had an opportunity to see how much more desolate was the prospect the nearer I approached it. Its desolation increased the feelings of awe with which the mystery of my own fate, the ambiguous words and manner of Bruno, and the vague conjectures I had formed in reference to my benefactress, had necessarily filled my mind; and I was conscious, on first standing in the presence of the baroness, of far more apprehension than gratitude — an apprehension not so creditable to my manhood, and only to be excused and accounted for, by the secluded and unworldly manner in which my education had been conducted.

The baroness met me with a smile, and such a smile! — I could not comprehend its language. It was clearly not that of affection; it did not signify hatred — shall I say that it was the desperate effort of one who seeks to look benevolence while feeling scorn; that it was a smile of distrust and bitterness, the expression of a feeling which seemed to find the task of receiving me too offensive and unpleasant even to suffer the momentary disguise of hypocrisy and art. I was confused and stupefied. I turned for explanation to Bruno, who had accompanied me into the presence; and the expression in his face did not less surprise me than that in the face of the baroness. His eyes were fixed upon hers, and his looks wore an air of pride and exultation; not dissimilar to that which I have already described as distinguishing them while our dialogue was in progress. There was something also of defiance in his glance, while gazing on the baroness, which puzzled me the more. Her eyes were now turned from me to him.

"And this then is the — the youth — the ——" She paused. I could no longer misunderstand those accents. They were those of vexation and annoyance.

"The same!" exclaimed Bruno, "the same, my lady, and a noble youth you see he is; well worthy of your patronage, your love!"

There was a taunting asperity in his tones which struck me painfully, and at length stimulated me to utterance and action. I rushed forward, threw myself at her feet, and, while I poured forth my incoherent acknowledgments for her benefactions, would have seized and carried her hand to my lips. But she shrunk back with an impulse if possible more rapid than my own, her hands uplifted, the palms turned upon me as if beckoning me away, her head averted, and her whole attitude and manner that of one suffering contact with the thing it loathes.

"No, no! None of this. Take him away. Take him away."

I rose upon my feet and turned to Bruno. His form was erect, his eye was full of a stern severity as he gazed upon the baroness, which seemed to me strangely misplaced when I considered his relative position with the noble lady to whom I owed so much, and, in respect to whom it would seem so unaccountable, so unnatural. Bruno paused and did not regard me as I approached him. His eyes were only fixed upon his mistress. She repeated her injunction, with a wild and strange addition:—

"Have you not had enough? Would you drive me mad! Away with him. Away!"

"Come!" he exclaimed, turning to me slowly, but with an eye still fixed upon the baroness, whose face was averted from us. He muttered something further which I did not understand, and we were about to depart, he frowning as if with indignation, and I trembling with equal apprehension and surprise.

"Stay!" she exclaimed, "where would you take him, Bruno?"

"To the hall below, your ladyship."

"Right, see to his wants. His chamber is in the northern turret."

"There!" was the abrupt exclamation of Bruno.

"There! There!" was all the reply; a reply rather shrieked than spoken, and the manner of which, as well as the look of Bruno, when he beheld it, convinced me that there was something occult and mysterious in the purport of her command. Nothing more, however, was spoken by either the baroness or himself, and we left the presence in silence together.

IV.

WE descended to the *salle a mangér*, where we found a bountiful repast prepared. But neither of us seemed disposed to eat, though the long interval of abstinence since the morning meal, would, at another time, and under different circumstances, have justified a vigorous appetite and an enormous consumption of the various viands before us. I remarked one thing in the management of the feast which occasioned my astonishment. There was a regular taster of the several dishes, who went through his office before Bruno invited me to eat. I had heard and read of this officer and the objects of this precaution in the history of past and barbarous centuries, but that he should be thought necessary in a modern household and in a Christian country was a subject of very natural wonder; and I did not hesitate to say as much to my companion and friend. But my comment only met his smile; he did not answer me, but contented himself with assuring me that I might eat in safety. He even enlarged on the excellence of some of the dishes, most of which were new to me. I did little more in the progress of the repast than follow the example of the taster, who, his office over, had instantly retired, but not before casting a glance, as I fancied, of particular meaning toward Bruno, who returned it with one similarly significant! I observed that all the retainers exhibited a singular degree of deference to this man, that his wishes seemed anticipated, and his commands were instantly obeyed. Yet he spoke to them rather in the language of an intimate companion than a master. He was jocose and familiar, made inquiries into their exclusive concerns, and seemed to have secured their affections entirely. It was not long before I discovered that this was the case. From the *salle à mangér*, as neither of us cared to eat, we retired after a brief delay, and, leaving the castle, emerged by a low postern into an open court which had once been enclosed and covered, but of the enclosure of which only one section of the wall remained, connecting the main building with a sort of tower, which, as I afterward found, contained the apartments assigned me by the baroness. To this tower Bruno now conducted me. Crossing the court, we entered a small door at the foot of the tower, which my conductor carefully bolted behind him. We then ascended a narrow and decaying flight of steps, which, being circular, gradually conducted us to an upper chamber of greater height from the ground than, looking upward from below, I had at first esteemed it. This chamber was in very good repair, and at one time seemed, indeed, to have been very sumptuously furnished. There was, however, an air of coldness and damp about the apartment that impressed me with unpleasant sensations. But a single window, and that a small one, yielded the daylight from the eastern sky, while two small narrow doors, that appeared to have been shut up for a century and more, occupied opposite sections of the northern and southern walls. The little aperture at the head of the stairs was closed by a falling trap, and fastened or not at the pleasure of the incumbent, by a bolt in the floor above. A massive bedstead, of carved columns and antique pattern, stood almost beside the trap, making flight easy by that means in the event of such a proceeding seeming desirable. A venerable table, of the same style and century as the bedstead, stood in the middle of the apartment, sumptuously covered with a rich damask cloth, the massive fringes of which swept the floor around it. The solitary window of the apartment was shaded by a curtain of similar hue, but of softer and finer material. But the upholstery and decorations of my chamber, or my prison—for such it seemed with all its decaying splendor—called for little of my notice then, and deserves not that of my reader. A casual glance sufficed to show me the things of which I have spoken, and I do not think I bestowed upon them more. There were matters far more serious in my mind and important to my interest. Two stools which the apartment contained, afforded seats to Bruno and myself; and I scarcely allowed myself to be seated before I demanded an explanation of the strange scene through which we had gone with my benefactress.

"A little longer, dear Herman—be patient a little longer—and then you shall have no cause to complain of me. I shall strive soon to convince you of my wishes for your happiness and welfare, and, perhaps, of the continued labors which I have undergone, having your fortunes in view only. Yet, I do not promise you to unfold the mystery entirely, or even partially, which enwraps this castle and its unhappy mistress. Perhaps I can not. I confess freely there is something beyond my knowledge, though not, I trust, beyond my power. Should I succeed in what I purpose, and this very night may show, then may you expect such a revelation as will satisfy your curiosity and make you better content with your position. Of one thing I may assure you; your fortunes are better than you think them, the prospect is favorable before you, and the time is not far distant when you may realize my hopes in your behalf, and reap some of the fruits of my toils. But I must leave you now. Nay, do not stay me, and do not seek to question me further. I can not now, I will not, speak more on this subject. It is your interest that calls me from you."

I would have detained him for further questions, spite of his admonition, but he broke away from me, and was hurrying through the small southern door of the apartment when he suddenly stopped.

"Herman, I had almost forgotten a most important matter. I must give you some cautions. This door, you perceive, has a bar, which drops within these fissures of the wall and secures it thoroughly. You will close it after me, and keep it fast at all hours. Do not open it to any summons unless it be mine, and even my voice, or what may seem to be my voice, must not persuade you to violate this caution. When I desire entrance, you will hear these sounds, but no words"—here he breathed, rather than whistled, a slight note, interrupted by a singular quaver, which seemed the very soul of mystery—"above all," he continued, "let no woman's voice persuade you to undo the bar."

"But suppose the baroness should send?"

"Do not you hear. She may send—nay, I am sure she will—she may come herself."

"But I must then open?"

"No, not then! Not for your life."

"Ha, Bruno! What may this mean?"

"Inquire not now, my son; but believe me that my precautions are not idle, not unnecessary. I live but to serve and save you."

"Save me! You confound me, Bruno."

"Yes, I have saved you until now, and require nothing but your obedience to be your preserver still. Do as I ask, as I command you! and all will be well, and we shall be triumphant."

His words were no less strange to me than had been those of the baroness, and what was more strange than all was that sudden air of authority, parental indeed, which he now assumed for the first time. I did not, at the moment, feel the greater singularity of my own tacit obedience, without disputation, to the authority of this man. I acted, all the while, as if under the sway of an instinct. His eye, in the next moment, gave a hasty glance to the solitary window of my chamber and to the door in the southern wall of the apartment.

"That door is almost unapproachable," he said, seeing that my eye followed the direction of his; "it leads to an abandoned terrace which overhangs the lake. The portion of wall which connected it with the castle is almost in ruins. Still it may be well that you should keep it bolted. The window, which is grated and inaccessible, will yet afford you a pretty view of the neighboring mountains; these, as there is a lovely moon to-night, you will be able to distinguish readily. Should the hours seem tedious in my absence, you can amuse yourself by looking forth. But, let me warn you at parting, Herman, open to no summons but mine."

V.

He left me at these words, and left me more perplexed, if not more apprehensive, than ever. My meditations were neither clear nor pleasant. Indeed, I knew not what to think, and, perhaps naturally enough, ended by distrusting my counsellor. The change in his deportment and language had been no less marvellous than was the reception which I had met with from the baroness. The inference seems usually justified that where there is mystery, there is guilt also; and Bruno had evidently been more mysterious and inscrutable than the baroness. She, indeed, had spoken plainly enough. Looks, words, and actions, had equally denounced and driven me from her presence; and, ignorant and innocent of any wrong, performed or contemplated, I necessarily regarded my benefactress as the victim of sudden lunacy. Still, it was impossible to reconcile the conduct of Bruno, however strange and unaccountable it might seem, with the idea of his unfaithfulness. He certainly, so far as I knew, had ever been true to my interests. He had been something more. He had shown himself deeply attentive to all my feelings. Never had father bestowed more tender care on a beloved son, and shown more of parental favor in his attachments, than had been displayed toward me from the first by this person. It was not easy now to distrust him; and, racked by conflicting conjectures, I passed two weary hours before anything happened to divert my thoughts from speculations which brought me no nigher to the truth. In the meanwhile, I had made sundry attempts, by looking around me, to lessen the influence of my thoughts upon my feelings. I examined my chamber with the appearance, if not the feeling, of curiosity. I mounted to the window, and for a little while was soothed by the soft, silvery light of the moon, as it seemed to trickle down the brown, discolored sides of the rocks that rose in the distance, hill upon hill, until the last was swallowed up in the gloomy immensity beyond. The moon herself, in the zenith, was beyond my glance. But this prospect did not relieve the anxiety which it failed to divert. I turned from the pleasing picture, and, resuming my seat beside the table in my gloomy apartment, again surrendered myself up to those meditations which, however, were soon to be disturbed. My attention was called to the door through which Bruno had taken his departure, and which—though I did not then know the fact—led through a long, dismal corridor, to a suite of rooms beyond. A distinct tap, twice or thrice repeated, was made upon the door. I was on the eve of forgetting the solemn injunctions of my companion, and had nearly risen from my seat for the purpose of opening it. I recollected myself, however, before doing so, and maintained an inflexible silence. But I could not stifle the beatings of my heart, which, on a sudden, seemed to have acquired fourfold powers of pulsation. I almost tottered under my emotion; and nothing but a resolution of the most stern character, and the feeling of shame that came to my relief and reproached me with my weakness, enabled me to preserve a tolerable degree of composure. I kept silence and my seat; suppressed my breathings as well as I could; and, with ears scarcely less keen than those of the watch-dog when the wolf-drove trots about the enclosure, did I listen to the mysterious summons from without. Again and again, though still in moderate force, as if some caution was necessary to prevent the sounds from reaching other senses than my own, were the taps repeated upon the door; and, after a full quarter of an hour, passed in a condition of suspense the most trying and oppressive, I was at length relieved by hearing the tread of retiring footsteps, preceded by the murmurs of a voice which I had never heard before, and none of the words of which could I distinguish.

I breathed more freely for a while, but for a while only. Perhaps an hour elapsed—it might have been less—it certainly could not have been more; I had fallen into a sort of stupor, akin to sleep, for nature was not to be denied her rights, even though care had begun to insist on hers; when the summons was renewed upon the entrance, and, this time, with a considerable increase of earnestness. Still, I followed the counsel of Bruno, returned no answer, and strove to retain my position in the most perfect silence. The knocking was repeated after a little interval, but with the same want of success. Then I heard voices. A whispering dialogue was evidently carried on between two persons. How acute will the ears of anxiety become when sharpened by apprehension. I heard whispers, evidently meant to be suppressed, through a stone wall nearly three feet in thickness. The whispering was succeeded by a third summons, to which I paid as little attention as before, and then the whispers were exchanged for murmurs—sharp, quick murmurs—in the tones of that voice, which, once heard, could never have been forgotten. It was the voice of the baroness. I could now distinguish her words; for, in her passion, she lost all her prudence. "Said you not that you saw them enter together?" The reply was not audible, though the whisper which conveyed it was sufficiently so.

"And you saw Bruno go forth alone?"

Again the whisper, which must have been affirmative.

"And he took the way to the convent?"

The response was immediate, and, I suppose, affirmative also, though still in a whisper too soft for me to hear.

"Then *he* must be here!"

The remark was followed by a louder knocking, in the intervals of which my name was called three several times in the voice of the baroness; each time with increased emphasis, and evidently under the influence of a temper, roused from the first, and growing momently more and more angry, under disappointment. I began to reproach myself with my conduct. How could I justify this treatment of my benefactress? By what right did I exclude her, and what reason could I give to myself or others for such disrespectful treatment? The discussion of this question in my own mind led to various and conflicting resolves. My reflections all required that I should answer the summons, and open the door to the mistress of the castle; but my feelings, swayed equally by the mystery of my situation, and the singular influence which Bruno had acquired over me, were opposed to any compliance. While I debated, however, with myself, I heard another voice without—the voice of Bruno —which seemed to produce as much annoyance and fluttering among my nocturnal visiters, as their summons had occasioned in my own excited heart. His tones were loud, and he seemed to be under as much excitement as the baroness. The words of his first address were clearly audible.

"Ah, madam," he exclaimed, "it is as I apprehended; you have then violated your promise—you have dared!"—

"Dared—dared!" was the almost fierce exclamation in reply.

"Ay, madam, dared. You know the penalty of faithlessness when you complied with the conditions; can it be that you would defy it. How is it then—"

"Stand from my way, insolent!" cried the baroness, interrupting him in haughty accents, and evidently moving forward.

"Willingly," was the answer; "willingly, but I go with you for awhile. Dismiss the girl."

Strange to say, this command, for command it was, was instantly obeyed. I heard the baroness clearly address a third person, of whom I knew nothing, but whom I conceived to be the person meant by Bruno, in terms which despatched her from the presence. The dialogue between the two was then resumed, but the sounds gradually died away from my ears, as it seemed in consequence of the parties retiring to some more distant spot. My agitation may be fancied all the while. So long as the interlocutors were within hearing, I was more composed and quiet. When I ceased to hear them and to be conscious of their neighborhood, my anxiety became utterly unrestrainable. I defied the fears which oppressed me, the warning which had been given me, the nice scruples of propriety and delicacy, which, at another time, I should have insisted upon as paramount to every other law. I lifted the bar from the door, which I opened, and emerged into the long and gloomy gallery, of which I have already briefly spoken. I was resolved to pursue the parties, and satisfy that intense curiosity — a curiosity which was strictly justified by my own entire dependence upon the circumstances in progress — possibly, for life and death, weal and wo, bondage and freedom — which was preying upon me like a fever. With many misgivings, some momentary scruples, and a few fears, all of which I contrived to keep in subjection, I pursued this gallery with the most cautious footstep, resolved to hear the dreadful truth, for such I now esteemed it to be, upon which turned the mysterious history of my birth and fortunes. I groped my way, almost in entire darkness, along a ruinous part of the castle. The gallery seemed to be winding, and there were openings in the wall, which I felt on either hand at intervals, and which seemed to indicate other chambers and apartments. Through these a chill wind passed, confirming me in the belief that they were ruinous and deserted, and satisfying me that the parties I pursued were not to be found in either of them. At the end of the gallery I was stopped by a door, and beyond it the voices were again heard, sometimes low, at other times in angry emphasis, but seemingly with little or no cessation either of one or of the other. The words were seldom sufficiently audible to be syllabled clearly, and my curiosity would not suffer me to remain satisfied. I tried the door, which, to my great joy, was unfastened, and advanced with increased caution into a second and small apartment which seemed a dressing-room. A faint light gliding through a chink in the opposite wall, together with the distinct voices of the persons I sought, guided me to a spot where I could see them with tolerable ease, and hear all their words distinctly. The chamber into which I looked was similarly furnished with my own. It seemed to have been equally unoccupied. An ancient ottoman received the form of the baroness, who, as she spoke, alternately rose from, or sunk back upon its cushions. She scarcely uttered a sentence without accompanying it with great and corresponding action; now rising from her seat and advancing passionately upon her companion with hand uplifted as if to strike, her eye flashing fury and resolution while her lips poured forth a tor rent of impetuous indignation and rage;—then suddenly receding at the close of her words, she would sink back as if exhausted upon the ottoman, burying her face within her hands and sobbing with disappointed anger. Bruno, meanwhile, looked the very embodiment of coolness and resolution.

"Ulrica," I heard him say, as I approached the aperture, "these are follies from which you should be now freed. They are frenzies which must only destroy you, while they do no good to your purpose, enfeeble you in my sight and humble you in your own. Of what avail is all this violence—of what avail your further struggles to prevent that consummation which is, at length, at hand: let me implore you to be wise ere it be too late. Welcome with a smile the necessity which you can baffle no longer."

"Welcome it with a curse—welcome it with death, rather. Well do you call it a necessity; it is a necessity like death, and as such, and such only, shall it have my welcome."

"And the wise welcome death with a smile, if only because it is a necessity," replied Bruno. "You can not now escape me, you can not longer evade compliance with my wishes. Long, long, and wearisome indeed, have been my labors. I have at length triumphed! I have succeeded in my purpose, and am, at length the master of your fate! I witness your struggles with sorrow, as they only drive you on the more certainly to humiliation—perhaps to madness. It is pity, Ulrica, genuine pity, and no other feeling, which would move me to implore of you a willing concession of that which you can no longer avoid to make. The necessity is now inevitable, and I would spare you those further struggles which tend only to your exhaustion. You are so completely in my power, that your hatred and fury no longer awaken my indignation."

"Do you exult, wretch—do you then exult? Beware! You are not yet secure of your triumph."

"I am. Let this night pass only without harm to the boy, and all is well, and our triumph is complete. I am then your master."

"Master! master! Away, insolent, and leave me. You are still my slave."

"No, Ulrica, you know better than this. The epithet is no

longer applicable. I am your master, and the master of your fate."

"Slave! slave! slave!" was the oft-repeated and bitter exclamation, which came forth from her lips in foamed impotence.

"If to conquer is to acquire the rights of a master, then are these rights mine. Still I say not 'Wo to the conquered.' No, Ulrica, again and again, I conjure you to seek favor and to find it. It is still in your power—it is in your power while this night lasts—to receive indulgence. Be merciful to yourself as well as to him, the youth, who now, for the first time, from that awful hour of storm and meditated crime, the hour of his birth, enters the dwelling of ——"

"Say it not, man—wretch, fiend! Hell's curses and consuming fire be upon that hour, and the vile thing of which you speak. Slave! Hence! hence and leave me! and hear from my lips—lips which have seldom spoken the language of vengeance and of hate in vain, that the night is not yet over, and he who shouts at the close of one day may howl ere the beginning of another."

"I do not despise your threats, Ulrica—I fear them;—but I guard against them also. Did you fancy that you could penetrate to that chamber undiscovered by the watchful eyes that for the last seventeen years have been busy in penetrating every movement of your mind and soul?"

"Accursed period! Fiend, wherefore will you torment me with the recollections of that time?"

"Curse not the time, Ulrica, but the deed which it witnessed, and the worse deeds to which it led—your deeds, Ulrica, not mine—your free and voluntary deeds, to which neither the counsels of wisdom, nor of others, but your appetites and evil passions impelled you. You have called me slave repeatedly to-night—it is your favorite epithet when you deign to speak of, and to me. It is now time that I should relieve myself from the epithet, as I am now able to prove myself your master, and the master of your fate. If, seventeen years ago, I was the bondman of your father, annexed to the soil, his serf—your slave—I have been emancipated from all such relationships by your crime. You asserted the power which was transmitted you, to command my obedience. You required of me a service as a slave, which released me from all obligations of that condition; and though I wore the aspect, the demeanor, the burden of the slave, from that moment I resolved to be one no longer. When that boy ——"

"Curse him!—Hell's curses be upon him and you!" was the fiendish exclamation, accompanied by looks equally fiendish.

"Those curses, Ulrica, will cling to your neck and strangle you for ever!" was the stern and indignant answer of Bruno to this interruption. "Of one thing be certain, they neither vex me nor baffle me in my purpose. They have never hitherto done so, nor shall they now, when my labors are on the eve of successful completion. But I resume: When that boy was born, I resolved to secure him from the fate of the others! Did it not prove my fitness for freedom when my mind was successful in the struggle with my master? How long has that struggle continued—what has been its history—what now is its termination? My triumph—my continued triumphs—my perfect mastery over you! I have baffled you in your purposes—prevented many—would I could have prevented *all*—of your evil deeds and desires; protected the innocent from your hate—preserved the feeble from your malice, and secured, to this moment, the proofs equally of your crime and my superiority. Did these achievements seem like the performances of a slave? Did these betray the imbecility, the ignorance, or the pliability of the slave? No, Ulrica, no! He who can rank with his master has gained a sufficient, perhaps the only sufficient title to his freedom! But that title was already gained when you descended to the level, and contented yourself with sharing the pleasures of the slave; when you were willing——"

A torrent of the most terrific imprecation, in a voice more like the bursting of a thunderbolt, drowned the narrative of the speaker, and prevented me from hearing the conclusion of a speech, the tenor of which equally surprised and confused me. What Bruno said was just enough to advance me to a mental eminence whence I could survey only a sea of fog, and haze, and mystery, much deeper than before. When his words again became intelligible, he had discontinued his reminiscences.

"Hear me, Ulrica. You know not yet the extent of my knowledge. You dream not that I am familiar with your secrets even beyond the time when I was called to share them. Till now I have kept the knowledge from you, but when I name to you the young but unhappy Siegfried! His fate—"

"Ha! Can it be! Speak, man, monster, devil! How know you this? Hath that vile negress betrayed me?"

"It needs not that you should learn whence my knowledge comes. Enough that I know the fate of the unhappy Siegfried—unhappy because of your preference, and too vain of his elevation from the lowly condition of his birth, to anticipate the fearful doom which in the end awaited him; and to which I, too, was destined. But the kind Providence which has preserved me, did not suffer me to be blinded and deceived by the miserable lures which beguiled him to his ruin, and which you vainly fancied should mislead me. You would have released my limbs from fetters to lay them the more effectually upon my soul. You commanded my submission, you enforced it, but you never once deceived me. I saw through you from the first, and prayed for the strength to baffle and overcome you. I obtained it through prayer and diligence; and more than once it was my resolution, as it long has been in my power, to destroy you, and deliver you without time for repentance, to the fearful agent of evil which has so long had possession of your heart. That boy has saved you more than once. The thought of him, and the thought of what he was, and should be, to *you*, has come between me and my purpose. You have been spared thus long, and it is with you to declare, in this place, and at this moment, whether you will be wise in season, whether you will forego the insane hatred which has filled your bosom from the hour of his birth, and accept the terms of peace and safety which I now offer you for the last time. Hear me through, Ulrica, and know that I do not heed your curses. I am too strong, too secure in my position, to be moved by the idle language of wrathful impotence. This night must determine equally for him and yourself. To-morrow, which witnesses his public triumph, will be too late for you unless to share it. I have already seen his holiness, who will be here at noon, armed with plenary powers to search and examine; and it needs only that I should point my finger, and your doom is written, here and eternally. You are not in the temper to die; and you may escape for repentance

Nor is the condition a hard one. The youth is noble, intelligent, and handsome; he will do honor to any house. It is only to acknowledge——"

"Say no more, slave! Base, blackhearted, bitter slave! Say no more to me on this hateful subject. You have deceived me long; but you have not yet baffled me, as you insolently boast. Still less are you the master of my fate!—The master of *my* fate! Ha! ha! ha! That were, indeed, to be humbled to the dust. Away, fool, and know that my foot shall yet be upon your neck, while your false tongue licks the ground in which you grovel. Away! I defy you now, and spit upon you with disgust and scorn. Give me way, that I may lose sight of your false and hateful aspect."

The words of the man were full of a calm, but bitter sorrow, as he stood before her.

"For your own sake and safety, Ulrica, I implore you. Be not rash; yield to the necessity which must go forward; yield to it with grace, and all may yet be well. There is still time for safety and for repentance. On my knees, Ulrica, I supplicate you to be more merciful to yourself, to me, to him!"

"Never, never!" she exclaimed, as, with violent hand and sudden blow, she struck the speaker, who had knelt before her, over the yet unclosed lips, and rapidly passed toward an opposite entrance. He did not rise, but continued to implore her.

"This, too, I forgive, Ulrica. Once more I pray you!"

"Slave! Slave! Slave! Do your foulest—base traitor, I defy you!"

She disappeared in the same instant, and Bruno rose slowly and sorrowfully to his feet; while, trembling with equal wonder and apprehension, I stole back with hurried but uncertain footsteps to my chamber, and hastily fastened the door behind me.

VI.

I NATURALLY expected that Bruno, in a short time, would follow upon my footsteps, and deep indeed was the solicitude with which I waited for his coming. No words could convey to the understanding of another the singular and oppressive feelings, doubts and anxieties which had been awakened in my mind by the strange and terrible scene which I had witnessed. The curious relation in which the parties stood to each other—the calm assurance and stubborn resolution which was shown by Bruno, in defiance of one whom I had regarded only in the light of a mistress equally without reproach or fear—her fury, which, as it awakened no respect in him, was the sufficient proof of the weakness and his power—his mysterious accusations, which I was too young to comprehend and too inexperienced to trace;—and, not least, the fearful threats to which every sentence which he uttered tended—subdued all my strength, and made me weaker in limb and in heart than the infant for the first time tottering on uncertain footsteps. There was something, also, in the brief space which he allowed the baroness—but the single night on which she had already entered—for repentance before doom, which fearfully increased the terrors with which my imagination invested the whole fearful subject. And what could be the judgment—what the penalty—for those crimes, of which, as nothing was known to me, all seemed vast, dark, and overwhelming? The more I strove to think, the more involved I became in the meshes of my own wild-weaving fancies; and, failing to fix upon any certain clue which might lead me to a reasonable conclusion, I strove, at length, in headache and vexation, to dismiss all thought from my mind, patiently awaiting the approach of Bruno and the morning for the solution of my doubts and conjectures. But Bruno and the morning promised to be equally slow in their approaches. The stillness of death now overspread the castle, and the buzzing of a solitary insect within my chamber, acquired, in the tomb-like silence of the hour, a strange and emphatic signification in my ear. Hopeless of Bruno's immediate return—as nothing could be more natural than the conclusion that his labors must be great that night in preparation for those morning results of which he had spoken so confidently—I determined to yield myself to slumber; and, without undressing, I threw myself upon the massive and richly decorated couch of my chamber. But I might as well have striven for flight to the upper clouds, as to win the coy and mocking sleep which I desired. My imagination was wrought up to an almost feverish intensity. The breathing of the wind through a crevice startled and distressed me, and in the very silence of the scene and hour I felt a presence which stimulated my fancies and increased my anxiety and dread. I no longer strove for sleep. I rose and approached the little window, and looked down upon the court. There the moonlight lay, spread out like a garment, so soft, so spiritual, that thought naturally became mysticism as I surveyed it, and the vague uncertainties of the future crowded upon the arena of the present world. I could fancy shadows—which were images rather than shadows—which passed to and fro in the cold, thin, but hazy atmosphere; that tossed their wild arms above their marble brows, as, melting away in the distance, they gave place to wilder and pursuing aspects. Sounds seemed, at length, to accompany these movements, and that acute sense of the marvellous, which all men possess in proportion to their cultivated and moral nature, and which seems a quality of sight and hearing only—a thing all eyes and ears—conjured syllables from the imperfect sounds, and shrieks of pain from the vague murmurs which now really reached my ears from a distance, and which, probably, were only murmurs of the wind over the little lake that lay at the foot of the castle. As this conviction stirred my mind, I remembered the door to which the attention of Bruno had been drawn for a moment while he was discussing the securities of my chamber. I remembered that this door, as he described it, led to the terrace which immediately overlooked the lake. The remembrance, in my feverish state of mind, led me to desire to survey this scene, and I approached the door, and had already begun to undo the fastenings, which, by the way, I found far less firm and secure than my friend had imagined. The niches of the wall, into which the bar was dropped, were crumbling, and decayed to so great a degree, that the shoulder of a vigorous man, from without, might, without much effort, have driven it from the slight fragments which still held it in its place. Nor was even this degree of violence necessary to effect an entrance. From a further examination I discovered that the wall had been tampered with—a fragment of the stone dislodged, though not withdrawn, through the opening of which a hand from without might readily lift the bar and obtain access. The cement having been carefully scraped away, the stone was suffered to remain, so nicely adjusted to the place, that it was only from one point of view that I could discern a faint glimmer of the moonlight through the aperture. The suspicions of Bruno, not to speak of my own, received strong confirmation from this discovery; and my apprehensions being naturally aroused, I now strove for means to secure the door which I had been about to open. It was apparent to me that I was now threatened with danger from without. I looked about my chamber, and my eye rested upon the massive table standing in the midst. I immediately seized upon that, and placed it, though with some difficulty, against the door. While I meditated in what manner to increase my defences, my ear, which had acquired all the keen sensibilities of an Indian scout on the edge of an enemy's encampment, detected a light buzzing sound, which drew my attention to the terrace. But I had scarcely stooped to the aperture, when a scream—a torrent of screams—rang so suddenly on the late silent atmosphere, that I was staggered, almost stunned, as if a thunderbolt had on the instant fallen at my feet in the deep stillness of the unbroken forests. The sounds came from the terrace; and as soon as I could recover from the enfeebling effect of my first surprise, hearing the screams still repeated as wildly as ever, I obeyed the natural impulse of my feelings, and prepared to rush out to the scene of clamor. I dashed the table from the door, against which I had taken such pains to bear it, and tearing the slight fastenings away which otherwise secured the entrance, I threw it open and darted out upon the scene. The object that met my eyes, that instant, fastened my feet. There stood the baroness, about twenty steps from me, and at nearly the same distance from a door in the opposite wall, which was open, and from which she had evidently emerged. Behind her stood a negress—a dwarf—the blackest, strangest and most hideous-looking animal I had ever in my life beheld. The baroness had been approaching my apartment—her face was toward me, but her eyes were turned—nay, fixed and frozen, it would seem, as if in the contemplation of some object upon the parapet which overlooked the lake. Her attitude exhibited the intense and strained action of insanity. One hand—the left—was uplifted, and averted, as if to hide her eyes from the object which they yet resolutely strained to see. In the other hand, glistening in the moonlight, was a poinard, bared and borne aloft, as if designed for immediate service. I shuddered with an uncontrollable emotion of sickness — heart-sickness — as I associated the dialogue to which I had listened, with this instrument of death. But, though her progress had evidently been toward my chamber, her eyes were not now given to me. Her thoughts — if thought she had — were all elsewhere. Her fancies were hurrying her to other worlds, and scenes, and objects, visible to no senses but her own. Wildly she pointed to the parapet overlooking the lake, and gazed and spoke — a speech whose every accent was a scream of agony — as if still in sight lay some object of hate and fear, which she vainly struggled not to see.

"There — there — will it never sink — will it never die — will those hideous eyes never turn away! Down, down! — Thrust it down when I command ye — the rock is heavy in its garments — the lake is deep, deep, and still and silent — down with it, slave — for ever from my sight! Or, if ye tremble, set me free and I will do it — I have no fears — none! none!"

Thus, fixed and terrible, ghastly and staring wild, with idiot frenzy, she stood gazing and intent upon the fancied object in her sight — immovable, seemingly, as a statue, and conscious of nothing beside. I lost my fears in the contemplation of hers, and approached her, though hardly with any distinct purpose. She seemed not to notice my approach — not even when the negress who followed in her train rushed to her at my appearance and strove, with an excitement of manner only less than her own, to direct her attention upon me. But the wretched one turned not once aside at the interruption. Her eyes took but the one direction, and could not be averted; and her incoherent language was poured forth in rapid, though inconsecutive syllables, to the object of her mind's vision, which so effectually froze to darkness all her capacities of sight. Never did I behold — never could I have fancied or believed a spectacle so wild and fearful. Imagine for yourself a woman, once eminently beautiful — of a dark and mysterious beauty — tall in form — majestic in carriage — in little more than the prime of life — wearing the dignity of age, yet, in every look, movement, feature, and gesture, exhibiting the impulsive force and passionate energy of youth; — her person bending forward — her eyes straining as if to burst from the burning sockets—her lips slightly parted, but with the teeth gnashing at occasional intervals with a spasmodic motion—her hair, once richly black and voluminously massive, touched with the gray that certainly ensues from the premature storms of a winter of the soul, escaping from all confinement, and streaming over her cheeks and neck—the veins of her neck and forehead swelling into thick ridges and cording the features with a tension that amply denoted the difficulty of maintaining any such restraint upon them!—Imagine such a woman!—the ferocity of the demon glaring from her eye, in connection with the strangest expression of terror which that organ ever wore—the raised dagger in her hand—her hand uplifted—her foot advanced—and so frozen!—so fixed in the rigidity of marble!—the image above the sepulchre!—no unfitting emblem of the dread and enduring marriage, which nothing can ever set asunder, between unrepented Guilt, and unforgiving Death!

I was nearly maddened even to behold this spectacle, and it was a relief to me, when, with a no less terrible and terrifying energy she shook off the torpor which stifled life in all its wonted forms of expression, and renewed those fearful tones of memory and crime, which, though revealing nothing, amply testified to a long narrative equal of shame, and sin, and suffering.

"There! there!" she exclaimed, still addressing herself to some imaginary object which seemed to rest or to rise before her upon the parapet which overhung the lake—"There again!—its hands—its little hands—will nothing keep them down! They rise through the water—they implore—but no! no! It were a mistaken mercy now to save!—let me not look--let me not see—will you not fling it over—the lake is deep—the rock is heavy in its little garments—it will soon sink from sight for ever, and then—then I shall be safe. Ha! it goes—it goes at last!—Do you not hear the plunge!—the water gurgles in its nostrils—closes over it, and—God spare me, what a piercing shriek—Another! another!—Keep me not back—I will look if it be gone!—No! no! its little face smiles upon me through the white water!"

And this was followed by a shriek, piercing like that which she described, which penetrated to the very marrow of my bones. With the cry she bounded toward the parapet, looked wildly lewn into the lake at the foot of the castle, then recoiled with a scream to which every previous cry from her lips was feeble and inexpressive. The climax of her frenzy had been reached. I was just in time to save her. She fell backward and I received her in my arms. The shock seemed to bring her back to a more human consciousness. Her eyes were turned upon my own; a new intelligence seemed to rekindle them with their former expression of hate—her hand vainly strove to use the dagger against my person. In the effort, it fell nerveless at her side, while a sudden discharge from the mouth and nostrils drenched my garments with her blood.

VII.

Bruno at that instant appeared and received her from my arms. The relief was necessary to me—I could not have sustained her much longer. I was sick almost to exhaustion. I felt unable to endure a sight to me so strange and terrible, yet I strove in vain to turn my eyes away. They were fixed as if by some fearful fascination. Hers, too, were now riveted upon me. At first, when I transferred her to the arms of Bruno, they were turned upon him; but, in the next moment, as suddenly averted, with an expression of loathsomeness and hate, which suffering had not softened, nor the seeming approach of death diminished of any portion of intensity. On me they bestowed a more protracted, but scarcely a more kindly expression. Broken syllables, stifled and overcome by the discharge of blood, struggled feebly from her lips; and, fainting at last, she was borne to the chamber from which she had emerged at the beginning of that scene, the purposes of which seemed to me so inscrutable, and the progress of which was in truth so terrible. Medical assistance was sent for, and every succor bestowed in the power of skill and humanity. Need I say that a deep interest in her fate affected my bosom. A vague conjecture, dark and strange, which coupled the fate and history of this noble but wretched lady with my own, had naturally arisen in my mind, from the dialogue to which I had been a listener. What was she to me? I shuddered with an apprehension and painful terror whenever this question suggested itself to my thoughts. What was she not? What had she not been? and what had been her purposes—her baffled purposes! Let me not fancy them lest I madden.

"It is no subject of regret, Herman," were the first words of Bruno, when, yielding the baroness up to her attendants, we retired to another apartment. "God has interposed to save us from a greater trial, and to save her from an exposure even more humbling than this. The dawn of another day, the sight of which she will now be spared, would have been worse than death to a spirit such as hers."

"But, will she die, Bruno? Can she not be saved? is it certain?"

"It is; and I am glad of it for your sake, as well as hers."

"For my sake?"

"Ay! the moment of her death puts you in possession of this castle and all her estates."

"Me!"

"You."

"And I am"——

"Her heir—yet not *her* heir. You are the heir to a power beyond hers, and which proved her destiny. Her death makes atonement at once to the living and to the dead. She now, involuntarily, compensates for a long career of injustice. But, inquire no further; death, which will place you in possession of your rights, will, at the same time, deprive you for ever of a knowledge of certain secrets, which, had she lived till to-morrow's noon, must have been revealed in order to compel that justice which has been too long denied. It is fortunate that she will perish thus—fortunate for her—for you—for——"

He paused, and with an impulse which I could not withstand, I desperately concluded the sentence—

"And for yourself!"

"For me! Ha!—Can it be?—Herman, my son, what have you done?"

"Followed you through the corridor, when, this evening, you 'ed the baroness away from my apartment."

"And did you trace our footsteps—did you find us where we were—did you hear what was spoken?"

"All! All!"

He covered his face with his hands, and groaned aloud in the bitterness of an anguished and disappointed spirit.

"This pang," he exclaimed at length, "I had hoped to spare you. I have toiled for this at all seasons and hours, by night and day, in crowds and solitudes. Unhappy boy! your curiosity has won for you that partial knowledge of the truth which must only bring delusion, doubt, and anxiety."

"But why should it be partial, Bruno. I know from what you have already said, that you know more, that you know all. You will complete my knowledge, you will terminate my doubts."

"Never! Never! If God has spared me, by his act this night, that dire necessity from which he well knows I would have shrunk, shall I now voluntarily seek it? No! No! The fearful chronicle of shame is sealed up for ever in her death. Blessed dispensation! Her lips can no longer declare her folly, and mine shall be silent on her shame. You have heard all that you can ever hear of these dreadful mysteries."

"Nay, Bruno! Say not this, I implore you. Tell me, at least, tell me, that this most fearful woman is not——"

I shrunk from naming the word, the word signifying the relationship which I suspected to exist between us, which, indeed, seemed now to be infinitely more than a doubt, a suspicion. I looked to him to comprehend, to answer, without making necessary the expression of my fear. But he was silent, and I forced out the reluctant word:—

"Tell me, Bruno, tell me at least, that this fearful woman is not—my mother."

"And of what avail if I should tell you this? Would that terminate your doubts—would that satisfy your curiosity?"

"It would—it would."

"No, Herman, I know your nature better—to know this would only lead to other and more annoying questions, questions which, if answered, would take peace from your mind for ever. You would know next—"

He now paused.

"Yes!" I exclaimed, "I would then seek to know—and I now do—what was he, Bruno—my father—and what is the secret of your power over her—and who are you?"

"Let it be a matter of thanks with you Herman, in your

nightly prayers, that you can never know these things," was the hoarsely spoken reply. I threw myself at his feet, I clasped his knees, I implored him in tears and supplications, but he was immovable. He pressed me to his heart, he wept with me, but he told me nothing.

VIII.

At dawn we were summoned to the chamber of the baroness. A crisis was at hand. His reverence, the cardinal ——, whose presence had been expected at a late hour in the day, and for another purpose, had been solicited to attend in haste, and had complied with Christian punctuality, with the demands of mortal suffering. But his presence effected nothing. The miserable woman clearly enough comprehended his words and exhortations. She listened without look of acknowledgment, or regret, or repentance. She heard his prayers for her safety, and a smile of scorn might be seen to mantle upon her lips. The Host was elevated in her sight, and the scorn deepened upon her countenance as she beheld it. Truly was she strong in her weakness. The sacred wafer was presented to her lips, but they were closed inflexibly against it. The death struggle came on; a terrible conflict between fate on the one hand and fearful passions on the other. The images of horror will never escape from my memory. They are engraven there for ever. She raised herself to a sitting posture in the bed without assistance. The effort was momentary only. But, in that moment, her glance, which was fixed on me, was the very life-picture of a grinning and fiendish malice. The expression horrified the spectators. His eminence once more lifted the sacred emblem of salvation in her sight, and the last effort of her struggling life was to dash it from his hands. In that effort she sank back upon the pillows, a fresh discharge of blood took place from her mouth, and strangulation followed. The sufferings of the mortal had given place to those of which there can be no mortal record.

* * * * * * * * * *

And I was the master, undisputed, of all these domains. And Bruno had gone, none knew whither. Nothing more could I fathom of these mysteries, but there was one search that I instituted, one discovery that I made, which tended to deepen them yet more, in seeming to give them partial solution. That little lake, I had it drained, and, just beneath the wall of the parapet, we found the tiny skeleton of an infant — bleached and broken into fragments, but sufficiently perfect to leave no doubt of its original humanity. A rude fragment of stone such as composed the outer wall enclosing the castle, lay upon its little ribs. Need I say that I gathered up, with the solicitude of a nameless love, every remnant of this little relic, that it was inurned with the tenderest care, and consigned to sacred keeping, with the feelings of one who knew not well that he might not even then possess, though he had never known, the love of an angel sister.

CHAPTER XII.

"To-morrow, gentlemen," said our captain, as we ascended from the supper-table to the deck, "is the ever-memorable anniversary of our national independence. I shall prepare, in my department, that it shall be welcomed with due honors. It will be for you to do your part. A committee, I suppose—eh, gentlemen?"

Here was a hint; and the excellent Captain Berry never looked more like a stately Spanish Don, in a gracious moment, than when delivering that significant speech.

"In plain terms, captain, we are to have a dinner corresponding with the day. I have pleasant auguries, my mates, of puddings and pasties. There shall be cakes and ale, and ginger shall be hot i' the mouth too. Nay, because thou art a Washingtonian, shall there be no wine? Shall there not be temperance—after the manner of Washington—namely, that goodly use, without abuse, of all the precious gifts of Heaven? The hint is a good one, captain. We thank you for your benevolent purposes. It will be for us to second your arrangements, and prepare, on our parts, for a proper celebration of the Fourth of July."

"I rejoice that I am understood, gentlemen. It is usual, on board this ship, to show that we duly sympathize with the folks on shore. We are still a part of the same great family. There will be shoutings in the cities to-morrow. The country will shake with the roar of cannon from Passamaquoddy to the Rio Grande. Boston will blaze away, and Gotham will respond, and Baltimore and Norfolk will cry aloud, 'What of the day?' to Charleston and Savannah; and these in turn will sing out to Mobile and New Orleans, and the whole gulf, to the Rio Grande, will catch up the echoes with a corresponding uproar of rejoicing. And shall *we* say nothing? we who sail under the name of the great partisan warrior of the Revolution? Gentlemen, those pretty little brass pieces, that now sleep at your feet, are stuffed to the muzzle with eloquence. They will give tongue at the first signs of the dawn, and I trust that all on board this ship will be prepared to echo their sentiments."

"In other words, captain, we must have a celebration."

"Even so, gentlemen, if it be your pleasure. We shall have a dinner—why not an oration? Why not our toasts and sentiments, as well as our friends in Charleston and New York. We are here a community to ourselves, and I venture to say that no community is more unanimous in regard to the dinner at least."

"Or the drink."

"Or the puddings."

"Or the pies."

"The pasties."

"The ices."

"The—the—"

There was no end to the enumeration of the creature comforts which were to prove our unanimity of sentiment, and a feeling of the mock-heroic prompted us to take up with due gravity the hints of our captain.

We agreed upon a president, and he was—the captain; a vice, and he was—no matter who.

We appointed a committee of arrangements, with instructions to prepare the regular toasts. And—we appointed an orator! This was a little shrivelled-up person in striped breeches, with a mouldy yellow visage, and green spectacles. Nobody knew anything about him, or, in fact, why he came to be chosen. He was at his books all day; but it was observed that whenever he had condescended to open his jaws it was to say something of a dry satirical character. He was accordingly appealed to, and made no scruple about consenting; only remarking, by way of premonitory, that "it was no easy matter to know the opinions of all on board ship; he should therefore simply unfold his own, satisfied that if they were not exactly those of the company, it was only their misfortune, which it should make them highly grateful to enjoy that opportunity of repairing."

Some of us thought this speech smacked not a little of a delightful self-complacency, but it was said so easily, so naturally, and so entirely as if the speaker had no consciousness of having delivered himself other than modestly, that we concluded to leave the matter in his hands, and forebore all comment. In this resolution we were confirmed by seeing him begin his preparations the next moment by an enormous draught from the bar; the potency of which, judging from the infinite depth of its color, was well calculated to afford to the orator all the inspiration that could ever be drawn from an amalgam of Snake and Tiger. Such was the title which he gave to a curious amalgam of the sweet, the sour, the bitter, and the strong — bitters and brandy, lemon and sugar, and, I think, a little sprinkling of red pepper, being the chief elements in the draught. We felt persuaded, after this specimen of his powers, that his tastes would be sufficiently various, and his fancies sufficiently vivid; and we saw him pull off his spectacles, and put off to bed, with full confidence that neither sleeping, dreaming, drinking or waking, would he defraud our honest expectations.

His departure did not constitute a pernicious example. It was followed by no other of the party. Soon, the ladies appeared on deck, and we grouped ourselves around them, my Gothamite friend planting himself on the right of Selina Burroughs, closely, but a little in the rear, as if for more convenient access to her ear.

"So squat the serpent by the ear of Eve," I whispered him in passing.

"Ah! traitor," quoth he, *sotto voce* also, "would you betray me?"

"Do not too soon betray yourself."

"Hem! a sensible suggestion."

We were not allowed to proceed any farther. The lady began with reproaches.

"I am told, gentlemen, that you took advantage of our departure last night to say some of your best things — told, in fact, some of your best stories. How was this? But we must not be made to suffer again in like manner, and I propose that we begin early to-night. Signor Myrtalozzi"— turning to an interesting professor of Italian, who formed one of the party — "we should hear from you to-night. If I did not greatly misunderstand you, there were some curious histories recalled to you this morning in our conversation touching the 'Tarchun,' and 'Sepulchres of Etruria,' by Mrs. Hamilton Gray?"

"You did not err, señorita. In my own poor fashion, I have gleaned from these and other picturesque chronicles a story of three thousand years ago, which may be sufficiently fresh for our present audience."

"In this salt atmosphere?"

"Precisely. With your permission, señorita, I will narrate the legend thus compiled from the antique chronicle, and which I call—

THE PICTURE OF JUDGMENT; OR, THE GROTTA DEL TIFONE

A TALE OF THE ETRURIAN.

> Ma se conoscer la prima radice
> Del nostri, amor, tu hai cotanto affetto
> Faro come colui che piange e dice.—DANTE.

CHAPTER I.

THE "Grotta del Tifoné"—an Etruscan tomb opened by the Chevalier Manzi, in 1833—discovered some peculiarities at the time of its opening, which greatly mystified the cognoscenti of Italy. It was found, by certain Roman inscriptions upon two of the sarcophagi, that the inmates belonged to another people, and that the vaults of the noble Tarquinian family of Pomponius had, for some unaccountable reasons, been opened for the admission of the stranger. No place was so sacred among the Etruscans as that of burial; and the tombs of the Lucumones of Tarquinia were held particularly sacred to the immediate connections of the chief. Here he lay in state, and the scions and shoots of his blood and bosom were grouped around him, being literally, as the old Hebrew phraseology hath it, "gathered to their fathers." It was not often—and then only under peculiar circumstances which rendered the exception to the rule proper—that the leaves of stone which closed the mausoleum were rolled aside for the admission of foreigners. The "Grotta del Tifoné"—so called from the Etruscan Typhon, or Angel of Death, which appears conspicuously painted upon the square central pillar—was the last resting-place of the distinguished family of Pomponius. It is a chamber eighteen paces long and sixteen broad, and is hewn out in the solid rock. The sarcophagi were numerous when first discovered. The ledges were full — every place was occupied, and a further excavation had been made for the reception of other tenants. These tombs were all carefully examined by the explorers with that intense feeling of curiosity which such a discovery was calculated to inspire. The apartment was in good preservation; the paintings bright and distinct, though fully twenty-two centuries must have elapsed since the colors were first spread by the hands of the artist. And there were the inscriptions, just declaring enough to heighten and to deepen curiosity. A name, a fragment — and that in Latin. That a Roman should sleep in a tomb of the Etruscan, was itself a matter of some surprise; but that this strangeness should be still further distinguished by an inscription, an epitaph, in the language of the detested nation — as if the affront were to be rendered more offensive and more imposing — was calculated still further to provoke astonishment! Why should the hateful and always hostile Roman find repose among the patriarchs of Tarquinia? — the rude, obscure barbarian, in the mausoleum of a refined and ancient family? Why upon an Etruscan tomb should there be other than an Etruscan inscription? One of the strangers was a woman! Who was she, and for what was she thus distinguished? By what fatality came she to find repose among the awful manes of a people, between whom and her own the hatred was so deep and inextinguishable — ending not even with the entire overthrow of the superior race? The sarcophagus of the other stranger was without an inscription. But he, too, was a Roman! His effigy, betraying all the characteristics of his people, lay at length above his tomb; a noble youth, with features of exquisite delicacy and beauty, yet distinguished by that falcon visage which so well marked the imposing features of the great masters of the ancient world.

The wonder and delight of our visitors were hardly lessened, while their curiosity was stimulated to a still higher degree of intensity, as their researches led them to another discovery which followed the further examination of the "Grotta." On the right of the entrance they happened upon one of those exquisite paintings, in which the genius of the Etruscan proves itself to have anticipated, though it may never have rivalled the ultimate excellence of the Greek. The piece describes a frequent subject of art—a procession of souls to judgment, under the charge of good and evil genii. The group is numerous. The grace, freedom and expression of the several figures are beyond description fine; and, with two exceptions, the effect is exquisitely grateful to the spectator, as the progress seems to be one to eternal delights. Two of the souls, however, are not freed, but convict; not escaping, but doomed; not looking hope and bliss, but despair and utter misery. One of these is clearly the noble youth whose effigy, without inscription, appears upon the tomb. He is one of the Roman intruders. Behind him, following close, is the evil genius of the Etruscan—represented as a colossal negro—brutal in all his features, exulting fiendishly in his expression of countenance, and with his claws firmly grasping the shoulders of his victim. His brow is twined with serpents in the manner of a fillet, and his left hand carries the huge mallet with which the demon was expected to crush, or bruise and mangle, the prey which was assigned him. The other unhappy soul, in similar keeping, is that of a young woman, whose features declare her to be one of the loveliest of her sex. She is tall and majestic; her carriage haughty even in her wo, and her face equally distinguished by the highest physical beauty, elevated by a majesty and air of sway, which denoted a person accustomed to the habitual exercise of her own will. But, through all her beauty and majesty, there are the proofs of that agony of soul which passeth show and understanding. Two big drops of sorrow have fallen, and rest upon her cheeks, the only tokens which her large Juno-like eyes seem to have given of the suffering which she endures. They still preserve their fires undimmed and undaunted, and leave it rather to the brow, the lips, and the general features of the face to declare the keen, unutterable wo that swells within her soul, triumphant equally over pride and beauty. Nothing can exceed in force the touching expression of her agony unutterable, unless in the sympathizing imagination of him who looks for the sources of the painter's pencil into the very bosom of the artist. Immediately behind this beautiful and suffering creature is seen, close following, as in the case of the Roman youth already described, the gloomy and brutal demon—the devil of Etruscan superstition—a negro somewhat less dark and deformed than the other, and seemingly of the other sex, with looks less terrible and offensive, but whose office is not less certain, and whose features are not less full of exultation and triumph. She does not actually grasp the shoulders of her victim, but she has her, nevertheless, beneath her clutches, and the serpent of her fillet, with extended head, seems momently ready to dart its venomous fangs into the white bosom that shrinks, yet swells, beneath its eye.

Long indeed did this terrible picture fix and fascinate the eyes of the spectators; and when at length they turned away, it was only to look back and to meditate upon the mysterious and significant scene which it described. In proceeding further, however, in their search through the "Grotta," they happened upon another discovery. They were already aware that the features of this beautiful woman were Roman in their type. Indeed, there was no mistaking the inexpressible majesty of that countenance, which could belong to no other people. It was not to be confounded with the Etruscan, which, it must be remembered, was rather Grecian or Phœnician in its character, and indicated grace and beauty rather than strength, subtlety and skill rather than majesty and command. But, that there might be no doubt of the origin of this lovely woman, examining more closely the effigy upon the sarcophagus first discovered—having removed the soil from the features, and brought a strong light to bear upon them—they were found to be those exactly of the victim thus terribly distinguished in the painting.

Here, then, was a coincidence involving a very curious mystery. About the facts there could be no mistake. Two strangers, of remarkable feature, find their burial, against all usage, in the tumulus of an ancient Etruscan family. Both are young, of different sexes, and both are Roman. Their features are carved above their dust, in immortal marble—we may almost call it so, when, after two thousand years, it still preserves its trust; and in an awful procession of souls to judgment, delineated by a hand of rare excellence and with rare precision, we find the same persons, drawn to the life, and in the custody, as doomed victims, of the terrible fiend of Etruscan mythology. To this condition some terrible tale was evidently attached. Both of these pictures were portraits. For that matter, all were portraits in the numerous collection. With those two exceptions, the rest were of the same family, and their several fates, according to the resolve of the painter, were all felicitous. They walked erect, triumphant in hope and consciousness, elastic in their tread, and joyous in their features. Not so these two: the outcasts of the group—*with* but not *of* them—painfully contrasted by the artist,—terribly so by the doom of the awful Providence whose decree he had ventured thus freely to declare. The features of the man had the expression of one whom a just self-esteem moves to submit in dignity, and without complaint. The face of the woman, on the contrary, is full of anguish, though still distinguished by a degree of loftiness and character to which his offers no pretension. There were the portraits, and there the effigies, and beneath them, in their stone coffins, lay the fragments of their mouldering bones—the relic of two thousand years. What a scene had the artist chosen to transmit to posterity, from real life! and with what motive? By what terrible sense of justice, or by what strange obliquity of judgment and feeling, did the great Lucumo of the Pomponii suffer the members of his family to be thus offensively perpetuated to all time, in the place of family sepulture? Could it have been the inspiration of revenge and hatred, by which this vivid and terrible representation was wrought; and what was the melancholy history of these two strangers—so young, so beautiful—thus doomed to the inexpiable torments of the endless future, by the bold anticipatory awards of a successor or a contemporary? To these questions our explorers of the "Grotta del Tifoné" did not immediately find an answer. That they have done so since, the reader will ascribe to the keen anxiety with which they have groped through ancient chronicles, in search of an event which, thus wonderfully preserved by art for a period of more than twenty centuries, could not, as they well conjectured, be wholly obliterated from all other mortal records.

CHAPTER II.

The time had passed when Etruria gave laws to the rest of Italy. Lars Porsenna was already in his grave, and his memory, rather than his genius and spirit, satisfied the Etruscan. The progeny of the She Wolf* had risen into wondrous strength and power, and so far from shrinking within their walls at the approach of the vulture of Volterra, they had succeeded in clipping her wings, and shortening, if not wholly arresting her flight. The city of the Seven Hills, looking with triumph from her eminences, began to claim all within her scope of vision as her own. Paralyzed at her audacity, her success, and her wonderful genius for all the arts of war, the neighboring cities began to tremble at the assertion of her claims. But the braver and less prudent spirits of young Etruria revolted at this assumption, and new wars followed, which were too fierce and bloody to continue long. It needs not that we should describe the varying fortunes of the parties. Enough for our purposes that, after one well-fought field, in which the Romans triumphed, they bore away, as a prisoner, with many others, Cœlius, the youthful Lucumo of the Pomponian family. This young man, not yet nineteen, was destined by nature rather for an artist than a soldier. He possessed, in remarkable degree, that talent for painting and statuary, which was largely the possession of the Etrurians; and, though belonging to one of the noblest families in his native city, he did not think it dishonorable to exercise his talent with industry and devotion. In the invasion of his country by the fierce barbarians of Rome, he had thrown aside the pencil for the sword, in the use of which latter weapon he had shown himself not a whit less skilful and excellent, because of his preference for a less dangerous implement. His captivity was irksome, rather than painful and oppressive. He was treated with indulgence by his captors, and quartered for a season in the family of the fierce chief by whose superior prowess he had been overthrown. Here, if denied his freedom, and the use of the sword, he was not denied a resumption of those more agreeable exercises of art to which he had devoted himself before his cap-

* Rome.

tivity. He consoled himself in this condition by his favorite studies. He framed the vase into grace and beauty, adorned its sides with groups from poetry and history, and by his labors delighted the uninitiated eyes of all around him. The fierce warrior in whose custody he was, looked on with a grim sort of satisfaction at the development of arts, for which his appreciative faculties were small; and it somewhat lessened our young Etruscan in his esteem, that he should take pleasure in such employments. At all events, the effects, however disparaging, were so far favorable that they tended to the increase of his indulgences. His restraints were fewer; the old Roman not apprehending much danger of escape, or much of enterprise, from one whose tastes were so feminine; and the more gentle regards of the family, in which he was a guest perforce, contributed still more to sweeten and soften the asperities of captivity. As a Lucumo of the first rank in Etruria, he also claimed peculiar indulgencies from a people who, conscious of their own inferior origin, were not by any means insensible to the merits of aristocracy. Our captive was accordingly treated with a deference which was as grateful to his condition as it was the proper tribute to his rank. The wife of the chief whose captive he was, herself a noble matron of Rome, was as little insensible to the rank of the Etrurian, as she was to the equal modesty and manliness of his deportment. Nor was she alone thus made aware of his claims and virtues. She had a son and daughter, the latter named Aurelia, a creature of the most imposing beauty, of a lofty spirit and carriage, and of a high and generous ambition. The brother, Lucius, was younger than herself, a lad of fifteen; but he, like his sister, became rapidly and warmly impressed with the grace of manner and goodness of heart which distinguished the young Etrurian. They both learned to love him; the youth, probably, with quite as unreckoning a warmth as his sister. Nor was the heart of Cœlius long untouched. He soon perceived the exquisite beauties of the Roman damsel, and, by the usual unfailing symptoms, revealed the truth as well to the family of the maiden as to herself. The mother discovered the secret with delight, was soon aware of the condition of her daughter's heart, and, the relations of the several parties being thus understood, it was not long before they came to an explanation, which ended to their mutual satisfaction. Cœlius was soon released from his captivity, and, to the astonishment of all his family, returned home, bearing with him the beautiful creature by whom his affections had been so suddenly enslaved.

CHAPTER III.

His return to Tarquinia was hailed with delight by every member of his family but one. This was a younger brother, whose position had been greatly improved by the absence and supposed death of Cœlius. He cursed in the bitterness of his heart the fate which had thus restored, as from the grave, the shadow which had darkened his own prospects; and, though he concealed his mortification under the guise of a joy as lively as that of any other member of the household, he was torn with secret hate and the most fiendish jealousy. At first, however, as these feelings were quite aimless, he strove naturally to subdue them. There was no profitable object in their indulgence, and he was one of those, cunning beyond his years, who entertain no moods, and commit no crime, unless with the distinct hope of acquisition. It required but a little time, however, to ripen other feelings in his soul, by which the former were rather strengthened than diminished, and by which all his first, and perhaps feeble, efforts to subdue them were rendered fruitless. In the first bitter mood in which he beheld the return of his brother, the deep disappointment which he felt, with the necessity of concealing his chagrin from every eye, prevented him from bestowing that attention upon the wife of Cœlius which her beauty, had his thoughts been free, must inevitably have commanded. With his return to composure, however, he soon made the discovery of her charms, and learned to love them with a passion scarcely less warm than that which was felt by her husband. Hence followed a double motive for hating the latter, and denouncing his better fortune. Aruns—the name of the younger brother—was, like Cœlius, a man of great talent and ingenuity; but his talent, informed rather by his passions than by his tastes, was addressed to much humbler objects. While the one was creative and gentle in his character, the other was violent and destructive; while the one worshipped beauty for its own sake, the other regarded it only as subserving selfish purposes. Cœlius was frank and generous in his temper, Aruns reserved, suspicious and contracted. The one had no disguises, the other dwelt within them, even as a spider girdled by his web, and lying secret in the crevice at its bottom. Hitherto, his cunning had been chiefly exercised in concealing itself, in assuming the port of frankness, in appearing, so far as he might, the thing that he was not. It was now to be exercised for his more certain profit, in schemes hostile to the peace of others. To cloak these designs he betrayed more than usual joy at the restoration of his brother. His, indeed, seemed the most elated spirit of the household, and the confiding and unsuspecting Cœlius at once took him to his heart, with all the warmth and sincerity of boyhood. It gave him pleasure to perceive that Aurelia, his wife, received him as a brother, and he regarded with delight the appearance of affection that subsisted between them. The three soon became more and more united in their sympathies and objects, and the devotion of Aruns to the Roman wife of Cœlius was productive of a gratification to the latter, which he did not endeavor to conceal. It was grateful to him that his brother did not leave his wife to that solitude in her foreign home, which might sometimes have followed his own too intense devotion to the arts which he so passionately loved; and, without a fear that his faith might be misplaced, he left to Aruns the duty which no husband might prudently devolve upon any man, of ministering to those tastes and affections, the most delicate and sacred, which make of every family circle a temple in which the father, and the husband, and the master, should alone be the officiating priest.

Some time had passed in this manner, and at length it struck our Lucumo that there was less cordiality between his brother and his wife than had pleased him so much at first. Aurelia now no longer spoke of Aruns—his name never escaped her lips, unless when she was unavoidably forced to speak it in reply. His approaches to her were marked by a timidity not usual with him, and by a *hauteur* in her countenance which was shown to no other person. It was a proof of the superior love of Cœlius for his wife that he reproached her for this seeming dislike. She baffled his inquiry, met his reproaches with renewed shows of tenderness, and the fond, confiding husband resumed his labors on the beautiful, with perhaps too little regard to what was going on around him. Meanwhile, the expression in the face of Aurelia had been gradually deepening into gravity. Care was clouding her brow, and an air of anxiety manifested itself upon her cheek—a look of apprehension—as if some danger were impending—some great fear threatening in her heart. This continued for some time, when she became conscious that the eye of her husband began to be fixed inquiringly upon her, and with the look of one dissatisfied, if not doubtful—disturbed if not suspicious—and with certain sensibilities rendered acute and watchful, which had been equally confiding and affectionate before. These signs increased her disquiet, deepened her anxiety. But she was silent. The glances of her husband were full of appeal, but she gave them no response. She could but retire from his presence, and sigh to herself in solitude. There was evidently a mystery in this conduct, and the daily increasing anxieties of the husband betrayed his doubts lest it might prove a humiliating one at the solution. But he, too, was silent. His pride forbade that he should declare himself when he could only speak of vague surmises and perhaps degrading suspicions He was silent, but not at ease. His pleasant labors of the studio were abandoned. Was it for relief from his own thoughts that he was now so frequently in company with Aruns, or did he hope to obtain from the latter any clue to the mystery which disturbed his household? It was not in the art of Aurelia so to mould the expression of her countenance as to hide from others the anxiety which she felt in the increasing and secret communion of the brothers. She watched their departure with dread. and witnessed their return together with agitation. She saw, or fancied she saw, in the looks of the younger, a malignant exultation which even his habitual cunning did not suffer him entirely to conceal.

CHAPTER IV.

At length the cloud seemed to clear away from the brow of her husband. He once more resumed his labors, and with an avidity which he had not betrayed before. His passion now mounted to intensity. He gave himself no respite from his toils. Late and early he was at his task — morning and night — without intermission, and with the enthusiasm of one who rejoices in the completion of a favorite and long-cherished study. Aurelia was not unhappy at this second change; to go back to his old engagements and tastes seemed to her to indicate a return to his former equanimity and waveless happiness. It was with some surprise, however, and not a little concern, that she was not now permitted to watch his progress. He wrought in secret — his studio was closed against her, as, indeed, it was against all persons. Hitherto it had not been so in her instance. She pleasantly reproached him for this seclusion, but he answered her — "Fear not, you shall see all when it is done." There was something in this reply to disquiet her, but she was in a state of mind easily to be disquieted.

She was conscious also of a secret withheld from her husband — and her reproaches sunk back upon her heart, unuttered, from her lips. She could not, because of what she felt, declare to him what she thought; and she beheld his progress, from day to day with an apprehension that increased momently, and made her appearance, in one respect, not unlike his own. She was not aware that he was the victim of a strange excitement, in which his present artist labors had a considerable share. He seemed to hurry to their prosecution with an eager impatience that looked like frenzy — and to return from his daily task with a frame exhausted, but with an eye that seemed to burn with the subtlest fires. His words were few, but there was a strange intelligence in his looks. His cheeks had grown very pale, his frame was thinned, his voice made hollow, in the prosecution of these secret labors; and yet there was a something of exultation in his glance, which fully declared that, however exhausting to his frame might be the task he was pursuing, its results were yet looked to with a wild and eager satisfaction. At length the work was done. One day he stood before her in an attitude of utter exhaustion. "It is finished!" he exclaimed. "You shall see it to-morrow."

"What is it?" she asked.

"Nay, to-morrow! to-morrow!"

He then retired to sleep, and rested several hours. She looked on him while he slept. He had never rested so profoundly since he had begun the labor from which he was now freed. The slumber of an infant was never more calm, was never softer, sweeter, or purer. The beauty of Cœlius was that of the most peaceful purity. She bent over him as he slept, and kissed his forehead with lips of the truest devotion, while two big tears gathered in her large eyes, and slowly felt their way along her cheeks. She turned away lest the warm drops falling upon his face might awake him. She turned away, and in her own apartment gave free vent to the feelings which his pure and placid slumbers seemed rather to subdue than encourage. Why, with such a husband—her first love—and with so many motives to happiness, was she not happy? Alas! who shall declare for the secret yearnings of the heart, and say, as idly as Canute to the sea, "thus far shalt thou go, and no farther—here shall thy proud waves be stayed." Aurelia was a creature of fears and anxieties, and many a secret and sad presentiment. She was very far from happy—ill at ease—and—but why anticipate? We shall soon enough arrive at the issue of our melancholy narrative!

That night, while she slept—for grief and apprehension have their periods of exhaustion which we misname repose—her husband rose from his couch, and with cautious footsteps departed from his dwelling. He was absent all the night and returned only with the dawn. He re-entered his home with the same stealthy caution with which he had quitted it, and it might have been remarked that he dismissed his brother, with two other persons, at the threshold. They were all masked, and otherwise disguised with cloaks. Why this mystery? Where had they been—on what mission of mischief or of shame? To Cœlius, such a necessity was new, and scarcely had he entered his dwelling than he cast aside his disguises with the air of one who loathes their uses. He was very pale and haggard, with a fixed but glistening expression of the eye, a brow of settled gloom, from which hope and faith, and every interest in life seemed utterly to be banished. A single groan escaped him when he stood alone, and then he raised himself erect, as if hitherto he had leaned upon the arms of others. He carried himself firmly and loftily, his lips compressed, his eye eagerly looking forward; and thus, after the interval of a few seconds, he passed to the chamber of his wife. And still she slept. He bent over her, earnestly and intently gazing upon those beauties which grief seemed only to sadden into superior sweetness. He looked upon her with those earnest eyes of love, the expression of which can never be misunderstood. Still he loved her, though between her heart and his, a high, impassable barrier had been raised up by the machinations of a guilty spirit. Tenderness was the prevailing character of his glance until she spoke. Her sleep, though deep, was not wholly undisturbed. Fearful images crossed her fancy. She started and sobbed, and cried, "Save, O save and spare him— Flavius, my dear Flavius!" and her breathing again became free, and her lips sunk once more into repose. But fearful was the change, from a saddened tenderness to agony and despair, which passed over the features of Cœlius as he listened to her cry. Suddenly, striking his clenched hands against his forehead, he shook them terribly at the sleeping woman, and rushed wildly out of the apartment.

CHAPTER V.

It was noon of the same day—a warm and sunny noon, in which the birds and the breeze equally counselled pleasure and repose. The viands stood before our Cœlius and his wife, the choicest fruits of Italy, and cates which might not, in later days, have misbeseemed the favorite chambers of Lucullus. The goblet was lifted in the hands of both, and the heart of Aurelia felt almost as cheerful as the expression on her face. It was the reflection in the face of her husband. His brow was gloomy no longer. The tones of his voice were neither cold, nor angry, nor desponding. A change—she knew not why—had come over his spirit, and he smiled, nay, laughed out, in the very exultation of a new life. Aurelia conjectured nothing of this so sudden change. Enough that it was grateful to her soul. She was too happy in its influence to inquire into its cause. What heart that is happy does inquire? She quaffed the goblet at his bidding—quaffed it to the dregs—and her eye gleamed delighted and delightfully upon his, even as in the first hours of their union. She had no apprehensions—dreaded nothing sinister—and did not perceive that ever, at the close of his laughter, there was a convulsive quiver in his tones, a sort of hysterical sobbing, that he seemed to try to subdue in vain. She noticed not this, nor the glittering, almost spectral brightness of his glance, as, laughing tumultuously, he still kept his gaze intently fixed upon her. She was blind to all things but the grateful signs of his returning happiness and attachment. Once more the goblet was lifted. "To Turmes [Mercury] the conductor," cried the husband. The wife drank unwittingly — for still her companion smiled upon her, and spoke joyfully, and she was as little able as willing to perceive that anything occult occurred in his expression.

"Have you drank?" he asked.

She smiled, and laid the empty goblet before him.

"Come, then, you shall now behold the picture. You will now be prepared to understand it."

They rose together, but another change had overspread his features. The gayety had disappeared from his face. It was covered with a calm that was frightful. The eye still maintained all its eager intensity, but the lips were fixed in the icy mould of resolution. They declared a deep, inflexible purpose. There was a corresponding change in his manner and deportment. But a moment before he was all life, grace, gayety and great flexibility; he was now erect, majestic and commanding in aspect, with a lordly dignity in his movement, that declared a sense of a high duty to be done. Aurelia was suddenly impressed with misgivings. The change was too sudden not to startle her. Her doubts and apprehensions were not lessened when, instead of conducting her to the studio, where she expected to see the picture, he led the way through the vestibule and into the open court of the palace. They lingered but for a moment at the entrance, and she then beheld his brother Aruns approaching. To him she gave not a look

"All is right," said the latter.

"Enter!" was the reply of Cœlius; and as the brother disappeared within the vestibule, the two moved forward through the outer gate. They passed through a lovely wood, shady and silent, through which, subdued by intervening leaves, gleamed only faintly the bright, clear sun of Italy. From under the huge chestnuts, on either hand, the majestic gods of Etruria extended their guiding and endowing hands. Tina, or Jupiter, Aplu, or Apollo, Erkle, Turmes, and the rest, all conducting them along the *via sacra*, which led from the palaces to the tombs of every proud Etruscan family. They entered the solemn grove which was dedicated to night and silence, and were about to ascend the gradual slopes by which the tumulus was approached. Then it was that the misgivings of Aurelia took a more serious form. She felt a vague but oppressive fear. She hesitated.

"My Cœlius," she exclaimed, "whither do we go? Is not this the passage to the house of silence?"

"Do you not know it?" he demanded quickly, and fixing upon her a keen inquiring glance. "Come!" he continued, "it is there that I have fixed the picture!"

"Alas! my Cœlius, wherefore? It is upon this picture that you have been so deeply engaged. It has made you sad—it has left us both unhappy. Let us not go—let me not see it!" Her agitation was greatly increased. He saw it, and his face put on a look of desperate exultation.

"Ay, but thou must see it—thou shalt look upon it and behold my triumph, my greatest triumph in art, and perhaps my last. I shall never touch pencil more, and wilt thou refuse to look upon my last and noblest work. Fie! this were a wrong to me, and a great shame in thee, Aurelia. Come! the toil of which thou think'st but coldly, has brought me peace rather than sadness. It has made of death a thing rather familiar than offensive. If it has deprived me of hopes, it has left me without terrors!"

"Deprived you of hopes, my Cœlius," said the wife, still lingering, and in mortal terror.

"Even so!"

"And, wherefore, O, my husband, wherefore?"

"Speak not, woman! See you not that we are within the shadow of the tomb?"

"Let us not approach—let us go hence!" she exclaimed entreatingly, with increasing agitation.

"Ay, shrink'st thou!" he answered; "well thou may'st. The fathers of the Pomponii, for two thousand years, are now floating around us on their sightless wings. They wonder that a

Roman woman should draw nigh to the dwellings of our ancient Lucumones."

"A Roman woman!" she exclaimed reproachfully. "My Cœlius, wherefore this?"

"Art thou not?"

"I am thy wife."

"Art sure of that?"

"As the gods live and look upon us, I am thine, this hour and for ever!"

"May the gods judge thee, woman," he responded slowly, as he paused at the gate of the mausoleum, and fixed his eyes intently upon her. Hers were raised to heaven, with her uplifted hands. She did not weep, and her grief was still mixed with a fearful agitation.

"Let us now return, my Cœlius!"

"What, wilt thou not behold the picture?"

"Not now — at another season. I could not look upon it now!"

"Alas! woman, but this can not be. Thou must behold it now or never. Hope not to escape. Enter! I have a tale to tell thee, and a sight to show thee within, which thou canst not near or see hereafter. Enter!" As he spoke, he applied the key to the stone leaf, and the door slowly revolved upon the massy pivots. She turned and would have fled, but he grasped her by the wrist, and moved toward the entrance. She carried her freed hand to her forehead — parted the hair from her eyes, and raised them pleadingly to heaven. Resistance she saw was vain. Her secret was discovered. She prepared to enter, but slowly. "Enter! Dost thou fear now," cried her husband, "when commanded? Hast thou not, thou, a Roman, ventured already to penetrate these awful walls, given to silence and the dead — and on what mission? Enter, as I bid thee!"

CHAPTER

SHE obeyed him, shuddering and silent. He followed her, closed the entrance, and fastened it within. They were alone among the dead of a thousand years — alone, but not in darkness. The hand of preparation had been there, and cressets were burning upon the walls; their lights, reflected from the numerous shields of bronze within the apartment, shedding a strange and fantastic splendor upon the scene. The eyes of Aurelia rapidly explored the chamber as if in search of some expected object. Those of Cœlius watched them with an expression of scornful triumph, which did not escape her glance. She firmly met his gaze, almost inquiringly, while her hands were involuntarily and convulsively clasped together.

"Whom dost thou seek, Aurelia?"

"Thou know'st! thou know'st!—where is he? Tell me, my Cœlius, that he is safe, that thou hast sped him hence— that I may bless thee."

He smiled significantly as he replied, "He is safe—I have sped him hence!"

"Tinai [Adonai], my husband, keep thee in the hollow of his hand."

"How! shameless! dost thou dare so much?"

"What mean'st thou, my Cœlius?"

"Sit thou there," he answered, "till I show thee my picture." He pointed her, as he spoke, to a new sarcophagus, upon which she placed herself submissively. Then, with a wand in his hand, he, himself, seated upon another coffin of stone, pointed her to a curtain which covered one of the sides of the chamber. "Behind that curtain, Aurelia, is the last work of my hands; but before I unveil it to thine eyes, let me tell thee its melancholy history. It will not need many words for this. Much of it is known to thee already. How I found thee in Rome, when I was there a captive—how I loved thee, and how I believed in thy assurances of love; all these things thou know'st. We wedded, and I brought thee, a Roman woman, held a barbarian by my people, into the palace of one of the proudest families of all Etruria. Shall I tell thee that I loved thee still—that I love thee even now, when I have most reason to hate thee, when I know thy perjury, thy cold heart, thy hot lust, thy base, degrading passions!"

"Hold, my lord—say not these things to my grief and thy dishonor. They wrong me not less than thy own name. These things, poured into thine ear by some secret enemy, are false!"

"Thou wilt not swear it?"

"By all the gods of Rome—"

"And of what avail, and how binding the oath taken in the names of the barbarian deities of Rome."

"By the Etrurian—"

"Perjure not thyself, woman, but hear me."

"Go on, my lord, I will hear thee, though I suffer death with ery word thou speak'st."

"It is well, Aurelia, that thou art prepared for this."

"Thy dagger, my Cœlius, were less painful than thy words and looks unkind."

"Never was I unkind, until I found thee false."

"Never was I false, my lord, even when thou wast unkind."

"Woman! lie not! thou wert discovered with thy paramour, here, in this tomb; thou wert followed, day by day, and all thy secret practices betrayed. This thou ow'st to the better vigilance of my dear brother Aruns — he, more watchful of my honor than myself—"

"Ah! well I know from what hand came the cruel shaft! Cœlius, my Cœlius, thy brother is a wretch, doomed to infamy and black with crime. I have had no paramour. I might have had, and thou might'st have been dishonored, had I hearkened to thy brother's pleadings. I spurned him from my feet with loathing, and he requites me with hate. Oh, my husband, believe me, and place this man, whom thou too fondly callest thy brother, before thine eyes and mine!"

"Alas! Aurelia, this boldness becomes thee not. I myself traced thee to this tomb — these eyes but too frequently beheld thee with thy paramour."

"Cœlius, as I live, he was no paramour — but where is he, what hast thou done with him?"

"Sent him before thee to prepare thy couch in Hades!"

"Oh, brother! — but thou hast not! tell me, my lord, that thy hand is free from this bloody crime!"

"He sleeps beneath thee. It is upon his sarcophagus thou sittest."

She started with a piercing shriek from the coffin where she sat, knelt beside it, and strove to remove the heavy stone lid, which had been already securely fastened. While thus engaged the Lucumo drew aside with his hand the curtain which concealed the picture.

"Look," said he, "woman, behold the fate which thou and thy paramour have received—behold the task which I had set me when first I had been shown thy perjuries. Look!"

She arose in silence from her knees, and turned her eyes upon the picture. As the curtain was slowly unrolled from before it, and she conceived the awful subject, and distinguished, under the care of the good and guardian genii, the shades of well-known members of the Pomponian family, her interest was greatly excited; but when, following in the train and under the grasp of the Etrurian demon, she beheld the features of the young Roman who was doomed, she bounded forward with a cry of agony.

"My brother, my Flavius, my own, my only brother!" and sunk down with outstretched arms before the melancholy shade.

"Her brother!" exclaimed the husband. She heard the words and rose rapidly to her feet.

"Ay, Flavius, my brother, banished from Rome, and concealed here in thy house of silence, concealed even from thee, my husband, as I would not vex thee with the anxieties of an Etrurian noble, lest Rome should hear and punish the people by whom her outlaw was protected. Thou know'st my crime. This paramour was the brother of my heart—child of the same sire and dame—a noble heart, a pure spirit, whose very virtues have been the cause of his disgrace at Rome. Slay me, if thou wilt, but tell me not, O, Cœlius, that thou hast put the hands of hate upon my brother!"

"Thy tale is false, woman—well-planned, but false. Know I not thy brother? Did I not know thy brother well in Rome? Went we not together oft? I tell thee, I should know him among a line of ten thousand Romans!"

"Alas! alas! my husband, if ever I had brother, then is this he. I tell thee nothing but the truth. Of a surety, when thou wert in Rome, my brother was known to thee, but the boy has now become a man. Seven years have wrought a change upon him of which thou hast not thought. Believe me, what I tell thee—the youth whom I sheltered in this vault, and to whom I brought food nightly, was, indeed, my brother—my Flavius, the only son of my mother, who sent him to me, with fond words of entreaty, when the consuls of the city bade him depart in banishment."

"I can not believe thee, woman. It were a mortal agony, far beyond what I feel in the conviction of thy guilt, were I to yield faith to thy story. It is thy paramour whom I have slain, and who sleeps in that tomb. His portrait and his judgment are before thee, and now — look on thine own!"

The picture, fully displayed, showed to the wretched woman her own person, in similar custody with him who was her supposed paramour. The terrible felicity of the execution struck her to the soul. It was a picture to live as a work of art, and to this she was not insensible. She clasped her hands before it, and exclaimed,

"Oh! my Cœlius, what a life hast thou given to a lie. Yet may I bear the terrors of such a doom, if he whom thou hast painted there in a fate full of dreadful fellowship with mine, was other than my brother Flavius — he with whom thou didst love to play, and to whom thou didst impart the first lessons in the art which he learned to love from thee. Dost hear me, my Cœlius, as my soul lives, this man was none other than my brother."

"False! false! I will not, dare not believe thee!" he answered in husky accents. His frame was trembling, yet he busied himself in putting on a rich armor, clothing himself in military garb, from head to foot, as if going into action.

"What dost thou, my lord?" demanded Aurelia, curious as she beheld him in this occupation.

"This," said he, "is the armor in which I fought with Rome when I was made the captive of thy people, and thine. It is fit that I should wear it now, when I am once more going into captivity."

"My husband, what mean'st thou — of what captivity dost thou speak?"

"The captivity of death! Hear me, Aurelia, dost thou feel nothing at thy heart which tells thee of the coming struggle when the soul shakes off the reluctant flesh, and strives, as it were, for freedom. Is there no chill in thy veins, no sudden pang, as of fire in thy breast? These speak in me. They warn me of death. We are both summoned. But a little while is left of life to either!"

"Have mercy, Jove! I feel these pains, this chill, this fire that thou speak'st of."

"It is death! the goblet which I gave thee, and of which I drank the first and largest draught, was drugged with death."

"Then—it is all true! Thou hast in truth slain my brother. Thou hast—thou hast!"

"Nay, he was not thy brother, Aurelia. Why wilt thou forswear thyself at this terrible moment? It is vain. Wouldst thou lie to death—wouldst thou carry an impure face of perjury before the seat of the Triune God! Beware! Confess thy crime and justify the vengeance of thy lord!"

"As I believe thee, my Cœlius—as I believe that thou has most rashly and unjustly murdered my brother, and put death in the cup which, delivered by thy hands, was sweet and precious to my lips, so must I now declare, in sight of Heaven, in the presence of the awful dead, that what I have said and sworn to thee is truth. He whom I sheltered within the tombs of thy fathers, was the son of mine—the only, the last, best brother of my heart. I bore him in mine arms when I was a child myself. I loved him ever! Oh, how I loved him! next to thee, my Cœlius—next to thee! Couldst thou but have spared me this love—this brother!"

"How knew I—how know I now—that he was thy brother?" was the choking inquiry.

"To save thee the cruel agony that thou must feel, at knowing this, I could even be moved to tell thee falsely, and say that he was not my brother; but, indeed, some paramour, such as the base and evil thought of thy brother has grafted upon thine; but I may not; thy love is too precious to me at this last moment even if death were not too terrible to the false speaker. He was, indeed, my Flavius, dear son of a dear mother, best beloved of brothers; he whom thou didst play with as a boy; to whom thou gav'st lessons in thy own lovely art; who loved thee, my Cœlius, but too fondly, and only forbore telling thee of his evil plight for fear that thou shouldst incur danger from the sharp and angry hostility of Rome. Seek my chamber, and in my cabinet thou wilt find his letters, and the letters of my mother, borne with him in his flight. Nay,—oh! mother, what is this agony?"

"Too late! too late: If it be truth thou speakest, Aurelia,

it is a truth that can not save. Death is upon us—I see it in thy face—I feel it in my heart. Oh! would that I could doubt thy story!"

"Doubt not—doubt not—believe and take me to thy heart. I fear not death if thou wilt believe me. My Cœlius, let me come to thee and die upon thy bosom."

"Ah! shouldst thou betray me—shouldst thou still practise upon me with thy woman art!"

"And wherefore? It is death, thou say'st, that is upon us now. What shall I gain, in this hour, by speaking to thee falsely? Thou hast done thy worst. Thou hast doomed me to death, and to the scornful eyes of the confiding future!"

She threw her arms around him as she spoke, and sunk, sunk sobbing upon his breast.

"Ah!" he exclaimed, "that dreadful picture! I feel, my Aurelia, that thou hast spoken truly—that I have been rash and cruel in my judgment. Thy brother lies before thee, and yonder tomb is prepared for thee. I did not yield without a struggle, and I prepared me for a terrible sacrifice. Upon this bier, habited as I am, I yield myself to death. There is no help—no succor. Yet that picture! Shall the falsehood overcome the truth. Shall that lie survive thy virtues, thy beauty, and thy life! No! my Aurelia, this crime shall be spared at least."

He unwound her arms from about his neck, and strove to rise. She sunk in the same moment at his feet. "Oh, death!" she cried, "thou art, indeed, a god! I feel thee, terrible in thy strength, with an agony never felt before. Leave me not, my Cœlius—forgive—and leave me not!"

"I lose thee, Aurelia! Where—"

"Here! before the couch—I faint—ah!"

"I would destroy," he cried, "but can not! This blindness. Ho! without there! Aruns! It is thy step I hear! Undo, undo—I forgive thee all, if thou wilt but help. Here—hither!"

The acute senses of the dying man had, indeed, heard footsteps without. They were those of the perfidious brother. But, at the call from within, he retreated hastily. There was no answer—there was no help. But there was still some consciousness. Death was not yet triumphant. There was a pang yet to be felt

—and a pleasure. It was still in the power of the dying man to lift to his embrace his innocent victim. A moment's return of consciousness enabled her to feel his embrace, his warm tears upon her cheek, and to hear his words of entreaty and tenderness imploring forgiveness. And speech was vouchsafed her to accord it.

"I forgive thee, my Cœlius—I forgive thee, and bless thee, and love thee to the last. I know that thou wouldst never do me hurt of thy own will; I know that thou wert deceived to this—yet how, oh, how, when my head lay upon thy breast at night, and I slept in peace, couldst thou think that I should do thee wrong!"

"Why," murmured the miserable man, "why, oh, why?"

"Had I but told thee, and trusted in thee, my Cœlius!"

"Why didst thou not?"

"It was because of my brother's persuasion that I did not—he wished not that thou shouldst come to evil."

"And thou forgiv'st me, Aurelia—from thy very heart thou forgiv'st me?"

"All, all—from my heart and soul, my husband."

"It will not, then, be so very hard to die!"

An hour after and the chamber was silent. The wife had yielded first. She breathed her last sigh upon his bosom, and with the last effort of his strength he lifted her gently and laid her in the sarcophagus, composing with affectionate care the drapery around her. Then, remembering the picture, he looked around him for his sword with which to obliterate the portraits which his genius had assigned to so lamentable an eternity: but his efforts were feeble, and the paralysis of death seized him while he was yet making them. He sunk back with palsied limbs upon the bier, and the lights, and the picture, faded from before his eyes, with the last pulses of his life. The calumny which had destroyed his hopes, survived its own detection. The recorded falsehood was triumphant over the truth; yet may you see, to this day, where the random strokes of the weapon were aimed for its obliteration. Of himself there is no monument in the tomb, though one touching memorial has reached us. The vaulted chamber buried in the earth was discovered by accident. A fracture was made in its top by an Italian gentleman in com pany with a Scottish nobleman. As they gazed eagerly through the aperture, they beheld an ancient warrior in full armor, and bearing a coronet of gold. The vision lasted but a moment. The decomposing effects of the air were soon perceptible. Even while they gazed, the body seemed agitated with a trembling, heaving motion, which lasted a few minutes, and then it subsided into dust. When they penetrated the sepulchre, they found the decaying armor in fragments, the sword and the helmet, or crown of gold. The dust was but a handful, and this was all that remained of the wretched Lucumo. The terrible picture is all that survives — the false witness, still repeating its cruel lie, at the expense of all that is noble in youth and manhood, and all that is pure and lovely in the soul of woman"

We all agreed that our professor, who delivered his narrative with due modesty, had made a very interesting legend from the chronicles — had certainly shown a due regard for the purity of the sex, in thus vindicating the virtuous sufferer from the malicious accusation which had been preserved by art, through the capricious progress of more than twenty centuries.

Several stories followed, short, sketchy, and more or less spirited, of which I could procure no copies. The ladies gave us sundry pleasant lyrics to the accompaniment of the guitar, and one or two male flute players contributed to our musical joys until we began to verge toward the shorter hours, when the fairer portion of the party bowed us good night — Duyckman nearly breaking his own and Selina Burroughs's neck, in helping her down the cabin-steps

CHAPTER XIII

"THE GLORIOUS FOURTH" AT SEA.

LET us skip over the small hours which were consumed by our little community — we may suppose — after a very common fashion on shore. There was silence in the ship for a space. But a good strong corps was ready, at the peep of day, to respond, with a general shout, to that salutation to the morn which our worthy captain had assigned to the throats of his pet brass pieces. We were not missing at the moment of uproar, and, as the bellowing voices roared along the deep, we echoed the clamor with a hurrah scarcely less audible in the courts of Neptune.

I need not dwell upon the exhibition of *deshabilles*, as we severally appeared on deck in nightgown and wrapper, with otherwise scant costume. But, as our few lady-passengers made no appearance at this hour, there was no need for much precaution. We took the opportunity afforded by their absence to procure a good sousing from the sea, administered, through capacious buckets, by the hands of a courteous coalheaver, who received his shilling a-head for our ablutions. By the way, why should not these admirable vessels, so distinguished by their various comforts, be provided with half-a-dozen bathing-rooms? We commend the suggestion to future builders. A bath is even more necessary at sea than on shore, and, lacking his bath, there is many a pretty fellow who resorts to his bottle. Frequent ablution is no small agent of a proper morality.

Outraging no propriety by our garden-like innocence of costume, we began the day merrily, and contrived to continue it cheerily. At the hour of twelve, the awning spread above us, a smooth sea below, a fine breeze streaming around us, we were all assembled upon the quarter-deck, a small but select congregation, to hear the man in a saffron skin and green spectacles.

We dispensed with the whole reading of the Declaration of Independence; our reader graciously abridging it to doggrel dimensions, after some such form as the following, which he delivered, as far as permitted, with admirable grace and most senatorial dignity:—

> "When in the course of human events,
> A people have cravings for eloquence.
> A decent regard for common-sense
> Requires——"

He was here broken in upon by a sharp shriek, rather than a voice, which we found to proceed from a Texan, who had worn his Mexican blanket during the whole voyage, and whom some of the passengers were inclined to think was no other than Sam Houston himself. His interruption furnished a sufficiently appropriate finishing line to the doggrel of our reader:—

"Oh, go ahead, and d——n the expense."

"'The very principle of the Revolution,' said the orator.

"Particularly as they never redeemed the continental money. My grandmother has papered her kitchen with the 'I. O. U's of our fathers of Independence."

This remark led to others, and there was a general buzz, when the orator put in, first calling attention, and silencing all voices, by a thundering slap with the flat of his hand upon the cover of a huge volume which he carried in his grasp.

"Look you, gentlemen," said he, with the air of a person who was not disposed to submit to wrong—"you asked me to be your orator, and hang me if I am to be choused out of the performance, now that I have gone through all my preparations. Scarcely had I received your appointment before I proceeded to put myself in training. I went below and got myself a dose of 'snake and tiger'—a beverage I had not tasted before for the last five months—and I commended myself, during a twenty minutes' immersion in the boatswain's bath at the fore—while you were all sleeping, I suppose—to the profound and philosophical thoughts which were proper to this great occasion With the dawn, and before the cannon gave counsel to the da. I was again immersed in meditation and salt-water; followed by a severe friction at the hands of one of the stewards, and another touch of 'snake and tiger' at the hands of the butler. I have thus prepared myself for the occasion, and I'll let you know I am not the man to prepare myself for nothing. Either you must hear me, or you must fight me. Let me know your resolution. If I do not begin upon you all, I shall certainly begin upon some one of you, and I don't know but that Texan shall be my first customer, as being the first to disturb the business of the day. An audible snort from the blanket was the only answer from that quarter; while the cry of—"An orator an orator!" from all parts of the ship, pacified our belligerent Demosthenes.

He began accordingly.

THE ORATION OF THE GREEN-SPECTACLED ALABAMIAN

"*Shipmates or Fellow-Citizens:* We are told by good authority that no man is to be pronounced fortunate so long as he lives, since every moment of life is subject to caprices which may reverse his condition, and render your congratulation fraudulent and offensive. The same rules, for the same reason, should be adopted in regard to nations, and no eulogy should be spoken upon their institutions, until they have ceased to exist. It would accordingly be much easier for me to dilate upon the good fortune of Copan and Palenque than upon any other countries, since they will never more suffer from invasion, and the scandalous chronicle of their private lives is totally lost to a prying posterity.

"In regard to our country, what would you have me say? Am I summoned to the tribune to deal in the miserable follies and falsehoods which now pervade the land? At this moment, from every city, and state, and village, and town and hamlet in the Union, ascends one common voice of self-delusion and deception. You hear, on all hands, a general congratulation of themselves and one another, about our peace, and prosperity and harmony About our prosperity a great deal may be said honestly, if not about its honesty. Never did a people so easily and excellently clothe and feed themselves. Our ancestors were very poor devils, compared to ourselves, in respect to their acquisitions Their very best luxuries are not now to be enumerated, except among our meanest and commonest possessions; and, without being better men, our humblest citizens enjoy a domestic condition which would have made the mouths to water, with equal delight and envy, of the proudest barons of the days of Queen Bess and Harry the Eighth. What would either of these princes have given to enjoy ices such as Captain Berry gave us yesterday, and the more various luxuries which (I see it in his face) he proposes to give us to-day! What would the best potentates, peers and princes of Europe, even at this day, give to be always sure of such oysters as expose themselves, with all their wealth of fat, buried to the chin, about the entrances of our harbors, from Sandy Hook to Savannah, in preference to the contracted fibres and coppery-flavored substitutes which they are forced to swallow, instead of the same admirable and benevolent ocean vegetable, as we commonly enjoy it here. And what—O Americans!—can they offer in exchange for the pear, the peach, the apple and the melon, such as I already taste, in anticipation of events which shall take place in this very vessel some two hours hence? It is enough, without enumerating more of our possessions—possessions in the common enjoyment of our people—that I insist on the national prosperity.

"But this is our misfortune. We are *too* prosperous. We are like Jeshuran, of whom we read in the blessed volume, who, waxing too fat, finally kicked. Fatal kicking! Foolish Jeshuran! In our fatness—in our excess of good fortune—we are kicking ungraciously, like him; and we shall most likely, after the fashion of the ungracious cow of which the Book of Fables tells us, kick over the bucket after we have fairly filled it.

"We admit the prosperity: but where's the peace? It is in the very midst of this prosperity that we hear terrible cries from portions of our country, where they have not yet well succeeded in casting off the skins of their original savage condition. There's Bully Benton, and Big-Bone Allen, and Humbug Houston, and Little Lion Douglass, and Snaky-Stealing Seward, and Copper-Captain Cass, and a dozen others, of bigger breeches than brains, and mightier maws than muscles—hear how they severally roar and squeak!* One would cut the carotid of corpu-

---

* Of course we are not responsible for the complimentary estimates here made of our men of mark, by our Alabama orator. We are simply acting as reporters, and taking down his language, *verbatim et literatim.*

lent John Bull; another would swallow the mines of Mexico; a third would foul the South, a fourth the North; and they are all for kicking up a pretty d——d fuss generally, expecting the people to foot the bill.

"And now, with such an infernal hubbub in our ears, on every side, from these bomb-bladders, should there be peace among us? We cry 'peace' when there is no peace! Their cry is 'war,' even in the midst of prosperity, and when short-cotton is thirteen cents a pound! And war for what? As if we had not prosperity enough, and a great deal too much, shipmates, since we do not know what to do with it, and employ such blatherskites as these to take it into their ridiculous keeping. In so many words, shipmates, these Beasts of Babylon, representing us poor boobies of America, are each of them, professedly on our part, playing the part of Jeshuran the Fat! They are kicking lustily, and will, I trust, be kicked over in the end, and before the end, and kicked out of sight, by that always-avenging destiny, which interposes, at the right moment, to settle accounts with blockhead statesmen and blockhead nations.

"Now, how are we to escape our own share of this judgment of Jeshuran? Who shall say how long it will be before we set our heels against the bucket, and see the green fields of our liberties watered with the waste of our prosperities! (I'm not sure of the legitimacy of this figure, but can't stop now to analyze it. We'll discuss it hereafter before the Literary Club of Charleston, which is said to be equally famous for its facts and figures.) But, so long as it is doubtful if we shall escape this disaster—so long as the future is still *in nubibus*, and these clouds are so full of growl and blackness—we may reasonably doubt if our prosperity is either secure or perfect. Certainly, it is not yet time either for its history or eulogy.

"But for our peace, our harmony, if not our prosperity?

"Believing ourselves prosperous, as we all do and loudly asseverate, and there should be no good reason why harmony should not be ours. But this harmony is of difficult acquisition, and we must first ask, my brethren, what is harmony?

"When we sit down to dinner to-day, it is in the confident expectation that harmony will preside over the banquet. There is no good reason why it should be otherwise. There will be ample at the feast for all the parties. Each will get enough, and probably of the very commodity he desires. If he does not, it is only because there is not quite enough for all, and the dish happens to be nearer me than him! Nevertheless, we take for granted that harmony will furnish the atmosphere of the feast to-day. It will render grateful the various dishes of which we partake. It will assist us in their digestion. We will eat and drink in good humor, and rise in good spirits. Each one will entertain and express his proper sentiments, and, as our mutual comfort will depend upon a gentlemanly conduct, so no one will say or do anything to make his neighbor feel uncomfortable. If you know that the person next to you has a corn upon his toe, you will not tread on it in order to compel his attention to your wants; and, should you see another about to swallow a moderate mouthful of cauliflower, it will not be your care to whisper a doubt if the disquiet of the person in the adjoining cabin was not clearly the result of cabbage and cholera. This forbearance is the secret of harmony, and I trust we shall this day enjoy it as the best salad to our banquet.

"And now, how much of this harmony is possessed among our people in the states? Are you satisfied that there is any such feeling prevailing in the nation, when, in all its states, it assembles in celebration of this common anniversary? Hearken to the commentary. Do you hear that mighty *hellabaloo* in the East? It comes from Massachusetts Bay. It is just such an uproar as we have heard from that quarter for a hundred years. First, it fell upon the ears of the people of Mohegan, and Naraganset, and Coneaughtchoke—the breechless Indians—and it meant massacre. The Indians perished by sword-cut and arquebus-shot and traffic—scalps being bought at five shillings per head, till the commodity grew too scarce for even cupidity to make capital with. Very brief, however, was the interval that followed. Our Yankee brethren are not the people to suffer their neighbors to be long at peace, or to be themselves pacific. Very soon, and there was another *hellabaloo!* The victims this time were the Quakers; and they had to fly from a region of so much prosperity, using their best legs, in order to keep their simple scalps secure under their broad brims. What was to be done to find food for the devouring appetite of these rabid wretches, who so well discriminated always as to seek their victims in the feeble, and rarely suffered their virtues to peril their own skins. They turned next, full-mouthed, upon the old women, and occasionally upon the young. At the new *hellabaloo* of these saints, these poor devils—and, unluckily, the devils whom they were alleged to serve were too poor to bring them any succor— were voted to be witches; they were cut off by cord and fire, until the land was purged of all but its privileged sinners.

"Short, again was the rest which these godly savages gave themselves or their neighbors. The poor Gothamites next fell beneath the ban, and the simple Dutchmen of Manhattan were fain to succumb under the just wrath of the God-appointed race. And now, all the neighboring peoples being properly subjected, the *hellabaloo* was raised against the cavaliers who dwelt south of the Potomac.

"These were ancient enemies of the saints in the mother-country. But there had been reasons hitherto for leaving them undisturbed. They had been good customers. They had been the receivers of the stolen goods brought them by these wise men of the East, and did not then know that the seller could give no good title to the property he sold. As long as our cavalier continued to buy the African, the saints hinted not a word about the imperfectness of the title. It was only when he refused to buy any more of the commodity that he was told it was stolen.

"And now the hellabaloo is raised against all those having the stolen goods in possession. Does this *hellabaloo* sound like harmony, my brethren? and don't you think there will be an answering hellabaloo to this, which will tend still more to disturb the harmonies? And, with these wild clamors in our ear, rocking the nation from side to side, who is it that cries 'peace! peace! peace!' when there is no peace? Am I to be made the echo of a falsehood? Shall my lips repeat the silly commonplace which cheats nobody, and persuades nobody, and makes nobody repent? No, my brethren! Let us speak the truth. There is no peace, no harmony, no union among us. As a people, we are already sundered. We now hate and strive against each other; and, until we come back to justice—to the recognition of all those first principles which led our ancestors into a league, offensive and defensive, for a common object and with a common necessity,—the breach will widen and widen, until a great gulf shall spread between us, above which Death will hang ever with his black banner; and across which terror, and strife, and vengeance, shall send their unremitting bolts of storm and fire! Let us pray, my brethren, that, in regard to our harmony, we arrest our prosperity, lest we grow too fat, and kick like Jeshuran!"

Here a pause. Our orator was covered with perspiration. He hemmed thrice with emphasis. He had reached a climax. The Texan was sleeping audibly, giving forth sounds like an old alligator at the opening of the spring. Our few Yankee voyagers had arisen some time before, not liking the atmosphere, and were now to be seen with the telescope, looking out into the East for dry land. The orator himself seemed satisfied with the prospect. He saw that his audience were in the right mood to be awakened. He wiped his face accordingly, put on his green spectacles, and in a theatrical aside to the steward—

"Hem! steward! another touch of the snake and tiger."

I do not know that I need give any more of this curious oration, which was continued to much greater length, and discussed a most amusing variety of subjects, not omitting that of Communism, and Woman's Rights. Know-Nothingism had not then become a fixed fact in the political atmosphere, or it would, probably, have found consideration also.

Very mixed were the feelings with which the performance was greeted. Our secessionists from South Carolina and other states, of whom there were several on board, were quite satisfied with our orator's view of the case; but our Yankees, reappearing when it was fairly over, were not in the mood to suffer it to escape without sharp censure. The orator was supposed to have made a very unfair use of the occasion and of his own appointment. But the orator was not a customer with whom it was politic to trifle; and as he seemed disposed to show his teeth, more than once, the discussion was seasonably arrested by the call to dinner.

They live well on the steamers between New York and Charleston. Both cities know something of good living, and in neither is the taste for turtle likely to die out. Why is the breed of aldermen so little honored in either? Our captain is proverbially a person who can sympathize duly with the exigencies of appetite, and his experience in providing against them has made him an authority at the table. Ordinarily admirable, our dinner on the *glorious Fourth* was worthy of the occasion. The committee of arrangements had duly attended to their duties.

The time at length arrived for that interchange of mortal and mental felicities which the literary stereotypists describe as the feast of reason and the flow of soul; and sentiment was to be indulged. Our excellent captain, sweetness in all his looks, homage in his eye, in every action dignity and grace, filling his glass, bowed to a stately matron, one of our few lady-passengers —

"The pleasure of a glass of wine with you, madam."

"Thank you, captain, but I never take wine," was the reply.

"Perfectly right, madam," put in the orator of the day; "Though written that wine cheereth the heart of man it is nowhere said that it will have any such effect on the heart of woman."

There was a little by-play after this, between the orator and the lady, the latter looking and speaking as if half disposed now to take the wine, if only to prove that its effects might be as cheering to the one sex as to the other. But the captain rising, interrupted the episode.

"Fill your glasses, gentlemen."

All charged," cried the vice.

1. *The day we celebrate!* — Dear to us only as the memorial of an alliance between nations, which was to guaranty protection justice, and equal rights, to all.

The batteries being opened, the play went on without interruption: I shall go on with the toasts. *seriatim*

2. *The Constitution.*—Either a bond for all, or a bond for none. Not surely such a web as will bind fast the feeble, and through which the strong may break away without restraint.

3. *The Union.*— The perfection of harmony, if, as it was designed to be, in the language of Shakspeare, — the "unity and married calm of States."—

4. *The Slave States of the South.*—The conservators of the peace, where faction never rears its head, where mobs tear not down, nor burn, nor destroy the hopes and habitations of the peaceful and the weak, and where reverence in the people is still the guarantee for a gentleman in the politician.

5. *The Agriculture of the South.*—The source of peace, hospitality, and those household virtues, which never find in business a plea against society.

6. *Cotton and Corn.*— The grand pacificators, which in *covering* and *lining* the poor of Europe, bind their hands with peace, and fill their hearts with gratitude.

7. *Washington.*— A Southron and a slaveholder—pious without cant; noble without arrogance; brave without boast; and generous without ostentation!—When the Free-Soilers shall be able to boast of such a citizen and son, it may be possible to believe them honest in their declarations, and unselfish in their objects — but not till then.

8. *The President of the United States.*—We honor authority and place; but let authority see that it do honor to itself. Let no man suppose that he shall play the puppet in his neighbors' hands, and not only escape the shame thereof, but win the good name of skilful play for himself. He who would wield authority, must show himself capable of rule; and he who has famously borne the sword, must beware lest other men should use his truncheon.

[*Par Parenthese.*— Brave old Zachary Taylor was the reigning president when this toast was given.

9. *The Native State.*—Yours or mine, no matter. We are all linked indissolubly, by a strange and more than mortal tie, to a special soil. To that soil does the true soul always hold itself firmly bound in a fidelity that loves to toil in its improvement, and will gladly die in its defence.

10. *Woman.* — Whether as the virgin she wins our fancies, as the wife our hearts, as the mother our loyalty, still, in all, the appointed angel to minister to our cares, to inspirit our hopes, to train our sensibilities, and to lift our sympathies, to the pure, the gentle, the delicate, and the true.

11. *Our Slaves.*—Like our children, minors in the hands of the guardian, to be protected and trained to usefulness and virtue

— to be taught service and obedience — love and loyalty — to be nurtured with a care that never wrongs, and governed by a rule that simply restrains the excesses of humanity.

12. *Our Captain and his Ship.*— A good husband for such a wife.— he lets her steam it, but keeps her in stays; — she may boil up, but never keeps the house in hot water — and all the *hellabaloo* finally ends in smoke. If she keeps up a racket below, he at least, trumpet in hand, walks the decks, and is still the master. May he always keep her to her bearings, and never suffer her to grow so old, as, like some other old woman, to become past bearing.

Here, the captain, overcome with emotion, his face covered with blushes, rose, and after the fierce plaudits of the table had subsided, replied in the most eloquent language to the compliment, concluding thus—

"And while I remain the master of this goodly creature, gentlemen, let me assure you, she will never discredit her breeding, certainly never while she continues to bear such children as I have the honor to see before me. Gentlemen, I give you—

"*The Fair*— Equally precious as fair weather, fair play, and fair women. While deriving from these the best welfare of the heart, may we be called upon to bid them *farewell* only when it is decreed that we shall *fare* better."

The regular toasts were resumed and concluded with the thirteenth :—

13. *The Orator of the Day.*— He hath put the chisel to the seam, the wedge to the split, the hammer to the head, the saddle on the horse. He has spoken well and wisely, and decently, without the *hellabaloo* which usually marks a fourth of July oration. Let him be honored with the mark of greatness, and if there be a place in senate and assembly which it would not discredit a wise man and a gentleman to occupy, send him thither.

Our orator was again on his feet. His green spectacles under them at the same moment — and, such a speech in reply : — there is no reporting it, but if Alabama does not yet ring with the voice of that nondescript, then hath she lost the taste for racy matters.

It will be seen that, thus far, the secessionists have pretty much had the affair in their own hands: and our brethren north of the Hudson were not in the best of humors — were somewhat *riled*, indeed, by the character of the oration and the toasts that followed. They attempted to reply, in the volunteer toasts which they offered, quoting Daniel Webster and others very freely, but without much visible effect. For once, the majority was against them. Our space will not suffice to report their toasts, the answers, or the discussions which ensued; but it is doing them justice only to give one of the several volunteer songs which were sung in honor of the Union. The secessionists had a poet on board, but his muse was suffering from sea-sickness or some other malady. She was certainly reluctant and made no sign. The lay that I give might have issued from the mint of Joel Barlow for aught I know: —

UNION AND LIBERTY.

[*Sung by a tall person in nankin pantaloons.*]

Oh, dear was the hour when Liberty rose,
   And gallant the freemen who came at her call,
Sublime was the vengeance she took on her foes,
   And mighty the blow which released her from thrall
     Down from its realm of blue,
     Proudly our Eagle flew,
Perched on our banner and guided us on;
     While from afar they came,
     Brave souls with noble aim,
Where at the price of blood, freedom was wooed and won

Ours was no trophy, the conquest of power,
   Heedless if triumph were sanctioned by right
We took not up arms in infuriate hour
   Nor thirsting for spoil hurried forth to the fight:
     Led by the noblest cause,
     Fighting for rights and laws,
Panting for freedom our fathers went forth;
     Nor for themselves alone,
     Struck they the tyrant down,
They fought and they bled for the nations of earth.

And dear be the freedom they won for our nation,
   And firm be the Union that freedom secures;
Let no parricide hand seek to pluck from its station,
   The flag that streams forth in its pride from our shores;
     May no son of our soil,
     In inglorious toil,

>   Assail the bright emblem that floats on our view.
>   Let not that standard quail,
>   Let not those stripes grow pale,
>   Take not one star from our banner of blue.

Pretty sharp were the criticisms of this ode on the part of our secessionists.

"It halts and hobbles like the Union itself," was the sneer of one.

"In truth," said another, "it is ominous, lacking, here and there, some very necessary feet."

"Its measures, like those of government are admirably unequal."

In short, politically, poetically, morally, and musically, the poor *ode* was declared, by a punster present, to be certainly within poetic rule, as it was decidedly *odeous*. At this—unkindest cut of all—the unhappy singer—author, too, perhaps—was suddenly seized with sea-sickness, and disappeared on deck. The day was at its close as we left the table. We came forth to enjoy a delicious sunset, and I was then officially notified that a story was expected from me that night. My turn had come. The ladies were graciously pleased to command that I should give them a tale of the Revolution, as appropriate to the day, and, after a fine display of fireworks, we composed ourselves in the usual circle, and I delivered myself of the following narrative, which I need not say to those who know me was founded on fact:—

THE BRIDE OF THE BATTLE.

A TALE OF THE REVOLUTION

CHAPTER I.

To the reader who, in the pursuit of the facts in our national history, shall confine himself only to those records which are to be found in the ordinary narrative, much that he reads will be found obscure, and a great deal absolutely untruthful. Our early historians gave themselves but little trouble in searching after details. A general outline was all that they desired, and satisfied with this, they neither sought after the particular events which should give rise to the narrative, nor into the latent causes which gave birth to many of its actions. In the history of South Carolina, for example, (which was one brimming with details and teeming with incidents,) there is little to be found—as the history is at present written—which shall afford to the reader even a tolerably correct idea of the domestic character of the struggle. We know well enough that the people of the colony were of a singularly heterogeneous character; that the settlers of the lower country were chiefly Cavaliers and Huguenots, or French Protestants, and that the interior was divided into groups, or settlements, of Scotch, Irish, and German. But there is little in the record to show that, of these, the sentiment was mixed and various without degree; and that, with the exception of the parishes of the lower country, which belonged almost wholly, though with slight modifications, to the English church, it was scarcely possible to find any neighborhood, in which there was not something like a civil war. The interior and mountain settlements were most usually divided, and nearly equally, between their attachments to the crown and the colony. A Scotch settlement would make an almost uniform showing in behalf of the English authority—one, two, or three persons, at the utmost, being of the revolutionary party. An Irish settlement (wholly Protestant, be it remembered) would be as unanimous for the colonial movements; while the Germans were but too frequently for the monarchical side, that being represented by a prince of Hanover. The German settlements mostly lay in the Forks of Edisto, and along the Congarees. The business of the present narrative will be confined chiefly to this people. They had settled in rather large families in Carolina, and this only a short period before the Revolution. They had been sent out, in frequent instances, at the expense of the crown, and this contributed to secure their allegiance. They were ignorant of the nature of the struggle, and, being wholly agricultural, could not well be taught the nature of grievances which fell chiefly upon commerce and the sea-board. Now, in Carolina, and perhaps throughout the whole south, the Revolution not only originated with the natives of the country, but with the educated portions of the natives. It was what may be termed the gentlemen of the colony—its wealth and aristocracy—with whom and which the movement began; and though it is not our purpose here to go into this inquiry, we may add that the motives to the revolutionary movement originated with them, in causes totally different from those which stimulated the patriotism of the people of Massachusetts Bay. The pride of place, of character and of intellect, and not any considerations of interest, provoked the agricultural gentry of the south into the field.

It was the earnest desire of these gentry, at the dawning of the Revolution, to conciliate the various people of the interior. At the first signs of the struggle, therefore, an attempt was made to influence the German population along the Edisto and Congaree, by sending among them two influential men of their own country, whose fidelity to the *movement* party was beyond dispute. But these men were unsuccessful. They probably made few converts. It is enough, if we give a glimpse at the course of their proceedings in a single household in the Forks of Edisto.* George Wagner and Felix Long arrived at the habitation of Frederick Sabb, on the 7th day of July, 1775. Frederick was an honest Dutchman of good character, but not the man for revolution. He was not at home on the arrival of the commissioners, but his good *vrow*, Minnicker Sabb, gave them a gracious reception. She was a good housekeeper, with but one daughter; a tall, silent girl, with whom the commissioners had no discourse. But Minnicker Sabb, had *she* been applied to, might have proved a better revolutionist than her spouse. It is very certain, as the results will show, that Frederica Sabb, the daughter, was of the right material. She was a calm, and sweetly-minded damsel, not much skilled in society or books — for precious little was the degree of learning in the settlement at this early period; but the native mind was good and solid, and her natural tastes, if unsophisticated, were pure and elevated. She knew, by precious instincts, a thousand things which other minds scarcely ever reach through the best education. She was what we call, a good girl, loyal, with a warm heart, a sound judgment, and a modest, sensible behavior. We are not seeking, be it remembered, a heroine, but a pure, true-hearted woman. She was young too — only seventeen at this period — but just at the season when the

---

* So called from the branching of the river at a certain point — the country between the two arms being called the Forks, and settled chiefly by Germans.

woman instincts are most lively, and her susceptibilities most quick to all that is generous and noble. She made the cakes and prepared the supper for the guests that evening, and they saw but little of her till the evening feast had been adjusted, and was about to be discussed. By this time old Frederick Sabb had made his appearance. He came, bringing with him three of his neighbors, who were eager to hear the news. They were followed, after a little space, and in season for supper, by another guest—perhaps the most welcome of all to the old couple—in the person of a favorite preacher of the methodist persuasion. Elijah Fields, was a man of middle age, of a vigorous mind and body, earnest and impetuous, and represented, with considerable efficiency, in his primitive province, the usefulness of a church which, perhaps, more than any other, has modelled itself after that of the Primitive Fathers. We shall see more of Elijah Fields hereafter. In the course of the evening, three other neighbors made their appearance at the farmhouse of Frederick Sabb; making a goodly congregation upon which to exercise the political abilities of Messrs. Wagner and Long. They were all filled with a more or less lively curiosity in regard to the events which were in progress, and the objects which the commissioners had in view. Four of these neighbors were of the same good old German stock with Frederick Sabb, but two of them were natives of the country, from the east bank of the north branch of the Edisto, who happened to be on a visit to an adjoining farmstead. The seventh of these was a young Scotchman, from Cross Creek, North Carolina, who had already declared himself very freely against the revolutionary movement. He had, indeed, gone so far as to designate the patriots as traitors, deserving a short cord and a sudden shrift; and this opinion was expressed with a degree of temper which did not leave it doubtful that he would gladly seek an opportunity to declare himself offensively in the presence of the commissioners. As we shall see more of this person hereafter, it is only right that we should introduce him formally to the reader as Matthew or Mat Dunbar. He went much more frequently by the name of Mat than Matthew. We may also mention that he was not entirely a politician. A feeling of a tender nature brought him to the dwelling of old Sabb, upon whose daughter, Frederica, our young Scotch man was supposed to look with hungry eyes. And public conjecture did not err in its suspicions.

But Mat Dunbar was not without a rival. Richard Coulter was the only native of the country present, Parson Fields excepted. He was a tall, manly youth, about the same age with Dunbar. But he possessed many advantages over the latter, particularly in respect to person. Tall, while Dunbar was short, with a handsome face, fine eye, and a luxuriant shock of hair, and a massive beard of the same color, which gave quite a martial appearance to his features, otherwise effeminate—the spectator inevitably contrasted him with his rival, whose features, indeed, were fair, but inexpressive; and whose hair and beard were of the most burning and unmitigated red. Though stout of limb, vigorous and athletic, Mat Dunbar was awkward in his movement, and wanting in dignity of bearing. Mentally, the superiority of Coulter was not so manifest. He was more diffident and gentle than the other, who, experienced by travel, bold and confident, never exhibited himself at less than his real worth. These preliminaries must suffice. It is perhaps scarcely necessary to say that Frederica Sabb made *her* comparisons between the two, and very soon arrived at one conclusion. A girl of common instincts rarely fails to discover whether she is sought or not; and the same instincts leads her generally to determine between rivals long in advance of the moment when they propose. Richard Coulter was certainly her favorite—though her prudence was of that becoming kind which enabled her easily to keep to herself the secret of her preference.

Old Sabb treated his guests with good Dutch hospitality. His wife and daughter were excellent housekeepers, and the table was soon spread with good things for supper. Butter, milk, and cream-cheeses, were not wanting; pones and hoe-cakes made an ample showing, and a few broiled chickens, and a large platter of broiled ham, in the centre of the table, were as much a matter of course in that early day, in this favorite region, as we find them among its good livers now. Of course, supper was allowed to be discussed before the commissioners opened their budget. Then the good *vrow* took her place, knitting in hand, and a huge ball of cotton in her lap, at the door, while the guests emerged from the hall into the piazza, and sweet Frederica Sabb quietly, as was her habit, proceeded to put away the *debris* of the feast, and to restore the apartment to its former order. In this she was undisturbed by either of her lovers; the custom of the country requiring that she should be left to these occupations without being embarrassed by any obtrusive sentiments, or even civilities. But it might be observed that Richard Coulter had taken his seat in the piazza, at a window looking into the hall, while Mat Dunbar had placed himself nearly at the entrance, and in close neighborhood with the industrious dame. Here he divided himself between attentions to her, and an occasional dip into the conversation on politics, which was now fully in progress. It is not our purpose to pursue this conversation. The arguments of the commissioners can be readily conjectured. But they were fruitless to persuade our worthy Dutchman into any change, or any self-committals, the issue of which might endanger present comforts and securities. He had still the same answer to every argument, delivered in broken English which we need not imitate.

"The king, George, has been a good king to me, my friends. I was poor, but I am not poor now. I had not a finger of land before I came hither. Now, I have good grants, and many acres. I am doing well. For what should I desire to do better? The good king will not take away my grants; but if I should hear to you, I should be rebel, and then he would be angry, and he might make me poor again as I never was before. No, no, my friends; I will sign no association that shall make me lose my lands."

"You're right!" vociferated Mat Dunbar. "It's treason, I say, to sign any association, and all these rangers here, in arms, are in open rebellion, and should be hung for it; and let the time come, and I'm one to help in the hanging them!"

This was only one of many such offensive speeches which Dunbar had contrived to make during the evening. The commissioners contented themselves with *marking* the individual, but without answering him. But his rudely-expressed opinions were not pleasing to old Sabb himself, and still less so to his worthy *vrow*, who withdrew at this into the hall; while the stern voice of Elijah Fields descended in rebuke upon the offender.

"And who art thou," said he abruptly, "to sit in judgment

upon thy brethren? And who has commissioned thee to lend thyself to the taking of human life? Life is a sacred thing, young man—the most precious of human possessions, since it depends on the time which is allowed us whether we shall ever be fit for eternity. To one so young as thyself, scarcely yet entered on thy career as a man, it might be well to remember that modesty is the jewel of youth, and that when so many of the great and good of the land have raised their voices against the oppressions of the mother-country, there may be good reason why we, who know but little, should respect them, and listen till we learn. If thou wilt be counselled by me, thou wilt hearken patiently to these worthy gentlemen, that we may know all the merits of their argument."

Dunbar answered this rebuke with a few muttered sentences, which were hardly intelligible, making no concessions to the preacher or the commissioners, yet without being positively offensive. Richard Coulter was more prudent. He preserved a profound silence. But he was neither unobservant nor indifferent. As yet he had taken no side in the controversy, and was totally uncommitted among the people. But he had been a listener, and was quietly chewing the cud of self-reflection.

After a little while, leaving the venerable seniors still engaged in the discussion—for Wagner and Long, the commissioners, were not willing to forego the hope of bringing over a man of Sabb's influence—the young men strolled out into the grounds where their horses had been fastened. It was almost time to ride. As they walked, the Scotchman broke out abruptly:—

"These fellows ought to be hung, every scoundrel of them; stirring up the country to insurrection and treason; but a good lesson of hickories, boys, might put a stop to it quite as well as the halter! What say you? They ride over to old Carter's after they leave Daddy Sabb's, and it's a lonesome track! If you agree, we'll stop 'em at Friday's flats, and trice 'em up to a swinging limb. We're men enough for it, and who's afraid?"

The proposition was received with great glee by all the young fellows, with one exception. It was a proposition invoking sport rather than patriotism. When the more eager responses were all received, Richard Coulter quietly remarked:—

"No, no, boys; you must do nothing of the kind. These are good men, and old enough to be the fathers of any of us. Besides, they're strangers, and think they're doing right. Let 'em alone."

"Well, if you wont," said Dunbar, "we can do without you. There are four of us, and they're but two."

"You mistake," replied Coulter, still quietly, "they are three!"

"How! who?"

"Wagner, Long, and Richard Coulter!"

"What, you! Will you put yourself against us? You go with the rebels, then?"

"I go with the strangers. I don't know much about the rebellion, but I think there's good sense in what they say. At all events, I'll not stand by and see them hurt, if I can help it."

"Two or three, boys," continued Dunbar, "will make no difference!"

This was said with a significant toss of the head toward Coulter. The instincts of these young men were true. They already knew one another as rivals. This discovery may have determined the future course of Coulter. He did not reply to Dunbar; but, addressing his three companions, he said, calling each by his Christian name, "You, boys, had better not mix in this matter before it's necessary. I suppose the time will come, when there can be no skulking, But it's no use to hurry into trouble. As for four of you managing three, that's not impossible; but I reckon there will be a fight first. These strangers may have weapons; but whether they have or not, they look like men; and I reckon, you that know me, know that before my back tastes of any man's hickory, my knife will be likely to taste his blood."

Dunbar replied rudely for the rest; and, but that Coulter quietly withdrew at this moment, seemingly unruffled, and without making any answer, there might have been a struggle between the two rivals even then. But the companions of Dunbar had no such moods or motives as prompted him. They were impressed by what Coulter had said, and were, perhaps, quite as much under his influence as under that of Dunbar. They accordingly turned a cold shoulder upon all his exhortations, and the commissioners, accordingly, left the house of old Sabb in safety, attended by young Coulter. They little knew his object in escorting them to the dwelling of Bennett Carter, where they stayed that night, and never knew the danger from which his prompt and manly courage had saved them. But the events of that night brought out Richard Coulter for the cause of the patriots; and a few months found him a second lieutenant in a gallant corps of Thompson's rangers, raised for the defence of the colony. But the commissioners parted from Frederick Sabb without making any impression on his mind. He professed to desire to preserve a perfect neutrality—this being the suggestion of his selfishness; but his heart really inclined him to the support of the "goot King Jorge," from whom his grants of land had been derived.

"And what dost thou think, brother Fields?" said he to the parson, after the commissioners had retired.

"Brother Sabb," was the answer, "I do not see that we need any king any more than the people of Israel, when they called upon Samuel for one; and if we are to have one, I do not see why we should not choose one from out our own tribes."

"Brother Fields, I hope thou dost not mean to go with these rebels."

"Brother Sabb, I desire always to go with my own people."

"And whom callest thou our own people?"

"Those who dwell upon the soil and nurse it, and make it flourish; who rear their flocks and children upon it, in the fear of God, and have no fear of man in doing so."

"Brother Fields, I fear thou thinkst hardly of 'goot King Jorge,'" said our Dutchman, with a sigh. "Minnicker, my vrow, get you de Piple."

CHAPTER II.

WE pass over a long interval of quite three years. The vicissitudes of the Revolution had not materially affected the relations of the several parties to our narrative. During this period the patriots of South Carolina had been uniformly successful. They had beaten away the British from their chief city, and had invariably chastized the loyalists in all their attempts to make a diversion in favor of the foreign enemy. But events were changing. These performances had not been effected but at great sacrifice of blood and treasure, and a formidable British invasion found the state no longer equal to its defence. Charleston, the capital city, after frequent escapes, and a stout and protracted defence, had succumbed to the besiegers, who had now penetrated the interior, covering it with their strongholds, and coercing it with their arms. For a brief interval, all opposition to their progress seemed to be at an end within the state. She had no force in the field, stunned by repeated blows, and waiting, though almost hopeless of her opportunity. In the meantime, where was Richard Coulter? A fugitive, lying *perdu* either in the swamps of Edisto or Congaree, with few companions, all similarly reduced in fortune, and pursued with a hate and fury the most unscrupulous and unrelenting, by no less a person than Matthew Dunbar, now a captain of loyalists in the service of George the Third. The position of Coulter was in truth very pitiable; but he was not without his consolations. The interval which had elapsed since our first meeting with him, had ripened his intimacy with Frederica Sabb. His affections had not been so unfortunate as his patriotism. With the frank impulse of a fond and feeling heart, he had appealed to hers, in laying bare the secret of his own; and he had done so successfully. She, with as frank a nature, freely gave him her affections, while she did not venture to bestow on him her hand. His situation was not such as to justify their union, and her father positively forbade the idea of such a connection. Though not active among the loyalists, he was now known to approve of their sentiments; and while giving them all the aid and comfort in his power, without actually showing himself in armor, he as steadily turned a cold and unwilling front to the patriots, and all those who went against the monarch.

The visits of Richard Coulter to Frederica were all stolen ones, perhaps not the less sweet for being so. A storm sometimes brought him forth at nightfall from the shelter of the neighboring swamp, venturing abroad at a time when loyalty was supposed to keep its shelter. But these visits were always accompanied by considerable peril. The eye of Matthew Dunbar was frequently drawn in the direction of the fugitive, while his passions were always eager in the desire which led him to seek for this particular victim. The contest was a well-known issue of life and death. The fugitive patriot was predoomed always to the halter, by those, who desired to pacify old revenges, or acquire new estates. Dunbar did not actually know that Coulter and Frederica Sabb were in the habit of meeting; but that they had met, he knew, and he had sworn their detection. He had become a declared suitor of that maiden, and the fears of old Sabb would not suffer him to decline his attentions to his daughter, or to declare against them. Dunbar had become notoriously an unmitigated ruffian. His insolence disgusted the old Dutchman, who, nevertheless, feared his violence and influence. Still, sustained by good old Minnicker Sabb, his *vrow*, the father had the firmness to tell Dunbar freely, that his daughter's affections should remain unforced; while the daughter herself, seeing the strait of her parents, was equally careful to avoid the final necessity of repulsing her repulsive suitor. She continued, by a happy assertion of maidenly dignity, to keep him at bay, without vexing his self-esteem; and to receive him with civility, without affording him positive encouragement. Such was the condition of things among our several parties, when the partisan war began; when the favorite native leaders in the south — the first panic of their people having passed — had rallied their little squads, in swamp and thicket, and were making those first demonstrations which began to disquiet the British authorities, rendering them doubtful of the conquests which they had so lately deemed secure. This, be it remembered, was after the defeat of Gates at Camden, when there was no sign of a Continental army within the state.

It was at the close of a cloudy afternoon, late in October, 1780, when Mat Dunbar, with a small command of eighteen mounted men, approached the well-known farmstead of Frederick Sabb. The road lay along the west bank of the eastern branch of the Edisto, inclining to or receding from the river, in correspondence with the width of the swamp, or the sinuosities of the stream. The farm of Sabb was bounded on one side by the river, and his cottage stood within a mile of it. Between, however, the lands were entirely uncleared. The woods offered a physical barrier to the malaria of the swamp; while the ground, though rich, was liable to freshet, and required a degree of labor in the drainage which it was not in the power of our good Dutchman to bestow. A single wagon-track led through the wood to the river from his house; and there may have been some half dozen irregular foot-paths tending in the same direction. When within half a mile from the house, Mat Dunbar pricked up his ears.

"That was surely the gallop of a horse," he said to his lieutenant — a coarse, ruffianly fellow like himself, named Clymes.

"Where away?" demanded the other.

"To the left. Put in with a few of the boys, and see what can be found."

Clymes did as he was bidden; but the moment he had disappeared, Dunbar suddenly wheeled into the forest also, putting spurs to his horse, and commanding his men to follow and scatter themselves in the wood. A keen suspicion was at the bottom of his sudden impulse; and, with his pistol in his grasp, and his teeth set firmly, he darted away at a rate that showed the eagerness of the blood-hound, on a warm scent. In a few moments the wood was covered with his people, and their cries and halloes answering to each other, turned the whole solitude into a scene of the most animated life. Accustomed to *drive* the woods for deer, his party pursued the same habit in their present quest, enclosing the largest extent of territory, and gradually contracting their *cordon* at a given point. It was not long before a certain degree of success seemed to justify their pursuit. A loud shout from Clymes, his lieutenant, drew the impetuous Dunbar to the place, and there he found the trooper, with two others of the party, firmly confronted by no less a person than Frederica Sabb. The maiden was very pale, but her lips were closely compressed together, and her eyes lightened with an expression which was not so much indicative of anger as of courage and resolve. As Dunbar rode up, she addressed him.

"You are bravely employed, Captain Dunbar, in hunting with your soldiers a feeble woman."

"In faith, my dear Miss Sabb, we looked for very different game," replied the leader, while a sardonic smile played over his visage. "But perhaps you can put us in the way of finding it. You are surely not here alone!"

"And why not? You are within hail of my father's dwelling."

"But yours, surely, are not the tastes for lonely walks."

"Alas! sir, these are scarcely the times for any other."

"Well, you must permit me to see that your walks are in no danger from intrusion and insult. You will, no doubt, be confounded to hear that scattered bands of the rebels are supposed to be, even now, closely harbored in these swamps. That villain, Coulter, is known to be among them. It is to hunt up these outlyers—to protect you from their annoyances, that I am here now."

"We can readily dispense with these services, Captain Dunbar. I do not think that we are in any danger from such enemies, and in this neighborhood."

It was some effort to say this calmly.

"Nay, nay, you are quite too confident, my dear Miss Sabb. You know not the audacity of these rebels, and of this Richard Coulter in particular. But let me lay hands on him! You will hardly believe that he is scarce ten minutes gone from this spot. Did you not hear his horse?"

"I heard no horses but your own."

"There it is! You walk the woods in such abstraction that you hear not the danger, though immediately at your ears. But disperse yourselves in pursuit, my merry men, and whoso brings me the ears of this outlaw, shall have ten guineas, in the yellow gold itself. No continental sham! Remember, his ears, boys! We do not want any prisoners. The trouble of hanging them out of the way is always wisely saved by a sabre-cut or pistol-bullet. There, away!"

The countenance of Frederica Sabb instantly assumed the keenest expression of alarm and anxiety. Her whole frame began to be agitated. She advanced to the side of the ruffianly soldier, and put her hand up appealingly.

"Oh! Captain Dunbar, will you not please go home with me, you and your men? It is now our supper-hour, and the sun is near his setting. I pray you, do not think of scouring the woods at this late hour. Some of your people may be hurt."

"No danger, my dear—all of them are famous fox-hunters."

"There is no danger to us, believe me. There is nobody in the woods that we fear. Give yourself no trouble, nor your men"

"Oh, you mistake! there is surely some one in this wood who is either in your way or mine—though you heard no horse."

"Oh! now I recollect, sir, I did hear a horse, and it seemed to be going in that direction."

Here the girl pointed below. The tory leader laughed outright.

"And so he went thither, did he? Well, my dear Miss Sabb, to please you, I will take up the hunt in the quarter directly opposite, since it is evident that your hearing just now is exceedingly deceptive. Boys, away! The back-track, hark you!—the old fox aims to double."

"Oh, go not—go not!" she urged, passionately.

"Will I not?" exclaimed the loyalist, gathering up his reins and backing his steed from her—"will I not? Away, Clymes,—away, boys; and remember, ten guineas for that hand which brings down the outlaw, Richard Coulter."

Away they dashed into the forest, scattering themselves in the direction indicated by their leader. Frederica watched their departure with an anxious gaze, which disappeared from her eyes the moment they were out of sight. In an instant all her agitation ceased.

"Now—thank Heaven for the thought!" she cried—"it will be quite dark before they find themselves at fault; and when they think to begin the search below, he will be wholly beyond their reach. But how to warn him against the meeting, as agreed on. The coming of this man forbids that. I must see—I must contrive it." And with these muttered words of half-meaning, she quietly made her way toward her father's dwelling, secure of the present safety of her lover from pursuit. She had very successfully practised a very simple *ruse* for his escape. Her apprehensions were only but admirably simulated; and, in telling Dunbar that the fugitive had taken one direction, she naturally relied on his doubts of her truth, to make him seek the opposite. She had told him nothing but the truth, but she had told it as a falsehood; and it had all the effect which she desired. The chase of the tory-captain proved unsuccessful.

CHAPTER III.

It was quite dark before Captain Dunbar reached the cottage of Frederick Sabb, and he did so in no good humor. Disappointed of his prey, he now suspected the simple *ruse* by which he had been deluded, and his first salutation of Frederica Sabb, as he entered the cottage, was in no friendly humor.

"There are certain birds, Miss Sabb," said he, "who fly far from their young ones at the approach of the hunter, yet make such a fuss and outcry, as if the nest were close at hand and in danger. I see you have learned to practise after their lessons."

The girl involuntarily replied: "But, indeed, Captain Dunbar, I heard the horse go below."

"I see you understand me," was the answer. I feel assured that you told me only the truth, but you had first put me in the humor not to believe it. Another time I shall know how to understand *you*."

Frederica smiled, but did not seek to excuse herself, proceeding all the while in the preparations for supper. This had been got in readiness especially for the arrival of Dunbar and his party. He, with Clymes, his first officer, had become inmates of the dwelling; but his troopers had encamped without, under instructions of particular vigilance. Meanwhile, supper proceeded, Sabb and his *vrow* being very heedful of all the expressed or conjectured wants of their arbitrary guests. It was while the repast was in progress that Dunbar fancied that he beheld a considerable degree of uneasiness in the manner and countenance of Frederica. She ate nothing, and her mind and eyes seemed equally to wander. He suddenly addressed her, and she started as from a dream, at the sound of her own name, and answered confusedly.

"Something's going wrong," said Dunbar, in a whisper, to Clymes; "we can put all right, however, if we try."

A significant look accompanied the whisper, and made the second officer observant. When supper was concluded, the captain of the loyalists showed signs of great weariness. He yawned and stretched himself amazingly, and without much regard to propriety. A like weariness soon after exhibited itself in the second officer. At length Dunbar said to Old Sabb, using a style of address to which the old man was familiar, "Well, Uncle Fred, whenever my bed's ready, say the word. I'm monstrous like sleep. I've ridden a matter of fifty miles to-day. In the saddle since four o'clock—and a hard saddle at that. I'm for sleep after supper."

The old man, anxious to please his guest, whom he now began rather to fear than favor, gave him soon the intimation which he desired, and he was conducted to the small chamber, in a shed-room adjoining the main hall, which had been assigned him on all previous occasions. Old Sabb himself attended his guest, while Lieutenant Clymes remained, for a while longer, the companion of the old lady and her daughter. Dunbar soon released his host from further attendance by closing the door upon him, after bowing him out with thanks. He had scarcely done so, before he approached one of the two windows in the chamber. He knew the secrets of the room, and his plan of operations had been already determined upon. Concealing his light, so that his shadow might not appear against the window, he quietly unclosed the shutter so as to rouse no attention by the sound. A great fig-tree grew near it, the branches, in some degree, preventing the shutter from going quite back against the wall. This afforded him additional cover to his proceedings, and he cautiously passed through the opening, and lightly descended to the ground. The height was inconsiderable, and he was enabled, with a small stick, to close the window after him. In another moment he passed *under* the house, which stood on logs four or five feet high, after the manner of the country, and took a crouching attitude immediately behind the steps in the rear of the building. From these steps to the kitchen was an interval of fifteen or eighteen yards, while the barn and other outhouses lay at convenient distances beyond. Shade-trees were scattered about, and fruit-trees, chiefly peach, rendering the space between something like a covered way. We need not inquire how long our captain of loyalists continued his watch in this unpleasant position. Patience, however, is quite as natural as necessary a quality to a temper at once passionate and vindictive. While he waited here, his lieutenant had left the house, scattered his men privily about the grounds, and had himself stolen to a perch, which enabled him to command the front entrance to the cottage. The only two means of egress were thus effectually guarded.

In a little time the household was completely quiet. Dunbar had heard the mutterings, from above, of the family prayers, in which it was no part of his profession to partake; and had heard the footsteps of the old couple as they passed through the passage-way to the chamber opposite the dining-hall. A chamber adjoining theirs was occupied by Frederica Sabb; but he listened in vain for her footsteps in that quarter. His watch was one calculated to try his patience, but it was finally rewarded. He heard the movement of a light foot over head, and soon the door opened in the rear of the dwelling, and he distinguished Frederica as she descended, step by step, to the ground. She paused, looked up and around her, and then, darting from tree to tree, she made her way to the kitchen, which opened at her touch. Here, in a whisper, she summoned to her side a negro—an old African who, we may at the same time mention, had been her frequent emissary before, on missions such as she now designed. Brough, as he was called, was a faithful Ebo, who loved his young mistress, and had shown himself particularly friendly to her *affaires de cœur*. She put a paper into his hands, and her directions employed few words.

"Brough, you must set off for Mass Richard, and give him this. You must keep close, or the soldiers will catch you. I don't know where they've gone, but no doubt they're scattered in the woods. I have told him, in this paper, not to come, as he promised; but should you lose the paper—"

"I no guine lose'em," said Brough seemingly rather displeased at the doubt, tacitly conveyed, of his carefulness.

"Such a thing might happen, Brough; nay, if you were to see any of the tories, you ought to destroy it. Hide it, tear it up, or swallow it, so that they won't be able to read it."

"I yerry, misses."

"Very good! And now, when you see Mass Richard, tell him not to come. Tell him better go farther off, across the fork, and across the other river; for that Mat Dunbar means to push after him to-morrow, and has sworn to hunt him up before he stops. Tell him, I beg him, for my sake, though he may not be afraid of that bad man, to keep out of his way, at least until he gathers men enough to meet him on his own ground."

The startling voice of Dunbar himself broke in upon the whispered conference. "Mat Dunbar is exceedingly obliged to you, Miss Sabb."

"Ah!" shrieked the damsel—"Brough—fly, fly, Brough." But Brough had no chance for flight.

"His wings are not sufficiently grown," cried the loyalist, with a brutal yell, as he grappled the old negro by the throat, and hurled him to the ground. In the next moment he possessed himself of the paper, which he read with evident disappointment. By this time the sound of his bugle had summoned his lieutenant, with half a dozen of his followers, and the kitchen was completely surrounded.

"Miss Sabb, you had best retire to the dwelling. I owe you no favors, and will remember your avowed opinion, this night, of Mat Dunbar. You have spoken. It will be for me yet to speak. Lieutenant Clymes, see the young lady home."

"But, sir, you will not maltreat the negro?"

"Oh! no! I mean only that he shall obey your commands. He shall carry this note to your favorite, just as you designed, with this difference only, that I shall furnish him with an escort."

"Ah!"

Poor Frederica could say no more. Clymes was about to hurry her away, when a sense of her lover's danger gave her strength.

"Brough," she cried to the negro; "you won't show where Mass Richard keeps?"

"Never show dem tory not'in', missis."

The close gripe of Dunbar's finger upon the throat of the negro stifled his further speech. But Frederica was permitted to see no more. The hand of Clymes was laid upon her arm, and she went forward promptly to save herself from indignity. She little knew the scene that was to follow.

CHAPTER IV.

The moment she had disappeared from the kitchen, the negro was taken forth by the captain of loyalists, who by this time had surrounded himself with nearly all his band. A single soldier had been stationed by Clymes between the house and kitchen, in order to arrest the approach of any of the whites from the former to the scene where Brough was about to undergo a certain painful ordeal. The stout old African, doggedly, with a single shake of his head, obeyed his captors, as they ordered him to a neighboring wood—a small copse of scrubby oaks, that lay between the settlement and the swamp forest along the river. Here, without delay, Brough was commanded, on pain of rope and hickory, to deliver up the secret of Richard Coulter's hiding-place. But the old fellow had promised to be faithful. He stubbornly refused to know or to reveal anything. The scene which followed is one that we do not care to describe in detail. The reader must imagine its particulars. Let it suffice that the poor old creature was haltered by the neck, and drawn up repeatedly to the swinging limb of a tree, until the moral nature, feeble at least, and overawed by the terrors of the last mortal agony, surrendered in despair. Brough consented to conduct the party to the hiding-place of Richard Coulter.

The savage nature of Matthew Dunbar was now in full exercise.

"Boot and saddle!" was the cry; and, with the negro, both arms pinioned, and running at the head of one of the dragoon's horses, leashed to the stirrup-leather, and in constant danger, should he be found tripping, of a sudden sabre cut, the whole party, with two exceptions, made their way down the country, and under the guidance of the African. Two of the soldiers had been placed in watch upon the premises, with instructions, however, to keep from sight, and not suffer their proximity to be suspected. But the suspicion of such an arrangement in existence was now natural enough to a mind, like that of Frederica Sabb, made wary by her recent misfortune. She was soon apprized of the departure of the loyalist troop. She was soon taught to fear from the weakness of poor Brough. What was to be done? Was her lover to be caught in the toils? Was she to become indirectly the agent of his destruction? She determined at all events to forego no effort by which to effect his escape. She was a girl of quick wit and prompt expedients. No longer exposing herself in her white cotton garments, she wrapped herself closely up in the great brown overcoat of her father, which buried her person from head to foot. She stole forth from the front entrance with cautious footsteps, employing tree and shrub for her shelter whenever they offered. In this way she moved forward to a spot inclining to the river, but taking an upward route, one which she naturally concluded had been left without a guard. But her objects required finally that she should change her course, and take the downward path, as soon as she could persuade herself that her progress was fairly under cover. Still she knew not but that she was seen, and perhaps followed, as well as watched. The spy might arrest her at the very moment when she was most hopeful of her object. How to guard against this danger? How to attain the necessary security? The question was no sooner formed than answered. Her way lay through a wilderness of leaves. The silent droppings from the trees for many years had accumulated around her, and their constant crinkling beneath her tread, drawing her notice to this source of fear, suggested to her the means of safety. There had not been a rain for many weeks. The earth was parched with thirst. The drought had driven the sap from shrub and plant; and just below, on the very route taken by the pursuing party, a natural meadow, a long, thin strip, the seat of a bayou or lake long since dried up, was covered with a rank forest of broom-grass, parched and dried by the sun. The wind was fresh, and driving right below. To one familiar with the effect of firing the woods in a southern country under such circumstances, the idea which possessed the mind of our heroine was almost intuitive. She immediately stole back to the house, her eagerness finding wings, which, however, did not betray her caution. The sentinels of Dunbar kept easy watch, but she had not been unseen. The cool, deliberate tory had more than once fitted his finger to the trigger of his horseman's pistol, as he beheld the approach toward him of the shrouded figure. But he was not disposed to show himself, or to give the alarm before he could detect the objects of his unknown visiter. Her return to the house was not beheld. He had lost sight of her in the woods, and fancied her still to be in the neighborhood. Unable to recover his clue, he still maintained his position waiting events.

It was not long before she reappeared upon the scene. He did not see the figure, until it crossed an open space, on his right, in the direction of the river. He saw it stoop to the earth, and he then bounded forward. His haste was injurious to his objects. He fell over the prostrate trunk of a pine, which had been thrown down for ranging timber only a few days before, and lay dark, with all its bark upon it, in the thick cover of the grass. His pistol went off in his fall, and before he could recover his feet, he was confounded to find himself threatened by a rapid rushing forest of flame, setting directly toward him. For a moment, the sudden blaze blinded him, and when he opened his eyes fully upon surrounding objects, he saw nothing human —nothing but the great dark shafts of pine, beneath which the fire was rushing with the roar and volume of swollen billows of the sea, breaking upon the shore which they promise to engulf. To save himself, to oppose fire to fire, or pass boldly through the flame where it burned most feebly, was now a first necessity; and we leave him to extricate himself as he may, while we follow the progress of Frederica Sabb. The flame which she had kindled in the dry grass and leaves, from the little old stable-lantern of the cottage, concealed beneath the great-coat of her father, had sufficed as a perfect cover to her movements. The fire swept below, and in the direction of the tory sentinels. The advance of the one, she had perceived, in the moment when she was communicating the blazing candle to the furze. She fancied she was shot when she heard the report of the pistol; but pressing her hand to her heart, the lantern still in her grasp, she darted headlong forward by one of the paths leading directly to the river. The fire was now raging over all the tract between her and the tory sentries. Soon, she descended from the pine ridge, and passed into the low flat land, strewed with gray cypresses, with their thousand *knees*, or abutments. The swamp was nearly dry. She found her way along a well-known path to the river, and from beneath a clump of shrouding willows, drew forth a little *dug-out*, the well-known cypress canoe of the country. This was a small egg shell-like structure, scarcely capable of holding two persons, which she was well accustomed to manage. At once she pushed boldly out into the broad stream. whose sweet rippling flow, a continuous and gentle murmur, was strangely broken by the intense roar and crackling of the fire as it swept the broad track of stubble, dry grass and leaves, which lay in its path. The lurid shadows sometimes passed over the surface of the stream, but naturally contributed to increase her shelter. With a prayer that was inaudible to herself, she invoked Heaven's mercy on her enterprise, as, with a strong arm, familiar in this exercise, she plied from side to side the little paddle which, with the favoring currents of the river, soon carried her down toward the bit of swamp forest where her lover found his refuge. The spot was well known to the maiden, though we must do her the justice to say she would never have sought for Richard Coulter in its depths, but in an emergency like the present. It was known as "Bear Castle," a close thicket covering a sort of promontory, three fourths of which was encircled by the river, while the remaining quarter was a deep swamp, through which, at high water, a streamlet forced its way, converting the promontory into an islet. It was unfortunate for Coulter and his party that, at this season the river was much lower than usual, and the swamp offered no security on the land side, unless from the denseness of the forest vegetation. It might now be passed dry shod.

The distance from "Bear Castle" to the farmstead of old Frederick Sabb, was, by land, but four or five miles. By water it was fully ten. If, therefore, the stream favored the progress of our heroine, the difference against Dunbar and his tories was more than equalled by the shorter route before him, and the start which he had made in advance of Frederica. But Brough was no willing guide. He opposed frequent difficulties to the distasteful progress, and, as they neared the spot, Dunbar found it necessary to make a second application of the halter before the good old negro could be got forward. The love of life, the fear of death, proved superior to his loyalty.

Brough could have borne any quantity of flogging—nay, he could, perhaps, have perished under the scourge without confessing, but his courage failed, when the danger was that of being launched into eternity. A shorter process than the cord or swinging limb would not have found him so pliant. With a choking groan he promised to submit, and, with heart swollen almost to bursting, he led the route, off from the main road now, and through the sinuous little foot-paths which conducted to the place of refuge of our patriots.

It was at this point, having ascertained what space lay between him and his enemy, that Dunbar dismounted his troopers. The horses were left with a guard, while the rest of his men, under his personal lead, made their further progress on foot. His object was a surprise. He designed that the negro should give the "usual" signal with which he had been taught to approach the camp of the fugitive; and this signal — a shrill whistle, three times sounded, with a certain measured pause between each utterance — was to be given when the swamp was entered over which the river, in high stages of the water, made its breach. These instructions were all rigidly followed. Poor Brough, with the rope about his neck, and the provost ready to fling the other end of the cord over the convenient arm of a huge sycamore under which they stood, was incapable of resistance. But his strength was not equal to his submission. His whistle was but feebly sounded. His heart failed him and his voice; and a repeated contraction of the cord, in the hands of the provost, was found essential to make him repeat the effort, and give more volume to his voice. In the meanwhile, Dunbar cautiously pushed his men forward. They passed through great hollows, where, at full water, the alligator wallowed; where the whooping crane sought his prey at nightfall; where the fox slept in safety, and the wild-cat in a favorite domain. "Bear Castle" was the fortress of many fugitives. Aged cypresses lay like the foundations of ancient walls along the path, and great thorny vines, and flaming, flowery creepers flaunted their broad streamers in the faces of the midnight gropers through their solitudes. The route would have been almost impassable during the day for men on horseback; it was a tedious and toilsome progress by night for men on foot. But Dunbar, nothing doubting of the proximity of his enemy, went forward with an eagerness which only did not forget its caution.

CHAPTER V.

The little party of Richard Coulter consisted of four persons besides himself. It was, perhaps, an hour before this that he sat apart from the rest conversing with one of his companions. This was no other than Elijah Fields, the methodist preacher. He had become a volunteer chaplain among the patriots of his own precinct, and one who, like the bishop of Beauvais, did not scruple to wield the weapons of mortal warfare as well as those of the church. It is true he was not ostentatious in the manner of the performance; and this, perhaps, somewhat increases its merit. He was the man for an emergency, forgetting his prayers when the necessity for blows was pressing, and duly remembering his prayers when the struggle was no longer doubtful. Yet Elijah Fields was no hypocrite. He was a true, strong-souled man, with blood, will, energies and courage, as well as devotion, and a strong passion for the soil which gave him birth. In plain terms, he was the patriot as well as the preacher, and his manhood was required for both vocations.

To him, Richard Coulter, now a captain among the partisans of Sumter, had unfolded the narrative of his escape from Dunbar. They had taken their evening meal; their three companions were busy with their arms and horses, grouped together in the centre of the camp. Our two principal persons occupied a little headland on the edge of the river, looking up the stream. They were engaged in certain estimates with regard to the number of recruits expected daily, by means of which Coulter was in hopes to turn the tables on his rival; becoming the hunter instead of the fugitive. We need not go over the grounds of their discussion, and refer to the general progress of events throughout the state. Enough to say that the Continental army, defeated under Gates, was in course of reorganization, and re-approaching under Greene; that Marion had been recently active and successful below; and that Sumter, defeated by Tarleton at Fishing creek, was rapidly recruiting his force at the foot of the mountains. Richard Coulter had not been utterly unsuccessful in the same business along the Edisto. A rendezvous of his recruits was appointed to take place on the ensuing Saturday; and, at this rendezvous, it was hoped that he would find at least thirty stout fellows in attendance. But we anticipate. It was while in the discussion of these subjects that the eyes of Coulter, still looking in the direction of his heart, were attracted by the sudden blaze which swept the forests, and dyed in lurid splendor the very face of heaven. It had been the purpose of Frederica Sabb, in setting fire to the undergrowth, not only to shelter her own progress, but in this way to warn her lover of his danger. But the effect was to alarm him for *her* safety rather than his own.

"That fire is at Sabb's place," was his first remark.

"It looks like it," was the reply of the preacher.

"Can it be that Dunbar has burnt the old man's dwelling?"

"Hardly!"

"He is not too good for it, or for anything monstrous. He has burnt others—old Rumph's—Ferguson's, and many more."

"Yes! but he prefers to own, and not destroy old Sabb's. As long as he has a hope of getting Frederica, he will scarcely commit such an outrage."

"But if she has refused him—if she answers him as she feels, scornfully—"

"Even then he will prefer to punish in a different way. He will rather choose to take the place by confiscation than burn it. He has never put that fire, or it is not at Sabb's, but this side of it, or beyond it."

"It may be the act of some drunken trooper. At all events, it requires that we should be on the look-out. I will scout it for a while and see what the mischief is. Do you, meanwhile, keep everything ready for a start."

"That fire will never reach us."

"Not with this wind, perhaps; but the enemy may. He evidently beat the woods after my heels this evening, and may be here to-morrow, on my track. We must be prepared. Keep the horses saddled and bitted, and your ears open for any summons. Ha! by heavens, that is Brough's signal now."

"Is it Brough's? If so, it is scarcely from Brough in a healthy state. The old fellow must have caught cold going to and fro at all hours in the service of Cupid."

Our preacher was disposed to be merry at the expense of our lover.

"Yes, it is Brough's signal, but feeble, as if the old fellow was really sick. He has probably passed through this fire, and has been choked with the smoke. But he must have an answer."

And, eager to hear from his beloved one, our hero gave his whistle in reply, and moved forward in the direction of the isthmus. The preacher, meanwhile, went toward the camp, quite prompt in the performance of the duties assigned him.

"He answers," muttered the tory captain; "the rebels are delivered to our hands!" And his preparations were sternly prosecuted to make a satisfactory finish to the adventure of the night. He, too, it must be remarked, though somewhat wondering at the blazing forest behind him, never for a moment divined the real origin of the conflagration. He ascribed it to accident, and, possibly, to the carelessness of one of the troopers whom he left as sentinels. With an internal resolution to make the fellow, if offending, familiar with the halberds, he pushed forward, as we have seen, till reaching the swamp; while the fire, obeying the course of the wind, swept away to the right of the path kept by the pursuing party, leaving them entirely without cause of apprehension from this quarter.

The plans of Dunbar, for penetrating the place of Coulter's refuge, were as judicious as they could be made under the circumstances. Having brought the troopers to the verge of the encampment, the negro was fastened to a tree by the same rope which had so frequently threatened his neck. The tories pushed forward, each with pistol cocked and ready in the grasp. They had scattered themselves abroad, so as to form a front sufficient to cover, at moderate intervals, the space across the isthmus. But, with the withdrawal of the immediate danger, Brough's courage returned to him, and, to the furious rage and discomfiture of Dunbar, the old negro set up on a sudden a most boisterous African howl—such a song as the Ebo cheers himself with when in the doubtful neighborhood of a jungle which may hide the lion or the tiger. The sound re-echoed through the swamp, and startled, with a keen suspicion, not only our captain of patriots, but the preacher and his associates. Brough's voice was well known to them all; but that Brough should use it after such a fashion was quite as unexpected to them as to Dunbar and his tories. One of the latter immediately dropped back, intending to knock the negro regularly on the head; and, doubtless, such would have been the fate of the fellow, had it not been for the progress of events which called him elsewhere. Richard Coulter had pressed forward at double quick time as he heard the wild chant of the African, and, being familiar with the region, it occupied but little space to enable him to reach the line across which the party of Dunbar was slowly making its way. Hearing but a single footfall, and obtaining a glimpse of a single figure only, Coulter repeated his whistle. He was answered with a pistol shot—another and another followed; and he had time only to wind his bugle, giving the signal of flight to his comrades, when he felt a sudden sickness at his heart, and a faintness which only did not affect his judgment. He could still feel his danger, and his strength sufficed to enable him to roll himself close beside the massive trunk of the cypress, upon which he had unhappily been perched when his whistle drew the fire upon him of several of the approaching party. Scarcely had he thus covered himself from a random search when he sunk into insensibility.

Meanwhile, "Bear Castle," rang with the signals of alarm and assault. At the first sound of danger, Elijah Fields dashed forward in the direction which Coulter had taken. But the private signal which he sounded for the other was unanswered, and the assailants were now breaking through the swamp, and were to be heard on every hand. To retreat, to rally his comrades, to mount their steeds, dash into the river and take the stream, was all the work of an instant. From the middle of the sweeping current the shouts of hate and defiance came to the ears of the tories as they broke from the copse and appeared on the banks of the river. A momentary glimpse of the dark bulk of one or more steeds as they whirled round an interposing headland, drew from them the remaining bullets in their pistols, but without success; and, ignorant of the effect of a random bullet upon the very person whom, of all, he most desired to destroy. Mat Dunbar felt himself once more foiled in a pursuit which he had this time undertaken with every earnest of success.

"That d——d African!" was his exclamation. "But he shall hang for it now, though he never hung before."

With this pious resolution, having, with torches, made such an exploration of Bear Castle as left him in no doubt that all the fugitives had escaped, our tory captain called his squad together, and commenced the return. The fatigue of passing through the dry swamp on their backward route was much greater than when they entered it. They were then full of excitement — full of that rapture of the strife which needs not even the feeling of hate and revenge to make it grateful to an eager and impulsive temper. Now, they were baffled; the excitement was at an end; and, with the feeling of perfect disappointment came the full appreciation of all the toils and exertions they had undergone. They had but one immediate consolation in reserve, and that was the hanging of Brough, which Dunbar promised them. The howl of the African had defeated their enterprise. The African must howl no longer. Bent on murder, they hastened to the tree where they had left him bound, only to meet with a new disappointment. The African was there no longer.

CHAPTER VI

It would be difficult to describe the rage and fury of our captain of loyalists when he made this discovery. The reader will imagine it all. But what was to be done? Was the prey to be entirely lost? And by what agency had Brough made his escape? He had been securely fastened, it was thought, and in such a way as seemed to render it impossible that he should have been extricated from his bonds without the assistance of another. This conjecture led to a renewal of the search. The rope which fastened the negro lay on the ground, severed, as by a knife, in several places. Now, Brough could not use his hands. If he could, there would have been no sort of necessity for using his knife. Clearly, he had found succor from another agency than his own. Once more our loyalists darted into the recesses of Bear Castle; their torches were to be seen flaring in every part of that dense patch of swamp-forest, as they waved them over every spot which seemed to promise concealment to the fugitive.

"Hark!" cried Dunbar, whose ears were quickened by eager and baffled passions. "Hark! I hear the dip of a paddle."

He was right. They darted forth from the woods, and when they reached the river's edge, they had a glimpse of a small dark object, which they readily conceived to be a canoe, just rounding one of the projections of the shore and going out of sight, full a hundred yards below. Here was another mystery. The ramifications of Bear Castle seemed numerous; and, mystified as well as mortified, Dunbar, after a tedious delay and a search fruitlessly renewed, took up the line of march back for old Sabb's cottage, inly resolved to bring the fair Frederica to terms, or, in some way, to make her pay the penalty for his disappointments of the night. He little dreamed how much she had to do with them, or that her hand had fired the forest-grasses, whose wild and terrific blaze had first excited the apprehensions and compelled the caution of the fugitives. It is for us to show what further agency she exercised in this nocturnal history.

We left her alone, in her little dug-out, paddling or drifting down the river with the stream. She pursued this progress with proper caution. In approaching the headlands around which the river swept, on that side which was occupied by Dunbar, she suspended the strokes of her paddle, leaving her silent boat to the direction of the currents. The night was clear and beautiful and the river undefaced by shadow, except when the current bore her beneath the overhanging willows which grew numerously along the margin, or when the winds flung great masses of smoke from the burning woods across its bright, smooth surface. With these exceptions, the stream shone in a light not less clear and beautiful because vague and capricious. Moonlight and starlight seem to make a special atmosphere for youth, and the heart which loves, even when most troubled with anxieties for the beloved one, never, at such a season, proves wholly insensible to the soft, seductive influences of such an atmosphere. Our Frederica was not the heroine of convention. She had never imbibed romance from books; but she had affections out of which books might be written, filled with all those qualities, at once strong and tender, which make the heroine in the moment of emergency. Her heart softened as, seated in the centre of her little vessel, she watched the soft light upon the wave, or beheld it dripping, in bright, light droplets, like fairy glimpses, through the overhanging foliage. Of fear—fear for herself—she had no feeling. Her apprehensions were all for Richard Coulter, and her anxieties increased as she approached the celebrated promontory and swamp-forest, known to this day upon the river as "Bear Castle." She might be too late. The captain of the loyalists had the start of her, and her only hope lay in the difficulties by which he must be delayed, going through a *blind* forest and under imperfect guidance—for she still had large hopes of Brough's fidelity. She *was* too late—too late for her purpose; which had been to forewarn her lover in season for his escape. She was drifting toward the spot where the river, at full seasons, made across the low neck by which the promontory of "Bear Castle" was united with the main land. Her paddle no longer dipped the water, but was employed solely to protect her from the overhanging branches beneath which she now prepared to steer. It was at her approach to this point that she was suddenly roused to apprehension by the ominous warning chant set up by the African.

"Poor Brough! what can they be doing with him?" was her question to herself. But the next moment she discovered that this howl was meant to be a hymn; and the peculiar volume which the negro gave to his utterance, led her to divine its import. There was little time allowed her for reflection. A moment after, and just when her boat was abreast of the bayou which Dunbar and his men were required to cross in penetrating the place of refuge, she heard the sudden pistol shooting under which Coulter had fallen. With a heart full of terror, trembling with anxiety and fear, Frederica had the strength of will to remain quiet for the present. Seizing upon an overhanging bough, she lay concealed within the shadow of the copse until the loyalists had rushed across the bayou, and were busy, with lighted torches, exploring the thickets. She had heard the bugle of Coulter sounded as he was about to fall, after being wounded, and her quick consciousness readily enabled her to recognise it as her lover's. But she had heard no movement afterward in the quarter from which came the blast, and could not conceive that he should have made his way to join his comrades in the space of time allowed between that and the moment when she heard whom taking to the river with their horses. This difficulty led to new fears, which were agonizing enough, but not of a sort to make her forgetful of what was due to the person whom she came to save. She waited only until the torrent had passed the straits—until the bayou was silent—when she fastened her little boat to the willows which completely enveloped her, and boldly stepped upon the land. With a rare instinct which proved how deeply her heart had interested itself in the operations of her senses, she moved directly to the spot whence she had heard the bugle-note of her lover. The place was not far distant from the point where she had been in lurking. Her progress was arrested by the prostrate trunk of a great cypress, which the hurricane might have cast down some fifty years before. It was with some difficulty that she scrambled over it; but while crossing it she heard a faint murmur, like the voice of one in pain, laboring to speak or cry aloud. Her heart misgave her. She hurried to the spot. Again the murmur—now certainly a moan. It is at her feet, but on the opposite side of the cypress, which she again crosses. The place was very dark, and in the moment when, from loss of blood, he was losing consciousness, Richard Coulter had carefully crawled close to the cypress, whose bulk, in this way, effectually covered him from passing footsteps. She found him, still warm, the flow of blood arrested, and his consciousness returning.

"Richard! it is me—Frederica!"

He only sighed. It required but an instant for reflection on the part of the damsel; and rising from the place where she had crouched beside him, she darted away to the upper grounds where Brough still continued to pour out his dismal ejaculations—now of psalms and song, and now of mere whoop, halloo and imprecation. A full heart and a light foot make quick progress when they go together. It was necessary that Frederica should lose no time. She had every reason to suppose that, failing to secure their prey, the tories would suffer no delay in the thicket. Fortunately, the continued cries of Brough left her at no time doubtful of his where-abouts. She soon found him, fastened to his tree, in a state sufficiently uncomfortable for one whose ambition did not at all incline him to martyrdom of any sort. Yet martyrdom was now his fear. His first impulses, which had given the alarm to the patriots, were succeeded by feelings of no pleasant character. He had already had a taste of Dunbar's punishments, and he dreaded still worse at his hands. The feeling which had changed his howl of warning into one of lament—his whoop into a psalm—was one accordingly of preparation He was preparing himself, as well as he could, after his African fashion, for the short cord and the sudden shrift, from which he had already so narrowly escaped.

Nothing could exceed the fellow's rejoicing as he became aware of the character of his new visiter.

"Oh, Missis! Da's you? Loose 'em! Cut you' nigger loose! Le' 'em run! Sich a run! you nebber see de like! I take d 'se woods, dis yer night, Mat Dunbar nebber see me 'gen long as he lib! Ha! ha! Cut! cut, missis! cut quick! de rope is wo.'r into my berry bones!"

"But I have no knife, Brough."

"No knife! Da's wha' woman good for! No hab knife! Take you teet', misses—gnaw de rope. Psho! wha' I tell you? Stop! Put you' han' in dis yer pocket—you fin' knife, if I no loss em in de run."

The knife was found, the rope cut, the negro free, all in much less time than we have taken for the narration; and, hurrying the African with her, Frederica was soon again beside the person of her lover. To assist Brough in taking him upon his back, to help sustain the still partially insensible man in this position until he could be carried to the boat, was a work of quick resolve, which required, however, considerable time for performance. But patience and courage, when sustained by love, become wonderful powers; and Richard Coulter, whose moans increased with his increasing sensibility, was finally laid down in the bottom of the dug-out, his head resting in the lap of Frederica. The boat could hold no more. The faithful Brough, pushing her out into the stream, with his hand still resting on stern or gunwale, swam along with her, as she quietly floated with the currents. We have seen the narrow escape which the little vessel had, as she rounded the headland below, just as Dunbar came down upon the beach. Had he been there when the canoe first began to round the point, it would have been easy to have captured the whole party; since the stream, somewhat narrow at this place, set in for the shore which the tories occupied, and a stout swimmer might have easily drawn the little argosy upon the banks.

CHAPTER VII.

To one familar with the dense swamps that skirt the rivers through the alluvial bottom lands of the South, there will be no difficulty in comprehending the fact that a fugitive may find temporary security within half a mile of his enemy, even where his pursuers hunt for him in numbers. Thus it happened that, in taking to the river, our little corporal's guard of patriots, under the direction of Elijah Fields, the worthy preacher, swimming their horses round a point of land on the opposite shore, sought shelter but a little distance below "Bear island," in a similar tract of swamp and forest, and almost within rifleshot of their late retreat. They had no fear that their enemy would attempt, at that late hour, and after the long fatigue of their recent march and search, to cross the river in pursuit of them; and had they been wild enough to do so, it was equally easy to hide from search, or to fly from pursuit. Dunbar felt all this as sensibly as the fugitives; and, with the conviction of his entire failure at "Bear Castle," he gave up the game for the present. Meanwhile, the little bark of Frederica Sabb made its way down the river. She made her calculations on a just estimate of the probabilities in the situation of Coulter's party, and was not deceived. As the boat swept over to the opposite shore, after rounding the point of land that lay between it and "Bear Castle," it was hailed by Fields, for whom Brough had ready answer. Some delay, the fruit of a proper caution, took place before our fugitives were properly sensible of the character of the stranger; but the result was, that, with returning consciousness, Richard Coulter found himself once more in safety with his friends; and, a still more precious satisfaction, attended by the woman of his heart. It was not long before all the adventures of Frederica were in his possession, and his spirit became newly strengthened for conflict and endurance by such proofs of a more than feminine attachment which the brave young girl had shown. Let us leave the little party for a season, while we return with the captain of loyalists to the farmstead of old Frederick Sabb.

Here Mat Dunbar had again taken up his quarters as before, but with a difference. Thoroughly enraged at his disappointment, and at the discovery that Frederica had disappeared—a fact which produced as much disquiet in the minds of her parents, as vexation to her tory lover; and easily guessing at all of the steps which she had taken, and of her object; he no longer imposed any restraints upon his native brutality of temper, which, while he had any hope of winning her affections, he had been at some pains to do. His present policy seemed to be to influence her fears. To reach her heart, or force her inclinations, through the dangers of her parents, was now his object. Unfortunately, the lax discipline of the British authority, in Carolina particularly, in behalf of their own followers, enabled him to do much toward this object, and without peril to himself. He had anticipated the position in which he now found himself, and had provided against it. He had obtained from Col. Nesbitt Balfour, the military commandant of Charleston, a grant of the entire farmstead of old Sabb—the non-committalism of the old Dutchman never having enabled him to satisfy the British authorities that he was a person deserving their protection. Of the services and loyalty of Dunbar, on the contrary, they were in possession of daily evidence. It was with indescribable consternation that old Sabb looked upon the massive parchment—sealed, signed, and made authoritative by stately phrases and mysterious words, of the purport of which he could only conjecture—with which the fierce Dunbar denounced him as a traitor to the king, and expelled him from his own freehold.

"Oh! mein Gott!" was his exclamation. "And did the goot king T'shorge make dat baber? And has de goot king Tshorge take away my grants?"

The only answer to this pitiful appeal, vouchsafed him by the captain of loyalists, was a brutal oath, as he smote the document fiercely with his hand and forbade all further inquiry. It may have been with some regard to the probability of his future marriage—in spite of all—with the old Dutchman's daughter, that he permitted him, with his wife, to occupy an old log-house which stood upon the estate. He established himself within the dwelling-house, which he occupied as a garrisoned post with all his soldiers. Here he ruled as a sovereign. The proceeds of the farm were yielded to him, the miserable pittance excepted which he suffered to go to the support of the old couple. Sabb had a few slaves, who were now taught to recognise Dunbar as their master. They did not serve him long. Three of them escaped to the woods the night succeeding the tory's usurpation, and but two remained in his keeping, rather, perhaps, through the vigilance of his sentinels, and their own fears, than because of any love which they entertained for their new custodian. Both of these were women, and one of them no less a person than the consort of Brough, the African. Mrs. Brough — or, as we had better call her—she will understand us better — Mimy (the diminutive of Jemima), was particularly watched, as through her it was hoped to get some clue to her husband, whose treachery, it was the bitter resolution of our tory captain to punish, as soon as he had the power, with exemplary tortures. Brough had some suspicions of his design, which it was no part of his policy to assist; but this did not discourage him from an adventure which brought him again very nearly into contact with his enemy. He determined to visit his wife by stealth, relying upon his knowledge of the woods, his own caution, and the thousand little arts with which his race usually takes advantage of the carelessness, the indifference, or the ignorance of its superior. His wife, he well knew, conscious of his straits, would afford him assistance in various ways. He succeeded in seeing her just before the dawn of day one morning, and from her discovered the whole situation of affairs at the farmstead. This came to him with many exaggerations; particularly when Mimy described the treatment to which old Sabb and his wife had been subjected. His tale did not lose any of its facts or dimensions, when carried by Brough to the fugitives in the swamp forests of Edisto. The news was of a character to overwhelm the affectionate and dutiful heart of Frederica Sabb. She instantly felt the necessity before her, and prepared herself to encounter it. Nine days and nights had she spent in the forest retreats of her lover. Every tenderness and forbearance had been shown her. Nothing had taken place to outrage the delicacy of the female heart; and pure thoughts in her mind had kept her free from any annoying doubts about the propriety of her situation. A leafy screen from the sun, a sylvan bower, of broad branches and thickly-thatched leaves, had been prepared for her couch at night; and, in one contiguous, lay her wounded lover. His situation had amply reconciled her to her own. His wound was neither deep nor dangerous. He had bled copiously, and swooned rather in consequence of loss of blood than from the severity of his pains. But the hands of Elijah Field—a rough but not wholly inexperienced surgeon—had bound up his hurts; which were thus permitted to heal from the first intention. The patient was not slow to improve, though so precious sweet had been his attendance—Frederica herself, like the damsels of the feudal ages, assisting to dress his wound, and so tender him with sweetest nursing, that he felt almost sorry at the improvement which, while lessening his cares, lessened her anxieties. Our space will not suffer us to dwell upon the delicious scenes of peace and love which the two enjoyed together in these few brief days of mutual dependence. They comprised an age of immeasurable felicity, and brought the two together in bonds of sympathy, which, however large had been their love before, now rendered the passion more than ever at home and triumphant in their mutual hearts. But, with the tidings of the situation in which her parents suffered, and the evident improvement of her lover, the maiden found it necessary to depart from her place of hiding—that sweet security of shade, such as the fancy of youth always dreams of, but which it is the lot of very few to realize. She took her resolution promptly.

"I must leave you, Richard. I must go home to my poor mother, now that she is homeless."

He would, if he could, have dissuaded her from venturing herself within the reach of one so reckless and brutal as Mat Dunbar. But his sense of right seconded her resolution, and though he expressed doubts and misgivings, and betrayed his uneasiness and anxiety, he had no arguments to offer against her purpose. She heard him with a sweet smile, and when he had finished, she said:—

"But I will give you one security, dear Richard, before we part, if you will suffer me. You would have married me more than a year ago; but as I knew my father's situation, his preferences, and his dangers, I refused to do so until the war was over. It has not helped him that I refused you then. I don't see that it will hurt him if I marry you now; and there is something in the life we have spent together the last few days, that tells me we ought to be married, Richard."

This was spoken with the sweetest possible blush upon her cheeks.

"Do you consent, then, dear Frederica?" demanded the enraptured lover.

She put her hand into his own; he carried it to his lips, then drew her down to him where he lay upon his leafy couch, and repeated the same liberty with hers. His shout, in another moment, summoned Elijah Field to his side. The business in prospect was soon explained. Our good parson readily concurred in the propriety of the proceeding. The inhabitants of the little camp of refuge were soon brought together, Brough placing himself directly behind his young mistress. The white teeth of the old African grinned his approbation; the favoring skies looked down upon it, soft in the dreamy twilight of the evening sunset; and there, in the natural temple of the forest—none surely ever prouder or more appropriate—with columns of gigantic pine and cypress, and a Gothic luxuriance of vine, and leaf, and flower, wrapping shaft, and cornice, capital and shrine, our two lovers were united before God—our excellent preacher never having a more solemn or grateful sense of the ceremony, and never having been more sweetly impressive in his manner of performing it. It did not impair the validity of the marriage that Brough honored it, as he would probably have done his own, by dancing *Juba*, for a full hour after it was over, to his own satisfaction at least, and in the absence of all other witnesses. Perhaps, of all his little world, there were none whom the old negro loved quite so much, white or black, as his young mistress and her youthful husband. With the midnight, Frederica left the camp of refuge under the conduct of Elijah Fields. They departed in the boat, the preacher pulling up stream—no easy work against a current of four knots—with a vigorous arm, which, after a tedious space, brought him to the landing opposite old Sabb's farm. Here Frederica landed, and the dawn of day found her standing in front of the old log-house which had been assigned her parents, and a captive in the strict custody of the tory sentries.

CHAPTER VIII.

It was with feelings of a tumultuous satisfaction that Mat Dunbar found himself in possession of this new prize. He at once conceived a new sense of his power, and prepared to avail himself of all his advantages. But we must suffer our friend Brough to become the narrator of this portion of our history. Anxious about events, Coulter persuaded the old African, nothing loath, to set forth on a scouting expedition to the farmstead. Following his former footsteps, which had been hitherto planted in security, the negro made his way, an hour before daylight, toward the cabin in which Mimy, and her companion Lizzy, a young girl of sixteen, were housed. They, too, had been compelled to change their abodes under the tory usurpation; and now occupied an ancient tenement of logs, which, in its time, had gone through a curious history. It had first been a hog-pen, next a hunter's lodge; had stabled horses, and had been made a temporary fortress during Indian warfare. It was ample in its dimensions—made of heavy cypresses; but the clay which had filled its interstices had fallen out; of the chimney nothing remained but the fireplace; and one end of the cabin, from the decay of two or more of its logs, had taken such an inclination downward, as to leave the security which it offered of exceedingly dubious value. The negro does not much regard these things, however, and old Mimy enjoyed her sleeps here quite as well as at her more comfortable kitchen. The place, indeed, possessed some advantages under the peculiar circumstances. It stood on the edge of a limestone sink-hole—one of those wonderful natural cavities with which the country abounds. This was girdled by cypresses and pines, and, fortunately for Brough, at this moment, when a drought prevailed, was entirely free from water. A negro loves anything, perhaps, better than water—he would sooner bathe in the sun than in the stream, and would rather wade through a forest full of snakes than suffuse his epidermis unnecessarily with an element which no one will insist was made for his uses. It was important that the sink-hole near Mimy's abode should be dry at this juncture, for it was here that Brough found his hiding-place. He could approach this place under cover of the woods. There was an awkward interval of twelve or fifteen feet, it is true, between this place and the hovel, which the inmates had stripped of all its growth in the search for fuel; but a dusky form, on a dusky night, careful to crawl over the space, might easily escape the casual glance of a drowsy sentinel; and Brough was partisan enough to know that the best caution implies occasional exposure. He was not unwilling to incur the risk. We must not detail his progress. Enough that, by dint of crouching, crawling, creeping, rolling, and sliding, he had contrived to bury himself, at length under the wigwam, occupying the space, in part, of a decayed log connected with the clayed chimney, and fitting himself to the space in the log, from which he had scratched out the rotten fragments, as snugly as if he were a part of it. Thus, with his head toward the fire, looking within—his body hidden from those within by the undecayed portions of the timber—with Mimy on his side of the fireplace, squat upon the hearth, and busy with the *hominy* pot; Brough might carry on the most interesting conversation in the world, in whispers, and occasionally be fed from the spoon of his spouse, or drink from the calabash, without any innocent person suspecting his propinquity. We will suppose him thus quietly ensconced, his old woman beside him, and deeply buried in the domestic histories which he came to hear. We must suppose all the preliminaries to be despatched already, which, in the case of an African *dramatis personæ*, are usually wonderfully minute and copious.

"And dis nigger tory, he's maussa yer for true?"

"I tell you, Brough, he's desp'r't bad! He tek' ebbry ting for he'sef! He sway [swears] ebbry ting for him—we nigger, de plantation, hoss, hog, hominy; and ef young misses no marry um—you yeddy? [hear]—he will hang ole maussa up to de sapling, same as you hang scarecrow in de cornfiel'"

Brough groaned in the bitterness of his spirit.

"Wha' for do, Brough?"

"Who gwine say? I 'spec he mus fight for um yet. Mass Dick no chicken! He gwine fight like de debbil, soon he get strong, 'fore dis ting gwine happen. He hab sodger, and more for come. Parson 'Lijah gwine fight too—and dis nigger gwine fight, sooner dan dis tory ride, whip and spur, ober we plantation."

"Why, wha' you tink dese tory say to me, Brough?"

"Wha' he say, woman?"

"He say he gwine gib me hundred lash ef I no get he breckkus [breakfast] by day peep in de morning!"

"De tory wha' put hick'ry 'pon you' back, chicken, he hab answer to Brough."

"You gwine fight for me, Brough?"

"Wid gun and bagnet, my chicken."

"Ah, I blieb you, Brough; you was always lub me wid you' sperrit!"

"Enty you blieb? You will see some day! You got 'noder piece of bacon in de pot, Mimy? Dis hom'ny 'mos' too dry in de t'roat."

"Leetle piece."

"Gi' me."

His creature wants were accordingly supplied. We must not forget that the dialogue was carried on in the intervals in which he paused from eating the supper which, in anticipation of his coming, the old woman had provided. Then followed the recapitulation of the narrative; details being furnished which showed that Dunbar, desperate from opposition to his will, had thrown off the restraints of social fear and decency, and was urging his measures against old Sabb and his daughter with tyrannical severity. He had given the old man a sufficient taste of his power, enough to make him dread the exercise of what remained. This rendered him now, what he had never been before, the advocate himself with his daughter in behalf of the loyalist. Sabb's virtue was not of a self-sacrificing nature. He was not a bad man —was rather what the world esteems a good one. He was just, as well as he knew to be, in his dealings with a neighbor; was not wanting in that charity which, having first ascertained its own excess of goods, gives a certain proportion to the needy; he had offerings for the church, and solicited its prayers. But he had not the courage and strength of character to be virtuous in spite of circumstances. In plain language, he valued the securities and enjoyments of his homestead, even at the peril of his daughter's happiness. He urged, with tears and reproaches, that soon became vehement, the suit of Dunbar, as if it had been his own; and even his good *vrow* Minnicker Sabb, overwhelmed by his afflictions and her own, joined somewhat in his entreaty. We may imagine poor Frederica's afflictions. She had not dared to reveal to either the secret of her marriage with Coulter. She now dreaded its discovery, in regard to the probable effect which it might have upon Dunbar. What limit would there be to his fury and brutality, should the fact become known to him? How measure his rage — how meet its excesses? She trembled as she reflected upon the possibility of his making the discovery; and, while inwardly swearing eternal fidelity to her husband, she resolved still to keep her secret close from all, looking to the chapter of providential events for that hope which she had not the power to draw from anything within human probability. Her eyes naturally turned to her husband, first of all mortal agents. But she had no voice which could reach him — and what was his condition? She conjectured the visits of old Brough to his spouse, but with these she was prevented from all secret conference. Her hope was, that Mimy, seeing and hearing for herself, would duly report to the African; and he, she well knew, would keep nothing from her husband. We have witnessed the conference between this venerable couple. The result corresponded with the anticipations of Frederica. Brough hurried back with his gloomy tidings to the place of hiding in the swamp; and Coulter, still suffering somewhat from his wound, and conscious of the inadequate force at his control, for the rescue of his wife and people, was almost maddened by the intelligence. He looked around upon his party, now increased to seven men, not including the parson. But Elijah Fields was a host in himself. The men were also true and capable — good riflemen, good scouts, and as fearless as they were faithful. The troop under Dunbar consisted of eighteen men, all well armed and mounted. The odds were great, but the despair of Richard Coulter was prepared to overlook all inequalities. Nor was Fields disposed to discourage him.

"There is no hope but in ourselves, Elijah," was the remark of Coulter.

"Truly, and in God!" was the reply.

"We must make the effort."

"Verily, we must."

'We have seven men, not counting yourself, Elijah."

"I too am a man, Richard," said the other, calmly.

"A good man and a brave; do I not know it, Elijah? But we should not expose you on ordinary occasions."

"This is no ordinary occasion, Richard."

"True, true! And you propose to go with us, Elijah?"

"No, Richard! I will go before you. I *must* go to prevent outrage. I must show to Dunbar that Frederica is your wife. It is my duty to testify in this proceeding. I am the first witness."

"But your peril, Elijah! He will become furious as a wild beast when he hears. He will proceed to the most desperate excesses."

"It will be for you to interpose at the proper moment. You must be at hand. As for me, I doubt if there will be much if any peril. I will go unarmed. Dunbar, while he knows that I am with you, does not know that I have ever lifted weapon in the cause. He will probably respect my profession. At all events, I *must* interpose and save him from a great sin, and a cruel and useless violence. When he knows that Frederica is irrevocably married, he will probably give up the pursuit. If Brough's intelligence be true, he must know it now or never."

"Be it so," said Coulter. "And now that you have made your determination, I will make mine. The odds are desperate, so desperate, indeed, that I build my hope somewhat on that very fact. Dunbar knows my feebleness, and does not fear me. I must effect a surprise. If we can do this, with the first advantage, we will make a rush, and club rifles. Do you go up in the dug-out, and alone, while we make a circuit by land. We can be all ready in five minutes, and perhaps we should set out at once."

"Right!" answered the preacher; "but are you equal to the struggle, Richard?"

The young man upheaved his powerful bulk, and leaping up to the bough which spread over him, grasped the extended limb with a single hand, and drew himself across it.

"Good!" was the reply. "But you are still stiff. I have seen you do it much more easily. Still you will do, if you will only economize your breath. There is one preparation first to be made, Richard. Call up the men."

They were summoned with a single, shrill whistle, and Coulter soon put them in possession of the adventure that lay before them. It needed neither argument nor entreaty to persuade them into a declaration of readiness for the encounter. Their enthusiasm was grateful to their leader, whom they personally loved.

"And now, my brethren," said Elijah Fields, "I am about to leave you, and we are all about to engage in a work of peril. We know not what will happen. We know not that we shall meet again. It is proper only that we should confess our sins to God, and invoke his mercy and protection. My brothers, let us pray."

With these words, the party sank upon their knees, Brough placing himself behind Coulter. Fervent and simple was the prayer of the preacher—inartificial but highly touching. Our space does not suffer us to record it, or to describe the scene, so simple, yet so imposing. The eyes of the rough men were moistened, their hearts softened, yet strengthened. They rose firm and resolute to meet the worst issues of life and death, and, embracing each of them in turn, Brough not excepted, Elijah Fields led the way to the enemy, by embarking alone in the canoe. Coulter, with his party, soon followed, taking the route through the forest.

CHAPTER IX.

In the meantime, our captain of loyalists had gone forward in his projects with a very free and fearless footstep. The course which he pursued, in the present instance, affords one of a thousand instances which go to illustrate the perfect recklessness with which the British conquerors, and their baser allies, regarded the claims of humanity, where the interests, the rights, or the affections of the whig inhabitants of South Carolina were concerned. Though resolutely rejected by Frederica, Dunbar yet seemed determined to attach no importance to her refusal, but, despatching a messenger to the village of Orangeburg, he brought thence one Nicholas Veitch, a Scotch Presbyterian parson, for the avowed object of officiating at his wedding rites. The parson, who was a good man enough perhaps, was yet a weak and timid one, wanting that courage which boldly flings itself between the victim and his tyrant. He was brought into the Dutchman's cottage, which Dunbar now occupied. Thither also was Frederica brought, much against her will; indeed, only under the coercive restraint of a couple of dragoons. Her parents were neither of them present, and the following dialogue ensued between Dunbar and herself, Veitch being the only witness.

"Here, Frederica," said Dunbar, "you see the parson. He comes to marry us. The consent of your parents has been already given, and it is useless for you any longer to oppose your childish scruples to what is now unavoidable. This day, I am resolved that we are to be made man and wife. Having the consent of your father and mother, there is no reason for not having yours."

"Where are they?" was the question of Frederica. Her face was very pale, but her lips were firm, and her eyes gazed, without faltering, into those of her oppressor.

"They will be present when the time comes. They will be present at the ceremony."

"Then they will never be present!" she answered firmly.

"Beware, girl, how you provoke me! You little know the power I have to punish—"

"You have no power upon my voice or my heart."

"Ha!"

The preacher interposed: "My daughter, be persuaded. The consent of your parents should be enough to incline you to Captain Dunbar. They are surely the best judges of what is good for their children."

"I can not and I will not marry with Captain Dunbar."

"Beware, Frederica!" said Dunbar, in a voice studiously subdued, but with great difficulty—the passion speaking out in his fiery looks, and his frame that trembled with its emotions.

"'Beware?'" said Frederica. "Of what should I beware? Your power? Your power may kill me. It can scarcely go farther. Know, then, that I am prepared to die sooner than marry you."

Though dreadfully enraged, the manner of Dunbar was still

carefully subdued. His words were enunciated in tones of a laborious calm, as he replied:—

"You are mistaken in your notions of the extent of my power. It can reach where you little imagine. But I do not desire to use it. I prefer that you should give me your hand without restraint or coercion."

"That, I have told you, is impossible."

"Nay, it is not impossible."

"Solemnly, on my knees, I assure you that never can I, or will I, while I preserve my consciousness, consent to be your wife."

The action was suited to the words. She sunk on her knees as she spoke, and her hands were clasped and her eyes uplifted, as if taking a solemn oath to heaven. Dunbar rushed furiously toward her.

"Girl!" he exclaimed, "will you drive me to madness? will you compel me to do what I would not?"

The preacher interposed. The manner of Dunbar was that of a man about to strike his enemy. Even Frederica closed her eyes, expecting the blow.

"Let me endeavor to persuade the damsel, captain," was the suggestion of Veitch. Dunbar turned away and went toward the window, leaving the field to the preacher. To all the entreaties of the latter, Frederica made the same reply.

"Though death stared me in the face, I should never marry that man!"

"Death *shall* stare you in the face!" was the fierce cry of Dunbar. "Nay, you shall behold him in such terrors as you have never fancied yet; but you shall be brought to know and to submit to my power. Ho, there! Nesbitt, bring out the prisoner."

This order naturally startled Frederica. She had continued kneeling. She now rose to her feet. In the same moment Dunbar turned to where she stood, full of fearful expectation, grasped her by the wrist, and dragged her to the window. She raised her head, gave but one glance at the scene before her, and fell back swooning. The cruel spectacle which she had been made to witness, was that of her father, surrounded by a guard, and the halter about his neck, waiting only the terrible word from the ruffian in authority.

In that sight, the unhappy girl lost all consciousness. She would have fallen upon the ground, but that the hand of Dunbar still grasped her wrist. He now supported her in his arms.

"Marry us at once," he cried to Veitch.

"But she can't understand—she can't answer," replied the priest."

"That's as it should be," answered Dunbar, with a laugh; "silence always gives consent'

The reply seemed to be satisfactory, and Veitch actually stood forward to officiate in the disgraceful ceremony, when a voice at the entrance drew the attention of the parties within. It was that of Elijah Fields. How he had made his way to the building without arrest or interruption is only to be accounted for by his pacific progress—his being without weapons, and his well-known priestly character. It may have been thought by the troopers, knowing what was in hand, that he also had been sent for; and probably something may be ascribed to the excitement of most of the parties about the dwelling. At all events, Fields reached it without interruption, and the first intimation that Dunbar had of his presence was from his own lips.

"I forbid this proceeding in the name and by the authority of God," was the stern interruption. "The girl is already married!"

CHAPTER X.

LET us now retrace our steps and follow those of Richard Coulter and his party. We have seen what has been the progress of Elijah Fields. The route which he pursued was considerably longer than that of his comrades; but the difference of time was fully equalized by the superior and embarrassing caution which they were compelled to exercise. The result was to bring them to the common centre at nearly the same moment, though the policy of Coulter required a different course of conduct from that of Fields. Long before he reached the neighborhood of old Sabb's farm, he had compelled his troopers to dismount, and hide their horses in the forest. They then made their way forward on foot. Richard Coulter was expert in all the arts of the partisan. Though eager to grapple with his enemy, and impatient to ascertain and arrest the dangers of his lovely wife, he yet made his approaches with a proper caution. The denseness of the forest route enabled him easily to do so; and, making a considerable circuit, he drew nigh to the upper part of the farmstead, in which stood the obscure outhouse, which, when Dunbar had taken possession of the mansion, he assigned to the aged couple. This he found deserted; he little dreamed for what reason,— or in what particular emergency the old Dutchman stood at that very moment. Making another circuit, he came upon a copse, in which four of Dunbar's troopers were grouped together in a state of fancied security. Their horses were fastened in the woods, and they lay upon the ground, greedily interested with a pack of greasy cards, which had gone through the campaign.

The favorite game of that day was *Old-Sledge*, or *All-Fours*, or *Seven-Up;* by all of which names it was indiscriminately known. Poker, and Brag, and Loo, and Monte, and *Vingt'un*, were then unknown in that region. These are all modern innovations, in the substitution of which good morals have made few gains. Dragoons, in all countries, are notoriously sad fellows, famous for swearing and gaming. Those of Dunbar were no exception to the rule. Our tory captain freely indulged them in the practice. He himself played with them when the humor suited. The four upon whom Coulter came were not on duty, though they wore their swords. Their holsters lay with their saddles across a neighboring log, not far off, but not immediately within reach. Coulter saw his opportunity; the temptation was great; but these were not exactly his prey — not yet, at all events. To place one man, well armed with rifle and pair of pistols, in a situation to cover the group at any moment, and between them and the farmstead, was his plan; and this done, he proceeded on his way.

His policy was to make his first blow at the head of the enemy — his very citadel — trusting somewhat to the scattered condition of the party, and the natural effect of such an alarm to scatter them the more. All this was managed with great prudence; and, with two more of his men set to watch over two other groups of the dragoons, he pushed forward with the remaining four until he reached the verge of the wood, just where it opened upon the settlement. Here he had a full view of the spectacle — his own party unseen — and the prospect was such as to compel his instant feeling of the necessity of early action. It was at the moment which exhibited old Sabb in the hands of the provost, his hands tied behind him, and the rope about his neck. Clymes, the lieutenant of Dunbar, with drawn sword, was pacing between the victim and the house. The old Dutchman stood between two subordinates, waiting for the signal, while his wife, little dreaming of the scene in progress, was kept out of sight at the bottom of the garden. Clymes and the provost were at once marked out for the doom of the rifle, and the *beads* of two select shots were kept ready, and levelled at their heads. But Dunbar must be the first victim — and where was he? Of the scene in the house Coulter had not yet any inkling. But suddenly he beheld Frederica at the window. He heard her shriek, and beheld her, as he thought, drawn away from the spot. His excitement growing almost to frenzy at this moment, he was about to give the signal, and follow the first discharge of his rifles with a rush, when suddenly he saw his associate, Elijah Fields, turn the corner of the house, and enter it through the piazza. This enabled him to pause, and prevented a premature development of his game. He waited for those events which it is not denied that we shall see. Let us then return to the interior.

We must not forget the startling words with which Elijah Fields interrupted the forced marriage of Frederica with her brutal persecutor.

"The girl is already married."

Dunbar, still supporting her now quite lifeless in his arms, looked up at the intruder in equal fury and surprise.

"Ha, villain!" was the exclamation of Dunbar, "you are here?"

"No villain, Captain Dunbar, but a servant of the Most High God!"

"Servant of the devil, rather! What brings you here — and what is it you say?"

"I say that Frederica Sabb is already married, and her husband living!"

"Liar, that you are, you shall swing for this insolence."

"I am no liar. I say that the girl is married, and I witnessed the ceremony."

"You did, did you?" was the speech of Dunbar, with a tremendous effort of coolness, laying down the still lifeless form of Frederica as he spoke; "and perhaps you performed the ceremony also, oh, worthy servant of the Most High!"

"It was my lot to do so."

"Grateful lot! And pray with whom did you unite the damsel?"

"With Richard Coulter, captain in the service of the State of South Carolina."

Though undoubtedly anticipating this very answer, Dunbar echoed the annunciation with a fearful shriek, as, drawing his sword at the same moment, he rushed upon the speaker. But his rage blinded him; and Elijah Fields was one of the coolest of all mortals, particularly when greatly excited. He met the assault of Dunbar with a fearful buffet of his fist, which at once felled the assailant; but he rose in a moment, and with a yell of fury he grappled with the preacher. They fell together, the latter uppermost, and rolling his antagonist into the fireplace, where he was at once half buried among the embers, and in a cloud of ashes. In the struggle, however, Dunbar contrived to extricate a pistol from his belt, and to fire it. Fields struggled up from his embrace, but a torrent of blood poured from his side as he did so. He rushed toward the window, grasped the sill in his hands, then yielded his hold, and sunk down upon the floor, losing his consciousness in an uproar of shots and shouts from without. In the next moment the swords of Coulter and Dunbar were crossed over his prostrate body. The struggle was short and fierce. It had nearly terminated fatally to Coulter, on his discovering the still insensible form of Frederica in his way. In the endeavor to avoid trampling upon her, he afforded an advantage to his enemy, which nothing prevented him from employing to the utmost but the ashes with which his eyes were still half blinded. As it was, he inflicted a severe cut upon the shoulder of the partisan, which rendered his left arm temporarily useless. But the latter recovered himself instantly. His blood was in fearful violence. He raged like a *Birserker* of the Northmen—absolutely mocked the danger of his antagonist's weapon —thrust him back against the side of the house, and hewing him almost down with one terrible blow upon the shoulder, with a mighty thrust immediately after, he absolutely speared him against the wall, the weapon passing through his body, and into the logs behind. For a moment the eyes of the two glared deathfully upon each other. The sword of Dunbar was still uplifted, and he seemed about to strike, when suddenly the arm sunk powerless—the weapon fell from the nerveless grasp—the eyes became fixed and glassy, even while gazing with tiger appetite into those of the enemy—and, with a hoarse and stifling cry, the captain of loyalists fell forward upon his conqueror, snapping, like a wand of glass, the sword that was still fastened in his body.

XI.

We must briefly retrace our steps. We left Richard Coulter in ambush, having so placed his little detachments as to cover most of the groups of dragoons—at least such as might be immediately troublesome. It was with the greatest difficulty that he could restrain himself during the interval which followed the entry of Elijah Fields into the house. Nothing but his great confidence in the courage and fidelity of the preacher could have reconciled him to forbearance, particularly as, at the point which he occupied, he could know nothing of what was going on within. Meanwhile, his eyes could not fail to see all the indignities to which the poor old Dutchman was subjected. He heard his groans and entreaties.

"I am a goot friend to King Tshorge! I was never wid de rebels. Why would you do me so? Where is de captaine? I have said dat my darter shall be his wife. Go bring him to me, and let him make me loose from de rope. I'm a goot friend to King Tshorge!"

"Good friend or not," said the brutal lieutenant, "you have to hang for it, I reckon. We are better friends to King George than you. We fight for him, and we want grants of land as well as other people."

"Oh, mine Gott!"

Just then, faint sounds of the scuffle within the house, reached the ears of those without. Clymes betrayed some uneasiness; and when the sound of the pistol-shot was heard, he rushed forward to the dwelling. But that signal of the strife was the signal for Coulter. He naturally feared that his comrade had been shot down, and, in the same instant his rifle gave the signal to his followers, wherever they had been placed in ambush. Almost simultaneously the sharp cracks of the fatal weapon were heard from four or five several quarters, followed by two or three scattering pistol-shots Coulter's rifle dropped Clymes, just as he was about to ascend the steps of the piazza. A second shot from one of his companions tumbled the provost, having in charge old Sabb. His remaining keeper let fall the rope and fled in terror, while the old Dutchman, sinking to his knees, crawled rapidly to the opposite side of the tree which had been chosen for his gallows, where he crouched closely, covering his ears with his hands, as if, by shutting out the sounds, he could shut out all danger from the shot. Here he was soon joined by Brough, the African. The faithful slave bounded toward his master the moment he was released, and hugging him first with a most rugged embrace, he proceeded to undo the degrading halter from about his neck. This done, he got the old man on his feet, placed him still further among the shelter of the trees, and then hurried away to partake in the struggle, for which he had provided himself with a grubbing-hoe and pistol. It is no part of our object to follow and watch his exploits; nor do we need to report the several results of each ambush which had been set. In that where we left the four gamblers busy at *Old-Sledge*, the proceeding had been most murderous. One of Coulter's men had been an old scout. Job Fisher was notorious for his stern deliberation and method. He had not been content to pick his man, but continued to revolve around the gamblers until he could range a couple of them, both of whom fell under his first fire. Of the two others, one was shot down by the companion of Fisher. The fourth took to his heels, but was overtaken, and brained with the butt of the rifle. The scouts then hurried to other parts of the farmstead, agreeable to previous arrangement, where they gave assistance to their fellows. The history, in short, was one of complete surprise and route — the dragoons were not allowed to rally; nine of them were slain outright — not including the captain; and the rest dispersed, to be picked up at a time of greater leisure. At the moment when Coulter's party were assembling at the dwelling, Brough had succeeded in bringing the old couple together. Very pitiful and touching was the spectacle of these two, embracing with groans, tears, and ejaculations—scarcely yet assured of their escape from the hands of their hateful tyrant.

But our attention is required within the dwelling. Rapidly extricating himself from the body of the loyalist captain, Coulter naturally turned to look for Frederica. She was just recovering from her swoon. She had fortunately been spared the sight of the conflict, although she continued long afterward to assert that she had been conscious of it all, though she had not been able to move a limb, or give utterance to a single cry. Her eyes opened with a wild stare upon her husband, who stooped fondly to her embrace. She knew him instantly—called his name but once, but that with joyful accents, and again fainted. Her faculties had received a terrible shock. Coulter himself felt like fainting. The pain of his wounded arm was great, and he had lost a good deal of blood. He felt that he could not long be certain of himself, and putting the bugle to his lips, he sounded three times with all his vigor. As he did so, he became conscious of a movement in the corner of the room. Turning in this direction, he beheld, crouching into the smallest possible compass, the preacher, Veitch. The miserable wretch was in a state of complete stupor from his fright.

"Bring water!" said Coulter. But the fellow neither stirred nor spoke. He clearly did not comprehend. In the next moment, however, the faithful Brough made his appearance. His cries were those of joy and exultation, dampened, however, as he beheld the condition of his young mistress.

"Fear nothing, Brough, she is not hurt—she has only fainted. But run for your old mistress. Run, old boy, and bring water while you're about it. Run!"

"But you' arm, Mass Dick—he da bleed! You hu't?"

"Yes, a little—away!"

Brough was gone; and, with a strange sickness of fear, Coulter turned to the spot where Elijah Fields lay, to all appearance, dead. But he still lived. Coulter tore away his clothes, which were saturated and already stiff with blood, and discovered the bullet-wound in his left side, well-directed, and ranging clear through the body. It needed no second glance to see that the shot was mortal; and while Coulter was examining it, the good preacher opened his eyes. They were full of intelligence, and a pleasant smile was upon his lips.

"You have seen, Richard; the wound is fatal. I had a presentiment, when we parted this morning, that such was to be the case. But I complain not. Some victim perhaps was necessary, and I am not unwilling. But Frederica?"

"She lives! She is here: unhurt but suffering."

"Ah! that monster!"

By this time the old couple made their appearance, and Frederica was at once removed to her own chamber. A few moments tendance sufficed to revive her, and then, as if fearing that she had not heard the truth in regard to Coulter, she insisted on going where he was. Meantime, Elijah Fields had been removed to an adjoining apartment. He did not seem to suffer. In the mortal nature of his hurt, his sensibilities seemed to be greatly lessened. But his mind was calm and firm. He knew all around him. His gaze was fondly shared between the young couple whom he had so lately united.

"Love each other," he said to them; "love each other—and forget not me. I am leaving you—leaving you fast. It is presumption, perhaps, to say that one does not fear to die—but I am resigned. I have taken life—always in self-defence—still I have taken life! I would that I had never done so. That makes me doubt. I feel the blood upon my head. My hope is in the Lord Jesus. May his blood atone for that which I have shed!"

His eyes closed. His lips moved, as it were, in silent prayer. Again he looked out upon the two, who hung with streaming eyes above him. "Kiss me, Richard—and you, Frederica—dear children—I have loved you always. God be with you—and—me!" He was silent.

Our story here is ended. We need not follow Richard Coulter through the remaining vicissitudes of the war. Enough that he continued to distinguish himself, rising to the rank of major in the service of the state. With the return of peace, he removed to the farmhouse of his wife's parents. But for him, in all probability, the estate would have been forfeited; and the great love which the good old Dutchman professed for King

George might have led to the transfer of his grant to some one less devoted to the house of Hanover. It happened, only a few months after the evacuation of Charleston by the British, that Felix Long, one of the commissioners, was again on a visit to Orangeburg. It was at the village, and a considerable number of persons had collected. Among them was old Frederick Sabb and Major Coulter. Long approached the old man, and, after the first salutation, said to him—" Well, Frederick, have we any late news from goot King Tshorge?" The old Dutchman started as if he had trodden upon an adder—gave a hasty glance of indignation to the interrogator, and turned away exclaiming—" D—n King Tshorge! I don't care dough I nebber more hears de name agen!"

CHAPTER XIV.

GLIMPSES ALONG SHORE OF THE OLD NORTH STATE.

If you have ever, in a past period of your life, been a coastwise voyager, south or north, along our Atlantic shores, and making your way, after an antique fashion, in one of those good old slow-and-easy coaches, called packet ships, brigs, or schooners, you must a thousand times have bewailed the eternal prospect, the endless length of waste and unprofitable shore, which the old North State continued to unfold to your weary eyes, creeping forward at a snail's pace under the influence of contrary winds, or no winds at all, with every now and then the necessity of *going about*, lest the nose of your vessel — having thereto a strong native tendency — should thrust itself into one of Peleg Perkin's tar barrels, close by Pamlico, or, worse still, into the ugly Scylla and Charybdis, the ship-traps of Cape Hatteras. From rise of morn to set of sun, still the same vague, faint, monotonous outline. You go to your berth at night, with a half-smothered curse at the enormous bulk of body which the good old state protrudes along your path. You rise in the morning and ask, with the smallest possible expectation, of the steward —

"Where are we now?" and still the same lamentable answer "Off North Carolina, sir."

You go on deck, and there, precisely as she lay last night, she lies this morning — a sluggish monster drowsing on the deep, like that to the back of which Sinbad had recourse, dreaming it a comfortable islet for hermit habitation.

"Hugest of fish that swim the ocean stream."

The annoyance was immeasurable, and, doubtless, to this feeling may be ascribed much of that sharp sarcasm to which, in its season, the good old North State has been exposed; she nevertheless, all the while, showing herself very scornfully indifferent to that vulgar thing, called, very ridiculously, "public opinion." Angry travellers were apt to assume an intellectual sluggishness on the part of her people corresponding to that which her vast outline along the sea seemed to indicate to the voyager. That she made no great fuss in the body politic—that she kept herself out of hot water of all kinds, and, in proportion to the exhibition of morbid energies on the part of her neighbors, seemed all the more resolute to subdue her own—these were assumed as proofs of a settled mental atrophy, which only made her enormous bulk of body show more offensively in the eyes of the impatient traveller. He visited upon her genius the very vastness of her dimensions, and fancied that her soul was small, simply because her physique was gigantic.

"And, by the way," answered my Gothamite, "a very reasonable assumption according to human experience."

"True enough," interposed our orator with a leer, "as instanced in your own state of Gotham."

Duyckman felt uneasy and looked savage for a moment. The Alabamian continued.

"What was felt of tedious, passing the shores of the old North State, was not a whit lessened when you took the land route, seeking to shorten the progress by the help of railroads and locomotives. A more dreary region than the track from Wilmington to Portsmouth is hardly to be found anywhere. The region through South Carolina, from Augusta to Charleston, is bad enough. That through her ancient sister is a fraction worse."

"Something is due to our own impatience. Our thoughts do not keep progress with our eyes. Were travellers observers, which they rarely are, and still less thinkers upon what they observe, they would make many more grateful discoveries along the route than they do. He who goes from Dan to Beersheba and reports nothing to be seen, is simply an animal that has not duly acquired the use of his eyes."

"My friend," quoth the Alabamian with green eyes—"your eyes have been indulgent. I have tried as much as possible to see something along your Carolina routes, but to little profit."

"Perhaps," put in a sharp, peppery, little fellow, whom we afterward ascertained to be from the old North State himself—

"perhaps, you did all your seeing through those tea-green spectacles."

"I surely have done so always when passing through North Carolina," answered the other quietly. "It was needful to give the trees, shrubs, fields and flowers, something of a natural complexion. Now, I will report briefly the result of several progresses, through that state, during the growing season. The whole country, so far as its agriculture is concerned, seemed wretchedly unpromising. The glimpse here and there of a tolerable farm, was only an oasis in the desert, which made the rest of the country more and more distressing to the eye. The cornfields were few, I could have covered half of them with a table cloth, and the crops raised seem all destined for the markets of Laputa."

"Laputa? Where's that, I wonder?" quoth North Carolina.

"Somewhere north of Brobdignag, I believe, and west of the tropics, between the equator and the Frozen sea, and crossed by the central fires of the Equinox, which enables the people to raise potatoes and barley with equal facility, but prevents them from growing corn. This commodity, of which they are passionately fond, eating an ear at a mouthful, and chewing the cob at their leisure, is brought to them only once a year by one Captain Gulliver, a native of Cape Cod, the only known trader between Laputa and North Carolina. I should not be surprised if he is even now taking in a cargo at Wilmington."

"I never heard of the man, and I reckon I know all the people that trade to Wilmington, captains and ships. Just say now, if you can remember, what's the vessel called that he navigates."

"The Long Bow," was the quiet and immediate answer. "This is a great craft for shallow waters. She certainly does trade with North Carolina somewhere — are you sure that you remember all the names of the vessels that ply to your ports."

"Every one of them?"

"You have a most wonderful memory, my friend. — But passing from the cornfields of your state, I am sorry to say that I can say as little for its habitations. The dwellings were all of the rudest construction, and signs of gardening, or culture of any kind, were as rare, almost, as you will find them along the waste places of the Tigris and the Dead sea. As for fruit, the peaches, and apples offered us along the route were such as nature seemed to have designed for the better encouragement of Cholera,—a sort of bounty offered for bile, indigestion, dyspepsia and riled intestines."

"But that's only along the railroad route," said our little North Carolina man, "and who ever expects to see a decent country along a railroad route in any agricultural region?"

Another party came to the succor of the North-Carolinian with whom our bilious orator was evidently disposed to amuse himself.

"He is right. You will form a very erroneous notion of this truly valuable state if you assume its general character from what you see along the railroad route. North Carolina is even now, in many respects, one of the most prosperous of all the states. She lacks nothing but population to exhibit incomparable resources, of vegetable and mineral treasure, such as in future days shall make us utterly forgetful of California. Penetrate the interior even now, and you will be rewarded in a thousand places by the beauties of a careful cultivation, the sweets of a mild and graceful society, and the comforts of a condition to which want and care are strangers, and where the real misfortune is that the means of life are so easily and abundantly found. North Carolina has suffered a greater drain upon her population, in emigration to the Southwest, than probably any of her Atlantic sisters. How often have I met, twenty years ago, her poor wayfarers—'from Tar River or thar' abouts,' trudging on by the side of their little wagons, from which the great eyes of a wilderness of young ones were peeping out, thick as the dogwood blossoms in the spring-time. The surplus population— the natural increase of this state, and that of South Carolina and Virginia — have thus for thirty years or more been carried off to the unrestoring West; and it is only within the last seven that the torrent seems to be measurably stayed. The prosperity of these states depends in great degree upon the arrest of this outflow; — since all the improvements ever effected in a state — all of its newer developments of resource — are only to be made by its own surplus, or natural increase, under the stimulus of necessities, the result of a more crowded condition, and a closer competition in the fields of labor. That portion of a population which has reached the age of forty seldom achieve any new development of the resources of a country. To hold their own — to be what they have been and keep as they are, — is all that can reasonably be expected at their hands. But they are doing much more than this. As a state, and as communities, they are making large general improvements, and as individuals, they are rising equally in education and in prosperity."

"Glad to hear it, but take leave to doubt," responded the man of bile. "You are evidently an enthusiast, my friend; a word in your ear—"

Here he slid up to the previous speaker, looked him slyly under his green spectacles, gave him a nudge in his side, and whispered:—

"Don't I know Rip Van Winkle as well as you or anybody else, but don't you see that this little fellow don't know me. We'll have some fun out of him. He has a large capital of patriotism out of which we shall manufacture many a broad grin, such as would do no discredit to a Washington politician. Listen now, while I touch him under his diaphragm.— It's something of a waste of words," he resumed aloud, "to be discussing North Carolina. But — one question. Have you ever been to Smithville? If you want to know something of her, go to Smithville. We once put into that port, somewhat in distress, making the voyage from Charleston to New York in one of those cockle shells which Pennoyer got up to run between the two places. She was the Davy Brown I think. She had very nearly carried me to Davy Jones'. It is a God's mercy that these miserable little mantraps had not gulfed their hundreds as did the 'Home.' Well, we put into Smithville — a gale blowing on deck, and fifty children squalling in the cabin. A few of us got to shore, counting on an oyster supper. We met a fellow seven feet high, with his back against a bank of sand that kept off the wind, while the fragment of an old cutter's deck, hanging over the bank, covered him from the rain — all except drippings and leakage.— There was the bottom of an old turpentine tub beside him from which he detached occasional fragments of gum to gnaw upon. We questioned him about oysters.

"'Reckon it's hard to find 'em now.'

"'Why?'

"'Why, you see, we've done cleaned off all a 'top, and them down low in the water's mighty hard to come at. Don't get much oysters at Smithville now. Reckon there mought have been a right smart chance of 'em long time ago—'bout the Revolution.'

"'Well, do you think we can get any broiled chickens anywhere?'

"'Chickens don't do so well at Smithville. I'm thinking they drink too much of the salt water, and the gravel's too coarse for 'em, but they die off mighty soon, and there's no cure for it.'

"'Eggs?'

"'Well now, as for eggs, somehow the hens don't lay as they used to. Folks say that there's a sort of happidemic among the poultry of all kinds. They don't thrive no more in Smithville.'

"'And what *have* you got in Smithville?'

"'I reckon there's pretty much all the Smiths here that was here at the beginning. Old granny Pressman Smith lives thar in that rether old house that looks a'most as if it was guine to fall. 'Lijah Smith keeps opposite. He had the grocery, but he's pretty much sold out—though they do say there's a schooner expected mighty soon with some codfish and p'taters for him, from down East. Rice Smith owns that 'ere flat. you sees thar' with its side stove; and the old windmill yander with the fans gone b'longs to Jackson W. Smith, the lawyer. He's pretty much broke up I hear, by buying a gold mine somewhere in the South. I'm a Smith myself—my name's Fergus Smith, but I'm the poorest of the family. I don't own nothing, no how, and never did.'

"Now there's a chronicle," said our orator. "Was there ever such a complete picture of all sorts of *debris* and ruin?"

"But Smithville is not North Carolina," was the reply of our little red-faced native, who seemed particularly to resent this portraiture.

"I am afraid it is," was the reply of the orator, coolly spoken, and without seeming to heed the evident ruffling of the young one's plumage. "I have seen somewhere," he continued, "a picture of the old North State, of which I remember just the heads. Doubtless there is some exaggeration in it, but on the whole the thing is true. It is true in generals if not details—

true to the spirit of the whole, if regardless of all occasional exceptions. We have had a picture of the Virginian. We can not object to one of the North-Carolinian, and he who objects to it as not true, will be wise enough to regard it as a jest, not wholly without body in the fact."

"Oh, you're only a-jesting, then?"

"Jesting, sir! I never jest. I am as serious as the Dutch Momus, and I never suffer myself to smile except in a thunderstorm."

"And what makes you smile then?"

"To hear so much ado about nothing."

"You're a mighty strange person, I'm a thinking."

"Ah! that's a practice, my young friend, you should not indulge in. Don't go out of your way, at any time, in search after vain things."

"You don't call thinking a vain thing?"

"By no means—only you search after it."

"I don't rightly understand you."

"The fault, I suspect, is rather yours than mine; and I don't see how we're to amend it. I must leave you to your unassisted efforts; and, if you will suffer me, I will resume my portrait of the old North State."

"That's right! Go ahead, old Bile!" cried the Texan, irreverently. The Alabamian glanced at him from under his green spectacles.

"Have you been eating cabbage, my friend?"

"Cabbage, no!"

"It must be the cocktails then! Either swear off from cocktails altogether, Texas, or go and get yourself another. Your complexion is rather the worse for wear."

"Oh! d—n the complexion," cried Texas, "and breeze away with what you've got. Hurrah for nothing—go ahead!"

"Thank you for permission," was the cool reply. "And now, gentlemen, for our unknown chronicler of the virtues of the old North State. I may not give his exact language always, but you will excuse my involuntary fault:—

"'The genius of North Carolina,' says he, 'is clearly masculine. He has no feminine refinements. You will not accuse him of unnecessary or enfeebling delicacies, and, one merit, he is totally free from affectation. You have strong smells of him before you approach his shores, but these occasion no concern in—'"

Here, however, a be . rang, which seemed to have some peculiar meaning in it. The Texan curled himself up only to stretch away for the cabin. His example was about to be followed by the rest, and our orator seeing this, judiciously proposed that we should for the present forbear the discussion of the old North State for the more grateful discussion of the supper — a proposition which was carried *nem. con.* We adjourned to meet again

CHAPTER XV.

MORE OF THE GENIUS OF THE OLD NORTH STATE.

"WE must not forget our pledges," said the sea-green orator, as we seated ourselves in a group near the wheel, after supper, cigars all lighted. "And, if not too full of better stuff, my friends, I propose to give you the chronicle of the old North State, of which I have spoken. As I have mentioned already, the matter is not my own. I gathered it from the correspondence of a traveller in some of the newspapers. It seemed so truthful, so appropriate, and confirmed so admirably my own experience, that I memorized it without any effort."

No one dissenting, the Alabamian proceeded with his narrative, very much as follows :—

"'The genius of the old North State,' said he, 'is decidedly masculine. With a large physical development, he is as conscious of his strength as totally indifferent to its uses. Indifference is his virtue. He would be as little interested if the scents which he gave forth were cologne instead of turpentine. There he stands or lies, an enormous waste of manhood, looking out upon the Atlantic. His form, though bulky, is angular— one shoulder rather higher than the other, and one leg standing awkwardly at ease. His breeches, you perceive, are of the most antique fashion—equally short and tight. He has evidently outgrown them, but the evidence is not yet apparent to his own mind. His meditations have not yet conducted him to that point, where the necessity of providing himself with a better fit, a more becoming cut, and a thoroughly new pair, comes upon him with the force of some sudden supernatural conviction. When they do, he will receive such a shock as will cover him with perspiration enough for a thousand years. He stands now, if you believe me, in pretty nearly the same attitude which he maintained when they were running the State Line between him and his northern brother (Virginia) to the great merriment, and the monstrous guffawing of the latter. He carries still the same earthen pipe, of mammoth dimensions, in his jaws; and you may see him, any day, in a fog of his own making, with one hip resting against a barrel of tar, and with his nose half buried in a fumigator of turpentine. He is the very model of that sort of constancy which may at least boast of a certain impregnableness. His tastes and temper undergo no changes, and are what they have been from the beginning. The shocks of the world do not disturb his gravity. He lets its great locomotives pass by, hurrying his neighbor through existence, and congratulates himself that no one can force him into the car against his will. He is content to be the genius of tar and turpentine only. His native modesty is quite too great to suffer him to pretend to anything better.

"'The vulgar notion is that this is due wholly to his lack of energy. But I am clear that it is to be ascribed altogether to his excessive modesty. He asserts no pretensions at all — he disclaims most of those which are asserted for him. Some ambitious members of his household have claimed for him the first revolutionary movements, and the proper authorship of the Declaration of Independence. But his deportment has been that of one who says, "What matter? I did it, or I did not! The thing is done! Enough! Let us have no botheration."

"'Do you ask what he does, and what he is? You have the answer in a nutshell. He is no merchant, no politician, no orator; but a small planter, and a poor farmer — and his manufactures are wholly aromatic and spiritual. They consist in turpentine only, and his modesty suffers him to make no brag even of this. His farm yields him little more than peas and pumpkins. His corn will not match with the Virginian's, and that is by no means a miracle. I have seen a clump of sunflowers growing near his entrance, and pokeberries and palma-christi are agreeable varieties in his shrubberies. Of groundnuts he raises enough to last the children a month at Christmas, and save enough for next year's acre. His pumpkins are of pretty good size, though I have not seen them often, and think they are apt to rot before he can gather them. His cabbage invariably turns out a collard, from which he so constantly strips the

SHIPPING OF THE OLD NORTH STATE.   821

under leaves that the denuded vegetable grows finally to be almost as tall as himself. His cotton crops are exceedingly small —so short in some seasons as not to permit the good wife to make more than short hose for herself and little ones. His historian is Shocco Jones.'"

"Where the d—l is Shocco Jones now?" was the inquiry of the little red-faced native, who tried to appear very indifferent to all that the orator was saying. "He wrote well, that Jones. His defence of North Carolina against Tom Jefferson was the very thing, and I have seen some of his sketches of the old State that were a shine above Irving's."

"No doubt! no doubt! Jones and Smith have possibly gone on a visit to their cousin German, Thompson. To proceed:—

"'His orators are Stanley and Clingman, who are by no means better than Webster and Calhoun—and his shipping consists of the "Mary and Sally," and "Polly Hopkins——"'

"He must have others, for I saw a wreck at Smithville in 1835, on the stern of which I read 'Still-Water.'"

"She is there still," said the orator, "and still-water at that. She was beached in 1824—the 'Sleeping Beauty' taking her place, between Squam Island, Duck's Inlet, Old Flats, and Smithfield, till, lingering too long in the river, the tide fell and left her on the Hognose Bank, where her beauty is somewhat on the wane. But to proceed with our authority—"

"Your authority is an abominable falsehood all throughout —a lie of whole cloth," said the fiery native—"so let's have no more of it."

"Go on! Go on! old Bile! It's prime!" quoth the Texan. Not heeding either, the Alabamian proceeded as if he were reading from a book:—

"'Wilmington is his great port of entry—his city by the sea. Here he carries on some of his largest manufactures, converting daily into turpentine a thousand barrels of the odoriferous gum. His dwellings here are of more pretension than elsewhere. He has lately been doing them up, rebuilding and retouching in a style that shows that he has suddenly opened his eyes upon what the world has been doing elsewhere. The change is really not in unison with his character. It sits unnaturally upon him, and gives him a slightly fidgetty manner which is no ways prepossessing. He seems to be impressed with an idea that the world requires him to bestir himself. He has a certain respect for the world, and is not unwilling to do what it requires, but he moves slowly and awkwardly about it, and he must not be hurried. If he can accomplish the new duty without disparaging the old habit, he has no objection, but he seems quite unwilling to give up his pipe, his tar barrel, and his luxurious position in the shade, just on the outer edge, of the sunshine. The superficial observer thinks him lazy rather than luxurious. But this is scandal surely. I am willing to admit that he has a Dutch infusion in his veins, which antagonizes the naturally mercurial characteristics of the South; but it is really a Dutch taste, rather than Dutch phlegm, which is at the bottom of his failings.

"'It has been gravely proposed to neutralize his deficiencies through a foreign graffing, and by the introduction of a colony from Bluffton in South Carolina—otherwise called Little Gascony—and no doubt an amalgamation with some of the tribes of that impatient little settlement would work such a change in his constitution as might lead to the most active demonstrations. It would be as the yeast in the dough, the hops in the beer, the cayenne in the broth. The dish and drink would become rarely palatable with such an infusion.

"'But, even if we allow our brother to be indolent, or apathetic, we are constrained to say that he is not without his virtues. His chief misfortune is, that knowing them to be such, he has grown rather excessive in their indulgence. His prudence is one of his virtues. For example, he will owe no money to his neighbors at a season when states beggar themselves in the wildest speculations, and dishonor themselves through a base feeling of the burden of their debts. Speculation can not seduce him into following their foolish and mean examples. He believes in none of the fashionable bubbles. Fancy stocks have no attractions for him. He rubs his forehead, feels his pockets, and remembers his old sagacity. Sometimes he has been beguiled for a moment, but a moment only, and his repentance followed soon. He has been known, for example, to lay down a railway, and has taken it up again, the more effectually to make himself sure of being able to meet his contracts. His logic is doubtful perhaps, his purpose and policy never. You can not gull him into banks, though, strange to say, he thinks Nick Biddle an ill-used man, and still halts with a face looking too much in the direction of Whiggery. And, with the grateful smell of his turpentine factories always in his nostrils, though with no other interest in manufactures, you can not persuade him that a protective tariff is any such monstrous bugbear, as when it is painted on the canvass of his southern sister.

"'Of this southern sister he is rather jealous. She is too mercurial to be altogether to his liking. He thinks she runs too fast. He is of opinion that she is forward in her behavior—too much so for his notions of propriety. A demure personage himself, he dislikes her vivacity. Even the grace with which she couples it, is only an additional danger which he eschews with warning and frequent exhortation. His error is, perhaps, in assuming her in excess in one way, and he only proper in the opposite extreme.

"'As little prepared is he to approve of the demeanor of his northern brother. Virginia is none of his favorites. He has never been satisfied with the high head she carries, from the day when that malicious Col. Byrd, of Westover, made fun of his commissioners.* The virtue of our North-Carolinian runs somewhat into austerity. We fear that he has suffered somehow a cross with the Puritans. His prudence is sometimes a little too close in its economies. His propriety may be suspected of coldness; and a very nice analysis may find as much frigidity in his modesty as purity and sensibility. He is unkind to nobody so much as to himself. He puts himself too much on short commons.† He does not allow for what is really generous in his nature, and freezes up, accordingly, long before the "Yule Log" is laid on the hearth at Christmas. His possessions constitute him, in wealth perhaps, no less than size, one of the first class states of the confederacy—yet he has failed always to put the proper value on them. His mountains—of which we shall give hereafter a series of sketches—are salubrious in a high degree—

---

* See the Westover Manuscripts, one of the pleasantest of native productions, from a genuine wit and humorist, and a frank and manly Southron.

† The venerable Nathaniel Macon, a very noble and virtuous gentleman, has been heard to say to his friends, "Don't come to see me this season for I've made no corn. I'll have to buy."

very beautiful to the eye, and full of precious minerals and metals.* But his metallurgists do precious little with the one, and he has failed to commission a single painter to make pictures of the other. He has some first rate lands scattered over his vast domains—the valleys between his mountains making not only the loveliest but the most fertile farmsteads, while along his southern borders, on the seaboard, it is found that he can raise as good rice as in any other region. But he is too religiously true to tar and turpentine to develope the rare resources which he possesses and might unfold by the adoption of only a moderate degree of that *mouvement* impulse which the world on every side of him exhibits.† He has tried some experiments in silk, but it seems to have given him pain to behold the fatiguing labors of his worms, and, averting his eyes from their sufferings, he has forgotten to provide the fresh mulberry leaves on which they fed. When they perished, his consolation was found in the conviction that they were freed from their toils; with this additional advantage over men, that their *works* would never follow them. His negroes are fat and lazy, possessing, in the former respect, greatly the advantage of their masters.

"'Our North-Carolinian will be a lean dog always—though it would be no satisfaction to him if the chase is to be inevitable from the leanness. His experience refutes the proverb. Certainly, the contrast is prodigious between his negroes and himself. They have the most unctuous look of all the slaves in the South—and would put to utter shame and confusion their brethren of the same hue in the Yankee provinces—the thin-visaged, lank-jawed, sunken-eyed, shirking, skulking free negroes of Connecticut and Rhode Island. Our North Carolina negro rolls rather than walks. His head is rather socketed between his shoulders than upon a neck or shaft. When he talks, it is like a heated dog lapping—his mouth is always greasy, and he whistles when-

---

* It is not so generally known that the only diamonds found in the United States have been found, of late years, in North Carolina. Some six or eight have been picked up without search, attesting the probable abundance of the region.

† Our orator must not forget the new railroad progress of the old North State. It strikes us she has already turned over a new leaf, and promises to become a *moving* character. ED.

ever he has eaten. He is the emblem of a race the most sleek, satisfied, and saucy in the world. You see the benevolence of the master in the condition of the slave. He derives his chief enjoyments, indeed, from the gay humors of the latter. He seems to have been chosen by Heaven as a sort of guardian of the negro, his chief business being to make him happy.

"'Our North-Carolinian, with all his deficiencies, is a model of simplicity and virtue. His commendable qualities are innumerable. He never runs into excesses. You will never see him playing Jack Pudding at a feast. He commits no extravagances. You will never find him working himself to death for a living. He is as moderate in his desires as he is patient in his toils. He seems to envy nobody. You can scarcely put him out of temper. He contracts no debts, and is suspicious of those who do. He pays as he goes, and never through the nose. He wastes none of his capital, if he never increases it, and his economy is such that he never troubles himself to furnish a reason for his conduct, before he is asked for it. In truth he is almost too virtuous for our time. He seems to have been designed for quite another planet. He is totally unambitious, and though you may congratulate yourself at getting ahead of him, you will be mortified to learn from himself that this is altogether because he prefers to remain behind. He has no wants now that I remember, with a single exception. Without having a single moral feature in common with Diogenes, he perhaps will be obliged to you if you will not interrupt his sunshine.'"

"Well, have you done at last?" demanded the fiery little son of the old North State, as the other appeared to pause.

"The chronicle?—yes."

"Well, I'll just take leave to say that it's a most slanderous and lying history from beginning to end."

"To what do you object?"

"To everything."

"But what is there that you deny to be true?"

"Well, there's that about our shipping. Why, instead of two vessels, Wilmington's got fifty, more or less, and some of them steamers, and some of them square-rigged, brigs and hermaphrodites."

"I admit the hermaphrodites. I have seen one of them myself."

"Ah! have you? and you'll admit the brigs and schooners too, I reckon, if you're put to it, and the steamers. Then, too, you don't say a word of our exports."

"Your produce, you mean! Didn't I admit the pumpkins and the peas?"

"As if six millions could be got out of peas and pumpkins."

"It does seem a large amount, indeed, from such a source, but of course there's the tar and turpentine."

"I say, young hoss," put in the Texan, "don't you see that old Bile is just putting the finger of fun into the green parts of your eye."

"Well said, son of Texas; the figure is not a bad one. The finger of fun! — green parts of the eye! Good — decidedly."

"He's poking fun at me, you mean to say."

"That's it!"

"Well, he shall see that he can't do that without risking something by the transaction. One thing, my friend, you forgot to say about the people of North Carolina in your chronicle. They won't stand impudence of any sort. And now I have just to ask of you for an answer, up and down, to one question."

"Propound!"

"Did you mean to make my state or me, personally, ridiculous by what you have been saying?"

"Ridiculous, indeed, my friend! How can you imagine such a vain thing. You are quite too sensitive. Your self-esteem is singularly undeveloped. Your state is a very great state, after a somewhat peculiar model, and no doubt, though a small man, you are one who need not be ashamed of yourself or your acquaintance."

We all assured the young Carolinian that there could be no purpose to give him offence — that the Alabamian was simply endeavoring to amuse the company with a salient view of men and communities.

"But he shan't do so at my expense."

"Oh! he means nothing of the kind.'

"If he did!"

"Well!" quoth the Alabamian. "If I did! what then?"

"Why, you'd only try it at some peril."

"Peril of what?"

"Of a fight to be sure! We'd see who was the best man after all."

"There is something in the warning to prompt a person to tread cautiously. The rattle announces the snake. Now, look you, my friend, once for all, I beg leave to disclaim all desire to offend you. I simply sought to enjoy my jest, in an innocent way, and to amuse other people by it. That ought to be sufficient; but, for my own sake and self-esteem, I must add that it is only as a good Christian that I say so much. I am apt to be *riled* rather, — feel skin and hair both raised unnaturally — when I am threatened; and, as for a fight, it sounds to me rather like an invitation than a warning. Were you now to desire to do battle with me how would you propose to fight?"

"Why, if I were really anxious, I shouldn't much care how. I am good at pistol and rifle, and have heft enough for a good bout at arms-length with a bigger man than myself."

"Well, my good fellow, for all that, you'd stand no chance with me at either. I should whip you out of your breeches, without unbuttoning mine."

"You?"

"Yes, I."

We were all now somewhat curious. The orator did not look half the man of his opponent.

"Now," said he, "without fighting, which wouldn't do here of course, we can test the chances of the two. Suppose you try and lift that little brass piece yonder," pointing to the cannon of the steamer, "our captain's brazen beauty."

"I can't do it, nor you."

"Answer for yourself. *I* can. But here is a test."

With these words he seized two chairs that stood at hand.

"Hold the backs of these firmly," he said to the bystanders.

He placed the chairs some five feet apart, and in the twinkling of an eye had stretched himself at length, the back of his head resting upon one chair, his heels upon the other.

"Now, some half dozen of you sit upon me."

To the astonishment of all, the slight-looking person, who seemed too frail to support himself, maintained two or three persons for several seconds sitting upon his unsupported body. He stretched out his arms to the group.

"Feel them."

They were all muscle — so much whip, cord and wire.

"You spoke of pistol and rifle," continued the orator. "You shall have a sample of shooting." He retired for a few moments, and returned, bringing with him a large case which, when opened, displayed a beautiful brace of pistols and a rifle of elegant proportions and high finish. The pistols were already charged. A bottle was thrown into the sea, and, at the flash of the pistol, was shattered to a thousand pieces.

"My friend," quoth the orator, "I have led just that sort of life which makes a man up to anything; and the use of the weapon, of every sort, is natural to me in any emergency."

"Well, t'aint your muscle and strength and good shooting that would keep me from having a trial with you, in case you show'd a disposition to insult me."

"But I avow no such disposition, my excellent friend of the old North State."

"Many's the man that's a good shot at a bottle, who can't take a steady aim, with another pistol looking him in the face."

"Nothing more true. But we need say no more on this head, unless you still think that I designed offence."

"Well, since you say you didn't, of course, I'm satisfied."

"I'm glad of it. There's my fist. I didn't mean offence to you, my friend; but I confess to amusing myself at all hazards and with any sort of customer. You happened in the way, and I stumbled over you. You are a clever fellow, and I don't like you the less for standing up for your state, which is a clever and most respectable state, — a state of size, and some sizable steamboats and schooners, — not forgetting the hermaphrodite. And now, let us have a touch of snake and tiger together."

"Where *were* you born?" demanded the North-Carolinian.

"I was born in a cloud and suckled by the east wind."

"Oh, get out! I reckon you're crazy, after all."

"I'll defend myself against the imputation when you'll prove to me that anybody is quite sane. It is but a difference in degree between the whole family of man."

"What's your business? You've served, I reckon, in the army."

"Yes, as a ranger."

"Been in many fights?"

"A few. The last I had was with seven Apache Indians. I had but one revolver, a six-barrel—"

"Well?"

"I killed six of the savages."

"And the seventh?"

"He killed me!—And now for the snake and tiger."

The two disappeared together, steering in the direction of the bar. When they next joined us, the North-Carolinian had his arm thrust lovingly through that of his tormentor, and came forward laughing uproariously, and exclaiming:—

"You should have heard him. Lord, what a fellow! He's mad as thunder—that's certain; but he's got a mighty deal of sense in him, in spite of all."

"We are about opposite Smithville now," said our captain, as the Alabamian came up. The latter turned to the North-Carolinian, and, with a poke in his ribs, said:—

"You thought me quizzing your state, when, in fact, I have more reverence for its antiquities than any person I know. This place, Smithville, for example, I have studied with great industry. It was settled—perhaps you have heard—by the first man of the name of Smith that came out of Noah's ark. It is supposed, indeed, to be the very spot where the ark rested when the waters subsided. There is an old windmill here, still to be seen, and the most picturesque object in the place, which is referred back to the period when Noah carried three sheets in the wind. The people here, of course, are all named Smith."

"Oh, that's a mistake, my dear fellow," put in the North-Carolinian. "You have been imposed upon. *I* know the place, and know that the Buttons live here, and the Black family; and there's another family——'

"Never mind—it is you who are mistaken. They are really all Smiths, however much they may disguise and deny. There's a family likeness running through all of them which nobody can dispute."

"That's true. There is such a likeness, I admit."

"Of course you must admit. Everybody sees it. The wonder is, that, boasting such a great antiquity, they are so little ambitious. Their enterprise is limited to an occasional visit to the oyster bank, where it is said they will feed for some hours at a stretch, but they never trouble themselves to carry any of the fruits away. The pearl-fisheries, which conjecture supposes to have been very active here at one period, were discontinued and fell into neglect somewhere about the time of the Babylonian captivity. Smithville is a place that should largely command the veneration of the spectator, apart from its antiquity of site, and the antiquities which may yet be found within its precincts after proper exploration; it is a study for the ethnologist. There is one peculiarity about the race — all the children here are old when they are born. The period of gestation seems to be about eighteen years. The child is invariably born with a reddish mustache and imperial, and a full stock of reddish hair."

"Bless me, what a story! Why, how they have imposed upon you, old fellow! I tell you, I myself know the families of Button and Black, and — and they all have children — real children, just like any other people's children — little, small, helpless, with hardly any hair upon their heads, not a sign of a moustache, and the color of the hair is whitish, rather than reddish, when they are born."

The assurance was solemnly given by our Carolinian.

"How a man's own eyes may deceive him! My dear friend, you never saw a child in Smithville of native origin at all. The natives are all full grown. If you saw children there — ordinary children — they were all from foreign parts, and grievously out of their element, I assure you. Your supposed facts must not be allowed to gainsay philosophy. I repeat, the region, on this score of idiosyncrasy in the race, should attract the ethnologists. In mere antiquities — in the proofs of ancient art — it is also rich. I have found curiously-wrought fragments of stone there, — sharp at the edges, somewhat triangular of shape—"

"Nothing but Indian arrow-heads, I reckon."

"My friend, why expose yourself? They were sacrificial implements, no doubt. Then, curious vases, in fragments, are to be still picked up, such as were probably employed for sacred purposes in the temples of their gods."

"As I live, old Bile," said the Texan—"nothing but Injun pots and pans for biling hominy."

"Get thee behind us, Texas—blanket thyself and be silent. The present inhabitants of Smithville are certainly the Autocthones—natives of the soil. They have never known any other. And yet, Smith is said to have been a common name among the Phœnicians. Its founder was undoubtedly Tubal-Cain. It is fortunate that we have a place like Smithville, destined for its perpetuation. We are, unhappily, fast losing all traces of the venerable name in every other quarter of the country."

"Why how you talk! There isn't a name so common as Smith in all our country."

"Ah, my dear fellow! do you not see that you are giving constant proof of what I said touching Smithville, that all the babies were grown men at birth?"

"That's somehow a fling at me, I reckon; but I sha'n't quarrel with you, now I know you."

At this moment, the tender tinkle of the guitar, in the hands of Selina Burroughs, announced that my friend Duyckman had succeeded in his entreaties; and we gathered around the ladies, and the mischievous fooling of our Alabamian ceased for a season,—but only for a season. The young lady sang very sweetly one of Anacreon Moore's best lyrics, accompanied by my friend from Gotham. When she had done, to the surprise of all, our orator, who seemed quite a universal genius, coolly took up the guitar when the damsel laid it down, and, without apology or preliminary of any kind, gave us the following sample of the mock-heroic with equal archness and effect:—

THE ANCIENT SUITOR.

OLD Time was an ancient suitor,
  Who, heedless of jury and judge,
Still kept to the saws of his tutor
  And held that all fashion was fudge:
He never kept terms with the tailors,
  The aid of the barbers he scorn'd,

And with person as huge as a whaler'd,
  His person he never adorn'd.
    Sing—Out on that ancient suitor.

What chance could he have with a maiden,
  When round her, the gallant and gay
Came flocking, their bravest array'd in,
  Still leading her fancies astray?
But he studied the chapter of chances,
  And having no green in his eyes,
He gallantly made his advances,
  As if certain to carry the prize.
    Sing—Hey for that ancient suitor.

But his beard had grown whiter than ever,
  He still made no change in his dress,
But the codger had Anglican clever,
  And was confident still of success;
And the ladies now smiled at his presence,
  Each eagerly playing out trumps,
And his coming now conjured up pleasance,
  Where before it but conjured up dumps.
    Sing—Ho for that ancient suitor!

And what were the arts of our suitor?
  Why, the simplest of all, to be sure
He took up Dan Plutus as tutor,
  Dan Cupid he kicked from the door.
Still sneering at sentiment-gammon,
  He found that whene'er he could prove,
That his Worship found favor with Mammon,
  His worship found favor with love.
    Hurrah! for that ancient suitor!

"Oh! most lame and impotent conclusion," cried the lady An old and stale scandal."

"What a slander of the sex," echoed Gotham, looking more sentimental than ever.

"I have given you but a true and common history," answered the orator. "It is within every man's experience; but here's a case that occurred in one of our own villages. The ladies there admit the fact to be undeniable, though they assert—*Credat Judæus!*—that the world can show no other such marvellous example."

Here he again fingered the guitar with the ease of one who had mastered all its pulses, and sung the following historical ballad, which he called—

LOVE'S CONTINGENT REMAINDER.

At eve, when the young moon was shining,
  And the South wind in whispers arose,
A youth, by the smooth stream reclining,
  Thus pour'd forth the stream of his woes;—
"I sigh and I sing for the maiden,
  Who dwells in the depths of yon grove;
Not the lily, its whiteness array'd in,
  So beautiful seems to my love."

And the maiden, she drank in the ditty
  With keen sense and a tremulous heart:
But there dwelt an old man in the city,
  And he in her musings had part:
She answer'd love's song by another,
  To the very same air, but less sweet,
And some sighs which she struggled to smother
  Found their way to the youth at her feet.

Ah! Dick, I confess you are dearest,
  But then you can buy nothing dear;
Your song is the sweetest and clearest,
  And I dote on your whiskers and hair;
But then, the old man in the city,
  Has bonds and bank-notes, and a store,
Such possessions, both costly and pretty,
  And he promises gold in galore.

With you I should find love in marriage,
  But love is poor feeding alone;
With him I have horses and carriage;
  With you but a crust and a bone;
He leaves me no time to consider,
  Still pressing with tongue and with pen,
But if ever he leaves me a widow,
  Oh! Dicky, come sing to me then!

"Worse and worse!" cried the lady.

"Truer and truer," answered the orator.

"Bless me, sir, for what reason is it that you so hate our sex?"

"Hate your sex! Nobody loves it better. I have been married three times!"

"That accounts for it all!" quoth Gotham, *sotto voce*, with the feeling of one who is amply avenged. Selina Burroughs whispered—

"The danger seems to be that he will leave just such an inscription upon his monument as the Hon. Mr. Custis of the Eastern Shore."

There was a pause.

"No story to-night?" inquired one of the party.

"By the way, yes—and our friend here from North Carolina, has been appointed to deliver it."

With a thousand excuses and apologies, some stammering and much confusion, our fiery little companion commenced his task, in a legend of the North Carolina shore, which he entitled

THE SHIP OF FIRE.

"THE State of North Carolina, the assumed poverty of which in material resources, and in mind, has been a little too much dwelt upon by some portions of this company, is, nevertheless, quite as rich, in all respects, as any of her sister states. Her deficiency seems to lie in her want of a seaport of capacity equal to her product, and in the lack of a population sufficiently dense for her territorial magnitude. We may never be able to supply the one deficiency, except possibly by railroads which shall give us the free use of the harbors of our sister states; but the latter will be developed on a magnificent scale, so soon as the population shall become sufficiently dense for the due exploration and working of our soil. Our productions, as the case stands, must now amount to fully eight millions, sent to market along shore. And this, be it remembered, is pretty much a surplus production. As an agricultural community, North Carolina supports herself apart from what she sells. Of the morals of the people of our State, I have only to say, that they shrink from comparison with none. We do no startling things, but we rob no exchequers. We attempt no wonderful works, but we repudiate none of our debts. In brief, we owe no debts. There is no State in the Union quite so independent as North Carolina. You may smile at her simplicity, but you must respect her honesty. You may see something green in her eye, but nothing jaundiced. If goaded by no wild ambition, she is troubled with no excess of bile. Her brains may never set rivers on fire, but they are sure not to blow up her locomotive.

"But, even in enterprises, such as are so largely assumed to be the signs of moral progress, she is not idle. In proportion to the strength of her population, her railroads are as extensive as those of any other Southern State; and when you consider the wide stretch of her territory and the difficulties of her situation, lacking an eligible seaport, she has done more and better than most. Her people are prosperous, making money fast; the results of tar and turpentine will put to shame those of your boasted regions of rice and cotton; and our railroads have brought into use, for these productions, vast territories which have hitherto yielded nothing. I repeat, that in the morals of her people, their physical prosperity, their virtues and advance in education, North Carolina need shrink in comparison with none of the states of this confederacy."

"Bravo!—spoken like a patriot! But what of the story all this time?"

"Patiently: I had first to fling off some of the feeling with which you, sir, have been stirring me up about my good old State for the last twenty-four hours."

"Well — you have relieved yourself?"

"Perhaps: but a few words more, before I begin my legend. I shall not say anything here about our lack of literature in North Carolina, since the argument necessarily belongs to most of the Southern States—in fact, to all the States—our national deficiency being still a reproach to us in the mouths of other nations. When the nation, as a whole, shall be able to answer this reproach satisfactorily, it will then be quite time enough for North Carolina to show her solicitude as to what people think of her shortcomings."

"Quite logical that."

"I have no doubt that the native genius of the old North State will bring her intellectual wares into the market in due season for her reputation."

"Save her distance, you mean."

"As you please. Her native material affords adequate stuff for the future author and artist. She is rich in traditions and unwritten histories. Her revolutionary chronicles are by no means meagre, and only lack the chronicler and author. They will be found as soon as our communities shall become sufficiently dense and numerous to afford the audience."

"Meanwhile, we will put off the requisition *ad Græcas Kalendas*. The argument is a good plea for all the states if admissible in the case of one. I doubt its propriety. I am not prepared to believe in that inspiration which waits upon the gathering of the audience. But the point needs no discussion. Go ahead with your story."

"My story must excite no expectations. I am no artist, and shall attempt nothing but a simple sketch — a bare outline of a legend which our simple people along the seashore, wreckers and fishermen, have told a thousand times with grave looks and a most implicit faith. It will add but another chapter to the vast chronicles of credulity which we possess, and skepticism will decide against it only as further proof of human superstitions which keep their ground even in the most enlightened ages. Be it so. The wise man will find much occasion for thought even where the subject is a vulgar superstition. The inventive genius may go further, and weave from it some of those beautiful fictions which need no better staple than the stuff which dreams are made of — which delight us in the fancies of Comus, and carry us into new creations, and new realms of exploration in the Tempest and Midsummer Night's Dream."

Thus far the preliminaries. Our raconteur then proceeded as follows: —

"You are then to know that annually, at a regularly-recurring period, the coast of North Carolina, even the very route over which we voyage now, is visited by a luminous object having the exact appearance, at a little distance, of a ship on fire. This appearance has been seen regularly, according to the tradition, and the fact has been certified by the sworn statements in recent times, of very credible witnesses. They affirm that nothing can be more distinct than the appearance of this ship, limned in fire, consuming, yet always unconsumed. She invariably appears approaching from the east. She speeds slowly toward the west, nearing the shores always until seemingly about to run aground, when she disappears, for a moment, only to re-emerge again from the distant east. Thus advancing perpetually, she appears to grow in bulk to grow more vivid and distinct as she draws nigh, until, when most perfect to the eye, and about to enter the harbor — when she flits from sight, only to shoot up in the distance and renew her fiery progress to the shore.

"Every part of her seems ablaze. Hull and gunwale, mast and spar, sail and cordage, are all distinctly defined in fiery mass and outline. Yet she does not seem to burn. No fiery flakes ascend, no smoke darkens her figure, no shroud or sail falls, no visible change takes place in her fate, or dimensions—and thus perfect, she glides onward to the shore, glides along the shore, skirts the breakers into which she appears about to penetrate, then suddenly goes out; but only, as I have said, to loom up once more upon the eastern edge of the sea. This operation continues for twenty-four hours, one day in every year."

"Bless me, how curious. I wish we could get an exhibition of it now. Is it a regular day in the year on which it appears?"

"So it is asserted, but I do not recollect the day, and I doubt if our chronicles determine the fact. But the affidavits of respectable witnesses give the date on which they declare themselves to have seen the spectacle, and that day, each year, may be assumed to be the one on which it annually reappears."

"Well, how do they account for this singular exhibition?"

"In the following manner. The tradition, I may add, is a very old one, and the historical facts, so far as they may, are found to confirm it.

"The burning vessel is known as 'The ship of the Palatines.' The story is that, some time during the region of the First George of England, and when it was the anxious policy of that monarch to encourage emigration to the Southern Colonies, a small company of that class of colonists who were known as 'German Palatines' having come from the Palatinate, arrived in London seeking means to get to America. They were sustained for a time at the public expense, until a vessel could be chartered for their use, when they took their departure for the New World. The public policy made it comparatively easy to persuade the crown to this sort of liberality; and succor of this character was frequently accorded to this class of adventurers, who were supposed to have a special claim on the bounty of the German monarch of the English. The emigrants, in the present instance, wore the appearance of poverty so common to their class, and studiously forebore to betray the fact that they had any resources of their own. But, as usual, in all such cases, they were far less destitute than they avowed themselves. Our Palatines, on this occasion, were in rather better condition, in pecuniary respects, than was commonly the fact with their countrymen. It was only a natural cunning which prompted their concealment of means which they preferred to keep in reserve for other uses. Upon their secresy, on this head, depended their hope of help from private bounty and the public exchequer. They kept their secret successfully while on shore. It was their great error and misfortune that they were less prudent when they put to sea. They had treasures — speaking with due heed to the usual standards of inferior castes — of considerable value; treasures of gold and silver, jewels and movables; old family acumulations, little relics of a former prosperity: relics of an affection which sometimes stinted itself in its daily desires, that it might provide token and trinket to give pleasure to a beloved one. The stock, in these things, which had been parsimoniously kept, and cunningly hidden away by this little community of adventurers, was by no means inconsiderable. A treasure of great value in their own eyes, it was a sufficient bait to lust and cupidity, when beheld by those of others. But I must not anticipate. These treasures of the precious metals, toys, and trinkets, were easily concealed in close nooks, among their common luggage, and, seeming no other than a poor peasantry, and mere destitutes of society, they went on board of the vessel which had been chartered for them, and soon after put out to sea.

"The voyage was a very tedious one, protracted by bad weather, and thwarting winds. The bark in which they sailed was one which would be likely, in our day, to be condemned as unseaworthy, except when soldiers, doing battle for the country, needed to be sent to Texas and California. It would answer even now for such purposes — perhaps find preference."

"A good hit, young Turpentine," quoth the Alabamian.

"Our Palatines were pretty well wornout by the tedium of the voyage, their miserable fare and more miserable accommodations. The ship was leaky, the stores stale, the storms frequent, and, our poor adventurers, new to such a progress, were terribly subdued in spirit long before they made soundings. When at length they did, when at length the low gray coast of North

Carolina, stretched its slight barriers across their western horizon, and the cry of 'land' sounded in their ears, they rose from the deeps of despondency into an extremity of joy. They were in ecstasies of hope, and, in their madness of heart, they forgot that prudence which had hitherto kept them humble and cautious. Seeing the shores so nigh, growing momently nearer, the great trees, the verdant shrubs, the quiet nooks and sheltering places for which their fancies had so long yearned, they felt that all danger, all doubt and delay was at an end, and all reserve and secretiveness were forgotten. They prepared to leave their gloomy prison-ship, and to taste the virgin freedom of the shores. Each began to gather up his stores, and to separate his little stock of worldly goods, from the common mass. They gathered their bales and boxes from below. They strapped and unstrapped them; and grouped themselves upon the decks, waiting to see the anchor dropped, and to dart into the boats which were to carry them ashore.

"Thus men for ever cheat themselves with their hopes, and the impatience of a single moment, will undo the work of years.

"They were destined to disappointment. To their surprise, the ship was suddenly hauled off from land. The sails were backed. The shores receded from sight. They could not land that day. The captain had his reasons. They were in dangerous soundings. There were treacherous currents. The insidious rocks were about to work them disaster. It was necessary that they should seek a more accessible region in which to effect their progress to the desired haven. These were the grounds for the movement which baffled their anticipations at the moment of seeming certainty.

"The last feather, it is said, breaks the camel's back. It is the last drop of bitter poured in the cup already full of bitterness. I can not say that our poor Palatines were utterly broken down by their disappointments; but it is very sure that they felt as wretched that night, as they receded from the land so freshly won, as if they were required to begin their voyage anew. Of course, the pretexts of the master were wholly false. He had made his port. He had reached his true destination. Had run his proper course, and might have landed all his Palatines that very night. That he did not, was due to their own error of policy — to that wild eagerness and childish hope, which made them heedless of a caution which they had hitherto preserved with a religious strictness, through long years in which they had known nothing but the caprice of fortune.

"The careless, or the ostentatious exhibition of their hitherto concealed treasures, now held to be secure, was the true cause of the master's change of policy. His greedy eye had caught golden glimpses among their luggage. He had seen the silver vessels and the shining jewels — he had detected the value of those heirlooms which had been accumulated and preserved by the tribe of adventurers, in spite of the trials of poverty, through long generations.

"These discoveries awakened the devil in his heart. His was the sort of honesty which kept steadfast only in the absence of the tempter. He had, otherwise, few or no human motives for its exercise. His life had been a reckless and a restless one, and sober business performance was only to be pursued by way of variety, and in the absence of more exciting stimulants. His mate, or second officer, was a person after his own heart. To him he dropped a hint of his discoveries. A word to the rogue is quite as sufficient as to the wise man. It required but few words between the two to come to a mutual understanding. The seamen were severally sounded; and the ship clawed off from the shore.

"In those days the profession of piracy had no such odious character as it bears in ours. Successful piracy was, in short, rather a creditable business. It was not dishonorable, and he who practised it with most profit, was likely to acquire from it the best credit. Great pirates were knighted by great kings in those periods. Witness the case of the monster Henry Morgan. The bloody hand was rather a noble badge indeed, provided it was shown at court *full*-handed. Then, as now, it was only your poor rogue who was hung for making too free with his neighbor's goods. Piracy was legitimated *beyond the line*, and found its national and natural excuse in Great Britain when it could prove that the victims were only Spaniards or Frenchmen. Like any other speculation, its moral depended wholly on its results. We are not to feel surprised, therefore, at the easy virtue of our mariners — a people in those days, whose lives and morals be casioned no such respectful concern or consideration among the pious as they command in ours.

"The devil, accordingly, found nothing to obstruct his machinations in the hearts of our captain and his subordinates. They determined upon possessing the goods and chattels of the poor emigrants, about whose fate the government was hardly likely to inquire. Hence the sudden purpose of drawing off from the shore, at the very moment of landing, to the mortification and final defeat of the hopes of our simple and unsuspecting Palatines.

"It was not found difficult to convince these ignorant people, that the safety of the vessel required these precautions — that they had erred somewhat in their reckoning — that they were still short of their promised port, and that a progress farther west was necessary. No matter what the plea, it was sufficient to silence complaint or murmuring. They were at the mercy of the master, whether he were pirate or honest mariner, and resigned themselves, with what philosophy they might, to the decree that told them of rolling a few days longer on the deep.

"They did not linger on deck after night, and when the shores were no longer visible. The hope deferred which maketh the heart sick, drove the greater part of them to their hammocks. Their baggage, with the unhappily exposed wealth, was again restored to the interior of the ship. But a few of the young men sat upon the deck, watching the faint lines of the land, until swallowed up in darkness; even then, with eyes straining in the direction of the shore for which they yearned, conversing together, in their own language, in hope and confident expectation of their future fortunes.

"While thus employed, the captain and his crew, in another part of the vessel, were concocting their fearful scheme of villany.

"The hour grew late, the night deepened; the few Germans who remained on deck, stretched themselves out where they were, and were soon composed in slumber.

"While thus they lay under the peaceful cope and canopy of heaven, in a slumber, which the solemn starlight, looking down upon, seemed to hallow, the merciless murderers, with cautious footstep and bared weapon, set upon them. The cabin-door of the vessel had been fastened, the entrance closed to the hold. Each seaman stood by his victim, and at a given signal they all struck together. There was no chance given for struggle—the murderers had planned their crime with terrible deliberation and consummate skill. A spasmodic throe of some muscular frame—a faint cry—a slight groan may have escaped the victims—but little more. At least, the poor sleepers below were unaroused by the event.

"The deck cleared of the murdered men, the murderers descended stealthily to the work below. Passing from berth to berth with the most fiendish coolness, they struck—seldom twice—always fatally—men, women, and children; the old, the young, the tender and the strong, the young mother and the poor angel-innocent but lately sent to earth—all perished; not permitted to struggle, or submitting in despair, incapable of arresting the objects of the criminals. We may fancy for ourselves the horror of such a scene. We may imagine some one or more of the victims awaking under the ill-directed knife—awaking to a vain struggle—unkindly alarming those into consciousness who had no strength for conflict. Perhaps a mother may have found strength to rise to her knees, imploring mercy for the dear child of her heart and hope;—may have been suffered to live sufficiently long to see its death struggle, its wild contortions, in the grasp of the unrelenting assassin. Art may not describe such a scene truly, as imagination can hardly conceive it. They perished, one and all—that little family of emigrants; and the murderers, grouped around the treasures which had damned their hearts into the worst hell of covetousness and crime, were now busied in the division of their bloody spoils.

"How they settled this matter among themselves—what division they made of the treasure—and with what temper they decided upon their future course, must be wholly matter of conjecture. Tradition rarely deals with the minor details of her subject, though sufficiently courageous always in the conception of leading events.

"The story further goes, that, having done the fearful deed without botching, thoroughly, effectively, suffering neither resistance nor loss—having possessed themselves of all that was valuable in the ship, as well as among the stores of their victims—the pirates proceeded to set the vessel on fire, as the safe mode for concealing all the proofs of their crime. They launched their boats. It was midnight. The night was calm and very beautiful—the stars looking down with serene eyes, as innocently and unconsciously, as if there were no guilt, and shame, and murder, anywhere visible; as if Death had not yet been born anywhere among the sons of men. No voices in the winds, no wail along the sea, arose to startle the secret consciences of the bloody-handed wretches, fresh from their cruel sacrifice. They worked as if Law and Love both presided gratefully over their labors; and, with jest and laughter, and perhaps song, they cheerily toiled away, until their ill-gotten spoils were all safely transferred to the stowage of the boats. They then set the condemned vessel on fire—

"'That fatal bark,
Built in th' eclipse, and rigg'd with curses dark;'"

and plied their prows in the direction of that shore, from the opening harbor of which they had withheld their longing victims. The fire, fed by tar and other combustible matter, seized instantly on every portion of the fabric. The pirates had made their arrangements for its destruction, in such a way as to leave no sort of doubt that the ship would be utterly destroyed. She was herself sufficiently old and combustible. The flames rose triumphantly in air, licking aloft with great, red, rolling tongues, far above the maintop, darting out to the prow, climbing along spar and shaft, from stem to stern, from keel to bulwark, involving the whole mass in inextinguishable fire. The pirates looked with satisfied eyes upon their work. Not the deluge now should arrest the conflagration. The deep should engulf its embers!

"Vain hope! The Providence still sees, though the stars prove erring watchers. Suddenly, as the receding criminals looked back, the ship had ceased to blaze! The masts, and spars, and sails, and cordage, still all alight, bright in fiery beauty, perfect in every lineament, no longer raged with the fire. The flames hissed and spread no longer. The fiery tongues no longer ascended like hissing serpents commissioned to destroy. They seemed each to sleep, long lines of red-hot glow, streaks of fire, shrouds of fire, sails of fire, hull and masts of fire,—fire alight—of a fierce red flame like that of an August sunset—but fire that would not consume the thing of which it seemed to have become the essential life!

"What a wonder! what a spectacle! To the murderers, the finger of God was present. He was present, beholding all, and his judgment of fire was already begun.

"For a moment every arm was paralyzed. The boats drifted idly on the waters. The oars dipped and dragged through the seas, undirected by the stroke, until the husky but harsh voice of the captain startled them into consciousness. He was a hardened sinner, but he too felt the terror. He was simply the first to recover from his paralysis.

"'Hell yawns! It is hell we see! Pull for dear life, men—pull for shore.'

"And they obeyed; and, fast as they fled, stoutly as they pulled for land, they looked back with horror and consternation at the sight—that terrible spectacle behind them—a ship all fire that would not burn—a fire that would neither destroy its object, nor perish itself, nor give out concealing smokes, shrouding the form with blackness,—shrouding the dreadful secret which they themselves had lighted up for the inspection of Heaven. Was God, in truth, presiding over that bloody deck? Was he then penetrating the secrets of that murderous hold? Did hell really yawn upon them with its sulphurous fires! Strange, indeed, and most terrific spectacle!

"They reached the land before the dawn of day. They drew their boats on shore upon a lonely waste, a few miles only from human habitations, but in a region utterly wild and savage. They had strength only to reach the land and draw the boats on shore in safety. Then they sank down, incapable of further effort, and gazed with vacant eyes upon the illuminated beacon of their hellish deeds. There was a God—there was a hell! They read both truths, for the first time clearly, in that awful picture of judgment.

"All night thus did the ship continue to glow with unconsuming brightness. The mortal fires had been extinguished in the supernatural. And thus articulately limned in phosphoric brightness, the fatal ship sped to and fro, now passing forward to the shore upon which they crouched—now suddenly lost to sight, and reappearing in the east only to resume the same fast fearful progress toward the shore. At moments when they lost her, they breathed freely in a relieving sigh, and cried out:—

"'She's gone—sunk at last—gone now—gone for ever!'

"A moment after, they would cry out in horror:—

"'Hell! There she is again!'

"And so the night passed.

"With the dawning of the day the vessel had ceased to burn. She was no longer illuminate. But she was there still—erect as ever—perfect in hull, and masts, and spars, and sails, and cordage—all unconsumed—everything in its place, as if she were just leaving port,—but everything blackened—charred to supernatural blackness—terribly sable—gloomy as death—solemn, silent, portentous, moving to and fro in a never-ceasing progress from east to west.

"With fascinated eyes the miserable murderers watched the dreadful spectacle all day. They ate nothing. They drank nothing. They had no sense but in their eyes, and these had but the one object. Every moment they watched to see the ship go down. When they spoke, it was with this hope; and sometimes, when for a moment the spectre vessel receded in the east, they cried this hope aloud in gasping accents full of a horrid joy. But the joy changed in a moment—as she reappeared quite near again—to a despair more horrid.

"With the return of night the terrible fascination increased. The sun went down in beauty; the stars came out in serene sweetness; the sky was without a cloud, the sea without a murmur; the winds slept upon the waves; the trees along shore hung motionless; and all gradually melted mistily into the sober darkness—all but the blackened vessel. Suddenly, she brightened. Suddenly, they beheld the snaky fires running up the cordage. They wound about the masts; they stretched themselves over the canvass; they glared out upon the broad black sea with a thousand eyes of fire; and the ship again went to and fro, from east to west, illuminate in supernatural fire. She bore down upon them thus, and stood off, then wore, then pressed with all canvass toward the beach upon which they crouched, until mortal weakness could no longer endure the terror. The dreadful horror could no more be borne. The murderers fled from the shore—fled to the cover of the forest, and buried themselves in the vast interior.

"According to tradition, the penalty of blood has never been fully paid; and the rule of retributive justice requires that the avenging fates and furies shall hang about the lives of the criminals and their children, unless expiated by superior virtues in the progeny, and through the atoning mercies of the Savior. Hence the continued reappearance, year after year, of the Ship of Fire. The immediate criminals seem to have gone free. At all events, tradition tells us nothing of their peculiar pains and penalties. Doubtlessly, Eternal justice followed on their footsteps. Their lives were haunted by terror and remorse. Horrid aspects crowded upon their souls in dreaming hours and in solitude. They lived on their ill-gotten spoils to little profit; and, according to the story, each year brought them down, as by a fearful necessity, to the seashore, at the very period when the spectre ship made her fiery progress along the coast. This spectacle, which they were doomed to endure, kept alive and for ever green in their souls the terrible memory of their crime. They have all met the common destiny of earth—are all dead; for the period of their evil deed extends back long beyond the usual limit of human life. Their descendants still enjoy the fruits of their crime, and hence the still-recurring spectacle of the Ship of Fire, which, according to the tradition, must continue to reappear, on the spot consecrated by the crime, until the last descendant of that bloody crew shall have expiated, by a death of shame and agony, the bloody offences of his miserable ancestor"

Our North-Carolinian paused.

"Have you ever seen this Ship of Fire?" was the question of one of the ladies.

"I have seen something like it—something so utterly unaccountable otherwise, under the circumstances, that I have been reluctantly compelled to account for the mystery by a reference to the tradition."

This was said somewhat hesitatingly. The Alabamian touched the narrator on the shoulder:—

"I do not censure your credulity, my dear young Turpentine, nor will I question your belief in any way; but suffer me to counsel, that, whatever you may believe, you never permit yourself to give a certificate of the fact. No affidavies, if you are wise."

CHAPTER XVI.

SPIRIT-WHISPERINGS.— REMINISCENCE.

THE thanks of our little company were frankly given to our young North-Carolinian, who had delivered himself much more successfully than we were prepared to expect, from the previous scenes in which his simplicity had quite failed to suspect the quizzings of the Alabamian. That satirical worthy joined in the applause with great good humor and evident sincerity, though he could not forbear his usual fling at the venerable North State.

"Verily, thou hast done well, my young friend from the empire of Terebinth; thou hast delivered thyself with a commendable modesty and simplicity, which merits our best acknowledgments. Pray, suppose me, among the rest, to be eminently delighted and grateful accordingly. That a tragedy so grave, and so symmetrical as the one you have told, could have been conjured out of any of the historical or the traditional material of North Carolina, I could scarcely have believed. I have been pleased to think her genius too saturnine or phlegmatic for such conceptions. If she lost the phlegm for a moment, it was to indulge in a spasmodic sort of cacchination. She relishes the ludicrous at times. Travelling last summer over her railroad to the east, we came to a place called 'Strickland.'

"'Strickland!' cries the conductor: and at the word, an old woman got out, and a group of smiling country-girls got in.

"'Strickland, indeed!' exclaimed one Jeruthan Dobbs, an aged person in a brown linen overall, and with a mouth from ear to ear, defiled at both extremities, with the brownest juices of the weed—'Strickland, indeed! that's one of them big words they've got up now, to take in people that don't know. The people all about here calls the place 'Tear-Shirt' and they kain't be got to l'arn your fine big name for it. Strickland's quite too big a mouthful for a corn-cracker.'

"Think of the pathetic susceptibilities of any people who call their village 'Tear-Shirt!' I could not well believe it, and knowing in what sort of ditch water hyperbole our common sort of people are apt to deal, I turned to the fellow and said— You don't mean that 'Tear-Shirt' is the real name of this place?'

"'Why to be sure I do,' said he 'that's what the people calls it all about; its only the railroad folks that names it 'Strickland';—and he then told a long cock-and-bull story of a famous fight in these parts, at the first settling of the place, in which one of the parties, though undergoing a terrible pummelling all the while continued to tear the shirt wholly from the back of his assailant; and this imposing event, seizing upon the popular imagination, caused the naming of the place—the ludicrous naturally taking much firmer hold with the vulgar than the sublime.

"The most pathetic circumstance that I ever witnessed, or, indeed, heard of in North Carolina, occurred in this very region, and on the same occasion. I mentioned that a group of country girls came into the cars, at this place of ragged-linen cognomen. They were pretty girls enough, and several beaux were in attendance; and such sniggering and smiling, and chirping and chittering, would have made Cupid himself ache to hear and witness, even in the arms of Psyche.

"'Ain't you going to take little *Churrybusco* along with you, Miss Sallie?' demanded one of the swains, holding up a pet puppy to the windows of the car.

"'Ef they'd let me,' answered one of the girls; 'but they'd want me to pay for his passage.'

"'He'll be so sorry ef you leave him!' quoth the lover.

"'Well, I reckon,' responded the girl, pertly enough, 'he won't be the only puppy that's sorry.'

"'You're into me, Miss Sallie!' was the answer; 'and I shall feel sore about the ribs for the rest of the day.'

"'I don't think,' answered the girl—'I never gin you credit for any feeling.'

"'Ah! you're too hard upon a body now.'

"'Well, I don't want to be; for when I think about leaving Churrybusco, I has a sorrowful sort of feeling for all leetle dogs.'

"'Well, take us both along. I'll pay for myself, and I reckon the conductor won't see Churry, and he won't say nothing ef he does.'

"'You think so?'

"'I does.'

"'Well, hand him up here. I'll try it.'

"And, with the words, the insignificant little monster, of gray complexion and curly tail, was handed into the window of the car, and carefully snuggled up in the shawl of Miss Sallie. Soon we were under way. Soon the conductor made his appearance and received his dues. If he saw the dog, he was civil enough not to seem to see. For a few miles, the puppy and the damsel went on quietly enough. But Churrybusco became impatient finally of his wrappings in the mantle, and he scrambled out, first upon the seat, then upon the floor of the car. Anon, we stopped for a moment at some depôt, where twenty-two barrels of turpentine were piled up ready for exportation. Here Churrybusco made his way to the platform, and, just as the car was moving off, a clumsy steerage passenger, stepping from one car to another, tumbled the favorite from the platform upon the track. Very terrible and tender was the scream of the young lady —

"'Churrybusco! Churrybusco! He's killed! he's killed!'

"But the whining and yelping puppy soon showed himself running with all his little legs in pursuit of the train, and bow-wowing with pitiful entreaty as he ran.

"'Stop the car! stop the car!' cried the young lady to the conductor passing through.

"'Stop h—l!' was the horrid answer of the ruffian.

"The lady sobbed and begged, but the obdurate monster was not to be moved by her entreaties. The damsel was whirled away, weeping all the while. If you ask tradition, it will probably tell you that the pup has kept on running to this day, on his stumps, as the fellow fought in the old English ballad. The whole scene was very pathetic — after a fashion. Now, that is the most tragic adventure that I ever had in North Carolina."

"You may find others more tragical," quoth our North-Carolinian, significantly, " if you travel frequently on that route, and use your tongue as freely as you do here."

We soon got back to the traditions of the great deep — its

storms and secrets. Our captain then told the following anecdote of his own experience:—

"You remember the fate of the Pulaski? Well, when she arrived from Savannah, full of passengers, and took in almost as great a number in the port of Charleston, the packet-ship Sutton, which I then commanded, was up for New York also. The Pulaski was all the rage, as she had announced that she was to be only one night at sea. My ship had a large list of her own passengers, some of whom were prudent enough to prefer our ancient slow and easy sailer. But two of them were now anxious to leave me, and take the Pulaski. Of course, I had no objections to their doing so; I simply objected to giving them back their money. They were not so anxious to get on as to make them incur double expense of passage, so they remained with me, growling and looking sulky all the way. Of course, my resolution saved their lives, but I do not remember that they ever thanked me for having done so, or apologized for their sulks upon the way. But, curious enough, before they left the port, and while they were clamoring for their discharge, there came a gentleman from the interior, who had taken passage in the Pulaski, and paid his money to that vessel. He implored a place in my ship, giving as his reason that he was afraid to go in the steamer. He was troubled with a presentiment of danger, and preferred to forfeit his money, rather than lose his life. His earnestness to get on board the Sutton, and to escape the Pulaski, was in amusing contrast with that of my two passengers who wished to escape from me. I had no berth for the stranger, but he insisted. He could sleep anywhere—any how—and desired conveyance only. He was accommodated, and was, of course, one of those who escaped the danger.

"It so happened that we had on board the Sutton several members of one of the most distinguished of the South Carolina families. A portion of this family, in spite of the wishes of the rest, had gone in the Pulaski. The steamer, of course, soon showed us her heels, and the Sutton went forward as slowly as the most philosophical patience could desire. We had light and baffling winds—nothing to help us forward—but no bad weather. The long-sided coast of North Carolina stretched away, never ending in length, for days upon our quarter. At length, by dint of patience rather than wind, we reached that latitude in which the Pulaski had blown up four days before. We must have been very nearly over the very spot, as we discovered by calculation afterward. Of course we were wholly in ignorance of the terrible catastrophe.

"That evening, one of the gentlemen of the Carolina family I have mentioned, came to me, and said that he had heard cries of distress and moanings, as of some persons upon the water. I immediately set watches about the vessel, examined as well as I might myself, but could neither hear nor see any object beyond the ship. He again heard the noises, and again I watched and examined. He was excited necessarily, and I greatly anxious. With the first dawn of morning I was up in the rigging, and sweeping the seas with my glass. Nothing was to be seen. We had no special fears, no apprehensions. There seemed no reason for apprehension. None of us thought of the Pulaski. She was a good seaboat, and, saving the presentiment of the one passenger, who did not again speak of the scruples he had expressed on shore, there were not only no apprehensions entertained of the steamer's safety, but our passengers, many of them, were all the while regretting that they had not gone in her. We never heard of her fate, or suspected it, till we took our pilot off Sandy Hook. Now, what do you say of the warning cries which were heard by the one gentlemen, whose kinsmen in the Pulaski were all lost. Four days before, they were perishing, without help, in that very spot of sea. The presentiments of the one passenger, before we started, the signs manifested to another after the terrible event, are surely somewhat curious, as occurring in the case of this single ship. I think that I am as little liable to superstitious fears and fancies as anybody present, and yet, these things, with a thousand others in my sea experience, have satisfied me to believe with Hamlet, that

"'There are more things in Heaven and Earth,
Than are dreamed of in our philosophy.'"

Once open the way for the supernatural, and it is surprising what a body of testimony you can procure. Most people are sensitive to ridicule on this subject, and will rarely deliver the secrets of their prison-house to other ears, unless the cue has been first given to the company by one bolder than the rest. Our captain's anecdote led to a variety of experiences and revelations, at the close of which, one of the party, being reminded of his appointment as next raconteur, bestowed the following dark fancy-piece upon us, which he assured us was woven in the world of dreams, and was, in most respects, a *bona fide* report of a real experience in the domain of sleep:—

THE WAGER OF BATTLE.

A TALE OF THE FEUDAL AGES.

CHAPTER I.

THE analysis of the dreaming faculty has never yet been made. The nearest approach to it is in our own time, and by the doctors of Phrenology. The suggestion of a plurality of mental attributes, and of their independence, one of the other, affords a key to some of the difficulties of the subject, without altogether enabling us to penetrate the mystery. Many difficulties remain to be overcome, if we rely upon the ordinary modes of thinking. My own notion is, simply, that the condition of sleep is one which by no means affects the mental nature. I think it probable that the mind, accustomed to exercise, thinks on, however deep may be the sleep of the physical man; that the highest exercise of the thinking faculty—that which involves the imagination—is, perhaps, never more acutely free to work out its problems than when unembarrassed by the cares and anxieties of the temperament and form; and that dreaming is neither more nor less than habitual thought, apart from the ordinary restraints of humanity, of which the memory, at waking, retains a more or less distinct consciousness. This thought may or may not have been engendered by the topics which have impressed or interested us during the day; but this is not necessary nor is it inevitable. We dream precisely as we think, with suggestions arising to the mind in sleep, spontaneously, as they do continually when awake, without any special provocation; and our dreams, in all probability, did not our memory fail us at awaking, would possess that coherence, proportion and mutual relation of parts, which the ordinary use of the ratiocinative faculties requires. I have no sort of doubt that the sleep of the physical man may be perfect, even while the mind is at work, in a high state of activity, and even excitement, in its mighty storehouse. The eye may be shut, the ear closed, the tongue sealed, the taste inappreciative, and the nerves of touch locked up in the fast embrace of unconsciousness, while thought, fancy, imagination, comparison and causality, are all busy in the most keen inquiries, and in the most wonderful creations. But my purpose is not now to insist upon these phenomena, and my speculations are only meant properly to introduce a vision of my own; one of those wild, strange, foreign fancies which sometimes so unexpectedly people and employ our slumbers—coherent, seemingly, in all its parts, yet as utterly remote as can well be imagined from the topics of daily experience and customary reflection.

I had probably been asleep a couple of hours, when I was awakened with some oppressive mental sensation. I was conscious that I had been dreaming, and that I had seen a crowd of persons, either in long procession, or engaged in some great state ceremonial. But of the particulars—the place, the parties the purpose, or the period,—I had not the most distant recollection. I was conscious, however, of an excited pulse, and of a feeling so restless, as made me, for a moment, fancy that I had fever. Such, however, was not the case. I rose, threw on my *robe de chambre*, and went to the window. The moon was in her meridian; the whole landscape was flickering with the light silvery haze with which she carpeted her pathway. From the glossy surface of the orange leaves immediately beneath the window, glinted a thousand diamond-like points of inexpressible brightness; while over all the fields was spread a fleecy softness, that was doubly pure and delicate in contact with the sombre foliage of the great forest, to the very foot of which it stretched. There was nothing in the scene before me that was not at once gentle and beautiful; nothing which, by the most remote connection, could possibly suggest an idea of darkness or of terror. I gazed upon the scene only for a few moments. The night was cold, and a sudden shivering chillness which it sent through all my frame, counselled me to get back to bed with all possible expedition. I did so, but was not successful in wooing the return of those slumbers which had been so unusually banished from mine eyes. For more than an hour I lay tossing and dissatisfied, with my thoughts flitting from subject to subject with all the caprice of an April butterfly. When I again slept, however, I was again conscious of a crowd. A multitude of objects passed in prolonged bodies before my sight. Troops of glittering forms then occupied the canvass, one succeeding to the other regularly, but without any individuality of object or distinct feature. But I could catch at intervals a bright flash, as of a plume or jewel, of particular size and splendor, leading me to the conviction that what I beheld was the progress of some great state ceremonial, or the triumphal march of some well-appointed army. But whether the procession moved under the eagles of the Roman, the horse-tails of the Ottoman, or the lion banner of England, it was impossible to ascertain. I could distinguish none of the ensigns of battle. The movements were all slow and regular. There was nothing of strife or hurry—none of the clamor of invasion or exultation of victory. The spectacle passed on with a measured pomp, as if it belonged to some sad and gloomy rite, where the splendor rather increased the solemnity to which it was simply tributary.

CHAPTER II.

THE scene changed even as I gazed. The crowd had disappeared. The vast multitude was gone from sight, and mine eye, which had strained after the last of their retreating shadows, now dropped its lids on vacancy. Soon, however, instead of the great waste of space and sky, which left me without place of rest for sight, I beheld the interior of a vast and magnificent hall, most like the interior of some lofty cathedral. The style of the building was arabesque, at once richly and elaborately wrought, and sombre. The pointed arches, reached by half-moon involutions, with the complex carvings and decorations of cornice, column, and ceiling, at once carried me back to those wondrous specimens which the art of the Saracen has left rather for our admiration than rivalry. The apartment was surrounded by a double row of columns; slender shafts, which seemed rather the antennæ of graceful plants than bulks and bodies of stone and marble, rising for near fifty feet in height, then gradually spreading in numerous caryatides, resembling twisted and unfolding serpents, to the support of the vast roof. All appearance of bulk, of cumbrousness, even of strength, seemed lost in the elaborate delicacy with which these antennæ stretched themselves from side to side, uniting the several arches in spans of the most airy lightness and beauty. The great roof for which they furnished the adequate support, rose too high in the but partial light which filled the hall, to enable me to gather more than an imperfect idea of its character and workmanship. But of its great height the very incapacity to define its character afforded me a sufficient notion. Where the light yielded the desired opportunity, I found the flowery beauty of the architecture, on every hand, to be alike inimitable. To describe it would be impossible. A thousand exquisite points of light, the slenderest beams, seemed to depend, like so many icicles, from arch and elevation—to fringe the several entrances and windows—to hang from every beam and rafter; and to cast over all, an appearance so perfectly aerial, as to make me doubtful, at moments, whether the immense interior which I saw them span, with the massive but dusky ceiling which they were intended to sustain, were not, in fact, a little world of wood, with the blue sky dimly overhead, a realm of vines and flowers, with polished woodland shafts, lavishly and artfully accumulated in the open air, so as to produce, in an imperfect light, a delusive appearance of architectural weight, magnificence and majesty. An immense avenue, formed of columns thus embraced and bound together by the most elaborate and fantastic carvings, linked vines, boughs, flowers and serpents, opened before me, conducting the eye through far vistas of the same description, thus confirming the impression of cathedral avenues of forest. The eye, beguiled along these passages, wandered into others quite as interminable, with frequent glimpses into lateral ranges quite as wonderful and ample, until the dim perspective was shut, not because of the termination of the passage, but because of the painful inability in the sight any further to pursue it. Each of these avenues had its decorations, similarly elaborate and ornate with the rest of the interior. Vines and flowers, stars and wreaths, crosses and circles—with such variety of form and color as the kaleidoscope only might produce in emulation of the fancy—were all present, but symmetrically duplicated, so as to produce an equal correspondence on each side, figure answering to figure. But these decorations were made tributary to other objects. Numerous niches opened to the sight, as you penetrated the mighty avenue, in which stood noble and commanding forms;—statues of knights in armor; of princes; great men who had swayed nations; heroes, who had encountered dragons for the safety of the race; and saintly persons, who had called down blessings from heaven upon the nation in the hour of its danger and its fear. The greater number of these stood erect as when in life; but some sat, some reclined, and others knelt; but all, save for the hue of the marble in which they were wrought—so exquisite was the art which they had employed—would have seemed to be living even then. Around the apartment which I have been describing, were double aisles, or rather avenues, formed by sister columns, corresponding in workmanship and style, if not in size, with those which sustained the roof. These were deep and sepulchral in shadow, but withal very attractive and lovely places; retreats of shade, and silence, and solemn beauty; autumnal walks, where the heart which had been wounded by the shafts and sorrows of the world, might fly, and be secure, and where the form, wandering lonely among the long shadows of grove and pillar, and in the presence of noble and holy images of past worth and virtue, might still maintain the erect stature which belongs to elevated fancies, to purest purposes, and great designs for ever working in the soul.

But it would be idle to attempt to convey, unless by generalities, any definite idea of the vast and magnificent theatre, or of that singular and sombre beauty with which I now found myself surrounded. Enough, that, while I was absorbed, with my whole imagination deeply excited by the architectural grandeur which I surveyed, I had grown heedless of the progress of events among certain human actors—if I may be thus permitted to designate the creatures of a vision—which had meanwhile taken their places in little groups in a portion of the ample area. While mine eyes had been uplifted in the contemplation of things inanimate, it appears that a human action was in progress on a portion of the scene below. I was suddenly aroused by a stir and bustle, followed by a faint murmur, as of applauding voices, which at length reached my ears, and diverted my gaze from the remote and lofty, to the rich tesselated pavement of the apartment If the mere splendor of the structure had so fastened upon my imagination, what can I say of the scene which now commanded my attention! There was the pomp of courts, the pride of majesty, the glory of armor, the grace and charm of aristocratic beauty, in all her plumage, to make me forgetful of all other display. I now beheld groups of noble persons, clad in courtly dresses, in knightly armor, sable and purple, with a profusion of gold and jewels, rich scarfs, and plumes of surpassing splendor. Other groups presented me with a most imposing vision of that gorgeous church, whose mitred prelates could place their feet upon the necks of mightiest princes, and sway, for good or evil, the destinies of conflicting nations. There were priests clad in flowing garments, courtiers in silks, and noblest dames, who had swayed in courts from immemorial time. Their long and rustling trains were upborne by damsels and pages, lovely enough, and richly enough arrayed, to be apt ministers in the very courts of Love himself. A chair of state, massive, and richly draped in purple and gold, with golden insignia, over which hung the jeweled tiara of sovereignty, was raised upon a *dais* some five feet above the level of the crowd. This was filled by a tall and slender person, to whom all made obeisance as to an imperial master. He was habited in sable, a single jewel upon his brow, bearing up a massive shock of feathers as black and glossy as if wrought out of sparkling coal. The air of majesty in his action, the habitual command upon his brow, left me in no doubt of his sovereign state, even had the obeisance of the multitude been wanting. But he looked not as if long destined to hold sway in mortal provinces. His person was meagre, as if wasted by disease. His cheeks were pale and hollow; while a peculiar brightness of the eyes shone in painful contrast with the pale and ghastly color of his face. Behind his chair stood one who evidently held the position of a favorite and trusted counsellor. He was magnificently habited with a profusion of jewels, which nevertheless added but little to the noble air and exquisite symmetry of his person. At intervals he could be seen to bend over to the ear of the prince, as if whispering him in secret. This show of intimacy, if pleasing to his superior, was yet evidently of different effect upon many others in the assembly. The costume of the place was that of the Norman sway in England, before the Saxons had quite succeeded,—through the jealousy entertained by the kings, of their nobles,—in obtaining a share of those indulgences which finally paved the way to their recognition by the conquerors. Yet, even in this respect of costume, I was conscious of some discrepancies. Some of the habits worn were decidedly Spanish; but as these were mingled with others which bore conclusive proof of the presence of the wearers in the wars of the Crusades, it was not improbable that they had been adopted as things of fancy, from a free communion of the parties with knights of Spain whom they had encountered in the Holy Land.

But I was not long permitted to bestow my regards on a subject so subordinate as dress. The scene was evidently no mere spectacle. Important and adverse interests were depending—wild passions were at work, and the action of a very vivid drama was about to open upon me. A sudden blast of a trumpet penetrated the hall. I say *blast*, though the sounds were faint as if subdued by distance. But the note itself, and the instrument could not have been mistaken. A stir ensued among the spectators. The crowd divided before an outer door, and those more distant bent forward, looking in this direction with an eager anxiety which none seemed disposed to conceal. They were not long kept in suspense. A sudden unfolding of the great valves of the entrance followed, when a rush was made from without. The tread of heavy footsteps, the waving of tall plumes, and a murmur from the multitude, announced the presence of other parties for whom the action of the drama was kept in abeyance. The crowd opened from right to left, and one of the company stood alone, with every eye of the vast assemblage fixed curiously upon his person.

CHAPTER III.

AND well, apart from every consideration yet to be developed, might they gaze upon the princely form that now stood erect, and with something approaching to defiance in his air and manner, in the centre of the vast assemblage. He was habited in chain armor, the admirable work, in all probability, of the shops of Milan. This, though painted or stained thoroughly black, yet threw out a glossy lustre of incredible brightness. Upon his breast, as if the love token of some noble damsel, a broad scarf of the most delicate blue was seen to float. A cap of velvet, with a double loop in front, bearing a very large brilliant from which rose a bunch of sable plumes, was discarded from his brows the moment that he stood within the royal presence. He stood for a brief space, seeming to survey the scene, then advanced with a bold and somewhat rapid step, as if a natural spirit of fearlessness had been stimulated into eagerness by a consciousness of wrong and a just feeling of indignation. His face was scarcely less noble than his form and manner, but it was marked by angry passions — was red and swollen — and as he passed onward to the foot of the throne, he glanced fiercely on either hand, as if seeking for an enemy. In spite of the fearlessness of his progress, I could now perceive that he was under constraint and in duresse. A strong body of halberdiers closed upon his course, and evidently stood prepared and watchful of his every movement. As he approached the throne, the several groups gave way before him, and he stood, with unobstructed vision, in the immediate presence of the monarch. For an instant he remained erect, with a mien unsubdued and almost haughty, while a low murmur — as I fancied, of indignation — rose in various portions of the hall. The face of the king himself seemed suddenly flushed, and a lively play of the muscles of his countenance led me to believe that he was about to give utterance to his anger; but, at this moment, the stranger sunk gracefully but proudly upon his knee, and, bending his forehead, with a studied humility in his prostration, disarmed, if it had been felt, the indignation of his sovereign. This done, he rose to his feet with a manly ease, and stood silent, in an attitude of expectation, but with a calm, martial erectness, as rigid as if cut from the inflexible rock.

The king spoke, but the words were inaudible to my ears. There was a murmur from various parts of the assembly. Several voices followed that of the monarch, but of these I could not comprehend the purport. I could only judge of the character of what was said by its startling effect upon the stranger. If excited before, he seemed to be almost maddened now. His eyes followed the murmuring voices from side to side of the assembly, with a fearful flashing energy, which made them dilate, as if endangering the limits of their reddened sockets. A like feverish and impatient fury threw his form into spasmodic action. His figure seemed to rise and swell, towering above the rest. His arms were stretched in the direction of the assailing voices. His clenched fist seemed to threaten the speakers with instant violence. Unintimidated by the presence in which he stood, his appearance was that of a subject, not only too strong for his superior, but too confident and presumptuous for his own self-subjection, even in the moment of greatest peril to himself.

He resumed his composure at last, and the murmur ceased around him. There was deep silence, and the eyes of the stranger were fixed rigidly upon those of his prince. The latter was evidently moved. His hand was extended—something he spoke which I again lost; but, strange to say, the reply of the stranger came sharply and distinctly to my ear.

"Swear! Why should I swear? Should I call upon the Holy Evangel as my witness, when I see not my accuser? Let him appear. Let him look me in the face, if there be lord or knight in this assembly so bold, and tell me that I am guilty of this treason. Sire! I challenge my accuser. I have no other answer to the charge!"

CHAPTER IV.

The lips of the king moved. The nobleman who stood behind his throne, and whom I conceived to be his favorite, bent down and received his orders; then disappeared behind one of the columns whose richly-decorated, but slender shafts, rose up directly behind him, like some graceful stems of the forest, over which the wildering vine, and the gaudy parasite clambers with an embrace that kills. But a few moments elapsed when the favorite reappeared. He was accompanied by a person, whose peculiar form and aspect will deserve especial description.

In that hall, in the presence of princes, surrounded by knights and nobles of the proudest in the land, the person newly come—though seemingly neither knight nor noble—was one of the most lofty in his carriage, and most imposing and impressive in his look and manner. He was not only taller than the race of men in general, but he was obviously taller than any in that select circle by which he was surrounded. Nor did his features misbeseem his person. These were singularly noble, and of Italian cast and character. His face was large, and of the most perfect oval. Though that of a man who had probably seen and suffered under sixty winters, it still bore the proofs of a beauty once remarkable. It still retained a youthful freshness, which spoke for a conscience free from remorse and self-reproach. His eyes were of a mild, but holily expressive blue; and beneath their rather thin white brows, were declarative of more than human benevolence. His forehead was very large and lofty, of great breadth and compass, in the regions of ideality and sublimity, as well as causality; while his hair, thick still, and depending from behind his head in numerous waving curls, was, like his beard, of the most silvery whiteness. This was spread, massively, upon his breast, which it covered almost to the waist. His complexion was very pale, but of a clear whiteness, and harmonised sweetly with the antique beauty and power of his head. His costume differed in style, texture and stuff, entirely from that which prevailed in the assembly. A loose white robe, which extended from his shoulders to the ground, was bound about his body by a belt of plain Spanish leather, and worn with a grace and nobleness perfectly majestical. His feet were clothed in Jewish sandals. But there was nothing proud or haughty in his majesty. On the contrary, it was in contrast with the evident humility in his eye and gesture, that his dignity of bearing betrayed itself. This seemed to be as much the fruit of pure and elevated thoughts, calm and resigned, as of that superior physical organization which made this aged man tower as greatly above the rest, in person, as he certainly did in air and manner.

He advanced, as he appeared, to the foot of the throne, gracefully sunk before it, then rising, stood in quiet, as awaiting the royal command to speak. His appearance seemed to fill the assembly with eager curiosity. A sudden hush prevailed as he approached, the natural result of that awe which great superiority usually inspires in the breast of ignorance. There was but one face among the spectators that seemed to betray no curiosity as he came in sight. This was that of the accused. With the first coming of the ancient man, I had instinctively fixed my gaze upon the countenance of the nobleman. I could easily discern that his lips were compressed as if by sudden effort, while his usually florid features were covered with a momentary paleness. This emotion, with the utter absence of that air of curiosity which marked every other visage, struck me, at once, as somewhat significant of guilt.

"Behold thy accuser!" exclaimed the sovereign.

"He! the bookworm!—the dreamer!—the madman!—sorcerer to the vulgar, but less than dotard to the wise! Does your majesty look to a star-gazer for such evidence as will degrade with shame the nobles of your realm? Sire!—if no sorcerer, this old man is verily distraught! He is lunatic or vile—a madman, or a bought servitor of Satan!"

The venerable man thus scornfully denounced, stood, meanwhile, looking sorrowful and subdued, but calm and unruffled, at the foot of the *dais*. His eye rested a moment upon the speaker, then turned, as if to listen to that speech, with which the favorite, behind the throne of the monarch, appeared to reply to the language of the accused. This I did not hear, nor yet that which the sovereign addressed to the same person. But the import might be divined by the answer of the accused.

"And I say, your majesty, that what he hath alleged is false—all a false and bitter falsehood, devised by cunning and malice to work out the purposes of hate. My word against his—my gauntlet against the world. I defy him to the proof! I defy all my accusers!"

"And he shall have the truth, your majesty," was the firm, clear answer with which the venerable man responded to this defiance. His tones rang through the assembly like those of a sweet bell in the wilderness.—"My life, sire, is sworn to the truth! I can speak no other language. That I have said nothing falsely of this lord, I invoke the attestation of the Lord of all. I have had his sacred volume brought into this presence You shall know, sire, what I believe, by what I swear!"

He made a step aside, even while he spoke, to a little girl whom I had not before seen, but who had evidently followed him into the assembly. She now approached, bearing in her hands one of those finely illuminated manuscripts of an early day of Christian history in Europe, which are now worth their weight in gold. I could just perceive, as he opened the massive volume, by its heavy metallic clasps, that the characters were strange, and readily conjectured them to be Hebrew. The work, from what he said, and the use to which he applied it, I assumed to be the Holy Scriptures. He received it reverently from the child, placed it deliberately upon one of the steps of the *dais*, then knelt before it, his venerable head for a moment, being bowed to the very floor. Then raising his eyes, but without rising from his position, he placed one hand upon this volume, raised the other to heaven, and, with a deep and solemn voice, called upon God and the Holy Evangelists, to witness that what he had spoken, and was about to speak, was "the truth, and the truth only—spoken with no malice—no wicked or evil intent—and rather to defeat and prevent the evil designs of the person he accused." In this posture, and thus affirming, he proceeded to declare that "the accused had applied to him for a potent poison which should have the power of usurping life slowly, and without producing any of those striking effects upon the outward man, as would induce suspicion of criminal practice." He added, with other particulars, that "the accused had invited him, under certain temptations, which had been succeeded by threats, to become one of a party to his designs, the victim of which was to be his majesty then sitting upon the throne."

CHAPTER V.

SUCH was the tenor of the asseverations which he made, fortified by numerous details, all tending strongly to confirm the truth of his accusations, his own testimony once being relied on. There was something so noble in this man's action, so delicate, so impressive, so simple, yet so grand; and the particulars which he gave were all so probably arrayed, so well put together, and so seemingly in confirmation of other circumstances drawn from the testimony of other parties, that all around appeared fully impressed with the most perfect conviction that his accusation was justly made. A short but painful silence followed his narration, which seemed, for an instant, to confound the guilty noble. The sad countenance of the monarch deepened to severity, while a smile of triumph and exultation rose to that of the favorite behind his throne. At this sight the accused person recovered all his audacity. With half-choking utterance, and features kindling with fury rather than faltering with fear, he demanded,

"Am I to be heard, your majesty?"

A wave of the monarch's hand gave him the desired permission, and his reply burst forth like a torrent. He gave the lie to his accuser, whom he denounced as an impostor, as one who was the creature of his and the king's enemies, and tampering, himself, with the sovereign's life while pretending to minister to his ailments. He ridiculed, with bitterness and scorn, the notion that any faith should be given to the statements, though even offered on oath, of one whom he affirmed to be an unbeliever and a Jew; and, as if to crown his defence with a seal no less impressive than that of his accuser, he advanced to the foot of the throne, grasped the sacred volume from the hands by which it was upheld, and kneeling, with his lips pressed upon the opened pages, he imprecated upon himself, if his denial were not the truth, all the treasured wrath and thunder in the stores of Heaven!

The accuser heard, with uplifted hands and looks of holy horror, the wild and terrible invocation. Almost unconsciously his lips parted with the comment:—

"God have mercy upon your soul, my lord, for you have spoken a most awful perjury!"

The king looked bewildered, the favorite behind him dissatisfied, and the whole audience apparently stunned by equal incertitude and excitement. The eyes of all parties fluctuated between the accused and the accuser. They stood but a few paces asunder. The former looked like a man who only with a great struggle succeeded in controlling his fury. The latter stood sorrowful, but calm. The little girl who had brought in the holy volume stood before him, with one of his hands resting upon her head. Her features greatly resembled his own. She looked terrified; her eyes fastened ever upon the face of her father's enemy with a countenance of equal curiosity and suspicion. Some conversation, the sense of which did not reach me, now ensued between the king and two of his counsellors, to which his favorite was a party. The former again addressed the accuser.

"Have you any other testimony but that which you yourself offer of the truth of your accusation."

"None, your majesty. I have no witness of my truth but God, and it is not for vain man to prescribe to him at what seasons his testimony should be given. In bringing this accusation, my purpose was not the destruction of the criminal, but the safety of my sovereign; and I am the more happy that no conviction can now follow from my charge, as from the dreadful oath which he has just taken, he places it out of the power of human tribunal to resolve between us. For the same reasons, sire, he is in no condition to suffer death! Let him live! It is enough for me that your majesty is safe from the present, and has been warned against all future danger at his hands."

"But not enough for me!" cried the accused, breaking in impetuously. "I have been charged with a foul crime; I must free my scutcheon from the shame. I will not rest beneath it. If this Jewish sorcerer hath no better proof than his own false tongue, I demand from your majesty the wager of battle! I, too, invoke God and the blessed Jesu, in testimony of my innocence. This enemy hath slandered me; I will wash out the slander with his blood! I demand the trial, sire, his arm against mine, according to the laws and custom of this realm."

"It can not be denied!" was the cry from many voices. The favorite looked grave and troubled. The eyes of the king were fixed sadly upon the venerable accuser. The latter seemed to understand the expression.

"I am not a man of blood, your majesty. Strife hath long been banished from this bosom; carnal weapons have long been discarded from these hands."

"Let him find a champion!" was the fierce answer of the accused.

"And of what avail to me," returned the accuser, "the brute valor of the hireling who sells for wages the strength of his manhood, and perils for gain the safety of his life. Little should I hope from the skill of such as he, opposed in combat to one of the greatest warriors of the realm."

"Ah, sorcerer! thou fearest!" was the exulting cry of the

accused; "but, if thy cause be that of truth, as thou hast challenged the Most High to witness, what hast thou to fear? The stars which thou searchest nightly, will they not do battle in thy behalf?"

"Methinks," said the favorite, who now advanced from behind the throne, "methinks, old man, thou hast but too little reliance on the will and power of God to assist thee in this matter. It is for him to strengthen the feeblest, where he is innocent, and in the ranks of war to do successful battle with the best and bravest. Is it not written, 'The race is not always to the swift, nor the triumph to the strong!'"

"Ah! do I not know this, my lord? Do not think that I question the power of the Lord to do marvels, whenever it becomes his will to do so; but who is it, believing in God's might and mercy, that flings himself idly from the steep, with the hope that an angel's wings shall be sent to bear him up. I have been taught by the faith which I profess, to honor the Lord our God, and not to tempt him; and I do not readily believe that we may command the extraordinary manifestations of his power by any such vain and uncertain issue as that which you would now institute. I believe not that the truth is inevitably sure to follow the wager and trial of battle, nor will I lean on the succor of any hireling weapon to avouch for mine."

"It need be no hireling sword, old man. The brave and the noble love adventure, for its own sake, in the paths of danger; and it may be that thou shalt find some one, even in this assembly, noble as him thou accusest, and not less valiant with his weapon, who, believing in thy truth, shall be willing to do battle in thy behalf."

"Thyself, perchance!" cried the accused, impetuously, and turning a fiery glance upon the speaker. In this glance it seemed to me that I could discover a far greater degree of bitterness and hate than in any which he had shown to his accuser. "It is thyself that would do this battle? Ha! thou art he, then, equally noble and not less valiant, art thou? Be it so! It will rejoice me shouldst thou venture thy body in this quarrel. But I know thee—thou lovest it too well—thou durst not."

"Choose me for thy champion, old man," was the further speech of the favorite, with a difficult effort to be calm. "I will do battle for thee, and with God's mercy, sustain the right in thy behalf."

"Thou shalt not!" exclaimed the king, vehemently, but feebly, half rising as he spoke, and turning to the favorite. "Thou shalt not! I command thee mix not in this matter."

More was said, but in such a feeble tone that it failed to reach my senses. When the king grew silent, the favorite bowed with submissive deference, and sunk again behind the throne. A scornful smile passed over the lips of the accused, who looked, with a bitter intelligence of gaze, upon a little group seemingly his friends and supporters, who had partly grouped themselves around him. Following his glance, a moment after toward the royal person, I was attracted by a movement, though for a single instant only, of the uplifted hand of the favorite. It was a sign to the accused, the former withdrawing the glove from his right hand, a moment after, and flinging it, with a significant action, to the floor behind him. The accused, whispered a page in waiting, who immediately stole away and disappeared from sight. But a little while elapsed when I beheld him approach the spot where the glove had fallen, recover it adroitly, and convey it, unperceived, into his bosom. All this by-play, though no doubt apparent to many in the assembly, was evidently unseen and unsuspected by the king. I inferred the rank luxuriance of the practice of chivalry in this region, from the nicety with which the affair was conducted, and the forbearance of all those by whom it had been witnessed, to make any report of what they had beheld. The discussion was resumed by the accuser.

"I am aware, your majesty, that by the laws and practice of your realm, the wager of battle is one that may be freely challenged by any one accused of treason, or other crime against the state, against whom there shall be no witness but the accuser. It is not the fear of danger which makes me unwilling to seek this conflict; it is the fear of doing wrong. Though the issues of battle are in the hands of the Lord, yet who shall persuade me that he has decreed the combat to take place. Now I do confess that I regard it as unholy, any invocation of the God of Peace, to be a witness in a strife which his better lessons teach us to abhor—a strife grossly at variance with his most settled and divine ordinances."

"I am grieved, old man, to hear you speak this language," was the grave censure of one who, from his garments, seemed to be very high in authority and the church. "What thou sayest is in direct reproach of holy church, which has frequently called in the assistance of mortal force and human weapons to put down the infidel, to crush the wrong-doer, and to restore that peace which can only owe her continued existence to the presence ever of a just readiness for war. Methinks thou hast scarcely shown thyself enough reverent in this thy bold opinion."

"Holy father, I mean not offence! I do not doubt that war, with short-sightedness of human wisdom, has appeared to secure the advantages of peace. I believe that God has endowed us with a strength for the struggle, and with a wisdom that will enable us to pursue it with success. These we are to employ when necessary for the protection of the innocent, and the rescue and safety of those who are themselves unwilling to do harm. But I am unwilling to believe that immortal principles — the truth of man, and the value of his assurances — are to depend upon the weight of his own blows, or the address with which he can ward off the assaults of another. Were this the case, then would the strong-limbed and brutal soldier be always the sole arbiter of truth, and wisdom, and all moral government."

We need not pursue the argument. It has long since been settled, though with partial results only to humanity, as well by the pagan as the Christian philosopher. But, however ingenious, true, or eloquent, was the venerable speaker on this occasion, his arguments were entirely lost upon that assembly. He himself soon perceived that the effect was unfavorable to his cause, and exposed his veracity to question. With a proper wisdom, therefore, he yielded promptly to the current. But first he asked:—

"And what, may it please your majesty, if I decline this ordeal?"

"Death!" was the reply of more than one stern voice in the assembly. "Death by fire, by the burning pincers, by the tortures of the screw and rack."

The venerable man replied calmly.

"Life is a duty! Life is precious!" He spoke musingly,

looking down, as he spoke, upon the little girl who stood beside him, while the big tears gathered in his eyes as he gazed.

"Do you demand a champion?" was the inquiry of the king.

"No, sire! If, in behalf of my truth, this battle must be fought, its dangers must be mine only."

"Thine!" exclaimed the favorite.

"Ay, my lord—mine. None other than myself must encounter this peril."

A murmur of ridicule passed through the assembly. The accused laughed outright, as the exulting warrior laughs, with his captive naked beneath his weapon. A brief pause followed, and a visible anxiety prevailed among the audience. Their ridicule afforded to the accuser sufficient occasion for reply:—

"This murmur of surprise and ridicule that I hear on every hand, is of itself a sufficient commentary upon this trial of truth by the wager of battle. It seems to all little less than madness, that a feeble old man like myself, even though in the cause of right, should oppose himself to the most valiant warrior in the kingdom. Yet, if it be true that God will make himself manifest in the issue, what matters it whether I be old or young, strong or weak, well-skilled or ignorant in arms? If there be a just wisdom in this mode of trial, the feeblest rush, in maintenance of the truth, were mighty against the steel-clad bosom of the bravest. I take the peril. I will meet this bold criminal, nothing fearing, and will, in my own person, engage in the battle which is thus forced upon me. But I know not the use of lance, or sword, or battle-axe. These weapons are foreign to my hands. Is it permitted me to use such implements of defence as my own skill and understanding may invent, and I may think proper to employ?"

"Thou shalt use no evil arts, old man," exclaimed the churchman who had before spoken, anticipating the answer of the monarch. "No sorcery, no charms, no spells, no accursed devices of Satan. I warn thee, if thou art found guilty of arts like those, thou shalt surely perish by fire."

"None of these, holy father, shall I employ. My arts shall be those only, the principles of which I shall proclaim to thyself, or to any noble gentleman of the king's household. My weapons shall be those only which a human intelligence may prepare. They belong to the studies which I pursue—to the same studies which have enabled me to arrive at truths, some of which thou thyself hast been pleased to acknowledge, and which, until I had discovered them, had been hidden from the experience of men. It can not be held unreasonable and unrighteous that I employ the weapons the virtues of which I know, when my enemy uses those for which he is renowned?"

Some discussion followed, the demand of the accuser being strenuously resisted by the friends of the accused.

"The weapons for knightly encounter,' said they, "have long since been acknowledged. These are sword, and battle-axe, and spear."

"But I am no knight," was the reply; "and as it is permitted to the citizen to do battle with staff and cudgel, which are his wonted weapons, so may it be permitted to me to make use of those which are agreeable to my strength, experience, and the genius of my profession."

Some demur followed from the churchman.

"Holy father," replied the accuser, "the sacred volume should be your guide as it is mine. My claim is such as seems already, in one famous instance, to have met the most decisive sanction of God himself."

Here he unfolded the pages of the Holy Scriptures.

"Goliah," said he, "was a Philistine knight, who came into battle with the panoply of his order. David appeared with staff, and sling, and stone, as was proper to the shepherd. He rejected the armor with which Saul would have arrayed him for the combat. The reproach of the Philistine knight comprises the objection which is offered here—'Am I a dog,' said Goliah, 'that thou comest to me with staves?' The answer of David, O king! shall be mine: 'And all this assembly shall know that the Lord saveth not with sword and spear; for the battle is the Lord's, and he will give you into our hands.' Such were his words—they are mine. God will deliver me from the rage of mine enemy. I will smite him through all his panoply, and in spite of shield and spear."

He spoke with a momentary kindling of his eyes, which was soon succeeded by an expression of sadness.

"And yet, O king! I would be spared this trial. My heart

loves not strife. My soul shrinks in horror from the shedding of human blood. Require not this last proof at my hands. Suffer me to keep my conscience white, and clear of this sacrifice. Let this unhappy man live; for as surely as we strive together, so surely must he perish."

"Now this passeth all belief, as it passeth all human endurance!" exclaimed the accused with irrepressible indignation. "I claim the combat, O king, on any condition. Let him come as he will, with what weapons he may, though forged in the very armory of Satan. My talisman is in the holy cross, and the good sword buckled at my thigh by the holiest prince in Christendom, will not fail me against the devil and all his works. I demand the combat!"

"Be ye both ready within three days!" said the king.

"I submit," replied the aged man. "I trust in the mercy of God to sustain me against this trial, and to acquit me of its awful consequences."

"Ready, ay, ready!" was the answer of the accused, as with his hand he clutched fiercely the handle of his sword, until the steel rang again in the iron scabbard.

CHAPTER VII.

The scene underwent a sudden change, and I now found myself in a small and dimly-lighted apartment, which seemed designed equally for a studio and a laboratory of art. The walls were surrounded by enormous cases, on the shelves of which were massive scrolls of vellum, huge parchment manuscripts, and volumes fastened with clasps of brass and silver. Some of these lay open. Charts hung wide marked with strange characters. Frames of ebony were thus suspended also bearing the signs of the zodiac. Other furniture, of quaint and strange fashion, seemed to show conclusively that the possessor pursued the seductive science of astrology. He had other pursuits — a small furnace, the coals of which were ignited, occupied one corner of the chamber, near which stood a table covered with retorts and receivers, cylinders and gauging-glasses, and all the other paraphernalia which usually belong to the analytic worker in chemistry. The old man, and the young girl described in the previous scene, were, at first, the only occupants of the apartment. But a few moments elapsed, however, when an inner door was thrown open, and a third party appeared, closely enveloped in a cloak of sable. This he threw aside, and I discovered him to be the same person who had been the chief counsellor of the king, and whom I supposed to be his favorite. At his entrance the damsel disappeared. The stranger then, somewhat abruptly, began in the following manner:—

"Why, O why did you not choose me for your champion?"

"And why, my lord, expose you to a conflict with one of the bravest warriors in all the realm?"

"He is brave, but I fear him not; besides, he who fights against guilt hath a strength of arm which supplies all deficiencies. But it is not too late. I may still supply your place."

"Forgive me, dear lord, but I have made my election."

"Alas, old man, why are you thus obstinate? He will slay you at the first encounter."

"And if he does, what matter! I have but a brief space to live, according to the common allotment. He hath more, which were well employed devoted to repentance. It were terrible, indeed, that he should be hurried before the awful tribunal of Heaven with all the blackness in his soul, with all his sins unpurged, upon his conscience."

"Why, this is veriest madness. Think you what will follow your submission and defeat? He will pursue his conspiracy. Others will do what you have refused. He will drag other and bitter spirits into his scheme. He will bring murder into our palaces, and desolation into our cities. Know you not the man as I know him? Shall he be suffered to escape, when the hand of God has clearly shown you that his purposes are to be overthrown, and his crime to be punished through your agency."

"And it shall be so, my dear lord. It is not my purpose to submit. The traitor shall be met in battle."

"But by thyself? Why not a champion? I am ready."

"Greatly indeed do I thank and honor thee, my lord; but it can not be."

"Methinks there is some touch of insanity about thee, old man, in spite of all thy wisdom. Thou canst not hope to contend, in sooth, against this powerful warrior. He will hurl thee to the earth with the first thrust of his heavy lance; or smite thee down to death with a single blow of battle axe or dagger."

"Hear me, my lord, and have no fear. Thou knowest not the terrible powers which I possess, nor should any know, but that this necessity compels me to employ them. I will slay my enemy and thine. He can not harm me. He will perish helplessly ere his weapon shall be twice lifted to affront me."

"Thou meanest not to employ sorcery?"

"Be assured, my lord, I shall use a carnal agent only. The instrument which I shall take with me to battle, though of terrible and destructive power, shall be as fully blessed of Heaven as any in your mortal armory."

"Be it so! I am glad that thou art so confident; and yet, let me entreat thee to trust thy battle to my hands."

"No, my dear lord, no! To thee there would be danger — to me, none. I thank thee for thy goodness, and will name thee in my prayers to Heaven."

We need not pursue their dialogue, which was greatly prolonged, and included much other matter which did not concern the event before us. When the nobleman took his departure, the damsel reappeared. The old man took her in his embrace, and while the tears glistened upon his snowy beard, he thus addressed her:—

"But for thee — for thee, chiefly — daughter of the beloved and sainted child in heaven, I had spared myself this trial. This wretched man should live wert thou not present, making it needful that I should still prolong to the last possible moment, the remnant of my days. Were I to perish, where wert thou? What would be the safety of the sweet one and the desolate? The insect would descend upon the bud, and it would lose scent and freshness. The worm would fasten upon the flower, and a poison worse than death would prey upon its core. No! my poor Lucilla, I must live for thee, though I live not for myself. I must shed the blood of mine enemy, and spare mine own, that thou mayest not be desolate."

CHAPTER VIII.

WHILE the tears of the two were yet mingling, the scene underwent a change corresponding with my anxiety for the *denouément*. A vast area opened before me, surrounded by the seats and scaffolding as if for a tourney, and the space was filling fast with spectators. I will not attempt to describe the splendor of the scene. Lords and ladies, in their most gorgeous attire, occupied the high places; princes were conspicuous; the people were assembled in thousands. At the sound of trumpets the king made his appearance. A grand burst of music announced that he was on his throne. Among the knights and nobles by whom he was attended, I readily distinguished "the favorite." He was in armor, but it was of an exceedingly simple pattern, and seemed designed for service rather than display. He looked grave and apprehensive, and his eyes were frequently turned upon the barriers, as if in anxious waiting for the champions.

The accused was the first to appear. He was soon followed, however, by the accuser, and both made their way through the crown to the foot of the throne. As the old man approached, the favorite drew nigh, and addressed him in subdued, but earnest accents.

"It is not yet too late! Call upon me as thy champion. The king dare not refuse thee, and as I live, I will avenge mine own and thy wrongs together."

"It can not be, my lord," was the reply, with a sad shake of the head. "Besides," he continued, "I have no wrongs to avenge. I seek for safety only. It is only as my life is pledged equally to the living and the dead, that I care to struggle for it, and to save."

The face of the favorite was clouded with chagrin. He led the way in silence to the foot of the throne, followed by the venerable man. There, the latter made obeisance, and encountered the hostile and fierce glance of his enemy, whom he regarded only with looks of sorrow and commiseration. A breathless silence pervaded the vast assembly as they beheld the white locks, the simple majesty of his face and air, and the costume — singular for such an occasion — which he wore. This did not in any degree differ from that in which he had always appeared habited before. It consisted of a loose, flowing robe of the purest white, most like, but more copious than the priestly cassock. His opponent, in complete steel, shining like the sun with helmeted head and gauntleted hand, afforded to the spectators a most astonishing difference between the combatants. The wonder increased with their speculations. The surprise extended itself to the king, who proffered, as Saul had done to David, the proper armor of a warrior to the defenceless man. But this he steadily refused. The king, himself, condescended to remonstrate.

"This is sheer madness, old man. Wouldst thou run upon thy death with uncovered head and bosom?"

"Oh! sire, I fear not death, and feel that I am not now to die. Yet would I still implore that I may be spared this trial. Once more I lay myself at the foot of the throne, to supplicate its mercy."

"For thyself!" cried his enemy, with a scornful taunt.

"For myself and for thee!" was the firm reply, "that I may be spared the pang of sending thee before the Eternal Judge, with all thy unatoned crimes upon thy head."

The voice and words of the venerable speaker, deep and solemn, thrilled, with a sensible effect, throughout the assembly. Whence should he derive this confidence? From heaven or from hell. The conclusion to which they came, more than ever confirmed their belief in his reputed sorceries; and his words inspired a deep and silent terror among the crowd. But the accused, strong in his skill, courage, and panoply of steel, if not in the justice of his cause, mocked scornfully, and defied the doom which was threatened. Some of his friends, however, shared strongly in the apprehensions of the vulgar.

"He hath no visible armor," was their cry; "with what would he defend himself? How know we that he hath not magic arts, and devices of hell, with which he secretly arms himself?"

"Thou hast weapons—visible weapons, as I hear"—remarked the king.

"They are at hand, sire—they are here."

"Thou hast dealt in no forbidden practice?"

"None, sire, as I stand uncovered in the sight of heaven. The reverend father in God, to whom thou didst give in charge this inquiry, is here, and will answer to your majesty. He hath heard and seen the secret of my strength — that strength which I know and declare is powerful to destroy my foe. He knows it to be a secret of mortal wisdom only, as patiently wrought out by human art and labor, as were the sword and axe of him who now seeks my destruction. I have warned him already of the fearful power which they impart. I would still have him live, unharmed by me."

"Peace, insolent!" cried the accused. "I am here, your majesty, to fight, not to prate! — to chastise, not to hearken to the speeches of this pagan sorcerer. Let his power be what he esteems it: I trust to my good sword and to the favor of the Mother of God; and I doubt not of this good steel, which hath been crowned with a threefold conquest, on the plains of the Saracen. I entreat that your majesty will give command for the combat."

CHAPTER IX.

The eye of the venerable accuser, regarded the face of the speaker with a sad and touching solemnity; but at this moment, the little girl who had before accompanied him, was conducted into the foreground by the archbishop. She bore in her hand a sarbacane — seemingly of brass, long and narrow like a wand, and crowned, at the extremity, by a small globe or bulb of the same material. The length of this instrument was fully six feet or more. The old man took it into his hands, and having unscrewed a part of the bulb — which seemed a mere sheathing of brass, he discovered beneath it another globe, similar, in shape and size, to that which had been removed; but the inner bulb was manufactured of glass, of a whiteness equally crystalline and beautiful. He then took from beneath his robes a little box of ebony, which he unlocked, and from which he produced a headpiece, the face of which, instead of being hard steel or iron, was of glass also, very thin, and quite transparent, through which every muscle and motion of the features might be seen with the greatest distinctness. To the thoughtless vulgar, such a shield seemed only a mockery of that more solid furniture of metal which, in those days, thoroughly encased the warrior for battle. The inference, accordingly, was very general, that if by any possibility, the accuser succeeded in the combat, he would be indebted solely to supernatural agency for his good fortune. His wand of brass, with its crystal bulb—his glassy vizor and helmet—were only regarded as designed to divert the scrutiny from the more secret agency which he employed.

"I am ready," said the accuser.

"Hast thou prayed?" demanded his enemy, in a mocking fashion. "If thou hast not, get thee to thy knees quickly, and renounce the devil whom thou servest. Verily, but little time is left thee."

"I have prayed, and confessed to the Holy Father. Do thou likewise, and make thyself humble and contrite. Repent thee—for, of a truth, my lord, if the king forbid not this combat, thou art doomed this day to go to judgment."

The heart of the accused was hardened within him. He replied with a hiss of defiance and contempt to this last appeal; at the same moment he declared himself in readiness also. They were then withdrawn from the presence for a brief space, and were severally approached by their friends and attendants. The archbishop, and the king's favorite went aside with the accuser, and when the latter returned to the arena, in order to the combat, the archbishop led away with him the little girl, upon whom, at parting, the old man bestowed many caresses, accompanied by many tears. The spectators were all very much moved by this tenderness, and now began to regard him as one set apart for sacrifice—doomed to be separated for ever, and by a violent death, from the object of his affections. And when the opponents stood, at length, confronting each other—with none to go between—awaiting only the word for the combat *à l'outrance;*—when they regarded the strong soldier-like frame, and the warlike bearing of the accused—beheld the ease with which he strode the lists, and displayed his weapon;—and contrasted this image of dire necessity and war, with the feeble, though erect form of his venerable accuser,—habited in vestments like a priest or woman—with the simple unmeaning wand within his grasp, and the frail mask of brittle crystal upon his face—a loud murmur of regret and commiseration prevailed among the multitude. But this murmur was soon quieted by the cry of the master of the tournay—

"Laissez aller!"

Then followed a painful silence.

"Now, sorcerer," cried the knight, raising his glittering sword and advancing deliberately and with the confident manner of the executioner. The aged accuser simply presented the bulbous extremity of his wand, and before the accused could smite, the frail glass was shivered against the bars of his enemy's mouth-piece. At this moment the knight was seen slightly to recoil; but it was for a moment only, in the next instant he darted forward, and with a fierce cry, seemed about to strike. The old man, in the meantime, had suffered his wand to fall upon the ground. He made no further effort—offered no show of fear or flight, but with arms folded, seemed in resignation to await the death-stroke of his enemy. But while the weapon of the man of war was in air, and seemingly about to descend, he was seen to pause, while his form suddenly became rigid. A quick and awful shudder seemed to pass through his whole frame. Thus, for a second, he stood paralyzed, and then a thin, mist-like vapor, which might be called smoke, was seen to creep out from various parts of his frame, followed by a thin but oily liquor, that now appeared oozing through all the crevices of his armor. His arm dropped nervelessly by his side; the sword fell from the incapable grasp of his gauntleted hands, and in an inconceivable fraction of time, he himself, with all his bulk, sunk down upon the earth—falling, not at length, prostrate, either backward or forward, but in a heap, even upon the spot which he had occupied when standing; and as if every bone had suddenly been withdrawn which had sustained them, the several parts of his armor became detached, and rolled away—his helmet, his gorget, his cuiras, his greaves, his gauntlets—disclosing beneath a dark, discolored mass—a mere jellied substance, in which bones and muscles were already decomposed and resolved into something less than flesh. Above this heap might be seen a still bright and shining eye, which, for a single second, seemed to retain consciousness and life, as if the soul of the immortal being had lingered in this beautiful and perfect orb, reluctant to depart. But in a moment it, too, had disappeared—all the brightness swallowed up and stifled in the little cloud of vapor which now trembled, heaving up from the mass which but a moment before had been a breathing, a burning, an exulting spirit. A cold horror overspread the field, followed by a husky and convulsive cry, as from a drowning multitude. The people gazed upon each other, and upon the awful, heap in unspeakable terror. It was annihilation which had taken place before them. Dead was the silence that prevailed for several minutes; a vacant consternation freezing up the very souls of the spectators. But the reaction was tremendous.

"Seize upon the sorcerer! Tear him in pieces!" was the cry from a thousand voices. This was followed by a wild rush, like that of an incoming sea struggling to overwhelm the headlands. The barriers were broken down, the cries swelled into a very tempest, and the mammoth multitude rolled onward, with souls on fire, eyes glaring with tiger fury, and hands outstretched, clutching spasmodically at their victim. Their course had but one centre, where the old man calmly stood. There he kept his immovable station, calm, firm, subdued, but stately. How will he avert his fate — how stay this ocean of souls, resolute to overwhelm him? I trembled — I gasped with doubt and apprehension. But I was spared the further contemplation of horrors which I could no longer bear to witness, by the very intensity of the interest which my imagination had conceived in the subject. There is a point beyond which the mortal nature can not endure. I had reached that point, and was relieved. I awakened, and started into living consciousness, my face covered with clammy dews, my hair upright and wet, my whole frame agitated with the terrors which were due wholly to the imagination.

It would be easy, perhaps, to account for such a dream, assuming, as we did at the outset, that the mental faculties never know abeyance — that the thought never sleeps. Any speculation, in regard to the transition periods in English history, would give the requisite material. From a survey of the powers of physical manhood to those rival and superior powers which follow from the birth of art and science, the step is natural enough; and the imagination might well delight itself by putting them in contrast and opposition. But we have no space left for further discussion.

CHAPTER XVII.

HOW THE BILIOUS ORATOR ESSAYED

"A GOOD deal has been said in respect to the monotony of the prospect while passing through the North-Carolina country. In respect to such influences as are derived from the moral world, and by which places are lighted up by a brilliancy not their own, the same thing may be said of most of the ordinary stage and railway routes everywhere in our country. Roads are usually drawn through the most accessible regions. The lands commonly surrendered for this purpose are generally the most inferior, and the man of taste rarely establishes a fine mansion upon the common highway. In the South, this is particularly the case. The finer dwellings of the planter are to be approached through long and sinuous avenues, that open only a green arch upon the roadside, and show you nothing to convey any tolerable idea of the beauty, taste and comfort which are buried in noble woods away from vulgar curiosity. The landscape, in the eye of the hurrying traveller, needs to possess but a single element — variety. Let it be broken into great inequalities — steep rocks, and deep dells and valleys, overhanging precipices, and thundering waterfalls — and the voyager, who is only the pendant to a locomotive for the nonce, is quite satisfied. Beauty of detail is, of course, quite imperceptible to his vision. In the old countries of Europe, the site is illustrated by tower and temple, picturesque ruin and votive tablet. The handbook which you carry distinguishes the spot with some strange or startling history. In our world of woods, we lack these adjuncts. If we had the handbook, we should doubtlessly discover much to interest us in the very scenes by which we hurry with contempt. Dull and uninteresting as the railroad route appears through North and South Carolina, were you familiar with the facts in each locality — could you couple each with its local history or tradition — the fancy would instantly quicken, and the mind would not only take a lively interest in the scene through which you pass, but would, by a naturally-assimilative process, begin to explore for its underlying beauties."

"What a pity that handbooks for the South are not provided by some patriotic author!"

"They will be furnished, no doubt, when the tide of travel sets in this direction, and you will then be surprised at the discoveries which shall be made. He who goes over these common routes has no idea of the wondrous scenic beauties which lie in wait to delight him, hidden from sight only by the roadside umbrage. With a considerable knowledge of the history of the country in all these states, I am able to identify scenes of interest as I pass; and I find, at every step, in my course along these regions which seem so barren to the stranger, fruitful interests and moving influences, which exercise equally the memory and the imagination — the imagination through the memory. There is scarcely a mile in the passage over the common roads, in South Carolina, which I do not thus find suggestive of events and persons, legends and anecdotes, which elevate the aspect of the baldest tracts, each with a befitting moral. To him who can recall these events and traditions, the scene becomes invested with a soft and rosy light — the sterile sands put on features which sublime them to the thought, and the gloomy wastes of pine and swamp forest commend themselves to sympathies which lie much deeper than any which we can reach through the medium of the external senses. No doubt this is the same in all the wild states of the South, to him who is of 'the *manor* born.' There will be a thousand local matters, of colonization, early adventure, peculiar strifes and endurances — the long records of history and tradition, from the first coming of the colonists — which, if known to the wayfarer, would make him forgetful of the monotonous features of his progress."

"It is a great pity that for these we have no guide-books — no monuments along the wayside — no 'Old Mortality' to show us where the stone lies half buried, and, with his chisel, to deepen all its features to our eyes. Some of these days, no doubt, we shall have rare chroniclers springing up, who shall reveal to our successors these things—these objects, as well of mind as of sight—which we hourly hurry by unseeing."

"Of this I have no sort of question. The development is in progress. The mines of the South have been struck. The vein is revealed. The quarry is discovered, and in due season it will be worked. The very impatience with which we complain that the thing is not done, is in some degree a guaranty for the performance. We must wait upon Providence. The great error of our people, as a whole, is that they live too fast, and endeavor at too much. If suffered to go ahead, according to the motive impulse in their veins, our posterity would have neither necessity nor field for achievement. I am for leaving something to be done by our children. To him who remembers the South—North Carolina, for example—but twenty, nay, ten years ago, her social and mental progress is absolutely wonderful."

"Hear that, young Turpentine, and be consoled at all my flings at the old North state."

"Ah, he knows it better than either you or me."

"But, without looking to the social progress of North Carolina, and regarding her as a region only for the exploration of the picturesque and adventure-seeking traveller—the artist, the man of taste, the lover of fine manly sports,—the good old North state is one of the most attractive in all the confederacy. Her vast ranges of mountain render her especially attractive to all these classes."

"Yet, how little promise of this is there along the Atlantic shore!"

"Even here, to the painter of detail, to the contemplative and musing taste and nature, there are thousands of scenes of great interest and beauty. To find these, however, you need the eye that sees; and the man whose eyes have been properly couched by art may spend months and years along the Atlantic coast, and discover new provinces of beauty with the ramble of each succeeding day. Nature, in her arrangement of the scenery of the South, differing from the rule of the artist, has thrown her most imposing forms and aspects into the background. Her mountains and majestic altar-places are nowhere visible along the sea; and the superficial traveller is prepared to doubt the existence of any such throughout our land. Their absence on the Atlantic would not, perhaps, be so greatly felt, if men were not always most easily taken by the bald outline, the mere surface, the simply salient and externally imposing. There is much in the scenery along our coast which, closely examined, would, by its exquisite delicacy and nice variety of detail, quite as much attract the mere explorer as the artist. One of the peculiarities of this region, as distinguished from the northern coasts, is the presence of the numerous beautiful islets, that seem to guard our shores and cities from the wave. Roving in boat or steamer along these islets, or among them, they appeal to a moral instinct, the exercise of which puts a thousand genial fancies into activity. They rise up suddenly around you, like gems from out the sea; fairy abodes at least; sometimes green in shrub, and vine, and tree, to the very lips of ocean; and again, spread out, a sandy plain, glittering with myriads of diamond sparks, garlanded with myriads of fantastic shells, and seeming, for all the world,—particularly when seen by the moonlight—to have been devised and chosen as favorite places for the sports of Oberon and Titania, of Puck and Little John, the capricious Loline and the tricksy Anatilla. Southward as you go, they spread away, diamonds or emeralds, till they conduct you to the great waters of the Mississippi. They grow in size and lose in beauty as you advance northwardly. But they still constitute a remarkable feature of our whole coast; and to him who spreads sail among them at moonlight, especially in the more southwardly points, they compel the thought of all the beings recognised by the old system of pneumatology. The terrors of Cape Hatteras might well make it to be supposed a region of mischief, upheaved from the sea, by races of ungentler beings than such as harbor in those little sand-dunes which lie so smilingly in the moonlight, with the sea moving between them in such placid currents. At Hatteras, we may supposes, the malicious elves, the grim Brownies, the savage Kobolds inhabit— demon tribes that lie waiting, in malignant watch for the unconscious bark—slyly slipping beneath the wave, seizing without noise upon the prow of the vessel, and drawing her into the insidious currents, and upon the sands of the treacherous islet. The fancy that peoples the innocent islets, which wreck no vessels with the 'good people,' may with equal propriety refer the dangerous capes and headlands to such hostile tribes of demons as haunt the wilds of Scotland, the Harz mountains and Black forests of the German, and the stormy shores of the Scandinavian."

"Not an unreasonable notion. But was not Hatterask the old Indian name of the cape and the sea about it, as given by the ancient chroniclers?"

"Yes: they varied, however; sounds imperfectly caught from the Indian tongue were imperfectly rendered in the various tongues of Dutchman, Spaniard, Frenchman, and Englishman. We must content ourselves with making them euphonious, and leave their absolute propriety in doubt."

"And a pretty sort of euphony we should have of it, if we leave the matter to American discretion."

"This need occasion no concern. The poets settle this for succeeding time, when our generations have no longer the power to pervert the ears of the future. The necessity of verse compels the gradual growth of harmony in every language. The oral authority lasts no longer than it can compel the echo. The poet, always resisted while he lives, leaves a voice behind him that survives all others. Let him make his record, and be satisfied to leave it to the decision of posterity. There is no speech of the future that rises in conflict with his own."

"Are the historical and traditional materiel of North Carolina of attractive character?"

"None more so. The very regions of country which are so barren in the eyes of the stranger, pursuing the railway routes along the Atlantic coast, would alone afford materials for a thousand works of fiction. I have identified, along this very route, the progress of more than one curious history. Take an example:—

"Our first serious war with the redmen of the South, broke out in 1712. The savages of the old North State took up the tomahawk and scalping knife in that year, with terrible effect. Numerous tribes were leagued together for the extermination of the whites of the colony of New Berne. This colony was of Swiss, from the Canton of Berne in Switzerland, and Germans of the Palatinate. They came out to America under the patronage of Queen Anne. They were led by the Baron De Graffenreidt, who was created a landgrave. He, with Louis Mitchell, a leading man among the Swiss, received a grant of ten thousand acres of land on either of the rivers Neuse and Cape Fear, or their tributary branches, at the rate of ten pounds sterling for every thousand acres, and a quitrent of five shillings. The number of Germans is unknown; but the Swiss were fifteen hundred. They reached the confluence of the Neuse and Trent in December, 1710, and laid off the limits of the colony in that neighborhood.

"The conditions upon which these people came to America, were specious and encouraging. Each of them received, in England, an outfit in clothes and money, of from five to ten pounds sterling; and two hundred and fifty acres were allotted to each family, which was to be five years exempt from rent or taxation. At the end of that time, they were to pay at the rate of half per cent, Carolina currency.—They were credited one year with provisions, and seven years with the *materiel* for a certain farming establishment. This included cows and calves, sows and pigs, lambs, &c. Tools and implements for clearing land and building, were furnished without any charge by the proprietors

"To a poor people, driven from their native abodes, the prospect was encouraging enough; and the treatment which they received seemed very liberal. Indeed, the colony very soon began to put on the most prosperous appearance — was flourishing in fact, growing daily in numbers and affluence. But the Indians, as the phrase goes, began to look on the whites with jealousy. Jealousy, it probably was not. In brief the savages coveted treasures which they beheld for the first time, and which were indifferently guarded.

"In the fall of 1711, certain tribes agreed to combine their forces for the purpose of massacre and plunder. The Tuscaroras undertook to cut the throats of the settlers upon the Roanoke, and between that river and Pamlico, otherwise Tar river. The Cotheckneys and Corees arranged to do the same benevolent office for the settlements on the Neuse and Trent. The Mattamaskettos and Matchapangos had the duty assigned them of scalping the whites in the neighborhood of Bath.

"The work was done with little reservation at the designated period. But a few days before the massacre, the Indians succeeded in taking captive the Baron De Graffenreidt and John Lawson, the surveyor-general of the province, whose book of travels, a highly-interesting narrative, constitutes one of the best of our Indian authorities of the South, and should be in every good American library.

"These distinguished persons, totally unsuspicious of danger, were engaged in an exploring expedition up the Neuse. Their vessel was a mere *dug-out*, a cypress canoe of native manufacture: and they were accompanied only by a negro, who paddled the canoe, right and left. They landed at evening with the view of encamping, when they were suddenly surrounded by more than sixty Indians. They were made prisoners and marched off to a village some distance up the river—a march that occupied the whole night. Here the tribe and their neighbors met in solemn consultation on the fate of their prisoners. The baron was an *intruder*, but Lawson was an *invader*. As it was after his surveys that they found their lands appropriated, they assumed him to be the source of the evil of which they complained. Both the captives underwent a severe preliminary beating, the better to prepare them for what was to follow. They were then deliberately doomed to the fire torture, carried to the field of sacrifice, kept there in durance vile, and in the most gloomy apprehensions for a day and night, when the number of the savages having greatly increased to behold the spectacle, the preparations were immediately begun for carrying the terrible judgment into effect. The orgies and phrensied brutalities of the Indians may be imagined. The hour for execution came. The parties were bound to the stake; but at this moment the baron pleaded his nobility, appealing to the chiefs for protection, for that he too was a chief.

"Strange to say, the appeal was entertained. They concluded to spare his life: but no entreaty could save Lawson and the negro. They were subjected to the fiery ordeal, and perished by a terrible and lingering death, protracted to their utmost capacity to endure, with all the horrid ingenuity of savage art. Then followed the general massacre, which spread consternation throughout the province. More than one hundred and sixty persons were butchered in a night."

"Certainly, the romancer could work up such a history with good effect. What a terrible scene, in these awful forests, with thousands of the begrimed and painted savages, howling terribly, and dancing fiercely about them. Did the affair end here?"

"How could it? It is the necessity of civilization that it must conquer. At the first tidings of the affair, the assembly of South Carolina, then in session at Charleston, called out her militia, and appropriated eighty thousand dollars to the relief of the sister province. Six hundred militiamen, under Col. Barnwell, immediately took the field. An auxiliary force of friendly Indians, consisting of two hundred and eighteen Cherokees, seventy-nine Creeks, forty-one Catawbas, twenty-eight Yemassees—all commanded by *white* officers—were joined to the force under Barnwell—the Indians being chiefly used as scouts and hunters.

Wild, tangled, gloomy, was the wilderness which they had to traverse—a region utterly savage, inhabited by bear and panther, or by tribes of men quite as ferocious and untameable. The governor of North Carolina called out the militia of North Carolina, but seemingly in vain. His proclamation was little heeded.

Barnwell crossed the country, in spite of all impediments, and came up with the Indians, who were in great strength upon the Neuse, where they had erected a strong fort of logs, at a point some thirty miles below the spot where the railroad crosses the river. The battle that followed resulted in the utter defeat of the Indians, and the annihilation of some of their tribes. More than three hundred of the redmen were slain—we have no report of the wounded—and one hundred were made prisoners. The battle had taken place without their fortress, the Indians having boldly become the assailants. The fugitives found shelter in the fort, which, after much loss and great suffering, they surrendered, and sued for peace; which was granted them by their conqueror. Barnwell was censured for being too indulgent to the vanquished; but what could he exact from the savages? They had nothing farther to concede than submission—could make no farther sacrifice but in their lives. The fortress thus captured was called after the conqueror, and you may still trace out its ruins. Would these have no interest in the eyes of the traveller who is familiar with the history?

"Now, if I say that all this region is marked in like interesting manner, by wild, savage, bloody, strange, and wonderful events, you will be no longer doubtful of the attraction with which an ordinary handbook, such as in Europe distinguishes every crumbling fabric or fortress with a human interest, would invest this seemingly barren country. There are true histories throughout all these old states of the south, not inferior to those of Powhatan and Pocahontas, and that remarkable old Roman red man of Virginia, the mighty Opechancanough."

"It is curious," said Selina Burroughs, "that our own people are quite as ignorant of these local histories as anybody else."

The remark stirred the bile in the bosom of our Alabama orator, who was never more ready to lift the tomahawk than when opportunity offered to indulge in a fling at the Yankees, and pour out his sarcasms at the expense of those of the South, who were adverse to decisive or hostile measures.

"Nothing curious about it, Miss Burroughs. We are a poor, mouthing, meanspirited people after all, with long tongues and soft brains, and no resolution. Our ignorance in respect to our own history and own resources, and our own rights, is sufficiently conclusive against our perpetually vaunted patriotism. Our constant travel at the North among a people who are for ever assailing us, is enough to shame and discredit all our boasting."

"But there is a great change going on in this respect, sir."

"Yes, indeed! I can acknowledge this, though the acknowledgment does not a whit lessen the necessity of denouncing the practice which is still too much continued. We must continue to denounce until the reform is complete. It is a great consolation, full of hope and promise, that it is at last begun."

Here the orator dashed off into an essay, somewhat in the vein of his anniversary oration, which, as it contains sundry startling things, and striking sarcasms, our reporter has thought it proper to preserve. In fact, there is a wholesome word for North and South, in the very energetic expression of this man's feelings. He is the true type and representative of a large portion of the southern people, speaking the bitterness which they have been taught to nourish, their jealous resentments, and the spirit with which they will seize upon any opportunity of obtaining redress and remedy for the evils and injuries of which they complain. Let North and South consider, and be wise in season. The usual caprice in the destiny of nations precipitates catastrophes which men may lament but never repair; and one of the most dangerous of the errors which prevail among the people of the North, is their obstinate faith in the integrity of the Union. It is a faith against which all histories, in all periods, bear the most unvarying testimony — testimony which we should be authorized to disregard and reject, only when we shall be able to assure ourselves that we have stronger claims, by reason of our greater virtues, upon the protecting care of God, than any of the myriad generations by which we have been preceded. But, to the essay of our orator, which, though extempore, was delivered as rapidly as an oration memorized; not as if read simply, but with the freedom of one who declaims passionately, in hot blood, and with the bold impetuous action of a fiery soul, in which the long-fettered torrents have at length broken all their barriers, and are dashing headlong, in foam and fury, over the still resisting but incapable rock.

"Yes, soft-heads! soft-heads! That is the word — soft-heads! But there is hope, even for a soft-head!"

"We should only be indulging in one of the commonest of all truisms, were we to protest that there is no such thing as unmixed evil in the world; and all the philosophy may be compassed in a nut-shell, which chuckles over the 'ill wind that blows nobody good.' It will suffice if we insist that our bitter is, frequently, the wholesome medicine whose benefit is in the future; and what we regard as the mishap of the day, and lament accordingly, becomes to our great surprise, the parent of a necessity that leads to most pleasant and profitable results. To bring our maxims to bear upon our present topic, we have but to remark, that the cholera, which devastated the cities of the North last summer, and the abolition mania, — which is destined to root them out, and raze them utterly from the face of the earth, if not seasonably arrested, — have proved, in some degree, highly serviceable, if not saving influences, for the people of the South. How many thousand of our wandering idlers, our absentees who periodically crave a wearisome pilgrimage to northern regions, in stead of finding greater good in a profitable investment of thought and curiosity at home — who wander away in mere listlessness and return wearied and unrefreshed — were denied their usual inane indulgences by the dread of pestilence. And how many other thousands, capable of appreciating the charms of nature, and the delights of a glorious landscape, were, in like manner, compelled to forego the same progress, by the patriotic sentiment which revolts at the thought of spending time and money among a people whose daily labor seems to be addressed to the neighborly desire of defaming our character and destroying our institutions.

"The result of these hostile influences has been highly favorable to the development of the resources of the soil. We have, in the South, a race of 'soft-heads,' — a tribe that corresponds admirably with the 'dough-faces' of Yankee-land. These are people born and wedded to a sort of provincial servility that finds nothing grateful but the foreign. They prefer the stranger to the native, if for no other reason than because they are reluctant to admit the existence of any persons, in their own precincts, who might come in conflict with their own importance. In like manner, and for a similar reason, they refuse to give faith to their own possessions of scenery and climate. Their dignity requires foreign travel for its proper maintenance. It is distance only, in their eyes, that can possibly 'lend enchantment to the view.' They are unwilling to admit the charms of a region which might be readily explored by humbler persons; and they turn up their lordly noses at any reference to the claims of mountain, valley, or waterfall, in their own section, if for no other reason than because they may also be seen by vulgar people. To despise the native and domestic, seems to them, in their inflated folly, the only true way to show that they have tastes infinitely superior to those of the common herdlings.

"For such people, it was absolutely necessary that they should speed abroad in summer. The habit required it, and the self-esteem, even if the tastes did not. It is true that they were wearied with the monotonous routine. It is true that they were tired of the scenery so often witnessed; tired of the flatness of northern pastimes, and outraged constantly by the bad manners, and the unqualified monstrosity of the bores whom they constantly encountered, from the moment that they got beyond the line of Mason and Dixon. All the social training of a polished society at home, was disparaged by the reckless obtrusiveness by which that was distinguished which they met abroad—the free, familiar pertness of moneyed vulgarity, or the insolent assumptions of a class whose fortunes have been realized at the expense of their education. A thousand offensive traits in the social world which they sought, added to the utter deficiency of all freshness in the associations which they periodically made, combined to lessen or destroy everything like a positive attraction in the regions to which they wandered; but, in spite of all, they went. Habit was too inflexible for sense or taste; and, possibly, the fear that the world might not get on so well as before, unless they appeared as usual at the opening of the season in Broadway, and found themselves, for a week at least each year, at Newport and Saratoga, seemed to make it a duty that they should, at large pecuniary sacrifice, submit to a dreary penance every summer.

"But the cholera came in conflict with the habit. It unsettled the routine which was only endurable in the absence of thought and energy. It suggested unpleasant associations to those who, perhaps, would suffer under any sort of excitement, the wholesome as well as the pernicious; and the idea of eating cherries and cream, at the peril of utter revolution in the abdominal domain, had the effect of startling into thought and speculation the inane intellect which, hitherto, had taken no share in regulating the habits of the wanderer. When, at the same time, it was found that the pestilence confined its ravages to the North,—that either the climate of the South was too pure, or the habits of its people too proper, to yield it the requisite field for operation,—and that Charleston, Savannah and other cities in the low latitudes, were not within the reach of its terrors,—then it was that patriotism had leave to suggest, for the first time, the beauties and attractions of home, and to make the most of them. Her argument found succor, as we have hinted, from other influences. Our 'Soft-heads' no longer found that unlimited deference, and servile acknowledgment, which the societies they visited had uniformly shown, in return for their patronage. Society at the North was in revolution. Old things were about to pass away; all things were to become new. Property was to undergo general distribution in equal shares. Every man, it was argued, had a natural right to a farmstead, and a poultry-yard; as every woman, not wholly past bearing, had a right to a husband. The old Patroons of Albany were not permitted to rent, but must sell their lands, at prices prescribed by the buyer, or the tenant. Debtors liquidated their bonds in the blood of their creditors. The law of divorce gave every sort of liberty to wife and husband. The wife, if she did not avail herself of the extreme privileges accorded to her by this benevolent enactment, was, at all events, allowed to keep her own purse, and to spend her money, however viciously, without accounting to her lord. If he was lord, she was lady. She was not simply his master, but her own; and a precious household they made of it between them. Churches multiplied, mostly, at the very moment when a restless and powerful party—avowedly hostile to all religion—was denouncing and striving to abolish the Sabbath itself, as immoral, and in conflict with the privileges of labor and the citizen.

"In this universal disorder in laws and morals—this confusion of society, worse confounded every day—in its general aspects so wonderfully like those which, in France, preceded, and properly paved the way for, a purging reign of terror—all the usual amenities and courtesies were fairly at an end, even in those places, hotels and haunts of summer festivity, in which decency and policy, if not charity and good-will to men, requires that everything should be foreborne, of manner or remark, that might be offensive to any sensibilities. But the cloud and blindness which everywhere overspread society, was a madness too sweeping to forbear any subject, in which envy, malice, conceit, and a peevish discontent, could find exercise at the expense of one's neighbor. In destroying, at home, the securities of religion, the domestic peace of families, the inviolability of the laws, the guarantees of the creditor—nay, taking his life, as that of an insolent, when he presumed to urge his bond—these reckless incendiaries (like the French, exactly) must carry their beautiful system to the hearts of other communities. They are by no means selfish. They must share their admirable blessings with others—nay, force them, even against their desires, to partake of their drunken mixtures. No situation, accordingly is sacred from their invasion. No refuge is left for society, unembarrassed by their presence. They rage in all places, fireside, street, exchange, hotel, and, not so much seeking to reform and teach, as to outrage and annoy, they studiously thrust upon you, at every turn, the picture of the miserable fanatic, whose vanity prompted him to fire a temple-only that he might be seen in its blaze.

"Our 'Soft-heads,' who have been busily engaged, for the last thirty years, in feeding these fanatics, by draining the profits from their own soil, are, at length, beginning to feel somewhat uncomfortable, sitting cheek-by-jowl, at Saratoga, and other places of vulgar resort, and hearing themselves described as robbers and wretches by the very people whose thieving ancestors stole the negro with whom to swindle our forefathers. They begin to suspect that their pride is not wholly unimpaired, when they hearken quietly to such savory communications. A lurking doubt whether they are not the persons meant, all the while, begins to stir uneasily within them; and in a half-drowsy state, between dozing and thought, they ask themselves the question, whether it were not much more to their credit to resolve, henceforward, neither to taste, nor touch, nor commune with a people, who, in mere wantonness and insolence, are making so free with all the securities of their country, its reputation, and its property!

"The 'Soft-head,' it is true, is not without grateful assurances, from one class of his neighbors, that his assailants are very sorry fanatics who deserve no sort of consideration; that, though Tray, Blanche, and Sweetheart, bark at him furiously, yet he, Dick, and his brother Tom, and his cousin, Harry, all tavern-keepers, living in the broad route of southern travel, are his friends—are the true, sturdy butcher's dogs, who will keep the curs in proper fear and at a proper distance. But, after a while, 'Softhead' asks himself—having asked the question fruitlessly of Tom, Dick, and Harry—why do these curs, which are said to be so despicable—why do they continue this barking? nay, why, when the barking becomes biting—why do not these famous butcher's dogs use their teeth for the protection of their friends? Why are Tray, Blanche, and Sweetheart—worthless puppies as they are—why are they in full possession of the roast? The fanatics of abolition are said to be few; but why do they shape the laws, dictate the policy, control the whole action of society? 'Soft-head' gets no answer to all this; and now naturally begins to suspect that all parties either think entirely with the offenders, or possess too little courage, honesty, or proper sympathy with the south, ever to be relied upon as allies. In fact, our 'soft-head' discovers that, whether guilty or otherwise, the party denounced as so weak and worthless, wields, in reality, the entire power, and represents wholly the principles and feelings of the north. The thing is not to be gainsayed. Your merchant, having large dealings with the 'soft-heads,' makes little of it; your hotel-keeper, entertaining large squadrons of 'soft-heads,' 'for a consideration,' every summer, gravely insists that it is nothing but the buzz of a bee in a tar-barrel; your Yankee editor, crossing the line of Mason and Dixon — a northern man with southern principles! who teaches the 'soft-head southron,' from 'hard-head northern school-books'—he is potent in the asseveration that there is no sort of danger—that it is the cry of 'wolf,' only, made by the cunning boys, who wish to see the fun of the false chase; and that, in his hands, as grand conservator of the peace, everything that's worth saving is in a place of eminent security. Your thorough slave of party, whig or democrat, who hopes for a secretaryship, or a vice-presidentship, or a foreign mission — or who, with commendable modesty, resigns himself to a postmastership, or a tide-waitership — all these come in to the assistance of our 'soft-heads,' and take monstrous pains to reassure them and restore their equanimity! Governed by self, rather than by nation or section, they cry 'peace'—all—when there is no peace! When there can not be peace, so long as the south is in the minority, and so long as the spirit and temper of the north are so universally hostile to our most vital and most cherished institutions. Until you reconcile this inequality, and exorcise this evil spirit, that now rages rampant through the Northern States — allied with all sorts of fanatical passions and principles — Agrarianism, Communism, Fourierism, Wrightism, Millerism, Mormonism, etc.,— you may cry peace and union till you split your lungs, but you will neither make peace nor secure union.

"Well, our 'soft-head' begins to discover this. He has been

weak and lazy—listless and indifferent—vain, and an idler; weary, and a wanderer; but he still has latent sympathies that remind him of his home, and he is not blind to the warnings which tell him that he has a property which is threatened, and may possibly be destroyed. He rubs his eyes, and shakes himself accordingly. He begins to bestir himself. It is high time. He is no longer in the condition to say with the sluggard, 'A little more sleep—a little more folding of the arms to slumber.' 'Tray, Blanche, and Sweetheart,' the full-mouthed abolition curs, are at his heels, and, with their incessant barking, they suffer nobody to sleep. 'Soft-head' soon finds that they are not satisfied to bark simply. They are anxious to use their teeth upon him as well as their tongues. His wife's maid, Sally, is persuaded to leave his bonds, for a condition of unexampled human felicity, which is promised her in the neighborhood of the Five Points; and his man, Charles, walks off with two loving white brothers, who soon show him how much more moral it is to become a burglar than to remain a slave. 'Soft-head' very soon hears of both in their new Utopia. Sally writes to him from the Tombs or Blackwell's Island, and Charley from Sing-Sing. They relate a most horrid narrative of their condition; their follies, their crimes, the sufferings and abuses they have undergone at the hands of their sympathizing brethren, whose object has been, not the good of the wretched slave, but the injury and annoyance of the 'soft-head' owner. They declare their repentance, and entreat his assistance. They beg that he will release them from prison, and make them once more humbly happy in the condition which was so justly suited to their intellect and morals. The heart of 'soft-head' is touched. In this region he is quite as tender as in his cranium. He obtains their discharge, gives bail, pays fees, and suffers a world of trouble and expense, in helping the poor wretches into daylight. But, will the abolitionists suffer this triumph? Will they let the prey escape them at the last? Oh no! They dart between, a mob at their heels, and rend Charley and Sally away once more—this time by violence—the poor darkies all the while struggling against the cruel fate of freedom, for which they are so totally unfit, and declaring, with tears in their eyes, how infinitely they prefer being slaves to a gentleman, than brethren of such a gang of blackguards. 'Soft-head,' himself, barely escapes by the skin of his teeth. He is compelled to cast off the indolence which he has hitherto fondly conceived to form a part of his dignity, and, with all haste, to throw the Potomac between him and the pursuing curs of abolition.

"Growling over the popular sentiment at the North, which thus dogs their footsteps and disturbs their equanimity, or grumbling at the sudden invasion of cholera, which makes them tremble for their bowels, it is probable that more than twenty thousand Southrons forebore, last summer, their usual route of travel. Mason and Dixon's line, that season, constituted the *ultima thule*, to which they looked with shiverings only. Thus 'barred and banned,' almost hopeless of enjoyment, but compelled to seek for it where they were, and to find their summer routes and recreations in long-neglected precincts, it was perfectly delightful! to behold the sudden glory which possessed them, as they opened their eyes, for the first time in their lives, upon the charming scenery, the pure retreats, the sweet quiet, and the surprising resources which welcomed them—at home! Why had they not seen these things before? How was it that such glorious mountain ranges, such fertile and lovely valleys, such mighty and beautiful cascades, such broad, hard and ocean-girdled beaches and islets, had been so completely hidden from their eyes? By what fatuity was it that they had been so blinded, to the waste of millions of expenditure, in the ungrateful regions in which they had so long been satisfied to find retreats, which afforded them so little of pleasure or content? Poor, sneaking, drivelling, conceited, slavish provincialism never received such a lesson of unmixed benefit before; and patriotism never a happier stimulus and motive to future enjoyment as well as independence.

"It is a too melancholy truth, and one that we would fain deny if we dared, that, in sundry essentials, the Southern people have long stood in nearly the same relation to the Northern states of this confederacy, that the whole of the colonies, in 1775, occupied to Great Britain. A people wholly devoted to grazing and agriculture are necessarily wanting in large marts, which alone give the natural impulse to trade and manufactures. A people engaged in *staple* culture are necessarily scattered · remotely over the surface of the earth. Now, the activity of the common intellect depends chiefly upon the rough and incessant attrition of the people. Wanting in this attrition, the best minds sink into repose, that finally becomes sluggishness. As a natural consequence, therefore, of the exclusive occupation of agriculture in the South, the profits of this culture, and the sparseness of our population, the Southern people left it to the Northern States to supply all their wants. To them we looked for books and opinion—and they thus substantially ruled us, through the languor which we owed to our wealth, and the deficient self-esteem naturally due to the infrequency of our struggle in the common marts of nations. The Yankees furnished all our manufactures, of whatever kind, and adroitly contrived to make it appear to us that they were really our benefactors, at the very moment when they were sapping our substance, degrading our minds, and growing rich upon our raw material, and by the labor of our slaves. Any nation that defers thus wholly to another is soon emasculated, and finally subdued. To perfect, or even secure, the powers of any people, it requires that they shall leave no province of enterprise or industry neglected, which is available to their labor, and not incompatible with their soil and climate. And there is an intimate sympathy between the labors of a people, and their higher morals and more ambitious sentiment. The arts are all so far kindred, that the one necessarily prepares the way for the other. The mechanic arts thrive as well as the fine arts, in regions which prove friendly to the latter; and Benvenuto Cellini was no less excellent as a goldsmith and cannoneer than as one of the most bold and admirable sculptors of his age. To secure a high rank in society, as well as history, it is necessary that a people should do something more than provide a raw material. It is required of them to provide the genius also, which shall work the material up into forms and fabrics equally beautiful and valuable. This duty has been neglected by the South; abandoned to her enemies; and, in the train of this neglect and self-abandonment, a thousand evils follow, of even greater magnitude. The worst of these is a slavish deference to the will, the wit, the wisdom, the art and ingenuity of the people to whom we yield our manufactures; making it the most difficult thing in the world, even when our own people achieve, to obtain for them the simplest justice, even among themselves. We surrendered ourselves wholly into the hands of our Yankee brethren—most loving kinsmen that they are—and were quite content, in asserting the rank of *gentlemen*, to forfeit the higher rank of *men*. We were sunk into a certain imbecility—read from their books, thought from their standards, shrunk from and submitted to their criticism—and (No! we have not yet quite reached that point—Walker still holding his ground in the South against Webster), almost began to adopt their brogue! They dictated to our tastes and were alone allowed to furnish the proper regions for their exercise. Above all, theirs was all the scenery; and the tour to Saratoga, West Point, Newport, Niagara, almost every season, was a sort of pilgrimage, as necessary to the eternal happiness of our race of 'soft-heads,' as ever was that made, once in a life, to Mecca, by the devout worshipper in the faith of Islam!

"But, owing to causes, already indicated, the change has come over the spirit of that dream which constituted too much the life of too large a portion of our wealthy gentry; and the last summer, as we said before, left them at liberty to look about their own homes, and appreciate their own resources. The discoveries were marvellous; the developments as surprising as those which followed the friction of the magic lamp in the hands of Aladdin. Encountered, on the opposite side of Mason and Dixon's Line, by the loathsome presence of Asiatic cholera and African abolition, they averted their eyes from these equally offensive aspects, and found a prospect, when looking backward upon the South, at once calculated to relieve their annoyances, and compensate admirably for all their privations. The tide of travel was fairly turned; and, through the length and breadth of the land, in the several States of Virginia, the two Carolinas, Georgia, and even Florida, nothing was to be seen but the chariots and the horsemen, the barge and the car, bearing to new and lately discovered retreats of health and freshness, the hungering wanderers after pleasure and excitement. For such an event, the country was almost totally unprepared. A few ancient places of resort excepted, the numerous points of assemblage had scarcely ever been indicated on the maps. The means for reaching them were rude and hastily provided. The roads were rough, and, with the vehicles employed to traverse them, admirably adapted to give wholesome exercise to rheumatic joints and dyspeptic systems. The craziest carriages were hastily put in requisition, to run upon the wildest highways. Paths, only just blazed out in the woods, conducted you to habitations scarcely less wild, of frames covered with clapboards,—queer-looking log tenements, unplastered chambers, and little uncouth cabins, eight by twelve—where pride, in the lap of quiet, at all events, if not of comfort, might learn upon what a small amount of capital a man may realize large results in health and independence. It was the strangest spectacle, in Georgia and South Carolina, to see the thousands thus in motion along the highways, and thus rioting in rustic pleasures. Such cars and carriages, as bore the trooping adventurers, never figured in fashionable use before. You might see the railway trains, long and massive frames of timber, set on wheels, with unplaned benches, an interminable range, crowded with the living multitudes, wedged affectionately together, like herrings in boxes—sorted, if not salted masses—without covering, speeding through sun by day, and rain by night, to the appointed places of retreat; and, strange to say, in the best of all possible humors with themselves and all mankind. A certain grateful determination to make the most of the novel *désagremens* of their situation, in acknowledgment of the substantial good, in healthy excitement, and moral compensation, which they enjoyed at home, operated to make cheerful all the aspects of the scene, and to afford a pleasing animation to the strangest combinations of society. Here encountered, to the common benefit, circles and cliques that had never before been subjected to attrition. The reserved gentleman of the lower country, nice, staid, proper and particular, was pleased to receive a freshening stimulus from the frank, free, eager and salient manners of the gentleman of the interior. The over-refined ladies of the city were enlivened by the informal, hearty, lively and laughing tempers of the buoyant beauties of the mountain and forest country. These shared equally in the benefits of the association. The too frigid and stately reserves of the one region were thawed insensibly by the genial and buoyant, the unsophisticated impulse of the other; while the latter, insensibly borrowed, in return, something of the elaborate grace, and the quiet dignity, which constitute the chief attractions of the former. The result has compassed something more than was anticipated by the several parties. Seeking only to waste a summer gratefully, to find health and gentle excitements,—the simple object of the whole,—they yet found more precious benefits in the unwonted communion. Prejudices were worn away in the grateful attrition; new lights were brought to bear upon the social aspects of differing regions; thought was stimulated to fresh researches; and the general resources of the country, moral as well as physical, underwent a development, as grateful and encouraging as they were strange and wonderful to all the parties.

"The *désagrémens* of these extemporaneous progresses were not limited to bad roads and clumsy or crazy vehicles, rude dwellings, and the absence of the usual comforts upon which the gentry of the low country of the South, trained in English schools, are apt to insist with, perhaps, a little too much tenacity. We are compelled to make one admission, in respect to our interior, which we do in great grief of heart and much vexation of spirit. If the *schoolmaster* is abroad, the *cook* is not! Our *cuisine* is not well ordered in the forest country. The '*Physiologie de Goût*' has never there been made a text-book, in the schools of culinary philosophy. We doubt if a single copy of this grave authority can be found in all the mountain ranges of the Apalachian. They have the grace and the gravy; but these are not made to mingle as they should. The art which weds the vinegar and the oil, in happiest harmonies, so that neither is suffered to prevail in the taste, has never, in this region, commanded that careful study, or indeed consideration, which their union properly demands. The rank of the *cuisinier* is not properly recognised. The weight and importance of a grain of salt in the adjustment (shall we say *compromise*?) of a salade, is, we grieve to say, not justly understood in our forest watering-places; and, skilful enough at a julep or a sherry-cobler, they betray but ''prentice han's' when a steak, or a sauce, is the subject of preparation. Monsieur Guizot, speaking in properly-dignified language of the common sentiment of France, insists that she is the most perfect representative of the civilization of Christendom. Of course, he bases her claims to this position entirely on the virtues of her cuisine. The moral of the nation comes from the kitchen. The 'good digestion' which should 'wait on appetite' must be impossible where the *chef de cuisine* falls short of the philosopher as well as the man of science. Now, of all that philosophy, which prepares the food with a due regard, not only to the meats and vegetables themselves, the graces and the gravies, but to the temperaments of the consumers, we are sorry to confess that we have but little in our vast interior. Our mountain cooks think they have done everything when they have murdered a fillet of veal or a haunch of venison,—sodden them in lard or butter, baked or boiled them to a condition which admirably resembles the pulpy masses of cotton rag, when macerated for paper manufacture,—and wonders to see you mince gingerly of a dish which he himself will devour with the savage appetite of a Cumanche! You have seen a royal side of venison brought in during the morning, and laid out upon the tavern shambles;—you have set your heart upon the dinner of that day. Fancy reminds you of the relish with which, at the St. Charles, in New-Orleans, or the Pulaski, in Savannah, or the Charleston Hotel, you have discussed the exquisitely dressed loin, or haunch, done to a turn; the red just tinging the gravy, the meat just offering such pleasant resistance to the knife as leaves the intricate fibres still closely united, though shedding their juices with the eagerness of the peach, pressed between the lips in the very hour of its maturity;—or you see a fine 'mutton' brought in, of the wild flavor of the hills; and you examine, with the eye of the epicure, the voluminous fat, fold upon fold, lapping itself lovingly about the loins. Leg, or loin, or saddle, or shoulder, suggests itself to your anticipation as the probable subject of noonday discussion. You lay yourself out for the argument, and naturally recur to the last famous dinner which you enjoyed with the reverend father, who presides so equally well at the Church of the St. Savori, and at his own excellent hotel in the Rue des Huitres. You remember all the company, admirable judges, every one of them, of the virtues and the graces of a proper feast. The reverend father, himself, belongs to that excellent school of which the English clergy still show you so many grateful living examples,—men whose sensibilities are not yielded to the barren empire of mind merely, but who bring thought and philosophy equally to bear upon the humble and too frequently mortified flesh. With the spectacle of the venerable host, presiding so gracefully and so amiably — the napkin tucked beneath his chin, and falling over the ample domain in which certain philosophers, with much show of reason, have found the mortal abiding place of the soul — you associate the happy action with which, slightly flourishing the bright steel before he smites, he then passes the scimitar-like edge into the rosy round before him. It is no rude or hurried act. He feels the responsibility of the duty. He has properly studied the relations of the parts. He knows just where to insinuate the blade; and the mild dignity with which the act is performed, reminds you of what you have seen in pictures, or read in books, of the sacrifices of the high priests and magi, at Grecian or Egyptian altars. What silence waits upon the stroke! and, as the warm blood gushes forth, and the rubied edges of the wound lie bare before your eyes, every bosom feels relieved! The augury has been a fortunate one, and the feast begins under auspices that drive all doubts of what to-morrow may bring forth, entirely from the thought.

"With such recollections kindling the imagination, our extempore hotels of the Apalachian regions will doom you to frequent disappointment. You see yourself surrounded by masses that may be boiled or roasted polypi for what you know. But where's the mutton and the venison?

"You call upon the landlord — a gaunt-looking tyke of the forest, who seems better fitted to hunt the game than take charge of its toilet. He is serving a score at once; with one hand heaping beef and bacon, with the other collards and cucumbers, into conflicting plates; and you fall back speechless, with the sudden dispersion of a thousand fancies of delight, as he tells you that the mutton, or the venison, which has been the subject of your revery all the morning, lies before you in the undistinguishable mass that has distressed you with notions of the polypus and sea-blubber, or some other unknown monstrosities of the deep or forest. But the subject is one quite too distressing for dilation. We have painful memories, and must forbear. But, we solemnly say to our Apalachian landlord: —

"'Brother, this thing must be amended. You have no right to sport thus with the hopes, the health, the happiness of your guests. You have no right, in this way, to mortify your neighbors' flesh. Have you no sense of the evil which you are doing — no bowels of sympathy for those of other people? Is it pride, or indolence, or mere blindness and ignorance, which thus renders you reckless of what is due to humanity and society, and all that fine philosophy which the Roman epicure found essential to reconcile to becoming sensibilities the mere brutish necessities of the animal economy? You must import and educate your cooks. You must appreciate justly the morals of the kitchen. You must study with diligence, night and morning, the profound pages of the Physiologie de Goût; you must forswear those streams of lard, those cruel abuses of the flesh, those hard bakings of meats otherwise tender; those salt and savage soddenings of venison, otherwise sweet; those mountains of long collards, inadequately; boiled and those indigestible masses of dough, whether in the form of pies, or tarts, or biscuit, which need a yesty levity before they can possibly assimilate with the human system. We have often thought, seeing these heavy pasties upon your tables, that, if they could only command a voice, they would perpetually cry out to the needy and devouring guest, in the language of the ghosts to Richard the Hunchback — 'Let us lie heavy on thy soul to-morrow.'"

Here was a pause. Our orator had fairly talked himself out.

"Have you been speaking, sir?" was the artlessly-expressed inquiry, of Selina Burroughs.

"Good heavens, my dear little creature, you do not mean to say that you have been sleeping all the while!"

Here was a laugh!

"Oh! no, sir, — I merely wished to suggest that there is a story due to us from some quarter, and if you are in voice, sir, — I do not see who can better satisfy our expectation than yourself."

"Voice! I never was in better voice in all my life! You shall have a story and, in tribute to yourself, it shall be a love-story."

"Oh! thank you — a love story."

"A love story, and of the red man."

'Oh! that will be curious enough."

"It shall be as malicious and pathetic, and sad and humorous, and sedate, and fantastical, as Kotzebue himself could have desired."

And the group composed itself around, and the bilious *raconteur* told the following legend:—

LEGEND OF MISSOURI:

OR, THE CAPTIVE OF THE PAWNEE.

"A token of the spirit land —
The fleeting gift of fairy hand:
A wither'd leaf, a flower whose stem
Once broke, we liken unto them;
Thus fleet and fading, ripe ere noon,
And vanishing like midnight moon;
A rainbow gleam, that now appears,
And melts, even as we gaze, to tears."

INTRODUCTION.

THERE are certain races who are employed evidently as the pioneers for a superior people — who seem to have no mission of performance, — only one of preparation, — and who simply keep the earth, a sort of rude possession, of which they make no use, yeilding it, by an inevitable necessity, to the conquering people, so soon as they appear. Our red men seem to have belonged to this category. Their modes of life were inconsistent with length of tenure; and, even had the white man never appeared, their duration must have still been short. They would have preyed upon one another, tribe against tribe, in compliance with necessity, until all were destroyed; — and there is nothing to be deplored in this spectacle! Either they had no further uses, or they never, of themselves, developed them; and a people that destroy only, and never create or build, are not designed, anywhere, to cumber God's earth long! This is the substantial condition upon which all human securities depend. We are to advance. We are to build, create, endow; thus showing that we are made in the likeness of the Creator. Those who destroy only, by laws of strict moral justice, must perish, without having been said to live!

And yet, surveying this spectacle thro' the medium of the picturesque, one naturally broods with sympathy over the fate of this people. There is a solitary grandeur in their fortunes, and the intense melancholy which they exhibit, which compels us, in spite of philosophy, to regret the necessity under which they perish. Their valor, their natural eloquence, their passionate sense of freedom, the sad nobleness of their aspects, the subtlety of their genius,—these forbid that we should regard them with indifference; and we watch their prolonged battle for existence and place, with that feeling of admiration with which we behold the "great man struggling with the storms of fate." The conflict between rival races, one representing the highest civilization, the other the totally opposite nature of the savage, is always one of exquisite interest; and not an acre of our vast country but exhibits scenes of struggle between these rivals, which, properly delineated, would ravish from the canvass, and thrill all passions from the stage. The thousand progresses, in all directions, of the white pioneer;—the thousand trials of strength, and skill, and spirit, between him and the red hunter;—make of the face of the country one vast theatre, scene after scene, swelling the great event, until all closes in the grand denouëment which exhibits the dying agonies of the savage, with the conquering civilization striding triumphantly over his neck. Tradition will help us in process of time to large elements of romance in the survey of these events, and the red man is destined to a longer life in art than he ever knew in reality.

> "Yet shall the genius of the place,
>   In days of potent song to come,
> Reveal the story of the race,
>   Whose native genius now lies dumb.
> Yes, Fancy, by Tradition led,
> Shall trace the streamlet to its bed,
> And well each anxious path explore,
> The mighty trod in days of yore.
> The rock, the vale, the mount, the dell,
> Shall each become a chronicle;—
> The swift Imagination borne,
>   To heights of faith and sight supreme,
> Shall gather all the gifts of morn,
>   And shape the drama from the dream."

The sketch which follows might as well be true of a thousand histories, as of the one which it records. It is one which the painter might crown with all the glories of his art; one which future invention may weave into permanent song and story, for generations, to whom the memory of the red man will be nothing but a dream, doubtful in all its changes, and casting doubts upo the sober history.

CHAPTER I.

The Pawnees and the Omahas were neighboring but hostile nations. Their wars were perpetual, and this was due to their propinquity. It was the necessity of their nature and modes of life. They hunted in the same forest ranges. They were contending claimants for the same land and game. The successes of the one in the chase, were so many wrongs done to the rights of the other; and every buck or bear that fell into the hands of either party, was a positive loss of property to the other. That they should hate, and fight, whenever they met, was just as certain as that they should eat of the venison when the game was taken. Every conflict increased the mutual hostility of the parties. Successes emboldened the repetition of assault; defeat stimulated the desire for revenge. Every scalp which provoked triumph in the conqueror, demanded a bloody revenge at the hands of the vanquished; and thus they brooded over bloody fancies when they did not meet, and met only to realize their bloody dreams. It was soon evident to themselves, if it was not known to other nations, that the war was one of annihilation — that there could be no cessation of strife between them, until one of the parties should tear the last scalp from the brows of his hateful enemy.

Such a conviction, pressing equally upon the minds of both people, forced upon them the exercise of all their arts, their subtlety, their skill in circumventing their opponents, their savage and unsparing ferocity when they obtained any advantages. It prompted their devotions, also, to an intensity, which rendered both races complete subjects of the most terrible superstitions. Their priests naturally fed these superstitions, until war, which is the usual passion of the red man, became their fanaticism. Wild, mystical, horrid, were their midnight orgies and sacrifices; and, when they were not in battle — when a breathing spell from conflict had given them a temporary respite, in which to rebuild and repair their burned and broken lodges, and store away the provisions which were to serve them in new trials of strength,—

then religion claimed all their hearts, and fed their souls upon the one frenzied appetite which it thus made the decree of providence. The red man's Moloch has always been supreme among his gods, and he now absorbed wholly the devotions equally of Pawnee and Omaha. And thus, from generation to generation, had the fierce madness been transmitted. Their oldest traditions failed to say when the hatred did not exist between the two nations; and the boy of the Pawnee, and him of the Omaha, for hundreds of moons had still been taught the same passion at the altar; and his nightly dream, until he could take the field as a man, was one in which he found himself bestriding an enemy, and tearing his reeking scalp from his forehead. And this, by the way, is the common history of all these Indian tribes. They were thus perpetually in conflict with their neighbors, destined to slaughter or be slain. What wonder the sad solemnity on their faces, the national gloom over their villages, their passions which hide darkly, as wolves in the mountain caverns, concealing, in the cold aspect, their silent wretchedness; their horrid rages, under the stolid, though only seeming, indifference in every visage. Their savage god was dealing with them everywhere, after his usual fashion. They were themselves the sacrifices upon his bloody altars, and he nursed their frenzies only for self-destruction.

Gloomy, stern, intensely savage, was the spirit thus prevailing over the minds of both people, at the time of which we speak. The season was approaching, when, their summer crops laid by, they were again to take the field, in the twofold character of warriors and hunters. The union of the two, in the case of people living mostly by the chase, is natural and apparent enough. The forests where they sought their prey equally harbored their enemies, and for both they made the same preparations. The period of these events is within modern times. The coasts of the great Atlantic have been populously settled by the white race. The red men have gradually yielded before their pioneers. The restless Anglo-Norman is pushing his way rapidly into the forests — into the pathless solitudes — into sullen mountain-gorges, and dense and gloomy thickets. He has possessed himself everywhere of some foothold, and converted every foothold into a fastness. The borderers were already known to both Pawnee and Omaha. But, while these raged against each other, they took little heed of that approaching power under which both were to succumb. Its coming inspired no fear, while the hate for each other remained undiminished.

The autumn campaign was about to open, and the Pawnees and the Omahas were soon busy in their preparations for it. Before setting out upon the war-path, many things had to be done — mystic, wild, solemn — by which to propitiate their gods, and consecrate their sacrifices. The youth of each nation, who had never yet taken the field, were each conveyed to the "Silent Lodges," where, for a certain time, under trials of hunger, thirst, and exposure, they were to go through a sort of sacred probation, during which their visions were to become auguries, and to shadow forth the duties and the events of their future career. This probation over, they took their part in solemn feast and council, in order to decide upon the most plausible plans of action, and to obtain the sanction and direction of the Great Spirit, as ascertained by their priests. You already possess some general idea of the horrid and unseemly rites which were held proper to these occasions. We are all, more or less familiar with that barbarous mummery, in which, on such occasions, most savages indulge; blindly, and to us insanely, but having their own motives, and the greatest confidence in the efficacy of their rites. These proceedings lasted days and nights, and nothing was omitted, of their usual performances, which could excite the enthusiasm of the people, while strengthening their faith in their gods, their priesthood, and their destiny. In the deepest recesses of wood the incantations were carried on. Half naked, with bodies blackened and painted, the priests officiated before flaming altars of wood and brush. On these they piled native offerings. The fat of the bear and buffalo sent up reeking steams to the nostrils of their savage gods, mingled with gentler essences, aromatic scents, extracted from bruised or burning shrubs of strong odorous properties. The atmosphere became impregnated with their fumes, and the audience — the worshippers, rather — grew intoxicated as they inhaled. The priests were already intoxicated, drinking decoctions of acrid, bitter; fiery roots of the forests, the qualities of which they thoroughly knew. Filled with their exciting fires, they danced, they sang, they ran, and sent up, meanwhile, the most horrid howls to their demon. Filled with a sacred fury, they rushed hither and thither, smiting themselves unsparingly with sharp flints, which covered their breasts and arms with blood. Thus maddened, they divined, and the nation hung trembling, as with a single heart, upon the awful revelations from their lips. The scene is one for the most vivid and intense of the melodramas. Talk of your Druid sacrifices, as seen in your operas. They are not, for the picturesque and terrible, to be spoken of in the same hour with those of our aboriginal tribes.

In the case of both nations, as might be expected, the priests divined and predicted general success. They took care, however, as is usually the case with the prophets of the superstitious, to speak in language sufficiently vague to allow of its application to any sort of events; or they rested solely upon safe predictions which commonly bring about their own verification. They did not, however, content themselves with prophesying the events of the war. They consulted as well the course of the action to be pursued—the plans to be adopted—the leaders chosen; and this, too, in such manner as to leave no loopholes for evasion. Thus they encouraged their favorites, rebuked and kept down leaders whom they feared, and kept the nation subject wholly to their own exclusive despotism.

The response especially made by the Pawnee priesthood, when consulting their gods with reference to the approaching campaign, announced the victory to rest with that nation which should first succeed in making a captive. This captive was doomed to the torture by fire. Such a response as this, however cruel and barbarous it may seem, was yet of a highly merciful tendency, calculated really to ameliorate the horrors of war, and to promote the safety of human life. The effect upon the Pawnees—a people eager and impetuous—was to restrain their appetite for battle. Their great policy was to escape unnecessary risks of any sort, while employing all their subtlety for the possession of a native Omaha. To this the warriors addressed themselves with wonderful unanimity, but to the grievous sacrifice of their chief appetites, all of which indicated the fiercer conflict as their true delight.

CHAPTER II.

The Omahas, on the other hand, had their favorite auguries also, and the response from their gods was not dissimilar to that which had been given to the Pawnees. It said that the nation should infallibly succeed in the campaign, *which should receive the first blow.* But nothing was said of captivity. Similar, but in conflict, were the predictions. In both cases, as in battles usually, everything was made to depend upon the first blow. While, therefore, the policy of the Pawnees was to escape from everything like conflict, that of the Omahas was to provoke action and hurry into danger. Their warriors assembled, accordingly, at all points, and issued from their lodges and towns, taking the trail for the enemy's country. This they soon penetrated. But the Pawnees were very wary. They stood only on the defensive, and wholly avoided action; retreated before equal numbers, and simply contented themselves with keeping out of danger, while keeping the Omahas for ever vigilant. Their caution, which was a very unwonted virtue, provoked the Omahas to desperation. Their effrontery was prodigious. They exposed themselves to the shaft on all occasions, rushing beneath the fastnesses of the Pawnees, striking their naked breasts, and defying their enemies to shoot. But the latter lay *perdu*. quietly, if not calmly, looking on, and apparently satisfied to keep their towns and camps in safety. They neither invited attack nor awaited it, and resolutely avoided giving—what the Omahas solicited—*that first blow!* It is true that the young Pawnee braves felt sorely the necessity to which they were required to submit. Bitterly, in their hearts, they cursed the decree which kept them inactive; forced to submit to taunts, reproaches, and invectives, from a people whom they loathed, and affected to despise. It was scarcely possible to restrain the young Pawnee bloods under such severe trials of their temper;—but the voice of the priesthood was paramount; and, blindly believing that safety lay only in their predictions, they were persuaded to suspend the thirst of blood, and to substitute subtlety for valor. To circumvent the enemy—to make the captive,—not to slay, not even to wound: this was the great duty and the eager desire with the warriors of the Pawnee.

But this was no easy matter. The Omahas longed for the conflict. They desired to be smitten. They would struggle to receive the stroke. They would force the captors to strike the blow, which was to defeat the one prophecy and satisfy the conditions of the other. They were not to be ensnared. They exposed themselves but seldom singly, and they were always armed for battle. Turn where the Pawnees would—set what snares they might—employ what arts,—still they found themselves met and foiled by their now strangely insolent and assailing enemies.

But the Pawnee warriors had some long heads among them, and they cogitated earnestly, and planned with equal deliberation and method. Among these was a fellow of great renown, with the uneuphonic name of Kionk, or as he was sometimes called, Awé-Kionk. He was as shrewd and sensible as he was brave and active, and was full of energy and spirit, being just about thirty years of age. He was what we might call a splendid looking savage—a sort of Mark Antony among the red men—fond of good living—a rather merry companion for an Indian, but in battle a genuine Birserker—becoming drunk and delirious with a Hunnish rapture at the sight or taste of blood. Such was the chief Kionk. He had his devices, and after a secret conference with the head men of the nation he suddenly disappeared with a small but select party of warriors, to put them into execution. What was this famous project about which so much mystery was thrown? So secretly did Kionk and his followers depart, that nobody dreamed of their absence, even when they were far away; and so wide was the circuit which they took that they passed unseen and unsuspected, meeting not one of the cloud of spies whom the Omahas had set to watch along the line separating them from their enemies. The object of Kionk was the captive, unhurt, unwounded, whose agonies, reserved for the fiery torture, were to satisfy all the demands of their gods and secure them the victory

Within the whole wide ranges of a country which boasts an almost perpetual spring, the Omaha village occupied one of the sweetest and most beautiful situations that could anywhere be seen. Their principal settlement was upon a small island, embosomed in a broad and glassy lake, which empties into the river Platte. The Pawnees had long looked with eager and lustful eyes upon this lovely abiding place. It seemed to realize to their imaginations the dream of the Indian heavens. It was so cool, so solitary, and, though an island, so shady with noble groves. There the banks seemed to wear the green of a perpetual summer. Never were there such flowers as bloomed for them by the wayside; and the singing birds loved the region, and dwelt there, cherished choristers, throughout the year. There were other luxuries in that little island home of the Omahas which were even more precious and wooing in the sight of the hungry Pawnees. The fish inhabiting the lake were in abundance, and of surpassing fatness and flavor. No wonder that the Loups hated a people in the exclusive possession of such a delicious home!

The great scheme of Kionk was to effect a descent upon the island, and carry off one at least of the inhabitants. This, it was assumed, it was quite easy to do, provided the utmost caution was observed, and that nothing happened to render the Omahas suspicious of their object. Kionk reasoned rightly, when he urged upon the chiefs that, while invading their enemy's country, the Omahas would never dream of any foray into their own! Their chief strength was well known to be in the field, hovering all about the Pawnee settlements. It was argued that the secluded situation of the village—its remoteness from the scene of active operations—and its natural securities would, in all probability, render the Omahas over-confident of its safety; that they had probably left few men upon the island, and those mostly the infirm and timid. These would offer but a weak defence; but as assault was not the object, only surprise, even this was not apprehended. Kionk, as we have seen, succeeded in persuading the chiefs in council, and departed with his chosen band, making a successful circuit, which enabled him to pass the scouts of the Omahas, his progress entirely unsuspected.

CHAPTER III.

MEANWHILE, the Omahas labored in vain to provoke their enemies to action. Never did warriors show themselves so solicitous of being beaten—struck at least—and never did Christian warriors show themselves more reluctant to bestow the much desired chastisement. This sort of strategy could not last for ever. Our Omahas began to be very impatient, and to curse the priesthood and its prophecies, in their heart of hearts. It is true that they were not kept idle, but constantly watchful and busy; true, also, that they kept their hands in for war, by practising a very slaughterous campaign against bear, buffalo, and buck. But this did not satisfy the national appetite for the blood of their hated rivals. And they groaned with impatience at the difficulty of complying with the conditions of the war, which the prophets had prescribed, in consequence of the most unnatural forbearance displayed by the Pawnees.

Among the young warriors of the Omahas who suffered from this impatience, there was one, a gallant youth, little more than grown to manhood, who had already made himself famous by his excellence in all the qualities of warrior and hunter. A more daring or accomplished fellow than Enemoya, the nation did not possess. Though quite young still, he had been tried in frequent battles, and had acquired such a reputation for equal spirit, skill, and understanding, that he took a foremost rank among his people, whether in action, or in the preliminary deliberations of the council. But Enemoya, though brave and savage in war, had yet his weaknesses. He was not insensible to the tender passion. There was a young woman of his tribe, known by the pretty poetical name of Missouri; and the first symptoms which Enemoya had that this young woman was of any importance in his eyes, consisted in his sudden discovery of the great beauties of this name.—The Indian warrior, like Richard Cœur de Leon, and the knights most famous of Provence, is something of a Jongleur.—At all events, every chief of the red men sings his war song, his battle hymn, his song of rejoicing, and his death chant. Of the quality of these songs, as works of art, we have not a syllable to say. They were probably not any better than those of Cœur de Leon and his brother bard-knights of Provence. Perhaps, metrical harmony considered, they were not half so good. In making songs for the fair Missouri, Enemoya did by no means set up for a poet; and that his song has been preserved at all, is due to the fact that it has been found to answer the purposes of other lovers among the red knights of the Omaha. It has even found circulation among the Pawnees, and, by the last advices from that tribe, it is said that this people actually claim the original verses for one of their own warriors—a claim which we need scarcely assure you is totally unfounded. Perhaps, however, it matters very little with whom the authorship properly lies. It is certain that Enemoya, stealing behind the lovely Missouri, while she played with her sister's children in a stately grove on the borders of the beautiful lake, chanted the following ditty in her ear. We make a close translation from the original, putting it, however, into good English rhymes, in the hope that it may be adopted by Russell, or some other popular singer, and become the substitute for the poor, flat, puny, mean-spirited love songs, which are at present so discreditable to the manhood of the Anglo-Saxon race. We are constrained to add that Enemoya, though he had a good voice, and could scream with any eagle, was yet rather monotonous in singing his ditty.

LOVE SONG OF ENEMOYA,

ONE OF THE GREAT WAR CHIEFS OF THE OMAHAS.

I.

Fawn of the forest isle, but see
The gifts that I have brought for thee,
  To please thy heart and win thine eyes,
Here are the loveliest beads, as bright
As flowers by day, and stars by night,
  All colored with the prettiest dyes!—
    Oh! take them, girl of Omaha!

II.

Take them, with other gifts as dear,
Which thou wilt make more bright to wear!
  This robe of calico but view—
From pale-faced trader bought, who swore
The world ne'er saw the like before,
  So softly red, so green, so blue—
    Oh! take it, girl of Omaha!—

III.

This shawl of scarlet, see—to fold
About thy neck, when days are cold—

How soft, and warm, and nice!—
A dozen beaver skins, three bear,
A score, and more, of fox and deer,
　　It cost;—a swinging price!
　　　Yet, take it, girl of Omaha!

IV.

And here are other gifts—this bowl,
Of tin—a metal, by my soul,
　　Most precious and most rare;
These little bells, but hear them ting—
Ting, tingle, tingle!—bird on wing
　　Ne'er sung so sweet and clear!
　　　Oh! take them girl of Omaha!

V.

Take them, *and me!* For I'm the man
To make you blest, if mortal can!
　　I'm six feet high and strong
As bull of all the buffaloes;—
I'm good for any thousand foes,
　　As I am good for song.
　　　So, take me, girl of Omaha!

VI.

Take me if you are wise; and know
My lodge is ready;—such a show
　　Of skins, and meat, is there!
I've thirty venison hams and more,
Five buffalo humps are in my store,
　　And twice as many bear!
　　　They're yours, sweet girl of Omaha!

VII.

Take me!—and know before we part,
No other shall possess thy heart;—
　　I'll take his scalp who tries:
Nay thine—before I see thee won,
By any but my father's son,
　　So listen, and be wise,
　　　And take me, girl of Omaha!

This will be called rather a rough style of wooing, in our softly sentimental society, but, among the red men, the chant of Enemoya, on this occasion, was deemed the very perfection of a love song. It dealt frankly with the maiden. It told her all that she ought to know, and warned her of what she had to expect, whether she took him or not. The lover never thought of the damsel's fortune; but he freely tendered everything that he himself possessed. It was herself only that he wanted. He was no fortune-hunter. He was a man, and he talked to her like a man. "See what provision I have made for you. Look into my lodge. See the piles of meat in yonder corner. They are humps of the buffalo. These alone will last us two all the winter. But look up at the thirty venison hams, and the quarters of the bear now smoking, hanging from the rafters. There's a sight to give a young woman an appetite. They are all your own, my beauty. You perceive that there's much more than enough, and in green pea season we can give any number of suppers. Lift yon blanket. That is our sleeping apartment. See the piles of bear skins: they shall form our couch. Look at the tin ware—that most precious of all the metals of the white man—yet I have appropriated all these to culinary purposes. As for jewels and ornaments, the beads, of which I have given you a sample, are here in abundance. These are all your treasures, and you will do wisely to accept. Now, my beauty, I don't want to coerce your tastes, or to bias your judgment in making a free choice; but I must say that you shall never marry anybody but myself. I'm the very man for you; able to fight your battles and bring you plentiful supplies; and feeling that I am the only proper man for you, I shall scalp the first rival that looks on you with impertinent eyes of passion; nay, scalp you too, if you are so absurd as to look on him with eyes of requital. I'm the only proper person for you, I tell you."

We need scarcely say that this performance made Enemoya as famous as a poet, as he had been as a warrior and hunter. It is now universally considered the *chef d'œuvre* of the Omahas. As a matter of course, it proved irresistible with the fair Missouri. It had an unctuous property about it, which commended the lover to all her tastes. She suffered him to put his arms about her, to give her the kiss of betrothal, which, among the Omaha women, is called the "kiss of consolation," and the result was, an arrangement for the bridal, with the close of the present campaign, and the opening of the spring—that is, taking for granted that Enemoya does not happen, by any chance, to leave his own scalp along the war-path. But neither party thought of this contingency, or they made very light of it. The courtship occurred that very autumn, and just as the warriors were preparing for the winter campaign. It was during the "windy month" (October), and they were to wait till May. And Enemoya was to be absent all the winter! It was quite a trial even for a Birserker Omaha!

CHAPTER IV.

His new relations with the damsel Missouri, and the impossibility of forcing the Pawnee Loups to make the assault, rendered Enemoya very impatient of the war. Day by day he became more and more restless — more and more dissatisfied — more and more troubled by the strongest longing to steal away, and take, if only a look, at the dusky but beautiful damsel, by the lake side, and among the thickets. He had picked up certain spoils among the villages of the Pawnees — for the decree of the Omaha prophets did not denounce the spoiling of the Egyptians; only the slaying of them — and, now that he was a betrothed lover, Enemoya was quite as avid after spoils as ever feudal chieftain in the palmy days of chivalry. And why should he not draw off from the camp, and carry home his treasures and his trophies? What was there to be done? The Pawnees would not fight — would not strike, at all events — and eluded all efforts to bring them to blows, and dodged admirably every sort of danger. He could do no more than he had done, and the business of the war having subsided into a question of mere vigilance and patience, he felt that this could be carried on quite as well by ordinary warriors as by the best. As for hunting, why should he fatigue himself in this business? Had he not already shown to Missouri the rafters of his cabin reeking of the most savory meats? Thus thinking, he daily grew more and more convinced of the propriety of returning home. His meditations influenced his dreams, and these filled him with trouble. An Indian is a great dreamer, and has a great faith in the quality of dreams. The practice of *oneirocromancy* is a favorite among his priests and prophets. The orientals were never such famous interpreters in the days of "the Elders." Being a poet also, Enemoya shared in the dreaming endowment of the priesthood. His sleep was wholly occupied with dreams. In all of these, Missouri was a conspicuous feature. Now he saw her in flight; now in tears, and trembling; anon he beheld her fettered; and again she seemed to float away from his embrace, a bleeding spectre, melting away finally into thin air. In most of these dreams, he beheld always, as one of the persons of the drama, a warrior in the hateful guise of a Pawnee. How should a Pawnee dare to hover, even in a dream, about the person of Missouri, the betrothed of a great chief of the Omahas? What had he to do there? and why did the spectre of one unknown, whom indeed he only saw dimly, and always with face averted, and looking toward Missouri—why did he presume to thrust himself between his visions and the object so precious and ever present to his dreams? The heart of the young warrior became uneasy, as he could conjecture no reasonable solution of his difficulty, unless, indeed, one of which he dared not think. Was Missouri the captive of the Pawnee? He recoiled at the notion—he laughed, but rather hollowly, and with great effort—and became more uneasy than ever. His waking dreams, shaped by those that came to him in sleep, became still more troublesome, and he resolved to depart secretly for the dear islet in the little lake, if only to disarm his doubts, and get rid of his vexatious fancies. An opportunity soon enabled him to do so. A large party of the Omahas had resolved upon a long hunt, and they applied to Enemoya to join them. The sport in no way promised to interfere with the *quasi* warfare which was carried on; and, finding it impossible to bring the Pawnees to the striking point, the Omahas contented themselves with the warfare upon the quadrupeds of the forest. Enemoya joined the hunt, but soon disappeared from the party. They did not miss him till nightfall, and in the meantime he had sped, fast and far, pushing backward along the paths leading to the little island, and the dusky damsel whom he loved.

But the young warrior was late, though no laggard. His enemy had been before him. That subtle and enterprising Kionk had led his party with surprising address, and had succeeded in fetching such a compass as brought him entirely without the *alignment* of spies and scouts, which the Omahas had stretched across the country, and, without impediment or interruption, had made his way successfully to the borders of the little lake in which the blessed island seemed to be brooding upon its own bosom in a dream of peace.—Nothing could look more calm, more inoffensive, more winning. One would think that, to behold it only, would disarm the hostile passions of the enemy. There lay the quiet groves beyond. There rose the soft white curling smokes from the little cabin; and see beneath the trees where the young damsels and the children are skipping gayly about, as little conscious of care as danger.

The prospect did not disarm the Pawnee chief. On the contrary, it rather strengthened his resolve, and stimulated his enterprise. "If we obtain this captive," he thought to himself, "we conquer these rascally Omahas; and then we take possession of this beautiful island, this fine lake always full of the sweetest fish, and these broad green meadows, where I can keep a score of horses without sending them out to grass." And the eye of Kionk already selected a particular site for his own future settlement, and by no means stinted himself in the number of his self-allotted acres. But he did not, while thus thinking of his own projects of plunder, become neglectful of the duties which he had undertaken. He looked about him, the better to prosecute his objects. We need not to be told that this inquiry was prosecuted with as much caution as energy. Everybody understands that the red men kept themselves well covered in the woods, so that none of the innocent children and the thoughtless girls, sporting along the banks of the islet, on the opposite shore, could get the slightest glimpse of their persons or their projects. The marauders stole up the stream, for the lake was simply formed by the expansion of a river, which the islet divided in the middle. The Pawnees kept under cover till they almost lost sight of the islet. At length they emerged upon the banks of the river. Here they found a canoe, with which they put out from shore, leaving it to the current to take them down to the islet, and using their paddles simply to shape their course, so as to touch the point aimed at only where its shrubs and willows would afford concealment. The whole affair was well managed, and was quite successful. The Pawnee warriors found themselves, for the first time, on the blessed island of the Omahas The reptile was in the garden. He crawled, and crept, or sneaked, crouching or gliding from cover to cover, from thicket to thicket, and stealing from side to side, wherever he thought it most probable that he should happen upon the victim he sought. More than once Kionk might have caught up a child, a nice little girl of seven or eight, or a stout chunk of a boy of similar age; but he had his doubts if such juveniles were contemplated by the oracle. He must do his work thoroughly, and having gone thus far in his enterprise, peril nothing upon a miserable doubt.

CHAPTER V.

LITTLE did the beautiful damsel Missouri fancy, as she sat singing that evening by the shore of the quiet lake, while the infant child of her sister, Tanewahakila, was rocking in a case of wicker work from the boughs of an outspreading tree, that danger hung about her footsteps. She sung, in the gladness of a young warm heart, scarcely knowing what she sang, and musing, in delicious reveries, upon the spring season, which it is so pleasant to think of when one is lonely in cold weather, and which was to bring back Enemoya to her arms, a triumphant warrior. Alas! what a happy dream the Fates are about to mock with their cruel performances. What a lovely picture of peace and felicity is about to be blackened with the thunderbolt and storm!

While Missouri sang, or mused, lost in her sweet reveries, the hand of the fierce Pawnee chief, Kionk, was laid upon her shoulder. Before she could turn to see who was the rude assailant, his shawl had been wound about her mouth, shutting in her cries. In another moment she was lifted in his powerful arms and borne into the thickets. The infant was left swinging in his basket rocker from the tree!

The lightfooted Enemoya, meanwhile, sped with all the impetuous diligence of a lover toward the precious little islet, so full of treasure for his heart. Pursuing a direct course, he was not long in consummating his journey, and at the close of a fine day in November we find him once more on the borders of the little lake, and looking across to the happy haven which he sought. He paused for an instant only to take from the bough from which it depended the clear yellow gourd, such as was everywhere placed conveniently for the wayfarer, and scooped up a sweet draught from the flowing waters. Then he sought out a little canoe,— one of many which lay along the shore,— and paddled out into the lake, making his way toward the well-remembered headlands, where Missouri was wont to play with the children of her sister, Tanewahakila, the wife of his cousin, the grim warrior of Ouanawega-poree. It somewhat surprised Enemoya that he seemed to be unseen by the villagers, of whom he himself beheld none; and it was with a feeling of inquietude that he looked vainly to the headlands he was approaching for some signs of Missouri herself.—But, when he reached the island, and his little boat shot up along the silvery beach, he began to tremble with a strange fear at the deep and utter silence which prevailed everywhere. He pushed rapidly for the lodge of Tanewahakila, but it was silent and untenanted. The fire had gone out upon the hearth. He was confounded, and hurried off to the village. Here he found the women and children gathered within the picketed enclosure, and, from a score of tongues, he soon learned the disaster. Missouri had disappeared. She had been seen borne upon strong Pawnee shoulders to the boat at the upper end of the island, and, before the alarm could be given, she had been carried safely to the opposite side Not knowing how many of the subtle Pawnees were about, the old and decrepit warriors of the village had all set off on the route said to be taken by the enemy. As yet, there was no report of the result. But what report, or what result, could be anticipated— unless that of disappointment—from a pursuit against young and vigorous foes, undertaken by the superannuated? Poor Enemoya listened with the saddest feeling of hopelessness and desolation. "One stupid moment motionless he stood;" then, having heard all which the women had to tell, he darted off in pursuit, resolved to perish or rescue his dusky beauty from the talons of her cruel ravishers!

While Enemoya was thus, with all his soul and strength, urging the pursuit, Kionk, with his captive and his companions, was equally earnest in pressing his retreat. But, to make this safe, he was compelled to make it circuitous. He had to fetch a wide compass, as before, to escape the scouts and war parties of the Omahas. Though indefatigable, therefore, in the prosecution of his journey, Kionk made little direct headway. But he was in no hurry. He could afford to lose time now that he had his captive. It was only required that he should keep his trophy. To do this needed every precaution. He knew that he would be pursued. He gave sufficient credit to his enemies to assume that they would not give slumber to their eyelids, nor rest to their feet, in the effort to rescue his prey, and to revenge the indignity which they had suffered. He also took for granted that they would bring to the work an ingenuity and skill, a sagacity and intelligence, very nearly if not equal to his own. He must be heedful, therefore, to obliterate all traces of his progress; to wind about and double upon his own tracks; to take to the streams and water-courses whenever this was possible, and to baffle by superior arts those of his pursuers. That there would be much energy in the pursuit, whatever might be its sagacity, he did not apprehend; for he knew that the guardians of the village were mostly superannuated, and a cold scent is usually fatal to enterprise. He knew that they would fight, perhaps as well as ever, upon their own ground, and in defence; but for a war of invasion, or one which involved the necessity of prompt decision and rapid action, old men are nearly useless. He was therefore cool, taking his leisure, but playing fox-work admirably, and omitting no precaution. He contrived to throw out the veterans after a brief interval, and to shake himself free of their attentions. But he did not dream of that fierce wolf-dog upon the scent—the young, strong, and audaciously-brave chief, Enemoya.

CHAPTER VI.

It was not long before Kionk began to take a curious interest in the looks and behavior of his captive. Very sad and wretched, indeed, was our dusky damsel; but she was very patient withal, and bore up firmly against fatigue, and never once complained, and seemed to show herself perfectly insensible to danger. She had been chosen as the wife of a great warrior, and she was resolved to show that she possessed a soul worthy of so proud a destiny. Kionk beheld her patience and endurance with a grim sort of satisfaction. Such a woman, he thought, deserves to have a famous husband: she will do honor to the fire torture. And yet, again, he mused upon the grievous pity of burning up so much fine flesh and blood; such a fine figure, such a pretty face; a creature of so many graces and beauties; and one who would bear such noble-looking men-children, gladdening a warlike father's heart. Kionk began to think how much better it would be if he could pick up another captive, and save Missouri from the fire-torture. She would make such a commendable wife. But Kionk had a wife already; for that matter, it must be confessed that he had three, and did not enjoy any great reputation as an indulgent husband. But great chiefs have peculiar privileges, and a chief like Kionk might as safely repudiate his wives as any of the Napoleons, or any of the Guelphs of Europe. Positively, the thought began to grow upon the mighty Kionk, of the beauties and virtues and excellent domestic nature of Missouri. More than once he caught himself muttering: "What a pity such a fine figure should be scorched and blackened by the fire!" He watched her pitifully as he mused. When they paused for food and rest, he attended kindlily to her wants. He brought her the food himself; he chose the ground where she slept, and threw his buffalo robe over her, and watched at her head during the brief hours at midnight which were accorded to rest. When, long before dawn, the party was again in motion, he himself gave her the signal to rise, and helped her up. He was curiously attentive for so rough a sort of Birserkir. Could Enemoya have witnessed these attentions! Could he have seen what thoughts were passing through the brain of Kionk—what feelings were working in his heart! But his jealous and apprehensive spirit conjectured all. What lover but apprehended the worst of dangers from a charming rival?

While such were the relations between the captor and the captive, Enemoya pursued the search with as much rapidity as consisted with the necessity of keeping on the track of the fugitives. He encountered the party of exhausted veterans at the spot where they were thrown out of the chase; and, while they returned sorrowfully to the little islet, no longer safe and happy, he contrived to catch up the traces which they had lost, and once more resumed the pursuit with new hopes and spirit. Under any circumstances, the free step, the bold heart, the keen eye, and prompt sagacity, of Enemoya would have made him fearful as a pursuer; but now, with jealous fire and a fierce anger working terribly in his soul, all his powers of mind and body seemed to acquire greater vigor than ever. Passion and despair gave him wings, and he seemed to carry eyes in his wings. Nothing escaped his glance. He soon persuaded himself that he gained upon his enemy. There are traces which the keen vision of the hunter will detect, even though another hunter shall toil to baffle him; and, in spite of the care and precautions of Kionk, he could not wholly succeed in obscuring the tracks which his party unavoidably made. Besides, anticipating pursuit, though certainly not that of her lover, Missouri had quietly done all that she might, in leaving clues of her progress behind her. She was not allowed to break the shrubs as she passed, nor to peal the green wands, nor to linger by the way. Where she slept at night the careful hands of her captors stirred the leaves, and smoothed out all pressure from the surface. But the captors were not always watchful, and Missouri noted their lapses very heedfully. As Enemoya hurries forward over a little sandy ridge, what is it that sparkles in the path? It is one of the bright blue beads which he himself has wound about the neck of the dusky maiden. His hopes rekindle and multiply in his breast. Anon he sees another, and another, dropped always on the clear track, and where it may imprison the glistening rays of the sun. Now he hurries forward, exulting in the certainty of his clues. Toward sunset he happens upon the clearly-defined track of a man's moccasin. The foot is large and distinct. There are other like tracks, set down without any reserve or seeming apprehension. Enemoya at once concludes that the Pawnee party, deeming themselves secure, no longer continue their precautions. This encourages him still further. He will now catch them napping. Again he darts forward, following the obvious tracks before him. But night came down, and he could only travel under the guidance of a star, chosen, as pointing in the seemingly given direction. Thus, for an hour or more after night, he followed on through the dim forest. Suddenly, as he rounds a water-course, which he can not wade, he is startled by the blaze of a camp-fire.

"Such a fire," quoth Enemoya to himself, "was never made by Pawnee warrior. He would never be the fool so to advertise his sleeping place to his enemies."

The prospect which would have cheered the white man, disappointed our chief of Omaha. He now knew that he had been misled, and had turned aside from the true path indicated by the beads of Missouri, to follow upon one which had been evidently made by quite another party. But, though mortified with himself at this blundering, and in allowing himself to reason from a false assumption—his pride as hunter and warrior being equally wounded—he cautiously approached the fire, around which the outlines of a group of persons, dimly seen by the blaze, were crouching. They proved to be a party of white men, and were busily engaged in the discussion of a supper of broiled venison and smoking hoecake.— The intercourse of Enemoya with the white traders, had, as we have already seen, been rather considerable, and the larger profits had not certainly lain with the red man. The chief had learned some little of the English tongue in this intercourse, however, and he suddenly stood among the strangers, introducing himself with a softly murmured: "Huddye do, brudder; I berry glad to see you in my country."

Our pioneers were fellows of "the true grit," to employ their own verbal currency,—as big-limbed, muscular, hardy, and daredevil scamps, as ever came from "Roaring river." They were taken by surprise, but were on their legs in the twinkling of an eye, each brandishing his rifle, club-fashion, and feeling that his knife was convenient to his grasp. They were on the old route looking for a new route; had drawn up stakes in a too thickly settled neighborhood, having three neighbors in a square league, and were seeking where to plant them anew in a less-crowded region. The gentle language of Enemoya reassured them.

"No fight—good friends—brudders all. The Omaha chief is a friend to the pale-faces."

And he extended his hand which they promptly shook, all round, and then frankly bade him sit and share of their provisions. Enemoya's heart was not in the feast, nor yet with his new companions. He would much rather never have encountered them, but still kept on the track of the true enemy, as pointed out by the occasionally dropped bead of the poor Missouri. Many were the secret imprecations which he muttered against the big feet of the pale-faces, which had diverted him from the true course. Weary, almost to exhaustion, he was for the moment utterly desponding. The last feather breaks the camel's back. Now Enemoya's spine was still, in sooth, unshaken, but the conviction that he had lost ground which he might never be able to recover, made him succumb, as the hardiest man is apt to do, for a time, under the constantly accumulated pressure of misfortunes. He did as the Kentuckians bade him, and sat down with them to the supper, but not to eat. The white men noted his despondency, and, little by little, they wound out of the warrior the whole history of his affairs — the present war between Pawnee and Omaha — the predictions upon which the result was to depend — the secret foray of the Pawnees, and their capture of the dusky beauty whom he was to carry to his lodge in the spring. He narrated also the details of his pursuit thus far, and confessed in what manner he had been misled, never dreaming of the moccasin track of a white man in the country of the red, at such a moment.

"Well, now, yours is a mighty hard case for a young fellow; I must say it though I'm rather an old one myself," was the remark of one of the elders of the white party — a grisly giant, some forty-five years of age, yet probably with a more certain vigor than he had at thirty-five. "It's not so bad to lose one's wife, after he's got a little usen to her; but where it's only at the beginning of a man's married life, and where it's nothing but the happiness of the thing that he's considerin', to have the gal caught up, and carried away by an inimy, makes a sore place in a person's feelings. It's like having one's supper snapped up by a hungry wolf, jest before he's tasted the leetlest morsel, and when he's a-wiping his mouth to eat. I confess, I feels oneasy at your perdicament. Now, what do you say ef we lends you a hand to help you git back the gal."

Enemoya was cheered by the prospect, and expressed his gratitude.

"Well, that's pretty well said for a red-skin. We are the boys to help you, my lad, for there ain't one of us that can't double up an Ingin in mighty short order. With these pretty little critters here," touching one of the rifles, "we can see to a mighty great distance, and can stretch the longest legs you ever did see after an inimy. And we're good at scouting, and can take a track, and sarcumvent the heathen jist as well as we can sarcumvent the b'ar and buffalo.—And we *will* sarve you, ef we can make tarms upon it."

Enemoya was willing to admit the prowess of the white men; but he didn't altogether comprehend the latter part of what was said about the "tarms."

"Oh! don't make out that you're so green as all that comes to. You've been trading with our people, and ought to know what we mean by 'tarms.' But, ef you don't, it's only to make it cl'ar to you by using some easier words. Tarms is conditions—that is, the pay, the hire, the salary—what you're to give us for helping to git the gal back, sound in wind and limb, and other sarcumstances. No cure, no pay—no gal, no tarms."

Enemoya was not long in comprehending the suggestion. He felt the importance of such an alliance, and well knew that the proffered assistance was highly valuable. It filled him with new hope and courage. He was accordingly as liberal as the sunshine in his gratitude and promises. He had deer, and bear, and buffalo skins, which were all at the service of his allies, if they were successful in the chase.

"Ay, ay, all them's mighty good things; but the gal's worth a great deal more. Now, you jist now spoke of this being your country. Ef we chose, 'twould be mighty easy to dispute that argyment; for what made it more your country than mine? It's all God's country, and God grants no pr'emptions to any but a Christian people. The heathen's got to die out, any how, some day. But I won't dispute with a man when he's in a peck of troubles, so we'll leave that argyment over for another time. We'll take the skins, but you'll throw in some rifle-shots of land with 'em, won't you, ef so be we gits back your gal?"

Enemoya required some further explanations, and finally

agreed that our pioneers, if successful in recovering Missouri, should have as much territory of Omaha, wherever they were pleased to locate, as they *could shoot round* in a day. He did not calculate the number of acres that could be thus covered by a score of long Kentucky rifles. The bargain was concluded. And here we may observe that such leagues were quite frequent from the earliest periods of our history, between the red men and the white pioneers. The latter most commonly took sides with the tribe with which they hunted, harbored, or trafficked. The trappers and traders were always ready to lead in the wars between the tribes, and their presence usually determined the contest. They were in fact so many bold, hardy, fighting men, and were always active in the old French war, in subsidizing the Indians for their respective nations, against French or English, as it happened. Let them fight as they pleased, however, the red men were losers in the end. The rifle shots invariably resulted in the absorption of their acres. But the bargain was concluded, and the supper. The squatters leaped to their feet, girded themselves up for travel, reprimed their rifles, and set off, under the guidance of Enemoya—now refreshed by rest, and a new stimulus to hope—to recover the trail of the fugitive Pawnees, which he had lost.

CHAPTER VII.

While Enemoya was thus strengthening himself for the pursuit, passions of a strange and exciting character were slowly kindling in the camp of the Pawnees. The growing sympathy which Kionk showed for the beautiful captive, became intelligible to his comrades a little sooner than to himself. They had no such feelings, and they were a little resentful of his, accordingly. Besides, one of his companions was a brother to one of his many wives, and was particularly watchful of those peculiar weaknesses of his kinsman, which were sufficiently notorious among his people. Like Mark Antony, to whom we have already compared him, Kionk had too tender a heart—he was a born admirer of the sex, and would cheerfully lose the world any day for any dusky Cleopatra. He suffered his companions to see the progress which Missouri had made in his affections.

by gravely proposing to them, as they rested in camp, the very hour that Enemoya was making his bargain with the white men, to "seek for another captive." He was not quite sure that a woman sacrifice was contemplated by the gods, or would be acceptable to them. He very much doubted it himself. Indeed, how should it be so. It was the war-god to whom the victim was to be offered, and what should the victim be but a warrior. They had seen the defenceless condition of the islet. It would surely be easy to cast the snare about the feet of some one of the veterans, and carry him off, as they had carried off Missouri." The brother-in-law answered with a sneer:—

"Is my brother prepared, when he hath taken the old warrior, to leave the damsel behind him?"

This was a puzzler, by which Kionk began to see that he was suspected. But he was a bold fellow, who did not care much to offer apologies or excuses. He answered with equal promptness and determination:—

"No, indeed; the captive woman is comely, and would be the mother of many braves to a chief among the Pawnees."

"As if the Pawnees had no women of their own," was the reply of the other; and his sentiments were clearly those of the larger number of his companions.—Kionk, bold as he was, was not prepared to take the bull by the horns at that moment. He saw that public opinion was against him, and he must wait events. And this forbearance became much more essential, when his savage brother-in-law deliberately urged upon the party "to subject Missouri to the fire torture where they then were, and thus render the matter certain. They would thus free themselves from an incumbrance; would be better able to turn upon their enemies; could then strike and scalp with impunity, and revenge themselves fearfully for all the taunts of their impudent assailants, made safe by the oracle, to which they had found it so painful to submit. The requisitions of the oracle once complied with, they would be free to use their scalping-knives on every side."

It required all the logic and eloquence of Kionk to silence this terrible suggestion, one which better taught him to understand the extent of his newly-awakened passion for his beautiful and dangerous captive. His argument proved conclusive with all but his savage brother-in-law. He urged that the sacrifice could only take place under the immediate sanction and sight of the high-priest. But before the decision of his companions could be made, the party had nearly come to blows. In the midst of the discussion between Kionk and his kinsman, and when both were nearly roused to madness, the latter sprang suddenly upon Missouri—who had tremblingly listened to the whole dispute—seized her by her long black hair, whirled her furiously around, and actually lifted his knife to strike, before any of them could interpose. Then it was that the whole lion nature of Kionk was in arms, and tearing her away from the brutal assailant, he hurled him to the earth, and, but for his companions, would have brained him with his hatchet on the spot. But he warned him with terrible eye, as he suffered him to rise, that if he but laid his finger on the damsel again, he would hew him to pieces. The kinsman rose, silent, sullen, unsubdued, and secretly swearing in his soul to have his revenge yet. These events delayed the party. It was long that night before they slept. It was late—after daylight, next day—before the journey was resumed. This gave new opportunities to the pursuers.

It was not difficult to retrace the steps of the white men, which Enemoya had so unwisely followed, until he reached the point where he had turned aside from the true object of pursuit. To this the squatters themselves, who were as good at scouting, any day, as the red men, very easily conducted. This brought them to a late hour in the night, and here our whites proceeded to make their camp, though, this time, without venturing to make a fire. The Omaha chief would have hurried on, but his companions very coolly and doggedly refused. He soon saw the wisdom of curbing his impatience, not only because of the inflexibility of his allies, but because, as they showed him, his impatience would only cause him again to lose the trail, which it was not possible to pursue by night. With the dawn, however, the whites were on the alert, and one of them soon appeared with a bead in his hand, the certain indication of the damsel's route and providence. Enemoya readily conjectured the general direction which would be taken by the Pawnees, and an occasional bead, glistening upon the sandy spots, sufficed every now and then to encourage the pursuers. At this period, the better knowledge of the country possessed by Enemoya, enabled him, by striking an oblique course for the head of a creek, which the Pawnees would be compelled to cross, to gain considerably upon them, ignorant as they were of this shorter route. The suggestion was fortunate; and, never once dreaming of the events which had delayed the fugitives the last night, the Omaha chief with his allies came unexpectedly upon them about midday, where, squat beside a brooklet, they were taking a brief rest and a little refreshment. This pause had become especially necessary for Missouri, who, with incessant travel, and the terror of the scene of the previous night, had succumbed, and actually fainted that morning along the route. Kionk was compelled to carry her, at various stages, in his arms—which he did with the greatest tenderness—till the moment when the party stopped for nooning beside the little brooklet, where Enemoya and his white allies came upon them.

The Pawnees were overtaken, but not taken by surprise. They did not certainly expect to be overtaken, but they had relaxed in none of their vigilance, and their scout reported the enemy before the latter had discovered the quarry. The Pawnees were sitting upon the ground, scattered around a small circuit, Missouri in the centre of the group, resting against a tree. Her long hair was dishevelled, and lay heavily upon the leaves; her face was sad and anxious, weary and without hope;—so woful was the sight that the impulses of Enemoya, as he beheld her, got for a moment the better of his prudence, and he rushed out of the covert, shouting his war cry, and bounding forward with uplifted tomahawk. It was with no scrupulous or gentle hand that the elder of the white men caught him in his sinewy grasp, and drew him back into the thickets.

With the signal whistle of their scout, the Pawnee warriors were at once upon their legs, each covering himself with a tree; and a dozen arrows were rapidly shot into the wood where our squatters had taken harbor. But they were as quick and as practised in woodcraft as the Pawnees, and laughed at this demonstration. In numbers they exceeded the small party of their enemies, and could have overwhelmed them probably by a sudden rush from opposite quarters; but they were warned against such audacity by beholding the danger of the dusky maiden, who was seized by the hair by one of the captors as soon as Enemoya had shown himself, while a knife lifted over her bosom threatened her with instant death at the first demonstration of attack. Never had Enemoya before found himself in a situation in which he was so little capable of resolving what should be done. But the squatters who accompanied him were persons of as much shrewdness and experience as daring. While they felt that confidence and boldness were prime qualities of the warrior, they also well knew that rashness and precipitance would be fatal to their object. They held counsel among themselves, never consulting the red chief, though he stood up and listened. The Anglo-Norman has profound faith in parliaments. "We must argyfy the case with these red devils," was the conclusion to which they came. They had profound faith in their ability for "argyment." The result of their deliberations was to send forth one of their number, accompanied by Enemoya, bearing a white handkerchief at the end of his rifle, and a long pipe in his left hand—both signs of truce and amnesty—the calumet that of the red men, the flag that of the white. The object was to ascertain upon what terms the maiden would be given up. Of course they did not know what issues hung upon her fate, or what was her destiny, or that she was the subject of an awful oracle.

CHAPTER VIII

At the appearance of the flag and the Omaha chief, Kionk, followed by three others, emerged from his place of shelter. They advanced to meet the flag without apprehension, though both parties kept their weapons ready, and their eyes bright. Treachery is a warlike virtue among the savages, and our squatters well understood the necessity of covering an enemy, each with his rifle, while their comrades were engaged in conference. How shall we report this conference? It would be impossible to follow step by step the details, as developed in the broken English of the one party, and the half savage Pawnee of the other. But the high contracting parties contrived, after a fashion, to make themselves separately understood. Our squatter embassador had little hesitation in coming as promptly to the point as possible. We sum up much in little, when we report the following:—

"'Taint a manly way of carrying on the war, catching a poor young woman. What's the sperrit of a man to lay hands upon a girl, onless for love and affection? And now you've got her, what's the use of her to you? You have plenty of gals in your own nation. What do you want with this Omaha?"

The Pawnee acknowledged that his people were by no means wanting in specimens of the tender gender. They had enough, Heaven knows, even if all their chiefs were of the Kionk temper.

"Well, then, let's have the gal. We'll buy her from you at a fair vallyation. What do you say now to half a dozen tomahawks, a dozen knifes, two little bells, a pound of fishhooks, four pounds of beads, and a good overcoat, handsome enough for a king."

The goods were all displayed. Kionk acknowledged that the offer was a liberal one. But—and here he revealed the true difficulty—the captive-girl was the subject of an oracle. The fate of Pawnees or Omahas depended upon her life. She was doomed to the fiery torture. In her ashes lay the future triumph of his people over the accursed tribe of the Omaha! There could be no trade; no price could buy the captive; no power save her life; he would forego his hold upon her only with his own life; and in a few days she should undergo the torture by fire. Such was the final answer.

"May I be etarnally burned myself, ef I stand by and see her burned; so look to it, red-skin! I'm a human, after all; and my rifle shall talk like blazes before you take her off!"

The conference had reached this point, and Kionk had been made to comprehend the fiercely-expressed declaration of the representative squatter, when Missouri, arousing from her stupor, caught a glimpse of Enemoya. The sight seemed to restore instantly her strength and energies. With a single bound, and a wild passionate cry, she darted suddenly away from the savage who stood over her, and who had somewhat relaxed his vigilance in the curiosity which he felt with regard to the conference. She flew, rather than ran, over the space which lay between, and Enemoya sprang forward to receive her. But before they could meet, a blow from the fist of one of the savages felled her to the earth.

In a moment the work of death had begun. The hatchet of Enemoya cleft the skull of the brutal assailant. Then rose his war-cry—then came the fierce shout of Kionk and the rest. Every arrow was drawn to its head. Every rifle-bead rested with dead aim upon the tree which gave shelter to an enemy. The *charge d'affaires* of the squatters, quick as lightning, tore the white kerchief from his rifle, and dodged into cover; while Enemoya, no longer capable of restraint, dashed forward to gather up the beautiful damsel from the ground where she still lay, stunned by the blow of the Indian. But he was not permitted to reach his object. It was now Kionk's turn. He threw himself into the path of the young chief of the Omahas, and together grappling they came together to the earth. It was the death grapple for one or both. In their hearts they felt mutually the instinct of a deadly personal hatred, apart from that which belonged to their national hostilities. Closely did they cling; sinuously, like serpents, did they wind about each other on the earth, rapidly rolling over, fiercely striving, without a word spoken on either part. But one weapon could either now use, and that was the scalp-knife which each bore in his belt. But to get at this was not easy, since neither dared forego his grasp, lest he should give his opponent the advantage.

Meanwhile the rest were not idle. The Pawnees, highly excited by the death of one of their number, and seeing but two enemies before them — never dreaming that there were no less than six Kentuckians in ambush — darted, with terrible yells, into the foreground. Two of them, in an instant, bit the dust; and the rest recoiled from the unanticipated danger. The Kentuckians now made a rush in order to extricate Enemoya, and to brain Kionk; and the aspect of affairs was hopeful in the last degree; when, at this very moment, one of the Pawnees darted out of cover. He was the brother-in-law of Kionk — the sullen chief whom he had overthrown, and whose black passions meditated the most hateful of revenges. Before the squatters could reach the scene of action, the murderous monster, whose purpose was wholly unexpected, threw himself upon the crouching Missouri, and with a single blow buried his hatchet in her brain. With a howl of mixed scorn and exultation he had shrouded himself in the woods, and among his comrades, a moment after

The wretched Enemoya beheld the horrid stroke, but, grappling with his own assailant he had not the power to interfere. In striving to loose himself for this purpose, he gave his enemy the advantage. In a moment both were on their feet, and Kionk already brandished his scalp-knife in his grasp. But the eyes of Enemoya swam in a blind horror. He had seen the whizzing tomahawk descend, crushing into the head of the dusky beauty whom he so much loved. He saw no more; and the uplifted knife of Kionk was already about to sheathe itself in his bosom, when a rifle bullet from one of the squatters sent him reeling to the earth in the last agonies of death. When Enemoya sunk beside the poor damsel, her eyes were already glazed. She knew him not. She looked on him no more. He took the scalp of Kionk, but it gave him no consolation. He fought like a demon — he slew many enemies,—took many scalps,—but never felt a whit the happier. His hope was blighted — he loved the dusky beauty of the blessed islet, much more tenderly than we should suppose from the manner of his wooing: and he never recovered from her loss. He moved among his people like a shadow, and they called him the ghost only of the great warrior.

The campaign that season was indecisive between the rival nations of the Pawnee and Omaha. Neither had succeeded in complying with the requisitions of the oracle. The Pawnees had forfeited their hope in failing to bring their captive to the torture of fire. The Omahas had been equally unfortunate in being compelled to strike the first blow. The first life taken in the war was that of the savage Pawnee who smote Missouri with his fist, and whom Enemoya immediately slew. But the campaign of the ensuing winter went against the Omahas. They had lost the soul of Enemoya; who ceased to exhibit any enterprise, though he fought terribly when the hour came for conflict. Meanwhile, our squatters from Kentucky were joined by others from that daring region. Their rifles helped the Omahas for a long time; but the latter were finally defeated. The remnant of the nation were ready to disperse; they knew not where to turn. The blessed island was almost the only territory remaining in their possession. But for this there suddenly appeared a new claimant.

"These are pleasant places, boys," said the head man of the

squatters, looking at the lovely region around; "it seems to me to be good if we drive stakes and build our cabins here — here by this quiet lake, among these beautiful meadows. — What say you, — shall it be here? I don't want to go further, 'till it comes to be crowded."

"But this is the abiding place of my people, my brother; — here is the wigwam of Enemoya, — yonder was the dwelling which I built for the wife of my bosom, the beautiful Missouri."

"Look you, Inimowya," answered the white chief, "the argyment of territory, after all, lies at the eend of my rifle. As I told you once afore, when we first met, I could dispute with you that pr'emption title, but I wouldn't; and I won't now; considering that you've had a bad time of it. But what's the use of your talking, when you see the country's got to be ours. Why, you know we kin shoot round it every day"— again touching his rifle. — "But that's not the argyment I want to use with you. Your brown gal, who was a beauty for an Ingin, I'm willing to allow, is a sperrit now in the other world. What sort of heaven they find for the red-skins, is unbeknowing to me; but I reckon she's living thar. Thar's no living for her hyar, you see, so what's the use of the cabin you built. But that's not to say I wants to drive you out. By no possible means. I like you — all the boys like you. For a red-skin you're a gentleman, and as you hev' no nation now, and hardly any tribe of your own, why squat down with us, by any man's fireside you choose, and ef you choose, you kin only set down and look on, and see how we'll take the shine out of these Pawnee cock-a-doodles. You kin share with us, and do as we do, with all the right nateral to a free white man; but as for your getting this island from us, now that we're all ready to plant stakes, it's a matter onpossible to be argyfied except with the tongue of the rifle. Thar's no speech that ever was invented that shall make us pull up stakes now."

And the rifle butt came down heavily upon the earth, as the chief of the squatters declared himself. Enemoya regarded him with a grave indifference, and said calmly: —

"Be it so: the island is young; the country! Why should you not have it? I need it not! neither I nor Missouri! I thank you for what you say. But though your cabin door is wide for my coming, I do not see Missouri beside the hearth."

"Oh! for that matter, as you are quite a gentleman for a red-skin, there's many a pretty white gal that would hev you for the axing."

"No! I shall follow my people to the black prairies, and wait for the voice of that bird of the Spirit, that shall summon me to the happy valley where Missouri walks."

"Well, as you choose, Inimowya; but let's to supper now and you'll sleep under my bush to-night."

The chief silently consented. But at the dawn he was no where to be seen, nor have the hunters ever heard of him since. Meanwhile the country of the Omaha, which includes the lake and the beautiful islet, has become the possession of the pale-faces, but they call it still after the dusky damsel of Omaha, the lovely and loving Missouri.

CHAPTER XVIII.

"WHAT CONSTITUTES A STATE?"

"WE are now within the atmosphere of your southern Hotspur," said our Gothamite. "Come, sir," addressing our cynical orator from Alabama, "come, sir, and let us have your portrait of the South-Carolinian. You have dealt freely with Virginia and North Carolina, showing us their more salient features, which are rarely the most comely for boast; let us see if you can not depict their southern brother with as free and dashing a pencil."

The Alabamian smiled, and looked to Miss Burroughs, as he replied :—

"I dare not; in this instance there is a lady in the case."

"Oh! most unlooked-for and most unseasonable gallantry!" exclaimed the lady. "Do you forget, Sir Orator, those wicked and scandalous ballads, to the grievous disparagement of the sex, which you not only sang to us of your own motion, a volunteer performance, but which you sang with such unction and effect, as if the execution were a sort of labor of love, which you would not escape, even if you might?"

"Ah! forgive the offence. It was in evil mood that I sang, and not because of any love for the subject."

"He's been kicked, I reckon, by some lady only t'other day," said the Texan, roughly, "and the shins of his affections are still sore with the bruises."

"'The shins of his affections!' That is surely new. What admirable cropping, in the way of metaphor and figure, might our young ballad-mongers find in the fields of Texas! Well I will submit to the imputation of the recent kicking, as an acknowledgment of the merits of that phrase. 'The shins of the affections!' We shall next hear something touching, 'the tederness of the corns on the big toe of the heart.' When shall there be a Texan poet."

"Lord save you, we've got a matters of more than fifty-five already. We've got a Texan Hemans, and a Texan Tennyson —nay, we've got three Tennysons, and more than thirteen Byrons. Oh! we are not so badly off for poets as you think. In Galveston there's a poet who weighs more than two hundred and eighty pounds, and he has sighed out love poetry enough to fill the sails of a California clipper. It's the opinion of some of our people that we owe most of our worthies to his love poems. Latterly, he's gone into the elegiac; and since Tennyson's 'In Memoriam,' he has done nothing but write 'In Memoriams.' He has mourned the loss of more dear friends since the date of that publication, than he ever knew people. In fact, not to be irreverent, speaking of poetry, there's hardly a person in all Texas that would lend him a picayune, though it should save his soul from the gallows."

"Save his soul from the gallows! A new idea of the punishments employed in Tophet. Fancy the soul of a poet weighing two hundred and eighty pounds hung up to dry in the devil's clothes garden!"

"But all this talk," interrupted the son of Gotham, "must not be suffered to deprive us of our portrait of the South-Carolinian."

"You get no such portrait from me," answered the Alabamian, abruptly.

"And why not?" interrupted the North-Carolinian. "You had no scruples in dealing with the Old Dominion and the old North State."

"Very true: but there are reasons why I should have scruples when we come to South Carolina. I know the faults and the foibles of that little state as well as any person in this crowd, and I am as well able, I reckon, to describe them. But I will not. In the first place, I look to that same state to set us right yet in this confederacy. I feel that she will be the first to dare and brave the struggle when it comes, and I will in no way, however small, do or say anything to weaken her hands by disparaging her features. Besides, Miss Burroughs—this to you— I owe my mother to South Carolina, and the cradle which has rocked a mother should be an ark of the covenant to a loving son."

Our Alabamian, by showing himself sentimental for a single moment, had once more put himself within the pale of the vulgar humanity. It was very clear that we should get nothing further out of him on the one subject. Our North-Carolinian endeavored to supply the desired portrait, but the limning was contradictory—in fact, the moral portrait of South Carolina is one of many difficulties, which it requires a rare and various knowledge, and no small skill of the artist to manage and overcome: and gradually, the embarrassments of the subject were felt, as the discussion of her traits proceeded, and the subject was finally abandoned as one totally unmanageable. Of course much was said of her luxury, her pride and arrogance, her presumption in leading, the vanity of her boasts, her short-comings in a thousand respects; all of which provoked keen retort, particularly from our secessionists—the Alabamian scarcely seeming to heed the controversy, and taking no part in it till its close, when he said briefly:—

"One word, gentlemen. South Carolina is the only state in the Union which grants no divorce. If there were nothing else, in the catalogue of her virtues to show the character of her virtues, this would suffice. It says two things. It declares for the steadiness and constancy of both sexes, and for the virtues that render such a measure unnecessary. Her morals prevent, instead of pampering, the caprices of the affections—"

"Yes, but there are some crimes! It would be monstrous to keep parties fettered, one of whom is a criminal——"

"I understand you! They do *not* keep together. In Carolina, in all such cases, the criminal dies—disappears, at all events, and the social world never mentions again the name of the offender."

"Very Roman, certainly."

The Alabamian did not heed the sneer, but proceeded—

"South Carolina is the only state in which there is anything like loyalty to the past remaining. She preserves her veneration. The state is protected from the people."

"How is that? Is not the state the people."

"No! very far from it. The state is a thing of thousands of

years, past and future, constituting a moral which is to be saved from the caprices of the people. People change daily, and in their daily change, filled with novel hopes and expectations, and urged on by eager passions and desires, would easily forego a thousand absolute possessions which no people at any one time sufficiently values. In truth, it is only when we tremble at the onward and reckless course of a majority, that we are awakened to the fact that there are some things which they have no right to sacrifice. It is then that we see that the possessions and accumulations of the past are not an inheritance, but a trust; and we who occupy only a moment of time, in the general progress of the ages, are taught by this fact that we have no absolute rights over possessions which belong to generations yet untold in the future, and but partially recorded in the past. To guard the state from the people, we resort to a thousand devices, such as constitutions, bills of rights, &c., none of which is satisfactory for the sufficient reason that the subject is one of singular subtilty which escapes practical definition. It is, however, within our instincts, and these work in a thousand ways, and in spite of us, for its preservation. When these fail us, the state is gone, and the people soon follow. They are then without God or country. The French revolution was an instance of the sacrifice of the state—that vague and vast idea, growing out of the gradual acquisitions of thousands of years of a common fortune in the family, or race—by a mere generation just passing off the stage. Look at the summary in France to-day. Where is the liberty, the equality, the republicanism, which were all their avowed objects? What is left them of sacred tradition, of past loyalty and acquisition, of moral security—which must precede if it would maintain physical—of all that was deemed certain in the characteristics of the race? The guardian securities and virtues of a people lie in that social ideal which is embodied in the notion of the state as a thing permanent, contradistinguished from a mere generation or government—things which contemplate only passing necessities, and continual fluctuations, and are required to contribute in passing only a certain portion of capital to that grand stock which has been already put away safely within the securities of the ideal state. The state is a guardian ideal, and the conservative check upon the caprices of time.

The state represents the eternity of a race — its whole duration whether long or short. Cut the sinews of the state, in obedience to the caprices of a generation, and they must perish. All this is very obscure, I know, and it can not well be otherwise, with such a subject, and in a mere casual conversation. It must necessarily elude all common demonstrative analysis, particularly as it lies based on great but mysterious secrets, in the general plan of Providence, which it is scarcely permitted to us to explore. The subject belongs to the spiritual nature in high degree and is not to be measured by the common rules of argument. It constitutes a study for the metaphysician who is at the same time, a religious man. It is one of those problems which the rulers of a people have need carefully to study, as it is upon the due knowledge and appreciation of 'the state,' that every people's future must depend. Nations perish really because of their simple failure to recognise this distinction between state and people: and it is thus that a capricious generation, perpetually bent on change, restless and impatient because of its atrocious vanity, still wrecks all the ideal morals of their ancestors, and all the hopes, born of those ideals, which would conduct their posterity to power."

"I confess this transcendentalism is quite too much for me. I do not see the meaning yet of your distinction. It appears to me only a dreamy sophism."

"Precisely, and if you will show me the man to whom a metaphysical subtilty is for the first time presented, who is prepared on the instant not only to argue it but to judge it, I shall be willing to attach some importance to your present cavalier dismissal of the topic. Your process seems to be that of one of our western members of Congress, who, some years ago, began his speech with, 'I don't know nothing, Mr. Speaker, of the subject hyar before us, but I intend to go on argyfying it ontil I gits all the necessary knowledge.' But even he, bold and brave and candid as he was, never ventured to decide. He only proposed to use 'argyment' as a means of getting his 'edication.'"

"Why, you are perfectly savage."

"No; searching only.— To resume our subject for a moment longer. There is a passage from one of our southern poets, who has endeavored to express something of this idea of 'the state' as it appears to my own mind. Like all others, who have spoken and written on the point, the subtilty still eludes him; but enough is said to give the clues into the hands of the metaphysician; and no other person, by the way, has any right to pass upon it."

"Let's have the passage."

The Alabamian delivered it, from memory, to the following effect:—

"THE STATE.

"The moral of the race is in the State,
The secret germ for great development,
Through countless generations:—all the hopes,
The aims, the great ambition, the proud works,
Virtues, performance, high desires and deeds,
With countless pure and precious sentiments,
Nursed in some few brave souls, that, still apart
From the rude hunger of the multitude,
Light fires, built altars, image out the God
That makes the grand ideal:—which, unknown,
Unconsciously, the thoughtless tribes conceive
In a blind worship; which is still content
To follow Duty through the bonds of terror,
And learn its best obedience through its fears.
. . . . . . A state's the growth
Of the great family of a thousand years,
With all its grand community of thoughts,
Affections, faith, and sentiments, as well
As its material treasures. These are naught,
If that the faith, the virtues, and the will,
Be lacking to the race. The guardian state
Keeps these immaculate. They are not yours,
Or mine; nor do they rest within the charge
Of the mere feeders at the common crib,
Of all the myriads, keeping pace with us,
Some seventy years of march. We are but links,
In a long-banded, many-fibred stock,
Branching and spreading out on every side,
With every day some change of hope and aim,
Rule, province and division of our tribes,
Each with a moment purpose, to pursue
Some passion or mere fancy — some caprice —
Which, as even evil works out ways for good,
Must, in its turn, contribute to the truths,

> That are still garnered safely in the state.
> Our march makes little in the grand design
> Save as a natural incident that grows,
> Inevitably, out of natural progress,
> Leaving its moral in its very loss.
> Our change must work no changes in the state,
> Which still maintains the original ideal germ,
> Sacred within its keeping, as the Romans,
> The sacred shields that fell to them from Heaven
> As in all nations there are fabled treasures,
> Shrined awfully apart, to which men look,
> For safety, when the temple rocks in fire,
> And the walled city totters in the storm.
> —March as we may and govern as we may,
> Change with what sad or wild caprice we may,
> The indisputable majesty which makes
> The sovereignty which harbors in each race,
> Knows never change of attribute, till ends
> The mission, which the endowment still declares!"

The orator paused.

"Is that all? Why, we are no nigher to the solution of the problem than before."

"I suppose not. Poetry, the profoundest of all human studies, itself requires the abstract mind and the contemplative mood; and the necessity for these is the greater when it deals in metaphysics and politics. Perhaps, if you weigh well this passage, you will gradually see the light through the cloud and curtain. Precious things rarely lie upon the surface. In proportion to the glory is the necessity of obscuration. God showed himself to the Jews only through clouds and fire. They could see him only through some material medium. It was the poet prophet only who could discover his awful features through less terrible agencies."

"You are getting more and more obscure. Now, pray tell us, what have all your metaphysics to do with South Carolina?"

"Nothing, that I can show you, unless you can take the first step with me—which, as yet, you can not. It may be enough to say of South Carolina, that it is a sufficient merit of hers, in my eyes, that her revolutionary spirit (so called) has been the result of her loyalty; that it was to check revolution that she interposed the state veto, and threw down her gauntlet to federal usurpation. You all feel and see, now, that she was right.

You are all in possession of free trade and a prosperous progress, the result of her course, which leaves the condition of the country unexampled in history for its growth and prosperity. Her conservatism, not her resolution, prompted her action; and she still adheres to her conservative tendencies, while all other states are rocking with the conflict of revolutionary ideas. She still preserves her veneration. There are still many classes within her limits, who maintain the morals of her dawn — who seek to preserve sacred that capital of ideal in the state which, kept always in view as a guiding light, renders progress a safe and natural development, and not an inane and insane coursing in a circle where we for ever come in conflict with one another. Here you find, still of force, the manners and customs, the sentiments and traditions, that she held to be great and glorious eighty years ago; and which have enabled her, though one of the smallest states in the confederacy, to contribute a large proportion of its greatest warriors, its noblest and wisest sages, its purest and most venerated men. You can not bully her out of her propriety, for she has unshaken courage; you can not buy her with any bribe, for she has always shown herself scornful of cupidity. She maintains still the haughty sentiments of a race of gentlemen who never descended to meanness. She has a thousand foibles, faults — nay, follies — perhaps, but she has some virtues which power can not crush out of her, or money buy: and she will be the state, let me tell you, who will save all that is worth saving in this confederacy, even when the confederacy itself perishes."

"Why, old Blast," interposed the Texan, "you must be thinking that you're on the stump. You do put your horns into the bowels of the argument, just as if you knew where you was a-going all the time. Lord, how Sam Houston would laugh if you was to tell *him* of such prophecies as that."

"Sam Houston! Sir, don't speak to me of Sam Houston. He's beyond the reach of prophecy, which is never addressed to any but living souls!"

"Well, I must say that's a settler for Sam. But he'll take the change out of you, I reckon, when he comes to be president. You'll never get a foreign appointment from him, I'm a-thinking; and I reckon Sam's chance for the presidency is about as good as that of any man going."

We put in here, several of us, to arrest the partisan tendency of the discussion, which evidently began to "*rile*" some of the parties; and our excellent captain came to our assistance, with his jest and smile, his quip and crank, which have always proved so effective in curing the *maladie du mer* among his passengers

"I'm president here, gentlemen," said he, "and I hold it to be good law to declare that it is high treason to discuss the succession. As there is some talk of appointments, I beg to say, that if any of you wish office, the governorship of Bull's is vacant."

And he pointed us to the island of that name which made the rim of the horizon for us on the north.

"There is an island, gentlemen, upon which a man might be a sovereign. Solitude in perfection, game in abundance, fine fish of all sorts, oysters to beguile even an alderman to fleshly and fishy inclination—such a realm as would satisfy Alexander Selkirk, and make Robinson Crusoe dance with delight. I have often thought of Bull's as an island upon which a man might be at peace with all the world, and with fortune and himself in particular."

"A sort of heaven on earth."

"And sea. It has fine harborage, too. The coast survey has made it a harbor of refuge, and we are soon to have a lighthouse upon it."

"The pirates knew it as a place of refuge a hundred years ago and more. Here Robert Kidd, 'as he sailed,' and that more monstrous ruffian Blackbeard, and a hundred other fierce outlaws of the same practice, found their place of refuge and rollicking. Nor here alone: all the range of islands which run along the coast, between which and the main there are numerous islets of great beauty and interest, are distinguished by traditions of wild and sometimes terrible attraction. Many of these have been marked as spots conspicuous in history, and all of them possess their legends and chronicles, which only need to be hunted up and put on record, to render all of them classical and interesting, apart from their natural attractions. The whole of this region was the favorite resort of the pirates, and at periods long anterior to the Revolution, —those periods when, as the phrase ran through the marine of Great Britain, 'there was no peace beyond the line!' In these snug harbors and safe retreats the mousing robber found his coverts. Here he lay close until he beheld, from afar, the white sails of the fair trader. Then he darted forth like the shark, a little black speck upon the waters, and tore his victim with angry and remorseless jaws, and dyed the blue waters in his blood. To these islets he hurried back to divide and to hide his spoil; and dark and terrible are the thousand stories which, could they speak, they might narrate of the wild orgies of the cruel bands by which they were infested — of the bloody sacrifices which they witnessed — and of the fate of the victims guilty of the inexpiable offence of possessing treasures which their neighbors coveted. Young eagles must be fed, and the eagles of the sea are proverbially the most voracious of all the eagle tribe. These were merciless. They hovered about the mouth of Charleston for long periods, and it was in vain that Britain kept watch with her frigates and guarda costas for the protection of her trade. Her wealth, as a colony, was at that time superior to most of the colonies, and demanded powerful protection. But so swift of foot, so keen of sight, so fierce of appetite, were these marauding wretches, that they too commonly evaded pursuit, and not only succeeded in capturing the outward-bound vessels continually, but sometimes laid the infant city, itself, under contribution.

"Our friend from North Carolina has bestowed upon us a very interesting narrative of the 'Ship of Fire.' The tradition is well known in portions of South Carolina; and to this day certain families are pointed out as the descendants of those cruel mariners who so mercilessly slaughtered that little colony of German palatines. Our traditions point out the progeny of these pirates as still under the avenging danger of the fates. They are marked by continuous disasters. The favorite son perishes, from some terrible accident, in the moment of his very highest promise; the favorite daughter withers away in consumption or some nameless disease, just as she nears that bloomy period when the mother thinks to place within her hair the bridal flower. The neighbors shake their heads and look knowingly when the bolt descends suddenly upon those families, and express no surprise. 'It must be so,' they say. 'The fates must have their prey. The blood of that massacre must be washed out in blood. All these families, the descendants of the murderers, must die out, till not one man-child shall survive.' Their ill-gotten wealth does them no good. Their fruits turn to ashes on their lips. The sword, suspended by a single hair, hangs for ever over their heads, and the bolt strikes them down from the bosom of an unclouded sky. So well has tradition retained these memories, that people will even give you the names of the families, still living, over which this terribly unerring destiny impends. I have had one or more domestic chronicles of this sort put into my possession within five years. Of course, the doomed victims have no sort of knowledge either of the fates reserved for them, or of the familiarity of their neighbors with the unwritten tradition. Old people point them out to their children; they repeat the story to their sons, and their fingers point always to the illustrative catastrophe. Every stroke of Providence is keenly observed and dwelt upon which touches them; and it may be safely affirmed that the tradition will survive them all, and point to the grave of the last supposed victim of a crime committed two hundred years ago or more."

"How very terrible!"

"These several islands which we approach after Bull's, Dewee's, Caper's, Long, and Sullivan, and the islets which lie within, between them and the main, are all thus fruitful in ancient pirate legends. One of these occurs to me at this moment; and, as I believe I am the next person chronicled on your list for a story, I may as well pursue the vein upon which we have struck, as it were, by chance."

"O, let us have it, by all means. I confess to a passion for such stories, which even the reading of the Book of the Buccaneers has not totally overcome."

THE STORY OF BLACKBEARD.

I.

"THE narrative," said our *raconteur*, "which I am about to give you, was related to me by one of our oldest inhabitants, a planter who is still living at the advanced period of eighty years, and who ranks not less venerably from worth than age. He heard it from those who claimed to have known personally some of the parties to the history, and who fully believed the truth of the story which they told. The period of the narrative was, perhaps, a quarter of a century before the Revolution.

"You are all aware that from 1670 to 1750, using round numbers, the buccaneers, leagued of all nations, no longer confining themselves to the Spanish galleons, which were always held to be fair prey to the British cruisers, made the commerce of Britain herself finally their prey, and literally haunted with daily terrors the coasts of Virginia and the two Carolinas, as well as the West Indies, making spoil of their rich and but little protected productions. Their crews, composed of the scum of all nations — British, French, Dutch, Portuguese, and Spaniards — discriminated in behalf of none; and so loose were British and American morals at that period — (have they very much improved since?) — that the people of the provinces themselves — their very governors — were greatly inclined to countenance the *flibustiers* (French corruption of freebooters) in all those cases of piracy where they themselves were not the immediate sufferers. They drove a profitable trade with the marauders, who were sometimes to be seen walking the streets of the Atlantic cities with the most perfect impunity. Captain Kidd, for a long time, was the great master-spirit of these wretches. His successor in audacity, insolence, and crime, was the infamous Blackbeard, the *nom de guerre* by which he preferred that the world should read his character. His proper name, Edward Teach, was, in itself, innocent enough.

"Blackbeard particularly affected the coasts of Carolina. The waters over which we now go were the favorite fields of his performance. Harbored among these islands — Bull's, Dewee's, Caper's, Sullivan, Seewee, and others — he lay in close watch for the white sails of commerce. He explored all these bays and harbors, and knew their currents and bearings well, from the cape of Hatteras to that of Florida reef. He had command of a complete squadron, including vessels of nearly all sizes. His flag was hoisted upon a forty-gun ship, the crew of which consisted of more than a hundred men. His captains were Vane, Bonnet, Warley, and others, inferior to himself only in hardihood and skill. Somewhere about 1713, a proclamation had been issued by the king in council, promising a pardon to all the pirates who should surrender themselves in twelve months. Blackbeard was one of those who, either through a cunning policy, meant to delude the powers which he feared he should not so readily escape, or under a sudden uneasiness of conscience, presented himself before Governor Eden, of North Carolina, pleaded the king's pardon, and received the governor's certificate. Eden, by the way, was one of those governors of whom history speaks, as having received the bribes of the pirates, and kept up a criminal but profitable connection with Blackbeard in particular.

"Blackbeard, the better to prove his resolve to demean himself for the future with Christian propriety, married his *thirteenth* wife, a young girl of Pamplico. But he could not long forbear his riotous habits, or forego his passion for adventures upon the sea. He was soon again on board a smart cruiser, and reaping the fields of ocean with the sword. He sailed upon a cruise, carrying his new wife with him, and shortly returned with a valuable prize, a French ship laden with sugar and cocoa, which he had no difficulty in persuading the court of admiralty he had found at sea, abandoned by her crew. She was adjudged as a lawful prize to her unlawful captors. Here our narrative begins. Thus far, our facts are strictly historical—except, perhaps, in regard to the fact stated, that his new wife, the girl of Pamplico, accompanied him on this cruise. But the fact, omitted by history, is supplied by tradition, which asserts that the girl herself figured somewhat in the incidents connected with the capture of the French prize.

"Blackbeard steered south when he left the river of Cape Fear. The season was mild, late spring—the seas smooth—the winds fresh and favorable. Soon they espied the French brigantine laying her course, due east from the tropical islands.

"As he beheld his new prey, the savage chief—who, in taking the oath and receiving the king's pardon from the royal governor, had not denuded himself of a single hair of that enormous forest of beard which literally covered his face, head, and breast, and from which he took his name—chucked his new wife under the chin, and swore a terrible oath that the girl should see sights, should drink of the wine of the Indies, and enjoy their fruits, and be clad in the beautiful silks of the Frenchman.

"All sail was clapped on for pursuit. The Frenchman knew his danger, at a glance. Not more certainly does the flying-fish know his enemy the dolphin, or the tunny the swordfish, or the sailor the shark, than the simple trader the deadly danger of that pirate foe, who combined all the terrible characteristics of these several marauders of the sea. Fleet was the Frenchman in flight, but, unhappily, fleeter far was the outlaw in pursuit. Very precious was the Frenchman's cargo; one more precious still, among his passengers, was the fair creole wife of the young merchant, Louis Chastaign, now, for the first time, preparing to visit the birthplace of her husband. They, too, were soon made aware of the danger, and, while the wife watched, and prayed, and trembled, the young husband got his cutlass and his carabine in readiness, and prepared to do battle to the last in defence of the precious treasure of his heart.

"But his resolution was not to be indulged. The captain of the merchantman had no adequate force for resistance, and he prepared for none. He shook his head when Louis Chastaign spoke of it, and appeared on deck with his weapons.

"'It will not do, Monsieur Louis.'

"'And shall we yield tamely to these wretches? They are pirates!'

"'I fear so. But they are two to one. We have no arms. What can a dozen swords and pistols do against a hundred men?'

"'Better die bravely fighting than basely to offer our throats to the knife.'

"'Nay, our hope is that they will content themselves with robbing us of our treasures.'

"The young merchant turned with a look of agony on his beautiful creole. He knew what the appetites of the pirates were. He feared for the one treasure, over all, and thought nothing of the rest, though the better portion of the ship's cargo was his own. The chase was nearing fast. The Frenchman continued to try his heels, but in vain.

"'He gains rapidly, Monsieur Louis. Put away your weapons, my friend; the very show of them may provoke him to cruelty.'

"The poor young man was compelled to submit, yet, in putting his weapons out of sight, he felt as if his treasure was already gone.

"'Is there really so much danger, Louis?' asked the trembling woman of her husband. He could only shake his head mournfully in reply. Then she kissed the cross which she had in her hand, and hid it away in her bosom, and followed her young lord upon the deck of the vessel.

"At that moment, the cannon belched forth its fires from the pursuing pirate; the iron missiles shot through the rigging of the Frenchman, and with a groan he ordered sail to be taken in; and prepared for submission to the enemy from whom there was no escape.

II.

"Very soon the pirate vessel came alongside of the peaceful trader. Her wild and savage crew were ranged along the bulwarks, each armed with cutlass and half a score of pistols conspicuous in belt and bosom. Very terrible was the exhibition which they made of wild beard and brutal aspect. With a torrent of oaths, Blackbeard himself hailed the Frenchman, who put on all his politeness in responding to the insolent demands of his assailant. The vessels were lashed together by grapplings, the pirates streamed on board, and a general search was begun. Meanwhile, the young creole bride of Louis Chastaign kept at her prayers below. Here she was found, and dragged up to the deck at the command of the pirate-chief. The passengers, all, and crew, were made to gather on the deck, under the pistols of a score of the marauders, while the rest ransacked the hold and cabin.

"The examination lasted not long. Blackbeard soon discovered that the cargo was one for which he should have to find a market. Its treasures were not readily portable, nor easily converted into money. The gold and silver, jewels, and precious stones, found in the trunks of the young French merchant, though of considerable value, bore no proportion to the value of the cargo, the bulk of which rendered it necessary that the vessel should be carried into port. This necessity implied another. The crew and passengers must be disposed of. As the scheme presented itself to the mind of Blackbeard to have the vessel condemned by the court of admiralty as a lawful prize, it needed that he should be prepared to report that she was found abandoned by her proper owners. This resolve required that he should suffer no witnesses to live who might expose the true nature of the transaction. He had no remorseful scruples, and the decree was soon pronounced. The unhappy captives were doomed to walk the plank.

"That is to say, all were thus doomed who should refuse to join the pirate party. There was this terrible alternative to be allowed them. Accordingly, having seen what were the treasures of the ship, and fully satisfied himself of what she contained, he reascended to the deck, where the unfortunate crew were held in durance, pale and trembling, in waiting for their fate. Brief consultation had been needed among the pirate-chiefs. Blackbeard had given his opinion, in which the lieutenants all concurred: and there was no consultation necessary when they reappeared on deck.

"The terrible chief, closely followed by his new wife, the girl of Pamplico, confronted the group of captives in all his terrors of aspect, costume, and furious speech. His wife was scarcely less a terror in the eyes of our young French creole woman She was habited only in part like a woman. She wore a skirt, it is true, but the pantaloons of a man appeared beneath, and she wore a sort of undress uniform frock-coat covered with rows of massive golden buttons. On her shoulders were heavy epaulets; on her head a dashing cap of fur, with a feather. Her belt contained pistols, and a middy's dirk with glittering handle. She lacked nothing but a heavy mustache to make her as terrible in the eyes of the young French husband as in those of his wife. To make the portrait more revolting, we must add that her face was reddened and bloated with free use of the wine cup. and her eyes fiery, yet moist, from the same unnatural practice. The rest of the pirates need not be described. It will suffice to say, that in their costume and equipment nothing had been omitted which might exaggerate to the mind of the captives, the terrible character of the profession they pursued.

"The pirate-chief addressed the captain of the Frenchman with words of blood and thunder. The latter answered with words of weakness and submission. The former without scruple declared the only alternative to death which he allowed.

"'Are you prepared to join us against the world? We are free men of the seas. We are of no nation. We own no laws except those of our own making. Swear to obey our laws, join our crews, sail under the black flag and the bloody head, and take your share with us, of the cargo of your ship!'

"A dead silence answered him.

"'Swear!' and the black flag was waved before their faces.

"'Will my lord pardon us?' answered the captain for the rest. 'Will my lord take what we have and suffer us to go in peace? I only plead that our lives may be spared.'

"'Your lives are our deaths, unless you join with us. You have five minutes for deliberation. Swear, by the black flag,— kiss the bloody head, and, on your knees, take the oath, or you walk the plank every mother's son of you.'

"A dead silence again followed. Meanwhile, the creole wife, crouching in the rear of her husband, who stood immediately behind the captain, involuntarily took from her bosom the cross of black ebony, and, sinking silently upon her knees, pressed it to her lips, while they parted, in unuttered prayers to Heaven.

"The movement did not escape the ruffian. He was now reminded of the woman whom he had sent up from below. In the dim light of the cabin, he had not distinguished her features. A single glance now sufficed to show him their loveliness.

"'Ha!' he exclaimed — 'who have we here?' and passing rapidly through the group of captives he seized her where she knelt. With a shriek she held up the cross. He tore it from her hand, looked at it but an instant, then dashed it to the deck, and crushed it under his feet — accompanying the profane act with a horrid oath. The captain of the Frenchman groaned aloud. The pirate-chief still held his grasp upon the lady. She struggled to free herself, and cried out:—

"'Save me, husband!'

"The appeal was irresistible. Desperate as was the attempt, the young French merchant, drawing forth a pistol concealed in his bosom, levelled it at the head of the pirate and drew the trigger. The bullet only ruffled the monstrous whisker of the ruffian. It had been aimed well, but, in the moment when the trigger was pulled, the arm of the young merchant had been struck up by one of the nearest pirates. Baffled in the desperate deed, the merchant dashed upon Blackbeard with the famishing cry of the panther striving for her young; and strove, with more certain dagger, to mend the failure of his first attempt. But he might as well have cast his slight form against the bulk of a mountain. His blow was thrown upward, the stroke parried, and he himself stricken down with a blow from the butt of a carbine, which covered his head and face instantly with blood.

"'My husband! oh! my husband!' cried the wretched woman, now seeking again to break away from that iron grasp which never once relaxed its hold upon her. In vain.

"'Fling the carrion overboard. Sharks are not made to go hungry.'

"He was remorselessly obeyed; and, partly stunned, but conscious, Louis Chastaign was lifted in half a dozen stalwart arms, and thrust over into the yawning sea. Then the wife broke away;—but, ere she reached the side of the vessel, she was again in the grasp of the ruffian. She never saw her husband more. His head appeared but a moment upon the surface—his hands were thrown upward, then his shriek was heard—a single piercing shriek of agony; and when the French captain looked upon the sea, it was colored with blood, and he could perceive the white sides of the glancing sharks, a dozen of them, as they were tugging, below the surface, at their living victim!

III.

There are some scenes which art does not attempt to delineate—some agonies which baffle the powers of imagination. Such was the terrible, though momentary, horror and agony, of the wretched wife of the young merchant. In such cases, Nature herself seems to acknowledge the same necessities with art,—acknowledges her own incapacity to endure, what art lacks the power to delineate; and interposes a partial death, to spare to the victim the tortures of a horrid dying. Pauline Chastaign swooned and lay unconscious upon the deck.

Meanwhile, the miserable captives stood silent, incapable, paralyzed with their own terrors at the dreadful tragedy which had been so suddenly conceived, and so rapidly hurried to its catastrophe. The French captain shrugged his shoulders and prepared for his own fate.

"'You have seen!' said Blackbeard addressing him and the rest. 'Trample on these colors'—pointing to the flag of the Lily; which had been torn down and thrown upon the deck;—'spit upon that cross!'—that of poor Pauline Chastaign, which lay half crushed before them;—'and swear on the bloody head obedience to the laws of the 'Brothers of the Coast!'—such was the name which the pirate fraternity bore among themselves;—'or you share the fate of that young fool, and find the sharks their supper this very night. Speak! You!'—addressing the captain of the Frenchman.

The days of Rousseau, Voltaire, and Robespierre, had not yet dawned. The Frenchman had not yet prepared to spit on Christ, and substitute himself for God! Our captain knew his fate, and was prepared for it. He took the broken cross reverently, and kissed it, then, with a faint smile, he politely bowed to the pirate-chief—in these gestures according his only answer.

"'To the plank with him!' was the command of Blackbeard in a voice of thunder. A dozen unscrupulous ruffians seized upon the Frenchman to hurry him to his doom. Then, for the first time, the rest of the crew seemed to awaken to a sense of desperation, as by a common instinct. With a wild cry they rushed upon the pirates, striking right and left with muscular arms, and all the reckless violence of despairing nature! Unhappily, the timid policy of their captain had denied them weapons. They had nothing upon which to rely but their own sinews; nevertheless, so sudden, so unlooked for was the assault, that the pirates bearing the captain, were overborne; he rescued; and, with a cheer, they all together darted again upon the foe, picking up knife or cutlass where they might. Alas the brave effort but shortened the pang of dying. A new flood of ruffians from the pirate vessel poured in upon them, and finished the struggle in a few moments; but Blackbeard himself, meanwhile, had been wounded with a knife, and his smart rendered him less than ever disposed to mercy. Maimed, slain, or only wounded, the captives were all hurried into the deep;—but one male being suffered to survive—a poor cabin-boy who, in the last moment, grappled the knees of Blackbeard, swore allegiance to his authority, and was admitted to mercy!

IV.

"But one captive remained living in the hands of the pirates. This was the young wife of the unhappy merchant, poor Pauline Chastaign. She had been taken to the cabin in her swoon, and had been laid, with a certain degree of tenderness, which had given no satisfaction to the girl of Pamplico, upon the couch of that Amazon. It was with a curious interest, which still further displeased that person, that Blackbeard hung over the unconscious woman, and scanned the beauties of her face and figure. His second officer and himself conferred upon her fate together, in the hearing of the wife of the latter—the thirteenth wife, as you will remember. The conversation was not of a sort to gratify her. She had no small portion of the green infusion in her system against the indulgence of which Iago counsels Othello, and the eager appetite, speaking in the eyes of Blackbeard, warned her of her own danger from a superior rival. The lieutenant of the pirate had his passions also. He boldly preferred his claim as custodian of the young widow.

"'You!' answered the chief. 'You?'

"'And why not me?' was the reply in a tone approaching defiance.

The pistol of Blackbeard was at his head in a moment and, with a horrid oath, he ordered the other on deck and to his duties. The lieutenant slowly, and with a growl, submitted. When he had gone, the girl of Pamplico interposed with the same question which had been uttered by the lieutenant.

"'And why not he? Why should he not have this thing?'

"'Because it does not please me that he should, my beauty!'

"'And why should it not please you?'

"'I prefer that the woman should keep my cabin for a while.'

"'Ha! and what of me?'

"'You! ah? You may go to his cabin for a while.'

"'What! You fling me off, do you, for this bloodless creature! And such as she is to pass between us? That shall never be. Don't think that I am a thing of milk and water, without strength or courage. No! you shall see that I have blood, and that I can take it too! I'm not afraid of your black looks and thundering oaths. No! indeed! You are mine; and while I am yours, I shall see that no living woman shall pass between us. You would fling me off, and quarrel with your best officer for this rag of a woman, would you. But you shall not!'

"With the words, quick as lightning, the unsexed creature shot round the little table that stood between herself and the seemingly insensible wife of the young Frenchman, her dirk flourishing in her grasp directly before the eyes of Blackbeard. She had rounded the table, and occupied a place between him and the threatened victim, before he could possibly conceive her purpose, and heave up his huge bulk from where he lay, to interpose for the prevention of the mischief. He roared out a terrible threat and horrid oath, but the Amazon never heeded a syllable, and the poor captive would have sunk beneath her dagger-stroke, but for the fact that, while the dispute was in progress between Blackbeard, his lieutenant, and the girl from Pamplico, the captive lady was slowly coming to her senses, and understood it all. She saw the movement of her wild assailant, and darting up from where she lay, gave one piercing scream, and rushed up the cabin steps to the deck, closely followed by the Amazon and the pirate-chief. They reached the deck only to behold the white flash of a glancing form as it shot over the side of the vessel, and to hear a single plunge into the gulfing billows of the sea. When they looked over the bulwarks, there was nothing to be seen. The wife of the young merchant had joined him in the deep.

"'It is just as well!' growled Blackbeard, turning away. 'It prevents mischief! Ha! you young devil!' he continued, throwing his arms about the neck of the she-demon who stood confronting him, 'you are a girl after my own heart; but if I served you rightly, I should pitch you over after her. No more of this. Do you hear! Another such piece of meddling, and I shall slash this pretty throat with a sharp dagger. Do you hear!'

"She laughed impudently and returned his caresses, and the deadly vessel went on her midnight course

V.

"Such was the true history of the captured Frenchman, whom our pirate-chief persuaded the court of admiralty to adjudge to him as a vessel picked up at sea, abandoned by its proper owners. Blackbeard was soon at sea again. He was even more successful in the results of his next cruise; gathering Spanish gold, ingots, and jewels of great value, the treasures equally of east and west. But he carried in no more vessels for the jurisdiction of the courts. He employed the shorter processes of firing and scuttling. He seldom found any prisoners. He kept none. The sea locked up his secrets—for a time at least; and his cruise was a long one in proportion to its successes.

"But news reached him of a suspicious character. He heard rumors of ships-of-war preparing to search for pirates. He was advised from North Carolina, that his own virtues were not beyond suspicion, and that, somehow, certain rumors had reached Virginia affecting his securities. It became necessary to hide away the treasures already procured, before again venturing within the waters of Cape Fear and Ocracocke. He must cleanse the aspect of his craft, so that she should be able to endure examination as a fair trader, and secure the bloody spoils of previous ventures, beyond the grasp of law and civilization. We all know how common was the practice among the pirates of establishing hoards in unfrequented places. All these islets, according to tradition, from the capes of Virginia to that of Florida conceals some buried treasure. On this occasion our pirates put into Bull's bay, the avenues to which they well knew. In this region, they selected a spot, either on Bull's island, or Long, or some one of the islands immediately contiguous—all of which were then uninhabited—in which to hide their treasures. Here, at midnight, they assembled. The hole was dug in the earth. The pirates all gathered around it. They bore the glittering piles—in kegs, boxes, sacks, jars. They saw them all deposited. Then they clasped hands, and each swore, several'y repeating the horrid oath which Blackbeard dictated.

"There was a pause. The rites were yet unfinished. The hole remained opened. Something was yet to be done, accord ing to which alone, in the superstitions of the pirates, could the treasure be securely kept. Meanwhile, there had been voices crying to them from the woods. The devil had been adjured by the terrible chief of the crew, and he had answered with awful sounds from a neighboring thicket. They could, most of them, believe in a devil, and tremble, where they tacitly renounced all faith in a God. Of course, this mummery had been devised by the cunning for the especial benefit of the ignorant. They had imprecated a horrid destiny upon their souls, in the event of their fraud or infidelity to their comrades, and the audible answers of the fiend declared their oaths to be registered in hell. Such was a part of the scheme by which the pirates bound each other to forbearance, and for the common security of their hidden treasures.

"But something more was necessary to the completion of these horrid rites. There was a needed sacrifice which murder always found it necessary to provide for superstition. But this portion of the ceremony was, of course, a mystery to all those whom the pirates had lately incorporated among their crews from among the captives they had taken.

"'And now that we have all secure, brothers of the coast, it still needs that one of us should remain to watch the treasure till our present cruise is over. Food he shall have in abundance, drink, and shelter. A boat shall be left for him with which to fish, and weapons with which to procure game of the woods and wild fowl along the shore. It must be a willing mind that must undertake this watch. Who volunteers? Let him speak boldly, like a man.'

"An eager voice answered—

"'I will remain and watch the treasure!'

"It was that of the poor cabin-boy, the sole survivor of the French merchantman. The trembling creature had shuddered with daily and nightly horrors since the hour of his captivity. He eagerly seized the present opportunity of escape from an association the terrors of which oppressed his soul. Blackbeard looked at him grimly, and with a dreadful smile. He saw through the wretched boy, and readily conjectured all his hopes They were those of all who had ever consented to watch the treasure. But it did not matter to the pirate's object whether the volunteer were honest or not. It was enough that he should volunteer. According to their laws none could be *compelled* to take this watch; and it was one of the secret tests, that of the volunteer, by which to discover who, of the crew, were in secret disloyal, and likely to prove treacherous.

"'You!' repeated Blackbeard. 'You, then, willingly choose to remain and keep watch over the treasure?'

"'I do!'

"'Then remain, and see that you watch well!'

"And, with the words, lifting the pistol which, all the while, had been secretly prepared in his grasp, he shot the wretched boy through the head. So sudden was the movement, that the miserable victim was scarcely conscious of his danger a single moment, before the bullet was crashing through his brains. He fell into the hole above the treasure, and the earth was shoveled in upon the victim and the spoils he had probably fancied he should be able to bear away.

"'There—see that you keep good watch, good fellow!'

"A wild howl of demoniac joy from the adjacent covert startled the superstitious of the crew. The sacrifice to the fiend in waiting had been graciously accepted; and a tacit pledge was thus given by the demon that, with his aid, the treasure should be kept safely by the vigilant spectre of the victim.

VI.

"The horrid orgies which succeeded to this murder, among the pirates, that night—their dance of maniac frenzy over the grave of their victim, and upon the spot of earth which concealed their buried deposite—exceeds the possibility of description, as it would be greatly offensive to propriety were we to describe it. They drank, they danced, they sang, they swore, they howled, they fought; and it was long after dawn of the day following before they proved able to return to their vessel, which lay at easy anchorage a short distance from the shore. Before leaving the island, they had obscured with trampling, then with turf and leaves, all external signs of the burial which they had made. The orgies of drunkenness which followed had served still more effectually to obliterate from the memories of most of them the impressions of the locality which they had gathered from the scene. It was with this policy that their more cunning chiefs had encouraged their bestial debauchery and excess. They, however (the former), had taken the precaution to establish certain guide-marks to the spot which nothing could obliterate. The extended branch of one tree was a pointer to the place; the *blaze* of another was made to bear a certain relation also to the spot, and so many paces east from the one, and so many paces west from the other, intersecting with a third line drawn from the position of another bough, or tree, or *blaze*, and the point of junction of the three was that under which the treasures lay. We are not required here to be more precise in its delineation.

"Their work done effectually, as usual, and our pirates all pretty well sobered, they sailed away upon another cruise, the fortunes of which we need not recount. But this time they were not long at sea. After awhile they returned to the waters of North Carolina, and gave themselves up to a week of riot in Pamplico.

"But, along with the evil deed are born always three other parties—the accuser, the witness, and the avenger! It is now difficult to say by what means the later crimes of Blackbeard became known. He had certainly obliterated all his own tracks of blood, almost as soon as he had made them. Still, these tracks had been found and followed, though covered up with earth and sea: as if the accuser and the avenger were endowed with a peculiar faculty, such as, in the case of the hound, enables him to detect the odor of blood even through the mould. Blackbeard, with the instinct of guilt, was soon aware that a secret enemy was dogging at his heels.

"So it was.

"There had suddenly appeared a stranger at Pamplico, who threw himself more than once in the way of Blackbeard's last wife, the Amazon. He was a fine-looking young fellow, of martial carriage, wearing the loose shirt of the Virginian hunter, carrying a rifle, and followed by a dog. He was tall, erect, and very powerfully built. There was a laughing mischief in his eye, a sly, seductive humor upon his tongue, and a general something in his free, dashing, and buoyant manner, which is apt to be rather pleasing to the women. At all events, the stranger found favor in the sight of the girl of Pamplico, and she invited him to her cabin—*but without Blackbeard's knowledge.*

"The stranger did not hesitate to accept the invitation; but he took care to visit the woman only when he knew that the pirate-chief was present. The girl was a little dashed when he suddenly pushed open the door of the dwelling, and stood in his forest-costume before the parties. With an oath, Blackbeard demanded for what he came. The stranger had his answer ready. He had peltry for sale—several packs—and he wished to barter it for powder and ball. Regarding the pirate only in his *shore* character, as a fair trader, there was nothing in the visit to occasion surprise.

"Blackbeard regarded the stranger with eyes of curious admiration. He observed with delight the magnificent proportions of the hunter.

"'You are a big fellow,' said he—'strong as a horse, no doubt, and as active as a wild cat.'

"'A match,' was the reply, 'for any man of my inches.'

"'We'll see that!' exclaimed the pirate, suddenly rising and grappling with the stranger in a friendly wrestle. The muscular and bulky forms of the two rocked to and fro, breast to breast for awhile, until, by an extra exertion of strength, the hunter laid the outlaw on his back. The latter was nowise ruffled.

"'You don't look the man to do it,' said he, 'but it was well done. You're a man, every inch of you. Have you ever been upon the sea? That's the field for such a man as you. Come! what say you to a v'yage with me? Good pay, good liquor, and fine girls.'

"Here the pirate winked at his wife, and pointed her out to the stranger. The latter seemed disposed to entertain the project. Blackbeard became earnest. He was anxious to increase the number of his marines, and he held out liberal promises and prospects to our hunter—but without suffering him to suppose that his vocation at sea was anything but honest. In those days, the fair traders required something of a warlike armament for defence, and usually had it to a certain extent.

"Our hunter offered only such objections as were easy to overcome; and the result of the conference was an arrangement between the parties to meet the next day on board of Blackbeard's vessel, when they should come to a more definite understanding; our hunter only insisting upon seeing the sort of world to which he was to be introduced, and the accommodations and the fare designed for him. This understood, they separated for the night—the stranger refusing to drink or eat with the pirate, much to the latter's annoyance. How much more would this annoyance have been increased, had he known how tender was the squeeze of the hand which, at parting, the girl of Pamplico had bestowed upon their guest!

"'With such a chap as that to lead the boarders, and I shall sweep every deck that ever showed it's teeth,' said Blackbeard when the stranger had gone.

"'All's well so far!' quoth the latter, as he passed from hearing of the cabin. 'All's well. To-morrow! to-morrow.'

"With the morrow the parties again met, and Blackbeard's welcome was singularly cordial. He took the hunter on board his vessel, showed him her appointments, her strength, and dilated upon the profit of the trade he carried on. The stranger looked about him, noted well what he saw, took particular heed of the pirate guns and sailors,—their number, their character; yet pursued his watch so casually as to occasion no suspicion. He was pleased with everything, and only forebore to drink, to eat, or to make any positive engagement, as before. He left all things in a fair way for arrangement; but it needed that he should bring in his peltry and secure his various hunter effects, in his distant foreign home.

"'We shall meet in seven days!'

"'Be sure of it,' answered the other, 'for in ten I must prepare to be at sea. But, by the way, you haven't in all this time told me your name, or I've forgot it.'

"'Well, when I go to sea, I must get a name. To confess to you a truth, the one I have borne, is rather in bad reputation.'

"'Ah! ha! I see then why you are here. You've been using your rifle on meaner brutes than buck and bear. Well! I don't think the worse of you for that. But give yourself a name that we may swear by.'

"'Or at! well, as I am to be a sailor, I'll take my name from the ship. Call me Mainyard, for lack of anything better.'

"So they parted.

"'Mainyard! Mainyard!' muttered Blackbeard to himself. 'Where have I heard a name like that only a day or two ago! It was from that bloody booby, Coleman. There's something about the name that — pshaw! what an ass I am! as if there should be anything strange to a sailor's ear in such a name. Yet, there is something!'

"And with a vague memory of — he knew not what, — running in his mind, Blackbeard felt mystified and curious for a good hour after the departure of the Hunter. Had he not been half drunk and very furious when Coleman brought his story to his ears, his doubts would have assumed a more definite form, and might have led to other results than followed his oblivion.

"Meanwhile the hunter had disappeared. What follows, almost literally drawn from history, may serve to put into your hands the clue which was all tangled in those of the maudlin pirate.

VII.

"BLACKBEARD, as the fair trader, Edward Teach, had provoked the hostility of the planters in and about Pamplico. The stranger hunter had been among them before he sought the pirate. He had gathered all their evidence, had learned, like them, to distrust the justice of the ruling authorities of North Carolina in their dealings with the pirates, and had secretly sought the succor of the government of Virginia. Governor Spotswood had used his influence with the British commodore on the Virginia station to employ an adequate force for the capture of Blackbeard. For the command of this enterprise a volunteer had been found, in the person of one *Robert Maynard*, a Virginian, but a lieutenant in the royal navy. To catch Blackbeard was no easy matter; and Maynard found it advisable to make himself personally acquainted with the force of the pirates, his place of harborage, and to plan, on the spot itself, his mode of operations. We have seen the progress which he has made, thus far, in the character of the Virginian hunter.

"While he thus employed himself two sloops were got in

readiness with equal secrecy and expedition. Blackbeard, as we have seen, was not left unapprized of his danger. But, in his debauch, he had made light of the intelligence, and moreover, it was not thought by those who bore the tidings that the expedition would have such early despatch. In those days enterprises were undertaken as pilgrimages, with great deliberation, the adventurer stopping to get himself well shod, to provide himself with a select staff, and, only after protracted meditation and perhaps devotions, to take the field. The enterprise of young Maynard proved an exception to the common practice, and his sloops were ready to go to sea, while he was discussing with Blackbeard the preliminaries and the profit of future voyages which they might take together.

"Beginning thus vigorously, Maynard did not relax in his exertions. His sloops left James river on the 17th November, 1718. When fairly at sea, he broke the enterprise to his followers, all of whom were picked men. He read to them the proclamation of Governor Spotswood, offering a reward of £100 for the apprehension of Blackbeard, £15 for every officer, and £10 for every common sailor made captive with him. The proclamation was received with three hearty cheers, and all parties braced themselves up for the conflict which, it was very well understood, would be anything but child's play. On the 21st of November, Maynard passed the bar of Ocracocke, and rapidly drew near to the pirate. At this period, his force was small, consisting of twenty-five men; the rest were at sea, with his other vessel, under the command of Vaughan and other lieutenants.

"Blackbeard was taken by surprise. He certainly would never have waited at his anchorage and with so small a force, had he dreamed of his enemy's approach so soon. In truth, he had been waiting for his hunter, Mainyard,— whom he looked to supply the place of his captain of marines, one Hornsby, who was very sick on shore, and not expected to recover. He did recover, as we shall see hereafter, but not in season to take part in the conflict.

"Though thus caught napping, Blackbeard was a man of resources, and prepared himself for defence. Maynard standing directly for the pirate, received his fire which was delivered with terrible effect. Unfortunately, his own vessel run aground, in the shallow water of the river, and this increased the odds against him. Before he could extricate himself, he had lost twenty of his men, and the pirate prepared to board him. Seeing this, Maynard hurried his men below, with orders to keep ready for the hand-to-hand conflict which was impending. Blackbeard bore down upon him, threw in his *granades*, and, seeing the decks bare of all but the slain and wounded, he boarded without hesitation. Then Maynard rushed upon deck, followed by his crew, and they fell together upon the assailants. Maynard's costume, on this occasion, was that in which he had made the pirate's acquaintance. Blackbeard knew him at a glance.

"'Ha! traitor! Ha! villain!' he cried as the young lieutenant confronted him; and with the words both of them fired. Then they closed with their dirks. Blackbeard was now reminded of the wrestle they had had together, and the recollection made him desperate. It was ominous of the result in the present contest. He was overmatched, and slashed almost to pieces, but fighting to the last, he fell at the feet of his conqueror, who immediately smote off his head with his cutlass, and lifted it, all reeking and streaming with blood, in the sight of the remaining pirates. As the black and bloody mass, with its wilderness of beard was raised on high, the horrid eyes glaring, and glazing even as they glared, the spectacle overwhelmed the pirate-crew. They threw down their weapons, such as still survived the combat, and were ironed on the spot. The capture of the pirate-vessel followed, but had nearly proved a fatal conquest; since a desperate negro stood over the magazine, stationed there by Blackbeard's orders, with a blazing match, prepared to apply it at a given signal. It was only when the gory head of his master was thrust before his eyes, that he consented to resign his torch and leave his perilous duty unattempted. The victory of Maynard was complete, and he sailed up to the town of Bath, and finally returned to James river. with the head of the pirate, *in terrorem*, hanging at the bowsprit of his vessel."

CHAPTER XIX.

FROM SHIP TO SHORE.

"THUS," continued our *raconteur*—"thus ended the career of one of the most terrible pirates that ever infested these waters. He has left memorable traces, in curious and startling legends, all along these shores. There is a sequel to this narrative which I have related, in the further history of that horde of treasure of which we have seen the burial."

The narrator was sharply interrupted with a cry from one of the party.

"There's the light!"

"The Charleston light!"

And the group of listeners were no longer to be spelled by the *raconteur*. They broke away with a rush; each eagerly straining his eyes for the pale star-like beacon, set by the guardian civilization, on the edges of the great deep, for the benefit of the benighted mariner. Meanwhile, the swarthy beauty, Night, enveloped in dark mantle, was passing with all her train of starry servitors; even as some queenly mourner, followed by legions of gay and brilliant courtiers, glides slowly and mournfully, in sad state and solemnity, on a duteous pilgrimage to some holy shrine. And, over the watery waste, that sad, sweet, doubtful light, such as Spenser describes in the cathedral wood:—

"A little glooming light most like a shade."

showed us the faint line of shore upon our right.

"That is Long Island which we are so rapidly passing. There it was that Sir Henry Clinton marshalled his array, grenadiers and marines, in order to make their valiant demonstration upon the little army of rifles, under Thompson, on the ever-famous 28th of June, 1776, while Sir Peter Parker was hammering away at Fort Sullivan within the harbor. The white mass which you see at the extremity of the dark line, shows you what is called 'the breach,'—where the ocean breaks through with foam and roar, and separates Long from Sullivan's island. To cross this 'breach' was Clinton's necessity. It was sometimes fordable; but on this occasion, according to the British report, a miracle took place in behalf of the Carolinians, not unlike that which divided the sea for the Israelites, yet raised it up, immediately after, in mountains to overwhelm the pursuing Egyptians. Here, the waters on 'the breach,' rose in the twinkling of an eye from two feet to seven. It ceased to be fordable to the grenadiers who, strangely enough, contended that they could not possibly hope to do fighting, to sight a carabine, or charge a bayonet, with their eyes under the water. In that only half-civilized period, the average height of a grenadier corps did not exceed six feet."

"But Clinton had his vessels for the passage."

"Oh! to be sure! And he did try to cross. But the rifles of Thompson proved an obstacle no less potent than the arm of the sea. Two little six-pounders, besides, planted on the opposite sand-hills, were mischievously stuffed with grape and cannister. Under the two fires, Sir Henry's rafts, flats, and schooners, were swept of their crews, and after two desperate attempts the assailant drew sullenly off, and waited the result of that more terrific conflict, which was going on, the while, within the harbor, and which continued throughout the day till nine at night."

"There you get a faint glimpse of the sand-hills on Sullivan's, crowned sparingly with shrubs, among which the rifles were posted. Behind those sand-hills there is quite a forest. The white line which you mark, fringing the dusky plain of the sea, is that famous beach, so broad, so hard, so long, of which the Charlestonians boast as so beautiful a seaside drive. It is second to few or none in the country. Now you see the houses dotting the sandy shores. That long dusky building is the Moultrie House, cool, airy, ample—a delicious retreat in the hot season. The darker compacter mass which you note west of it is the famous fort, formerly Sullivan, where the stout old patriot Moultrie, pipe in mouth, at the head of his little regiment, beat off the British fleet. From this point you perceive that the settlement grows denser; the white cottages standing out, distinctly though rather crowded, in the pleasant starlight."

"What line of shore is this upon the left?" asked Duyckman of Miss Burroughs. Our Gothamite never left that young lady's side, and preferred evidently to get his information from a feminine source.

"That is Morris island, upon which the lighthouse stands. It is also a pleasant and healthy retreat during summer, and beyond the sand-hills there is a little hamlet.

"Morris is divided by a creek from James island. Let your eye move alongshore in this direction, and you see Fort Sumter, a new fortress, raised upon a mole in the sea. It confronts Fort Moultrie obliquely, and the fires of the two combined would serve to keep an approaching fleet in hot water for a while. We are now passing between the two, and have reached a point where the whole harbor opens upon the eye. To the left, you follow the water-line till it brings you to Ashley river, descending west of the city to the embraces with the deep. Look across now, due north, and you see another long sandy tract stretching away till lost in the distance. This is Haddrill's, or Mount Pleasant village—a third retreat for the citizens in summer. Just before you, Castle Pinckney looms up, forming another fortress for the protection of the harbor. It lies within half a mile of the city, the long line of lights of which you see stretching up Cooper river, which passes down from the north between Haddrill's and the city."

"The harbor is an ample one," said Duyckman.

"Few more so, and few in this country more beautiful. The effect at this moment is very fine. The seas are as placid and subdued as the happy slumber of childhood. The breezes swell gently over these slight elevations of land along the south, and stoop down to the little waves, creasing them with rippling beauties, which the luminous brightness of the stars enables us to follow in long lines that are unbroken till they subside from sight in distance."

"I should like to explore these islets and rivers, and visit all the places you have named. Can this be done safely in midsummer?"

"This season—yes! Charleston is now very healthy. Were

it a yellow-fever season, you should not be here. If you say so, we will take a week or so for the city and the island, before we go to the mountain region."

"Hem! Ah! When—Miss Burroughs—do you think to leave the city for your excursion to the interior?' queried Duyckman of the lady.

"O, not for a week or two."

Gotham nodded to me as if to say—

"That will just suit us."

"Hark! the gun! Captain Berry has a private signal on his arrival which he communicates to all the public! Well, my friends, our voyage is over. In ten minutes we shall be ashore."

"I hear the ringing of bells," said Duyckman. "A fire, perhaps—or possibly the salutation of the city and its welcome, in response to the gun of the captain. Your method of returning a salute."

"No! it is our curfew? That bell rings for ten o'clock. It is a signal to Sambo and Cuffy, the darkies, that they had better retire to their several lodgings for the night; and when it begins, at a quarter before the stroke of ten, the parties thus especially notified begin to make tracks homeward. It is quite an amusing picture to see them, at that hour, scattering, each taking his separate way. One hurries home, bearing a string of blackfish. He has pleasant anticipations of a fry that night. Another carries a basket filled with a variety; he will scarcely be willing that you should see what he carries. A third has a bottle of whiskey in one pocket, and a pound of tobacco in the other. And, thus armed and charged, they linger with their comrades and acquaintance about the streets, till the stroke of that *curfew* bell. A last word, a hurried shake of the hand, as they meet and pass, and they retire from the sight as the bell ceases,—or rather, when the tattoo ceases which always is beaten when the ringing closes. But of Charleston—more soon. Give your arm to Miss Burroughs. This is her brother who approaches. Her carriage is on the wharf. I will see for us."

Our chronicle, for the present, is completed. The *raconteur* is silent. The circle is dispersed. The spirits have nothing further to reveal, of the secrets of their prison-house, at the present sitting. But, doubtless, we shall re-form the circle, and have new revelations. We shall seek new sources of inspiration — new media — and fresh materials; and soothe, for the reader as for ourselves, "as humor prompts," the "idle vein" of both. We shall assemble, among our southern forests and mountains, a portion at least, of our present company — perhaps add others to our circle. But we shall make no definite promise; being resolute not to fetter ourselves to hard conditions. We need say no more; and, just now, our Alabama cynic is at our elbow, with a courtly entreaty that we shall do him grace, ere we part, "over a coil of snake and tiger."

THE END.

www.ingramcontent.com/pod-product-compliance
Lightning Source LLC
Chambersburg PA
CBHW022056300426
44117CB00007B/484